Advanced Praise

'This book articulates a rich set of links between psychoanalysis and the philosophical mind-body problem. The psychoanalytic and the philosophical traditions have many points of overlap. Both traditions articulate distinctive frameworks for the relationship between brain and mind. Both focus especially on the role of conscious and unconscious processes. Both give distinctive roles to the body and to the emotions. The essays in this book examine these connections to show both how philosophy can shed light on psychoanalysis and how psychoanalysis can shed light on philosophy.'

—**David Chalmers**, *University Professor of Philosophy and Neural Science, New York University; author of The Conscious Mind and Reality+*

'Psychoanalysis has had a very difficult time evolving from its roots in Nineteenth Century positivism into the multiple perspectives which comprise contemporary psychoanalytic thought. Jon Mills' new book, *Psychoanalysis and the Mind-Body Problem* is a scholarly tour de force that brings psychoanalytic scholarship into the present. It is rare to find an anthology which can so clearly explicate contemporary, philosophical, ethical, theoretical, neuropsychological, cognitive, economic and psychedelic dimensions of the ongoing psychoanalytic conversation. Mills' strategy of focusing on the body as central to contemporary psychoanalysis achieves this goal and highlights the difficulties that the separation of mind and body has created for psychoanalytic theoreticians and clinicians. As both an author and a practicing psychoanalyst I have found the ideas in this book extremely useful in understanding persistent theoretical and clinical problems. Because of my interests, I found the chapters on the unconscious, mentalization, and Lacanian theory very thought provoking. Other readers will also find particular chapters which speak more directly to them. I highly recommend this very evocative book to psychoanalysts, psychologists, mental health practitioners and scholars who will find this to be an extremely valuable addition to their library.'

—**Joseph Newirth, PhD, ABPP**, *Emeritus Professor, Derner School of Psychology, Adelphi University; author of Between Emotion* *and Cognition: The Generative Unconscious and From Sign to Symbol: Transformational Processes in Psychoanalysis, Psychology and Psychotherapy*

'In this intriguing collection, the authors address the interaction of mental and bodily functions as these are experienced (or not experienced) consciously or outside of conscious awareness. The authors are experts in their wide-ranging areas—from the interior perspectives of soul to the scientific study of brain; and they address these dimensions with the complexity that the concepts demand. The editor and the authors have produced a volume to visit and revisit, for those who are interested in psychoanalysis, and more broadly in underlying theories of emotional, somatic and cognitive organization.'

—**Wilma Bucci PhD**, *author of Psychoanalysis and Cognitive Science: A Multiple Code Theory; Emotional Communication and Therapeutic Change; and Understanding Psychotherapy Through Multiple Code Theory*

'Psychology can be said to have begun with the mind body problem first made salient by Rene Descartes. What is the mind? How is it different from the body? How shall we study it? All of the early pioneers of the field attempted to deal with these problems. William James seems to have left psychology and devoted himself to philosophy (at least partly) in an effort to address it. The functionalists tried to finesse the problem by making the distinction a methodological one. The behaviorists tried to solve it by declaring only the body to be real, thereby eliminating the mind. And then, it seems, everyone in the field ignored and or forgot about the problem. Psychoanalysis, which focuses on unconscious mental processes, which do not fit into Cartesian dualism, would appear to offer fruitful and creative ways to tackle this issue. But the problem seems to have never been directly addressed in psychoanalytic circles. Until now.'

'Jon Mills has edited a book that tackles this difficult issue head on. He has assembled a group of distinguished scholars who, using a psychoanalytic framework, address important and thorny philosophical issues related to the relationship between mind and body. The chapters represent a feast of psychoanalytic diversity. Dr. Mills approaches the problem from a Hegelian dialectical angle. Adrian Johnston takes what might be described as an anal/Marxist dialectical/Lacanian approach. Yadlin-Gadot takes us on a tour of Lacan's views that pertain to this issue. Other chapters make use of too often neglected Jungian ideas (Goodwyn, Pacolet). Neuroscience is here as well, reviewed by Dr. Solms, an internationally renowned expert in the area. And Dr. Jurist reviews recent work on embodied cognition and mentalization that bears importantly on this topic.'

'Anyone wanting to be stimulated by what psychoanalysis can contribute to an age-old issue would do well to study the chapters in this text. This is not an easy read; many of the ideas are complex and original. But it is more than worth the effort.'

—**Joel Weinberger, PhD,** *Professor of Psychology, Adelphi University; author of The Unconscious*

Psychoanalysis and the Mind-Body Problem

In this volume, internationally acclaimed psychoanalysts, philosophers, and scholars of humanities examine the mind-body problem and provide differing analyses on the nature of mind, unconscious structure, mental properties, qualia, and the contours of consciousness.

Given that disciplines from the humanities and the social sciences to neuroscience cannot agree upon the nature of consciousness—from what constitutes psychic reality to mental properties, psychoanalysis has a unique perspective that is largely ignored by mainstream paradigms. This book provides a comprehensive exploration of the mind-body problem in various psychoanalytic schools of thought, including philosophical and metapsychological points of view.

Psychoanalysis and the Mind-Body Problem will be of interest to psychoanalysts, philosophers, neuroscientists, evolutionary biologists, academics, and those generally interested in the humanities, cognitive science, and the philosophy of mind.

Jon Mills, PsyD, PhD, ABPP is a philosopher, psychoanalyst, and retired clinical psychologist. He is on Faculty in the Postgraduate Programs in Psychoanalysis & Psychotherapy, Gordon F. Derner School of Psychology, Adelphi University, USA; Department of Psychosocial & Psychoanalytic Studies, University of Essex, UK; and is Emeritus Professor of Psychology & Psychoanalysis at Adler Graduate Professional School in Toronto, Canada. Recipient of numerous awards for his scholarship, he is the author and/or editor of 30 books in philosophy, psychoanalysis, psychology, and cultural studies.

Philosophy & Psychoanalysis Book Series
Jon Mills
Series Editor

Philosophy & Psychoanalysis is dedicated to current developments and cutting-edge research in the philosophical sciences, phenomenology, hermeneutics, existentialism, logic, semiotics, cultural studies, social criticism, and the humanities that engage and enrich psychoanalytic thought through philosophical rigor. With the philosophical turn in psychoanalysis comes a new era of theoretical research that revisits past paradigms while invigorating new approaches to theoretical, historical, contemporary, and applied psychoanalysis. No subject or discipline is immune from psychoanalytic reflection within a philosophical context including psychology, sociology, anthropology, politics, the arts, religion, science, culture, physics, and the nature of morality. Philosophical approaches to psychoanalysis may stimulate new areas of knowledge that have conceptual and applied value beyond the consulting room reflective of greater society at large. In the spirit of pluralism, *Philosophy & Psychoanalysis* is open to any theoretical school in philosophy and psychoanalysis that offers novel, scholarly, and important insights in the way we come to understand our world.

Titles in this series:

Shame, Temporality and Social Change: Ominous Transitions
Edited by Ladson Hinton and Hessel Willemsen

Psychoanalysis, Catastrophe & Social Action
Robin McCoy Brooks

Metaphysical Dualism, Subjective Idealism, and Existential Loneliness: Matter and Mind
Ben Lazare Mijuskovic

Jung's Alchemical Philosophy: Psyche and the Mercurial Play of Image and Idea
Stanton Marlan

Psychoanalysis and the Mind-Body Problem

Edited by Jon Mills

Routledge
Taylor & Francis Group

LONDON AND NEW YORK

Cover image: "Architects of Delusion," by Jon Mills, mixed media, 2009

First published 2022
by Routledge
4 Park Square, Milton Park, Abingdon, Oxon OX14 4RN

and by Routledge
605 Third Avenue, New York, NY 10158

Routledge is an imprint of the Taylor & Francis Group, an informa business

British Library Cataloguing-in-Publication Data
A catalogue record for this book is available from the British Library

Library of Congress Cataloguing-in-Publication Data
Names: Mills, Jon, 1964- editor.
Title: Psychoanalysis and the mind-body problem / edited by Jon Mills.
Description: New York, NY : Routledge, 2022. |
Series: Philosophy and psychoanalysis | Includes bibliographical references and index. |
Summary: "In this volume, internationally acclaimed psychoanalysts, philosophers, and scholars of humanities examine the mind-body problem and provide differing analyses on the nature of mind, unconscious structure, mental properties, qualia, and the contours of consciousness"-- Provided by publisher.
Identifiers: LCCN 2021051840 | ISBN 9780367548285 (hardback) | ISBN 9780367548308 (paperback) | ISBN 9781003090755 (ebook)
Subjects: LCSH: Mind and body. | Psychoanalysis. | Qualia. | Consciousness.
Classification: LCC BF161 .P7859 2022 | DDC 150.19/5--dc23/eng/ 20220103
LC record available at https://lccn.loc.gov/2021051840

ISBN: 978-0-367-54828-5 (hbk)
ISBN: 978-0-367-54830-8 (pbk)
ISBN: 978-1-003-09075-5 (ebk)

DOI: 10.4324/9781003090755

Typeset in Times New Roman
by MPS Limited, Dehradun

Contents

Contributors

Anna Aragno, PhD, born in Rome, Italy, educated in England, Universities of London and Paris, with a background in the arts, humanities and languages, came to New York on a Fulbright scholarship in the late 1960s. After an international career as prima ballerina, she resumed academic studies at the New School for Social Research, receiving her psychoanalytic training from multiple NYC institutes and graduating from Washington Square's Psychoanalytic and Post Graduate Institute's supervisory tracks. Named 'distinguished scholar in residence' at WSI, she is author of many scholarly papers, chapters, book reviews, and two revisionary books, *Symbolization* (1997/2016) and *Forms of Knowledge* (2008/2016). She is the recipient of numerous nominations and awards including a Gradiva Award in 2020. Since 2009, her metatheoretical interests led to annual presentations and affiliations with two international academic communities, biosemiotics and code biology, interdisciplinary fields that are forging bridges between biology and the humanities, dividing her time between private practice and scholarly writings recently focused on the possibility of uniquely psychoanalytic contributions to the evolution of mind.

Barnaby B. Barratt, PhD, DHS, ABPP is currently director of studies at the Parkmore Institute and senior research fellow with the WITS Institute for Social and Economic Research at the University of Witwatersrand (Johannesburg). For a significant portion of his mid-career, he was professor of family medicine, psychiatry and behavioral neurosciences at Wayne State University (Detroit).

Formerly a training analyst for a decade with the Michigan Psychoanalytic Institute, Dr Barratt is currently a training analyst with the South African Psychoanalytic Association and supervising analyst with the Indian Psychoanalytic Society. He is a member of the International Psychoanalytic Association, as well as a Fellow of the American Psychological Association and of the American Academy for Psychoanalysis in Psychology. Dr Barratt is the author of five books on psychoanalysis, all published by Routledge, and most recently completed a trilogy titled Rediscovering Psychoanalysis. Additionally, he has published several books in other areas (philosophy, sexuality, somatic psychology, and spirituality). He has authored over forty original papers on psychoanalytic topics (in refereed journals), as well as many other articles and reviews.

Gary Clark, PhD is an Australian writer and researcher. He is currently a visiting research fellow in the University of Adelaide Medical School. His research focus is in paleoanthropology and the evolution of music, language, and human ritual life. He has a particular interest in situating Jungian psychology in the context of current debates in evolutionary neuroscience.

Jurandir Freire Costa, MD is a psychiatrist, psychoanalyst, and distinguished professor of public health at the Institute for Social Medicine in the State University of Rio de Janeiro where he taught from 1985 to 2014. His main areas of interest are psychoanalysis and culture, subjectivity and psychopathology, autism, and first-person accounts. He is member of the Rio de Janeiro Psychoanalytical Circle. He has published several articles on psychoanalysis and culture and his most recent publications include: "Austism and First-Person Accounts: The Cognitive Problem" (with R. R. Grinker) In F. Elizabeth & C. Rios (Eds.) *Autism in Translation. An Intercultural Conversation on Autism Spectrum Conditions*. (Palgrave/Macmillan, 2018); "The Subject of Psychopathology: Of What Plural Is It Made?" (with J. Gama, B. Bezerra Jr., in C. Banzato & C.P Messas (Eds.), *Philosophy, Psychiatry, & Psychology* (John Hopkins University Press, 2019). He has also published several books in Portuguese, his latest book being, *O Ponto de Vista do Outro - Figuras da Ética na Ficção de Graham Greene e Philip K. Dick* (Garamond, 2010).

Erik Goodwyn, MD received his bachelor degree in physics and mathematics at Western Kentucky University and a master degree in anatomy and neurobiology at the University of Louisville where he coauthored several journal articles in cancer cell research. He graduated from the University of Cincinnati with an MD and went on to psychiatric residency training at Wright State University. He was an officer in the Air Force for seven years, during which time he cared for patients from both civilian and military backgrounds, including soldiers who have been deployed to Iraq and Afghanistan. He is now an associate professor at the University of Louisville, Department of Psychiatry. He has published numerous journal articles, which have generated scholarly debates among top theorists in Analytical Psychology from the United States, England, and Australia. He has also published articles on the dreams of soldiers in combat zones, on archetype theory and cognitive anthropology and folklore studies, on the psychology of rituals around the world, on combining depth psychology with symbolic anthropology, and the application of ritual theory to grief and mourning in clinical practice. His books *The Neurobiology of the Gods* (Routledge, 2012) and *A Psychological Reading of the poem Beowulf: Understanding Everything as Story* (Mellen, 2014) have been well received by scholars in diverse fields. Further publications include *Magical Consciousness* (Routledge, 2015), a book coauthored with Susan Greenwood on the intersection between psychology and anthropology with respect to altered states of consciousness, and *Healing Symbols in Psychotherapy: a Ritual Approach* (Routledge, 2016). His newest book is *Understanding Dreams and Other Spontaneous Images: The Invisible Storyteller* (Routledge, 2018). Dr. Goodwyn is currently the director of Psychotherapy Training at the University of Louisville and teaches residents and medical students dream interpretation methods along with psychodynamic theory and general subjects in psychiatry. He gives yearly invited talks in the United States and in Europe on dream interpretation, psycho-anthropology, neuroscience, and Jungian theory.

Adrian Johnston, PhD is chair of and distinguished professor in the Department of Philosophy at the University of New Mexico at Albuquerque and a faculty member at the Emory Psychoanalytic

Institute in Atlanta. He is the author of *Time Driven: Metapsychology and the Splitting of the Drive* (2005), *Žižek's Ontology: A Transcendental Materialist Theory of Subjectivity* (2008), *Badiou, Žižek, and Political Transformations: The Cadence of Change* (2009), and *Prolegomena to Any Future Materialism, Volume One: The Outcome of Contemporary French Philosophy* (2013), all published by Northwestern University Press. He also is the author of *Adventures in Transcendental Materialism: Dialogues with Contemporary Thinkers* (Edinburgh University Press, 2014). He is the coauthor, with Catherine Malabou, of *Self and Emotional Life: Philosophy, Psychoanalysis, and Neuroscience* (Columbia University Press, 2013). His most recent books are *Irrepressible Truth: On Lacan's "The Freudian Thing"* (Palgrave Macmillan, 2017), *A New German Idealism: Hegel, Žižek, and Dialectical Materialism* (Columbia University Press, 2018), and *Prolegomena to Any Future Materialism, Volume Two: A Weak Nature Alone* (Northwestern University Press, 2019). With Todd McGowan and Slavoj Žižek, he is a coeditor of the book series Diaeresis at Northwestern University Press.

Elliot Jurist, PhD, PhD is professor of psychology and philosophy at the Graduate Center and the City College of New York, CUNY. From 2004 to 2013, he served as the director of the Clinical Psychology Doctoral Program at CUNY. From 2008 to 2018, he was the editor of *Psychoanalytic Psychology*, the journal of Division 39 of the APA. He is also the editor of a book series, Psychoanalysis and Psychological Science, from Guilford Publications, and author of a recent book in the series Minding Emotions: Cultivating Mentalization in Psychotherapy (2018), from the same publisher (the book has been translated into Italian, will be translated into Chinese, and was named best theoretical book in 2019 by the American Board and Academy of Psychoanalysis). He is the author of *Beyond Hegel and Nietzsche: Philosophy, Culture and Agency* (MIT Press, 2000) and coauthor of *Affect Regulation, Mentalization and the Development of the Self* (Other Press, 2002), the latter of which has been translated into five languages and won two book prizes. He is also the coeditor of *Mind to Mind: Infant Research,*

Neuroscience, and Psychoanalysis (Other Press, 2008). His research interests concern mentalization and the role of emotions and emotion regulation in psychotherapy. His research lab has published a self-report measure, the Mentalized Affectivity Scale (MAS), which has now been translated into ten languages. In 2014, he received the Scholarship Award from Division 39 of the APA.

Alan Michael Karbelnig, PhD, ABPP is a training and supervising psychoanalyst, and provides psychoanalytically oriented individual and couples psychotherapy in Pasadena, California. Board certified in forensic psychology, he also offers psycholegal services—mostly in the realms of administrative and employment law. He earned doctorates in Counseling Psychology from the University of Southern California (USC) and in Psychoanalysis from the New Center for Psychoanalysis (NCP). He founded Rose City Center (RCC)—a non-for-profit psychoanalytic clinic serving the economically disadvantaged. He writes extensively, regularly posting on PsychoanalyzingLife.com and has published numerous scholarly articles and book chapters. He also lectures locally, nationally and internationally, including, most recently, in Beijing, Shanghai, Shenzen, and Hong Kong, China; and in Delhi and Ahmedabad, India.

Jon Mills, PsyD, PhD, ABPP is a philosopher, psychoanalyst, and retired clinical psychologist. He is on faculty in the Postgraduate Programs in Psychoanalysis & Psychotherapy, Gordon F. Derner School of Psychology, Adelphi University, United States; Department of Psychosocial & Psychoanalytic Studies, University of Essex, UK; and Emeritus Professor of Psychology & Psychoanalysis at Adler Graduate Professional School in Toronto, Canada. Recipient of numerous awards for his scholarship, including four Gradiva Awards, he is the author and/or editor of thirty books in psychoanalysis, philosophy, psychology, and cultural studies, including *Debating Relational Psychoanalysis: Jon Mills and his Critics* (Routledge, 2020); *Inventing God* (Routledge, 2017); *Underworlds* (Routledge, 2014); *Conundrums: A Critique of Contemporary Psychoanalysis* (Routledge, 2012); *Origins: On the Genesis of Psychic Reality* (McGill-Queens University Press, 2010); *Treating Attachment Pathology* (Rowman & Littlefield, 2005); *The*

Unconscious Abyss: Hegel's Anticipation of Psychoanalysis (State University of New York Press, 2002); and *The Ontology of Prejudice* (Rodopi, 1997).

Joeri Pacolet, PhD works as a high school teacher at Melanchthon Schiebroek in Rotterdam where he teaches philosophy. Joeri has a degree in cultural studies from the University of Maastricht, a PhD in arts from Radboud University Nijmegen and an educational master in philosophy from the University of Leiden. From 2013 to 2019, Joeri was a board member of the C. G. Jung Vereniging Nederland (Interdisciplinary Association for Analytical Psychology). Joeri's interests are the application of analytical psychology and philosophy to popular culture, philosophy of identity, and the influence of technology on psychological development. Recently his book *Transcendent Writers in Stephen King's Fiction* was published by Routledge.

Claudia Passos-Ferreira, PhD, PhD is assistant professor of bioethics at New York University. She studied psychology at the Rio de Janeiro State University and earned her MA and PhD in the program of human sciences and health sciences in public health. She obtained a second PhD in philosophy at the Federal University of Rio de Janeiro in Brazil. She has published on philosophy, psychology, and neuroethics. She has worked as a clinical psychologist and has collaborated in crosscultural research on moral development and social cognition. She has published several works in Portuguese, including a book on Freud and mental causation, *A Máquina Semântica de Freud: Entre Mecanismo e Intencionalidade*. In philosophy of mind, she has published on self-knowledge, introspection, and external mental content. Passos-Ferreira's current research program focuses on the development of consciousness, including what theories of consciousness say about infant consciousness and machine consciousness, and how these theories shed light on ethical issues.

Mark Solms is a Professor at the Neuroscience Institute of the University of Cape Town. He is a member of the South African and American Psychoanalytic Associations and the British Psychoanalytical Society. He has received numerous honours and awards, including the

Sigourney Prize. He has published 350 articles and chapters, and eight books, the latest of which is The Hidden Spring: A Journey to the Source of Consciousness (2021).

Shlomit Yadlin-Gadot, PhD, is a clinical psychologist, psychoanalyst, and teacher in the Tel Aviv Institute of Contemporary Psychoanalysis (TAICP). She teaches and supervises in the Interdisciplinary Study Program of the Humanities Faculty and in the Doctoral and Psychotherapy tracks in the School of Psychotherapy, Sackler School of Medicine, Tel-Aviv University. She is a member of the board of directors of the International Association for Relational Psychoanalysis. She writes and lectures on Freud, Lacan, and truth, integrating perspectives of psychoanalysis, philosophy, and cultural studies. Her book *Truth Matters: Theory and Practice in Psychoanalysis* was published by Brill in 2016. She lives and practices in Ramat-Hasharon, Israel.

Introduction: Minding the Body and the Embodied Mind

Jon Mills

The Greek conception of the psyche or soul (ψυχή) may be said to be ultimately concerned with the essence of the human being, and various dispositions, composites, or *natures* have been attributed to its organization. By today's standards, what we typically refer to as Mind as a totality, including the unique features that comprise individual personality and subjectivity, the Greeks tended to emphasize its multimodal features as universal dimensions of the human condition. Because the notion of consciousness is a modern (not an ancient) concept, early cultures did not have a word for the "unconscious" in the way it is commonly used today, therefore the nature of the soul was not examined in this light. But the unconscious depths of the soul were not entirely neglected, as many preSocratic philosophers attempted to delineate. Testimonia from Aristotle notes that it was Thales who attributed a "motive force" to the notion of the soul (*De Anima*, 405a20), hence a purpose or telos that animates mind as a life-principle. For Anaximenes, our souls "hold us together" (*Fr.* 2), what Democritus equates with thought (*De Anima*, 405a9) as well as a "lust for pleasure" (*Fr.* 159). Perhaps it is in Heraclitus where we first get some glimpse of unconscious process when he points out that the soul follows an inner law of growth (*Fr.* 115) that has no limit, "such is the depth of its meaning" (*Fr.* 45), yet one that is corrupted by "impulsive desire," for "whatever it wants it will buy at the cost of the soul" (*Fr.* 85).

The desirous or lustful features of the soul were often separated from its more rational faculties attributed to the intellect, reason, or mind (*nous*), the "bright jewel" of which is wisdom (Gorgias, *Fr.* 11).

DOI: 10.4324/9781003090755-1

For the Pythagorean school, like the Egyptians, the soul was immortal: life on earth was a sojourn and preparation (through purification, self-discipline, and self-harmonization) for entering the afterlife, the destiny of which was to prepare for eternity. And for Philolaus, a contemporary of Socrates, the immortal *harmonia* of the soul becomes "incorporeal" as it separates from the body upon death (*Fr.* 22). Because the ancients believed in reincarnation, metempsychosis, and the transmigration of the soul, they believed that they had lived before and that learning or education was a matter of recollection (*anamnesis*). Here, we can appreciate how the Socratic method of dialectic was designed to question truth claims imposed by others and elicit knowledge that was previously forgotten, such as was demonstrated in Plato's famous dialogue, *Meno*.

Plato's treatment of the psyche in his *Dialogues* is vast and varied, but he takes up the Pythagorean concept of the soul as comprising three parts: intelligence, reason, and passion. In the *Republic*, he discusses the desirous or appetitive soul as pursuing pleasure and avoiding pain, and that the "lawless," base, "beastly and savage part" concerned with gratifying "its own instincts" (9:571c) is found in everyone. Plato not only anticipates the Freudian unconscious, but he also stipulates how desire can override reason and a sense of shame belonging to our ethical compass. It is here that we may see how Plato was the first psyche-analyst when he articulates the intimate relationship between desire, reason, and morality, how the soul possess a natural constitution that is instinctually driven, develops habits in relating to others and the environment, and that our true characters awaken during sleep when the soul is at rest, whether this be the "rational, gentle and dominate part" (9:571c) or disquieted passion, unruliness, and anger (9:572). In fact, Plato accounts for good and evil within the soul, or a "better part and a worse part," which is subject to "control" and "self-mastery" (4:431a). When the soul is able to attain a sense of "self-consciousness" (9:571d), the more primitive forms of our nature are "tamed," which "settles down in a compromise" between our competing tendencies (9:572d), only to find a middle-ground or synthetic function where unbridled desires are transformed into lawful order and democratic inclinations. Here are the seeds of Freud's tripartite theory of the mind.

Although the ontological connection between the psyche and the body has been a philosophical preoccupation since antiquity, it still remains unresolved. Largely due to its religious overtones, today the term "soul" has been replaced with discourse on mind and its embodiment, which is often reduced, problematically, to the human brain. Discourse in the philosophy of mind and cognitive neuroscience have further subsumed mind under the rubric of consciousness, when philosophies of the unconscious and neuropsychoanalysis has cogently shown how mind is unconsciously organized and operative in all acts of consciousness. The ontic division yet interaction between consciousness and unconsciousness is further pondered in relation to its enmattered nature, the parameters, scope, and limits of which resist consensus. Complicating matters further, the disputes between what actually constitutes consciousness has been extended to metaphysics and cosmogony to the point that the ancient revival of animism and panpsychism has enjoyed renewed interest from the philosophy of mind to physics. Here, we may observe the recapitulation of an almost intractable binary between two categories that sets the stage for contemporary discussions, and hence which continues to inform the materialism-immaterialism, realism-antirealism, and monism versus dualism debates. Because the question of mind and matter remain hotly contested, this book is the first of its kind to introduce key ideas from psychoanalysis to weigh in on the matter, pun intended.

This collection of chapters is both diverse and weighty, tackling the mind-body problem (MBP) from sundry and nuanced perspectives with competing agendas, both complementary and critical. We have considered arguments from Freudian and post-classical revisionist psychoanalytic theory, Jungian, Lacanian, and Winnicottian thought, neuropsychoanalysis, mentalization theory, biosemiotics, evolutionary anthropology, literature, psychedelics, cyborg technology, and how practicing psychotherapy affects the analyst's mind and body. We also have metaphysical discourse on first principles—from causation to cosmopsychism—that engage traditional mind-body literature; and offer spirited critiques of materialism, dualism, monism, realism-irrealism, the hard problem of consciousness, psychic energy, and the question and unconscious agency. All of this makes for a most exciting and fresh take on the MBP from a cornucopia of comparative psychoanalytic approaches.

In the boon of medical, scientific, and technological progress, materialism has gained increasing explanatory power in deciphering the enigma of mind. But with the proliferation and acceptance of cognitive science, psychic reality has been largely reduced to a physical ontology. In our first chapter, I explore the ground, scope, and limits to the materialist framework and show that while bio-neurochemical-physiology is a necessary condition for mental functioning, it is far from being a sufficient condition for adequately explaining the human being. This becomes especially significant when examining the question of selfhood, freedom, personal autonomy, value inquiry, and the phenomenal quality of the lived experience.

In chapter 2, Barnaby Barratt argues that defining psychoanalysis as free-associative praxis suggests the extent to which this discipline is not to be determined or justified in terms of an epistemology (subjectivistic, objectivistic, or hermeneutic), but rather be appreciated as an ontoethical practice. This thesis empowers the rediscovery of psychoanalysis and challenges the uses and misuses that contemporary "neuropsychoanalysts" have typically made of Spinoza's "dual-aspect monism." He then argues that Freud's notion of "psychic energy," which has historically been ignored or misconstrued by his followers, should be considered ontologically as akin to Spinoza's notion of "substance" underlying both the material and the immaterial realities that we can come to know (or as initiating a triple-aspect monism). Psychic energy cannot be purely endogenous (as Freud, in the tradition of Helmholtz, wished to insist). Rather, as indigenous cosmologies worldwide have intimated or intuited, it is pervasively both/and yet neither/nor in the sense of possible ontological relations of (non)identicality between 'body' and 'mind.' The hegemony of analytico-referential epistemologies throughout the modern era in North Atlantic cultures would seem to have prevented appreciation of this distinctive approach to mind-body issues.

In our next chapter, Claudia Passos-Ferreira explores Freud's complex and fascinating views on the question of mental causation. She offers an interpretation of Freud's views on this question, bringing together ideas from psychoanalysis, philosophy of psychoanalysis, and philosophy of mind. Faced with the impasse of the problem of how the mind interacts with the body, Freud created a two-dimensional picture of mental causation, with one dimension involving mechanistic causes and the other involving intentional causes. Passos-Ferreira's thesis is that that Freud's best-developed picture of mental causation describes mental causes as intentional causes using psychological vocabulary. She analyzes three moments in Freud's work with a focus on mental causation. In the first topography, Freud uses a hybrid vocabulary, describing the mind in terms of both mechanistic causes and intentional causes. In his second topography, the mind increasingly assumes an intentional description. The third moment is Freud's theory of anxiety, in which the arational cause of the unconscious drives, initially presented as a motor of the mind, gives rise to "anxiety" as an intentional affect that forces the self to find a solution for its mental conflicts. In the last part, she discusses how new empirical evidence and new philosophical developments in the problems of mental causation and the mind-body relationship can support Freud's hypothesis that mental conflicts are the cause of neurotic symptoms.

Erik Goodwyn's contribution surveys the mind-body literature and offers an assessment and critique of how the MBP can be addressed through a revised Jungian metaphysics. Jung developed his theory of the psyche at first without concern for metaphysics using a biological formulation of archetypes as instinctual functions. Later in life, however, Jung ventured into metaphysical territory when he forwarded the idea that archetypes may be ordering principles behind both matter and psyche. Jung tried to avoid metaphysics along the way, but was ultimately unable to escape it, thus it remains to develop a way to integrate analytical psychology with a metaphysical system other than physicalism, with which it is incompatible. In this chapter, the primary objection to physicalism—the explanatory gap problem—is reviewed, and the alternative metaphysical systems that better fit analytical psychology are explored. Ultimately, we find that cosmopsychism is the system that appears to best ground analytical psychology metaphysically.

Lacan's views on mind and body are taken up in the next chapter by Shlomit Yadlin-Gadot. Acknowledging how Freud's theoretical starting point was rooted in physiology generally and in neural mechanisms particularly, he construed the psychic as emerging from the body and its drives, where Id was a great reservoir of bodily-generated energy, and ego was "first and foremost a bodily ego."

Freud described psychic development by analogy to biological development, namely, as the unfolding of pre-determined structures. This is the context for the centrality of sexuality in shaping personality and the basis for a psychoanalytic anatomy. The coordination of the psychic and the physiological is orchestrated in the context of societal prohibitions, represented in superego imperatives. Whereas Freud's work can be seen as a brave attempt at bridging mind and body, Lacan's work offers to deconstruct this binary and examine its significance in his notion of the subject articulated in three orders: the Symbolic, the Imaginary and the Real. In this chapter Yadlin-Gadot describes mind-body relations in the context of Lacan's developmental account. For Lacan, there are two logical moments in the formation of psychic life: the mirror stage and the Oedipal stage as he conceives of them. Both are predicated upon an Other, transforming the binary system of body-mind into a triangulation of *other*-mind-body.

In chapter 6, Jurandir Freire Costa analyses the problem of psychological interiority or the inner world of the self. He argues that the current use of the expression "psychological interiority" is based on two implicit premises. The first premise is cognitive and epistemologically flawed; the second is of the order of mental experience that is theoretically justified and, furthermore, psychologically imperative. Regarding the epistemic fragility of the sense of interiority, he appeals to a critique of the ordinary use of the term by authors from conceptual approaches such as phenomenology, ecological psychology, behaviorism, and the analytical philosophy of mind that emphasizes bodily action. Discussing the compulsory nature of psychological experience of the inner world, he explores psychoanalytic theses from Margolis, Castoriadis-Aulagnier, and above all, D.W. Winnicott.

In our next chapter, Mark Solms takes a neuropsychoanalytic approach to the "hard problem" of consciousness. The starting point is Freud's assertion that, although cognition is mostly unconscious, affect is intrinsically conscious. A feeling wouldn't be a feeling if you didn't feel it. This crucial difference between cognition and affect casts new light on David Chalmers's claim that consciousness cannot be explained mechanistically. If affect (unlike cognition) is indeed intrinsically conscious, then surely its mechanism must account for how and why it feels like something.

Like Solms, Elliot Jurist continues to mind the body by focusing on affect. Although the body has always been relevant in psychoanalysis, in recent years, the mind-body relation has received greater attention and new ways of conceiving the relation are being forged. The body is not simply the repository of emotions that are too threatening to acknowledge; rather, it is a source of information that we can tune into and that provides meaning. In this chapter, Jurist focuses on the turn toward "embodied mentalization" in mentalization theory; in particular, the important role that "interoception" plays in maintaining homeostasis, as well as the further processing of emotions that is a part of "mentalized affectivity," a kind of emotion regulation that is mediated by autobiographical memory. He also discusses cross-cultural research that suggests a revaluation of somatization as a construct: somatization can be regarded as a culturally legitimate form of communication, not as a failure to put feelings into words. Ultimately, he argues that both neuroscience and cross-cultural studies contribute to the development of a contemporary psychoanalytic perspective on the mind-body relation.

Born at the bedside of Anna O, whose plethora of symptoms had no physiological basis, Anna Aragno reminds us how the "talking cure" unfolded, uncovering that hysterics suffer mainly from reminiscences—a product of the mind. Freud's scientific method, psychoanalysis, eschewed the body-mind dilemma from the beginning, bursting in on the scene in his explosive *The Interpretation of Dreams*. For Freud, the deep unconscious is biological. Like Piaget after him, Freud's mind begins in the body, the first ego, a *body*-ego. After taking the common dream as a legitimate object of scientific scrutiny, Freud produced a masterwork of observation in which he arrives at his first *topographical* theory of mind, the cornerstone of early psychoanalytic metatheory. Chapters 6 and 7 of the dream book present a detailed analysis of the two-tiered structure, motive force, and formal properties and compositional grammar of a "Primary Process" vocabulary of the deepest unconscious, where linguistic dream interpretation offers *a bridge* between the Ucs. and Cs. systems. Freud believed his theory of dreams held promise for the study of mental evolution. Yet Freud's great edifice of observation and theoretical foundations lies on the bedrock of residues from his neurological days in a paradigm borrowed from physics, couched in metaphors of repressive forces and shifting forms of energy, a dynamic metatheory of mind in search of real functional processes as explanatory base. To the end, Freud lamented that the *Weltanschauung* of his day could not provide concepts to answer *how* the unconscious becomes conscious.

An overview of Freud's early core concepts is followed by Aragno's revision of his topographical model into a developmental bio-semiotic theory of mind as forms of human communication. Her epigenetic model of mind in *inter-action* illustrates how language and dialogues retain deep roots at less-differentiated interpersonal levels regardless of how abstractly a semiotic system is used, generating bi-directional *semantic fields*. Specifically, her model uncovers a psychoanalytic epistemology articulated through different semiotic forms. The model generates a shift towards an *inter-penetrative* paradigm rooted in functional organizations governing experience, knowledge, and communication, illustrating the semiotic advantage unique to our species as paramount in our adaptation.

In my own work on unconscious semiotics, the coming into being of psychic reality may be understood from the standpoint of a developmental monistic ontology whereby there is a progressive unfolding of desire into an organizing and unifying process system we equate with the unconscious ego as an impersonal executive-synthetic agency. This agency is merely formal; hence, it is not a personal agent or subject in any proper sense, which is commonly ascribed to human consciousness or selfhood. The unconscious abyss is initially immersed in its own corporeal sentient embodiment and awakens as appetitive motivational longing, its initial being-in-relation-to-lack. The unconscious erupts, I suggest, from its self-enclosed original unity as pulsional desire. Such desirous rupture is in response to feeling its need, urge, or craving to experience and satiate the lack, which takes various initial forms that eventually breach into consciousness as ego proper. Originally, desire takes itself as its initial object through a form of pre-reflective self-consciousness I refer to as *unconscious apperception*, the pure experiential self-sense belonging to precognitive unconscious thought. The development of unconscious subjectivity ultimately follows an organic process based on a series of dialectical mediations beginning as unconscious apperception and culminating in self-conscious reflection, the sublated domain of conscious human experience. Yet this initial rudimentary process of desirous rupture and apperception constitutes the birth of the human psyche, for mind is an epigenetic, architectonic self-organizing achievement expressed as a dynamic, self-articulated complex totality or psychic holism.

Unconscious mind, I argue, is a series of spacings that first instantiate themselves as a multitude of *schemata*, which are the building blocks of psychic reality. A schema is a desirous-apperceptive-ideational unit of self-experience that is teleologically oriented and dialectically constituted. Schemata may be viewed as microagents with semi-autonomous powers of telic expression that operate as self-states as they create spacings within the unconscious. Schemata may take various forms, from the archaic to the refined, and instantiate themselves as somatic, sensuous, affective, perceptual, and conceptual (symbolic) orders within the psyche, each having their own intrinsic pressures, valences, intensities, intentional and defensive strategies, and unconscious qualia. It is here that I wish to offer a potential answer to the mind-body problem.

In his chapter, Adrian Johnston begins by arguing in favor of interpreting Freud as a spontaneous dialectical materialist, particularly apropos the perennial philosophical mind-body problem. In this, he follows in the footsteps both of certain classical Freudo-Marxists (e.g., Reich, Fenichel, and Marcuse) as well as, more recently, of Lacan, Althusser, and those one might dub "Lacano-Marxists" (e.g., Žižek). Not only does he focus on the Freudian metapsychological concept of drive (*Trieb*) as pivotal to a psychoanalytic depiction of mind vis-à-vis body, but also he further zeros-in on the anal drive in particular as a Cartesian-style metaphorical pineal gland knotting together soma and psyche. Moreover, as he goes on to show, a Lacanian revisiting of Freud's musings about anal erotism and anal character traits enables a theory of mind/psyche taking these musings into account to proffer not only a dialectical materialist model of subjectivity but also a historical materialist one in which like-mindedness is shaped and mediated by the socioeconomic dimensions foregrounded by the Marxist critique of political economy. Johnston's intervention on this occasion ultimately aims to make progress on two fronts: first, within Marxism itself, facilitating further reconsideration of the infrastructure-superstructure distinction on the basis of what psychoanalysis suggests apropos the mind-body rapport; second, between Marxism and psychoanalysis, utilizing a Lacano-Marxist reconception of the anal drive to advance the radical leftist criticism of capitalism.

Findings from evolutionary neuroscience suggest that the human brain consists of ancient primary process affective systems and more recently evolved secondary process systems. This duality has been compared to Jung's concept of an archaic or collective unconscious shared by all humanity and a more recently evolved form of ego consciousness. In the next chapter, Gary Clark explores these concepts in the context of psychedelic neuroscience and a neurophenomenological approach to the mind-body problem. More specifically, researchers in this field have been able to demonstrate that chemically induced alterations to neural architecture correlate with experiences of "ego dissolution" and a phase transition to primary process styles of cognition. This suggests that brain states and the phenomenology of consciousness are two aspects of the same underlying phenomenon. Clark also explores the work of Goethe and Nietzsche in the context of a discussion of shamanism and ritual transformations of consciousness. He argues that all three thinkers were pioneer explorers of a domain of experience that has for centuries been marginalised by Western philosophy and science. With emerging research in psychedelic neuroscience, this seems to be no longer the case. Consequently, we can now come to appreciate more fully the truly innovative nature of Jung's theories and his extension of ideas that can be traced back to both Nietzsche and Goethe.

Did you know that cities have dominant colours? London, for example, is mostly gold and red. Lisbon is light yellow and turquoise and Madrid is amber and terracotta. Is it possible to compose music by looking at someone's face? Have you ever heard someone say that attending a music concert is a colourful experience, or that one can hear paintings? Imagine what a Picasso would sound like! In his TED Talk "The Human Eyeborg," cyborg artist Neil Harbisson reveals that he has these eccentric colourful experiences. So in order to understand why he named one of his paintings *Mozart,* we need to look beyond ordinary sensory abilities towards a particular type of self-enhancement. If Harbisson is to be believed, when he looks at the colour combinations in his painting, his device (an antenna implanted in his skull that transforms colour frequencies into tone frequencies) enables him to experience a transcendent soundscape comparable to listening to the classical music of Mozart.

In the next chapter, Joeri Pacolet draws on Harbisson's enhanced creativity, as reflected in his painting *Mozart*, to argue against dualistic distinctions in analytical psychology. In his *Structure and the Dynamics of the Psyche*, Jung sets forth his fog argument. This argument has triggered a debate among Jungian scholars about whether to understand it as exemplary for a mind-body dualism in which psychological life is encapsulated within the head. However, even if Jung's fog argument cannot be read as straightforwardly in favour of substance dualism, Pacolet argues that Jungian psychology still displays a value dualism regarding technology, where technology is downplayed in favour of nature. When we look at the meeting of sound and colour that Harbisson experiences through his device, it becomes clear that creativity can no longer be considered as detached from the body and from technology. He shows that the philosophical anthropology of the German biologist, sociologist, and philosopher Helmuth Plessner not only offers a useful framework for reconsidering Harbisson's creativity in a more embodied way but also shows that the deepest roots of creativity move beyond a psychological understanding, such as a Jungian reading of creativity, and call for an ontic foundation. Plessner provides this foundation in his philosophy of borders, relating creativity to human's eccentric position and constitutive homelessness.

In our final chapter, using the long-term practice of psychoanalytic psychotherapy to exemplify the mind-body problem, Alan Michael Karbelnig begins by establishing non-dualistic and perspectivist foundations. As he proceeds to explain the intricacies of psychoanalytic practice, four basic mental phenomena are emphasized, namely, the unconscious and its manifestation in repetition compulsion, transference, and dreams (or other signifiers of the unconscious). Karbelnig proposes an analogy to lovers, exorcists, and critics for understanding the nature of psychoanalytic work. He further shares private details of three medical incidents, which he developed over the course of a decade occupying these social roles. He explores the mind-body interactions likely contributing to his medical crises. Furthermore, he elaborates upon the unique mind-body interactions involved in his work—disappointing patients, absorbing intense emotional states, and involvement in countertransference enactments—through a vivid description of a typical morning involving his work. Examples include one patient experiencing abrupt, unexpected marital separation, another re-living exposure to the New York 9/11 attack, and a third expressing wild spikes of idealization and devaluation towards him. Clinical psychoanalytic work risks triggering psychoanalytic practitioners' childhood traumas, unmet need states, unresolved conflicts, and neurobiological vulnerabilities. The chapter concludes with reflections on the extremely interpersonal, even intimate nature of psychoanalytic work. It renders practitioners' heart-minds and psyche-somas subject to the slings and arrows of projection, introjection, empathy, and identification.

Taken as a whole, this eclectic volume in philosophical psychoanalytic studies on the mind-body problem from the domains of revisionist classical Freudian theory, neo-Jungian analytical psychology, Lacanian analysis, neuropsychoanalysis, mentalization theory, biosemiotics, and applications to the arts, humanities, technological science, and psychoanalytic practice offers a rich bounty of competing yet complementary persepctives on minding the body and the embodied mind. More than any other discipline, psychoanalysis has offered a unique contribution to the question and problem of unconscious processes that may further advance possible solutions to the mind-body problem in contemporary consciousness studies.

References

Anaximenes. Fragments. In Kirk, G.S., J.E. Raven, & M. Schofield (Eds.) (1957). *The Presocratic Philosophers*, 2nd Ed. Cambridge: Cambridge University Press.

Aristotle. De Anima (On the Soul). In Barnes, J. (Ed.) (1984). *The Complete Works of Aristotle. 2 Vols.* (The revised Oxford trans.) (pp. 641–692). Princeton, NJ: Princeton University Press.

Democritus. Fragments. In Kirk, G.S., J.E. Raven, & M. Schofield (Eds.) (1957). *The Presocratic Philosophers*, 2nd Ed. Cambridge: Cambridge University Press.

Gorgias. Fragments. In Kirk, G.S., J.E. Raven, & M. Schofield (Eds.) (1957). *The Presocratic Philosophers*, 2nd Ed. Cambridge: Cambridge University Press.

Heraclitus. Fragments. In Kirk, G.S., J.E. Raven, & M. Schofield (Eds.) (1957). *The Presocratic Philosophers*, 2nd Ed. Cambridge: Cambridge University Press.

Philolaus. Fragments. In Kirk, G.S., J.E. Raven, & M. Schofield (Eds.) (1957). *The Presocratic Philosophers*, 2nd Ed. Cambridge: Cambridge University Press.

Plato. Meno. In Hamilton, E. & H. Cairns (Eds.) (1961). *The Collected Dialogues of Plato*, Princeton: Princeton University Press, pp. 353–384.

Plato. Republic. In Hamilton, E. & H. Cairns (Eds.) (1961). *The Collected Dialogues of Plato*, Princeton: Princeton University Press, pp. 575–844.

Chapter 1

A Critique of Materialism

Jon Mills

Contemporary theories in cognitive science and the philosophy of mind lend burgeoning support for the materialist position regarding the mind-body problem. That is, naturalism, physicalism, and material monism are the preferred theories that explain the relationship between mental processes and physical brain states. While dualist and spiritualist approaches offer counter-arguments to materialism (Vendler, 1994; Warner, 1994), the preponderance of current research in the philosophical, natural, and social sciences concludes that mental states are nothing but physical states (Armstrong, 1968; Bickle, 1998; Churchland, 1981; Dennett, 1991; Dretske, 1995; Searle, 1994). From these accounts, mind *is* brain.

Throughout this chapter, I highlight five central dangers associated with materialism that ultimately result in (1) the displacement of an ontology of consciousness, (2) a simplistic and fallacious view of causality, (3) the loss of free will, (4) renunciation of the self, and (5) questionable judgments concerning social valuation practices. I will attempt to demonstrate that the physicalist position eliminates the possibility of free agency and fails to adequately account for psychic holism.

The Spectrum of Materialism

Dating as far back as Democritus and Epicurus, who conceived of nature as being composed of changeless atoms as indivisible material particles in empty space, to the scientific naturalism of Thomas Hobbes, materialism has become the most popular contemporary

DOI: 10.4324/9781003090755-2

perspective on the nature and character of mind-brain dependence (Bechtel, 1988). There are sundry forms of materialism, yet it is important to note that not even materialists can find unified agreement on what constitutes a definition of materialism. Most materialists insist that nothing but matter in motion exists. Any reference to consciousness, psyche, soul, spirit, or anything denoting mental life *is* nothing but active matter. Another extreme is epiphenomenalism, which is the belief that mind does exist but is caused by and emerges out of material changes, which remains completely dependent on matter. Consciousness is a by-product of material-efficient causal forces and is itself causally impotent: mind has no causal efficacy of its own. All materialists would agree that immaterial agencies or entities do not exist: spirits, ghosts, angels, and demons are illusory. This often leads to the conclusion that there is no God(s) or a supernatural realm, and if these so-called non-material entities are purported to exist, they would be characterized in naturalized terms.

These accounts of materialism may be said to conform to three theses: (1) *The identification thesis*: mind is identified as nothing more than physical states and processes of the brain and central nervous system; (2) *The explanation thesis*: all human and animal behavior is best and most fully explained by physicalistic interpretations, that is, through neuro-chemistry and neurophysiology; and (3) *The exclusion thesis*: there are no powers or properties to the mind that no physical object or system can possess. All mental activity, thought, and action is physically governed and excludes non-materialistic accounts of mental phenomena (Graham, 1993, pp. 128–129).

The most sophisticated form of materialism, in my opinion, is non-reductive materialism. Here the claim is that the phenomenology of consciousness—referred to as qualia or the lived experience—cannot be adequately explained from physicalistic accounts. Hence, assertions about the ontological status of consciousness are bracketed. But it is often the case that non-reductive materialist attempts to bracket or neutralize the ontological status of mind ultimately evade the metaphysical question that is precisely at issue—Is the mind merely brain? Even the term "non-reductive materialism" is itself an oxymoron: substance is reducible matter. While non-reductive materialists claim that mental phenomena (i.e., the appearance of consciousness) cannot be adequately explained by appealing to physical brain states alone, the tacit ontological belief is that mind at bottom is the unification of biological-neurochemical-physical brain processes.

Recent definitions of materialism which have come into vogue within contemporary philosophy of mind include the view that what is material is anything that perceives or exists in space and time. Flew (1984), among others, points out that the precise meaning and status of the materialist doctrine is far from clear. What are the properties, attributes, or qualities that matter can, cannot, or must possess? Furthermore, what are its essential properties? Is there a distinction to be made between its existence, being, and essence, its occurrence and phenomenology, its appearance and reality? What is the exact nature of *how* matter extends in space and time, the forces that operate on it, and how consciousness—itself conceived as matter—perceives and understands its dependence on it? What are the exact mechanisms by which thought occurs, and how do we know? How is it that we cannot directly intuit, feel, observe, or recognize those mechanisms or processes when they are occurring in our own minds? The range of attempted and possible answers to these questions makes materialism an ambiguous group of precepts rather than a unified doctrine.

One thing is clear about materialism: it is a reaction against and rejection of Cartesian dualism that posits a non-extended "thinking substance," which is associated with an immaterial mind (Descartes, 1984). It is worth noting, however, that there are many forms of dualism ranging from the Platonic distinction between appearance and reality, Kant's separation of phenomena from noumena, the ontological distinctions between being and essence, the dialectically opposed forces and manifestations of consciousness, to the epistemological chasms between the knowing subject and object. It is not my intention to defend ontological dualism, but only to show that materialist conceptions of mind pose many problems for understanding the complex psychological, psychosocial, and ontological configurations that constitute the human condition.

Rather than explicate the multitude of materialist positions ranging from identity theories (Armstrong, 1968; Lewis, 1966; Place, 1956), functionalism (Levin, 1986; Putnam, 1967; Smart, 1962; Sober, 1985), supervenience (Teller, 1983), eliminativism (Churchland, 1981;

Stich, 1994), representationalism (Dretske, 1988, 1995; Fodor, 1987, 1998), to anomalous monism (Davidson, 1980), I will refer to the materialist position collectively, which includes the following characteristics as operationally defined:

I   *Physical Reductionism*: (a) all mental states are simply physical states in the brain; there is nothing "over and above" biological-neurochemical-physiological structures, processes, and evolutionary pressures; (b) all mental events, properties, or processes arise out of physical preconditions whereby (c) the organism is conceived of as a matter-energy system composed solely of active material properties or substances reified through material-efficient causal attributions.

II *Naturalism*, which I define as (a) the belief that all knowledge comes from physical conditions governed by natural causal laws based upon an empirical epistemology; (b) supports realism,[1] which is often (but not always) incompatible with a priori truths or transcendental idealist positions; (c) is a form of positivism, in that truth claims about reality are quantifiable facts that can be directly observed, measured, or verified within systematic science relying on experience, experimentation, and rational methods of inquiry; (d) is anti-supernaturalistic, anti-theological, and anti-metaphysical (despite its metaphysical consequences); (e) is pro-scientific, that is, all natural phenomena are adequately explained or are in principle explainable through scientific methodology; and (f) displays tendencies toward non-teleological, non-anthropomorphic, and non-animistic explanations.

If materialism is going to make such ontological assertions, then it must be able to coherently defend its own self-imposed assumptions without begging the question. It becomes our task to ferret out the philosophical, humanistic, and ethical implications of the materialist project and expose the conundrums it generates if we are going to properly understand the question of mind. I will attempt to show that psychic holism becomes an alternative paradigm to the materialist position, which more successfully addresses the multifaceted domains of mental processes, personal experience, and discourse surrounding mind-body dependence without succumbing to a reductive metaphysics.

The Naturalistic Fallacy

Freud (1900) admonishes us to "avoid the temptation to determine psychical locality in any anatomical fashion" (p. 536), insisting that the mind should not be reduced to "anatomical, chemical or physiological" properties (Freud, 1916-1917, p. 21). Materialists, on the other hand, are dogmatic in their insistence that all mental events are ultimately reducible to physical events or brain states in the organism. Thus, physical reductionism is the *sine qua non* of materialism. Teller (1983) summarizes this position nicely: "Everything... is at bottom physical." In other words, there is no mind, only brain. One might ask materialists, How do you know that? To justify their claims, they will inevitably rely upon science, empirical psychology, the bare appeal to sensible and tangible experience, or naturalized or evolutionary accounts of epistemology (see Quine, 1969a; Vollmer, 1975; Wuketits, 1990). While science has its legitimate status, it must first establish a coherent criterion for truth. To fall back on the very criterion that it must set out to prove simply begs the question and envelopes materialist justifications in circularity.

Many criticisms have been launched on naturalized epistemology for (1) its attempt to naturalize mental notions of intentionality in materialistic and physically reductive terms, (2) its presupposition of a realist notion of truth, (3) its positivistic structure, and (4) its tendency to collapse into cultural relativism. Putnam (1983) charges that naturalized epistemology presupposes a metaphysical realism and a correspondence theory of truth in that truth corresponds to the "facts." He ultimately argues that this notion is incoherent, whereby "truth" is relevant to one's scheme of describing and explaining physical phenomena, hence embedded in a social language practice that determines how truth is to be defined and measured. This metaphysical assumption postulates a set of "ultimate" objects that are "absolute" and can be "objectively" measured, hence are "real," which essentially tries to revive the whole failed enterprise of the realism/anti-realism debate. Because realism and correspondence theory presuppose knowledge of an object world independent of the subject, such postulation becomes a meaningless proposition when one cannot talk about objectivity without importing subjectivity. It was Kant, followed by the German Idealism of Fichte and Hegel, who cogently demonstrated that the a priori structures of subjectivity make objectivity possible.

Post-structural and linguistic accounts characteristic of post-modernism maintain that truth claims are constructed by historical contingencies and socially defined language practices: our identification of Truth conforms to current rationally accepted standards of truth. From this account, any talk of absolute knowledge that exists objectively—as if it inheres as a property in an object independent of the subject—is vacuous. All interpretation rests on a theory of language, therefore objectivity is always interpreted through subjectivity. Yet language is instantiated in a social ontology and determines the definition of objectivity. However, what is agreed upon within a social context of linguistic practices and custom is determined by a collection of subjects. Traditionally, arguments against realism come from a priori epistemology and semantics, or theories of meaning. This strategy typically applies a theory of meaning or a philosophy of language to critique and abnegate any metaphysical claims to truth that naturalism holds, thus bringing into doubt serious questions about any mind-independent realms of existence. From this perspective, realism is an issue of interpretation, hence hermeneutics, instantiated in linguistic, semantic, and social practices. Even *facts* are language-formulable facts, and can be semantically captured in language-formulated truth (Dancy & Sosa, 1992, p. 188). This claim is that epistemically, naturalized accounts cannot make such realist assertions of mind.

Some philosophers such as Wittgenstein and Derrida seem to renounce (or perhaps elude) the whole debate itself. While Derrida deconstructs the distinction between the inner and the outer and treats them equiprimordially, from a Wittgensteinian stance, the whole debate becomes a "language game" (see Post, 1991). Because there are many equally privileged ways of communicating, each language has its own rules and vocabulary that determine what we are talking about within a social context. Therefore, no linguistic practice captures the ultimate structure of reality, including the nature of mind. Absolute naturalized claims about the being and essence of mind become a naturalistic fallacy. This is the tendency to believe that a complex whole is identical or reducible to its parts, causes, and natural origins, and that the mind's complexity may be entirely explained by appealing to such naturalistic conditions.

Notions of truth and rational acceptability are relative to social language practices within a particular cultural context. "Reason is always relative to context and institution" and "the ideal language," "inductive logic," and "the empiricist criterion of significance" are "fantasies of the positivist" (Putnam, 1983, p. 358). Furthermore, reason is informed by the cultural norms that determine what naturalistic views will be. Truth—the only notion of truth one can understand—is then defined by the norms of one's culture and the cultural criteria that is socially imposed. If left unchecked, the politicalization and privileged discourse of scientific naturalism can lead to a form of cultural imperialism—*My* culture (truth) is better than *yours*!

Destruction of an Ontology of Consciousness

Materialist conceptions of mind are highly problematic for several reasons. First of all, the individual is reduced to physical substance alone, which gives rise to an organismic, and in some cases, mechanistic views of the human being. By reducing the psyche to matter, an ontology of consciousness is displaced. That is, there is no *distinct* ontological status to mental events; psychic processes and properties are merely physical properties within a functional system that constitutes the organism. The transcendental properties of the mental are reduced to atomic and sub-atomic particles within a closed system of energetics constituted through quantum mechanics. In this sense, mind does not direct consciousness or action, matter does. In short, the human being is reduced to a *thing*—a reified biological machine engineered by evolution and stimulated by the environment.

This approach can potentially lead to a very dehumanizing account of the individual. The intrinsic uniqueness of individuality, personality, and the phenomenology of psychical experience collapses in reductionism. By making the human being merely an organism, one has stripped the uniquely personal and idiosyncratic dimensions of selfhood down to biology. While this ideology has its rudiments in natural science and evolutionary biology, from this standpoint, consciousness does not exist; that is, consciousness, intentionality, the phenomenal experience, qualia, the "aboutness" or "what it's like" to experience something and to live is reduced to changes in brain states engulfed in a language describing physical processes alone. Within this context, all conscious experience and behavior is a functional (and at times mechanical) operation that is organized within a systemic structure. What it means to be human and the existential questions and dilemmas that populate mental life are abandoned to sterile scientific depictions of animate organic matter. Although materialist theories vary in conceptual depth and locution, in the end there is no metaphysical mind, only physical-energetic substance.

Simplicity and Causal Fallacies

Materialism ultimately rests on a simplistic view of causality, which is inherently biased and conforms to the empirical positivist tradition: namely, psychic reality is that which is directly observable, measurable, and quantifiable, thus constituted as fact. We owe this to the law of parsimony, or Ockham's razor. The virtue of simplicity is intended to be in the service of economy; that is, anything intelligible can be explained in material terms. Abstract theories of complexity and ambiguity are less economical and do not neatly "fit" into ordinary belief systems; therefore, simplicity is preferred to complexity. However, the simplest explanation does not mean it is the most accurate. This position has been applied in the following way: If one cannot observe it or measure it, it does not exist. In my view, the value of simplicity has been abused. There is no value in reducing the human being to a thing. While the value of parsimony is appropriate for various types of social, professional, and pragmatic discourse, the qualitative aspect of what it is like to be human is sacrificed. Cognitive science today is content with explaining consciousness as experiential changes in brain states, which can in part be observed, measured, and quantifiably verified. Observation is one thing, but to make the generalized claim, "That is all there is!" is epistemically problematic. This positivistic account presupposes a "God's eye" view of reality and thus makes a sweeping metaphysical judgment.

Materialism fallaciously believes that if psychic events are realized physically, then their tenets are proved. At the very least, materialists are obliged to take an agnostic position with regard to an ontology of consciousness. Just because one cannot directly observe or measure conscious phenomena, this does not mean that neurophysiology is all there is. As previously mentioned, this is a naturalistic or reductive fallacy. The very idea of the mental is that it is something that is not tangible, it is literally *no-thing*, hence psychical. This is not to deny the interdependence and interpenetration of mind and body: while physical processes and properties are a necessary condition of mind, it is far from being a sufficient condition. Mind is embodied or instantiated physically, but by virtue of its transcendental and elusive functions and properties, it cannot be spatially localized or dissected. Most materialists want to eliminate this stance as a viable possibility and hold allegiance to a simple economy—that which is *real* is something that is tangible. This fixation with making metaphysical and epistemic pronouncements based on tangible evidence in the service of economy jeopardizes the integrity of psychical reality.

Another pitfall of the materialist position is the simplistic notion of causality as physical reduction. Thus, materialism relies on the interaction of two primary causal attributions: (1) physical causation and (2) environmental determinism. This position insists that the human being is, in Aristotelian terminology, the conglomeration of material and efficient causes: mind is caused by the matter or physical substance it is made of as well as causally affected by the material forces that constitute the flux of environmental events. This is the case for the most unrefined materialist positions, such as the type-type identity theory, to the more sophisticated functional monist approaches. It boils down to (a) the physical causing all mental events, thus instituting force and motion that bring about effects, and (b) environmental contingencies that cause the organism to respond to a stimulus prior to the effect in time. This is the theoretical foundation of most materialist theories as well as American behaviorism, which espouses the S-R paradigm of psychological processes.[2] In other words, some stimulus (whether internal or external) is prior to a response (whether it be changes in brain states, neurochemical networks and neural patterns of activity, or behavioral output due to environmental variables), thereby causing physiological, cognitive, and behavioral changes in the organism.

For example, early distinguished pioneers such as Armstrong and Lewis assign causal attributions to mental states, which therefore direct behavior. However, mental events are physically realized and caused by sensory input, thus environmentally determined as well. Functionalism, on the other hand, championed by Putnam and to-day's contemporaries, more successfully argues for an elaborate organization of mental life (e.g., a functional physical system directs the body and consciousness via CNS sensory inputs and motor outputs, thereby producing changes in neurochemical patterns of brain activity and biophysiological structures that parallel a cybernetic machine of input-output operations). Despite these sophisticated and cogent strategies, the dynamic processes and properties of mind arise from physical substance, hence are reductionistic and physically determined. This position also holds true for certain dualist perspectives such as epiphenomenalism and the "qualia freaks." Ultimately, all mental properties arise out of matter, thereby, they belong to *it* and have no causal powers over physical states. Where Jackson (1982) rejects physicalism due to epiphenomenal qualia, nevertheless, consciousness is rendered causally impotent. Thus, we are biologically pre-wired and caused by environmental conditioning based on various propositional expectancies. If one espouses this view, the human being is the product of biology and the environment, nothing more.

With the exception of teleological functionalism, which employs a formal and final causal thesis, materialist theories are essentially reductive. Even with teleological functionalism advanced by Sober (1985), he ultimately supports a biological teleology in that the functional organism is purposeful in its organization and behavior. In the end, this position is also a physical reductionism for the purposeful behavior and has its source in biology whose aim is functionally motivated. While an organism can have telic organization, it does not require the organism to be self-directed or have an active agent doing the directing. For example, a heart has a telos; its function is to pump blood. This is reminiscent of Freudian drive theory in that a drive (*Trieb*) has a functional telos but does not think; it is merely oriented toward tension reduction in the service of pleasure, or in this case, functional adaptation to biological and environmental demands.

In espousing reductive causality, materialism ignores the multicausal processes and over-determined forces of mind that, I argue, can never be exactly pinpointed as empirical science wants to profess. In David Hume's (1748) seminal work, *An Enquiry Concerning Human Understanding*, he shows that temporal sequence does not necessarily establish causal connection. In other words, the mere occurrence of event Z after event Y does not provide sufficient grounds for claiming that event Y caused event Z. Causality can never be ascertained with unequivocal precision or isolated as distinct or independent physical events without accounting for the multiple overdetermining forces that comprise causal complexity. For example, if I strike a match to light a fire, one could say that the physical-chemical properties of the match caused the fire (material cause), or that my action of striking the match caused the fire (efficient cause), or that the natural elements of the physical surroundings such as the arid temperature, wind velocity, dryness of the wood, and so on caused the fire (formal cause), or that my volitional intention and purposeful behavior caused the fire (final cause), or that all these conditions must be present in interactional causal harmony. Aristotle's meta-causal theory allows us to break down the constituents of causal conditions and events, but it would be a category mistake to simply reduce teleology to physical necessity alone.

In the service of parsimony or simplicity, the materialist insistence on physical ontology selectively ignores the multitudinous and overdetermined processes a meta-causal theory of explanation affords. This becomes particularly germane to the question of determination, purpose, intentionality, and choice. Maintaining a physical ontology of consciousness has even further pernicious repercussions when examining the question of freedom.

Loss of Freedom

Reliance on material and efficient causal explanations, the overvaluation of simplicity à la Ockham's razor, and consequently, physical reductionism, completely eliminates any possibility of free will. From this standpoint, the human being is not free. This position is summarized by the exclusion thesis, which posits that human beings have no properties or mental powers that no object or physical system can possess (Graham, 1993). Thus, if free will is a mental process or property, and no physical system is free, then we do not possess free choice and are consequently not free. This simplicity denies the possibility of final causal determinants and transcendental teleology characteristic of free agents. Agency is here defined as a subject who is telic, purposeful, and self-directed via choices and deliberation in judgments constituting self-conscious activity. Therefore, thoughts, volitional intentions, and behaviors are the activities of the will: freedom is ultimately defined as the ability to choose or *be* otherwise. Freedom, however, is not merely restricted to choice; it also encompasses the structural organization of the individual doing the choosing, namely the agent. In short, agency, free will, intentionality, and final causality (e.g., choosing the grounds for the sake of which to behave) are problematic for the materialist, for physical matter is caused rather than being freely causal or determinative.

Several philosophers have tried to give an adequate account of free will for the materialist position (Davidson, 1980; Dennett, 1984; Levin, 1979; Thalberg, 1983). Levin (1979) argues that materialism is compatible with free will, since he defines freedom as "doing what you want to do" (p. 228). However, materialists have a proclivity to define freedom in terms of action rather than agency. Levin continues: "one can be free even if one's acts are caused by wants, and one's wants are caused by other factors out of one's control" (p. 228). It is one thing to have control over one's actions that are "unconstrained" by external forces, yet it is another thing to say that one's thoughts or volitional intentions are caused by something outside of one's control. Within this naturalistic framework, free choice is based upon external contingencies and physical states in the organism. Thoughts and actions cannot be freely chosen if they are caused by preceding events that are environmentally or physically determined. For the materialist, desire and choice *is not* freely acquired: it is imposed upon the organism by intrinsic and extrinsic forces. Freedom involves the intentional states of the individual, not just actions, in that choice is defined as "I could have done or *thought* otherwise!" This is not the case if choice is directed by a functional system where matter causes mental events. Materialists have a difficult time explaining why we have the ability to freely choose the next thought we wish to think. Therefore, the locus of freedom resides in the agent's ability to freely will and determine one's own thoughts and actions.

Davidson (1980) attempts to account for a non-reductive materialism by claiming that the mental is anomalous for there are no precise or discernible laws that account for mental events. In other words, there are no laws connecting propositional attitudes with brain states.[3] However, the materialist's response to Davidson is that each propositional attitude might in fact be a complex brain state or network of processes, which he even seems willing to concede. Putnam (1975) also proposed the notion of "multiple realizability" of mental states as an anti-reductionist response to psychoneural identity theory. This position is also taken up by Fodor (1974) who argues that social sciences are generally irreducible to physical theory. More recently, Horgan (1994) has proposed a non-reductive materialism where he denies that mentalistic psychology can be reducible to neurobiology. He maintains that reductionism would be disproved if intentional mental state-types could be physically realized in multifarious ways. By adopting a realization-neutrality posture, the ontology of intentional states of consciousness may be preserved within a framework that gives psychological processes and properties explanatory power and autonomy.

Post (1987, 1995) and Dennett (1991) offer sophisticated non-reductive material accounts of mental phenomena that take into account the natural-selective history of ancestral organisms within their specific cultural environments. From these perspectives, the phenomenology of mind is better construed as adaptions, which are not rigidly reduced to bio-neurochemical-physiological brain processes, but rather further consist of natural-selective pressures operating on ancestral organisms over long periods of time. The usual reductive accounts, especially those insistent on individualistic and synchronic reductions, do not adequately address these evolutionary and cultural adaptations. Hence, these types of materialists would hold reservations about characterizing the mind as an energy-matter system simply because some key mental properties are not sufficiently understood by physicalist paradigms. A recent example of this trend in philosophy of mind is to espouse some form of panpsychism, animism, or vitalism as the ontological basis of the cosmos qua mental processes that condition the coming into being of consciousness, itself problematic.

Because non-reductive materialists acknowledge they have difficulty in accounting for certain aspects of mental reality, this leaves open the possibility for psychical interpretations of mental events that exist and manifest apart from or are at least co-extensive with physical brain processes. Essentially, this form of materialism holds an agnostic stance toward some possible form of dualism or compatibilism. But when we follow this line of thinking through to its end, there really is no materialist position that is truly non-reductive, for any position that ultimately posits mental life in physical-evolutionary terms is reductionary. Evolutionary adaptations are realized physical mutations of brain processes and organismic structures. Thus, there is no such thing as non-reductive materialism: it is merely a myth (Kim, 1994). The burden of proof lies on the shoulders of those materialists who wish to account for freedom within an entirely materialist framework.

Charles Hanly's (1979) solution to the question of materialism is to offer a compatibilist framework of psychic determinism. While deterministic forces populate mental life, the difference between a free and a compelled act is due to the nature of its causes, for all acts are caused. Therefore, the concepts of will, intentionality, autonomy, and responsibility may be seen as compatible operations within the mind in which the notion of freedom is preserved within a determinist model. Here the point is that while psychic life is bound to the necessity of its natural enmattered configurations, the psyche may still operate as a freely determining self-directed agent.

Dretske (1988) and Dennett (1981) attempt to explain meaning, intentionality, "aboutness" and the "what it's like" aspect of qualia by placing primacy on the internal states of the organism that cause experience and behavior due to the internal organization of the functional states, rather than assigning causal attributions to the environment. From this perspective, the structure of the organism *appears* to have free will; it interacts with the surround, structures meaning within its functional framework, assigns experience a job, indicates a role for it, thus allegedly produces meaning and chooses the grounds for the sake of which to behave. By making a functional organism assign meaning to experience, they preserve the self as a self-directed agent, so it seems. Despite this, freedom is still defined in material terms: the transcendental qualities of mind are still reduced to matter even though, in Dennett's words, we have a little "elbow room." While a functional organism can freely act, it cannot transcend, or in Hegelian terms, sublate (*aufheben*) its physical thrownness. Thus, within this context, freedom is still reduced to a physical ontology. For

Hegel, freedom is among other things freedom from natural determination. We are free but we are natural beings; thus freedom is the process of transcending nature while incorporating it in its spiritual embodiment. Having attained freedom from its mere natural, necessarily determined corporeality, *Geist* is actively free to determine itself as a dynamic, intelligible self-articulated complex whole.

A sophisticated materialist view claims to allow for conscious experience, but disavows the notion that an ontology of consciousness may be purported to exist above or even equiprimordially alongside neurophysiological properties of the brain. For Dretske and Dennett, we are an elaborately designed and malleable machine in which we are also the designers, yet the blueprints must conform to natural laws. When followed through to its end, the mind is ultimately explained by appeal to material and efficient causal-evolutionary forces that have their teleology in substance. Thus, in the end, we are not autonomous free agents because substance teleology is confined to the formal characteristics of a pre-determined design. While self-assigned meaning as a mental property has causal powers, meaning is ultimately a pattern of neurons firing in the brain or a realized state in the biological machine. Mental activity is merely the product of a physical apparatus. Consciousness, meaning, and intentionality are merely neurological structures and processes, and the "I" is the system itself. The human being is still a thing, a complex thing, but nevertheless, a physical system. The true test for materialism is to explain, if it can, how matter can have freely self-directed constituting agency. Agency from the physicalist standpoint is not free, for it is only the product and succession of material and efficient properties of the brain.

A Word from Physics

What is particularly interesting is that those social scientists and philosophers of mind discussed previously seem to be unaware of the recent discoveries in the natural sciences (see Anderson & Stein, 1987; Atmanspacher, 1997; Atmanspacher, Amann, & Müller-Herold, 1999; Penrose, 1989; Primas, 1993). Many thoughtful scholars in experimental and theoretical physics as well as biophysics, biochemistry, genetics, and mathematics oppose reductionism on ontological, methodological, and epistemological levels (Yates, 1987). Because the procedures, observations, terms, and patterns of explanation in some sciences are entirely unconnectable to those of other disciplines (Ayala, 1987), reductive strategies that wish to collapse one branch of science into another is neither possible nor desirous. For example, physicists Anderson and Stein (1987) compared dissipative structures with thermodynamic equilibrium systems and conclude that complex physical systems exhibit emergent properties unrelated to those of their constituents. While higher order novelties and complexities arise out of simpler events, such complexifications are hardly reducible to their previous states.

Following the work of Hans Primas (1993, 1994), Otto Rössler (1994) has also provided support for a "parallelism" between phenomenology and science. In his assessment, endophysics offers a two-level interpretation of objective reality (endo and exo) that preserves the dualism inherent in both Cartesian and Kantian philosophy. While the endo-questions pertinent to quantum mechanics may be potentially resolved, the exo level remains, with qualifications, directly inaccessible. This is why physicists speak of probabilities rather than locality (see Gustafson, 1999; Sudarshan, 1999) and of correlations rather than causation (Atmanspacher, Amann, & Müller-Herold, 1999).

Atmanspacher et al. (1999) further contend that the multi-level structure of generalized quantum theories is too simplistic if epistemic and ontic elements are considered on the same level of description. Following Quine (1969b), they conclude that ontological descriptions are relative to the conceptual scheme one espouses. Because *both* mind and matter are emergent domains of description that are fundamentally symmetrical, they further speculate that the distinction between mental and physical polarities becomes irrelevant.

It is unfortunate that such ardent materialists are not acquainted with the advancements made by the natural sciences and their subsequent implications, such as the momentous discovery of the energetic stratification of material interactions; if they were, the whole reductionist enterprise would be recognized for what it is: an ideological artifact that is scientifically indefensible. These arguments radically change the whole issue. Until the relation between quanta, mind, and matter is examined from a holistic paradigm (see Shimony, 1999), the illusion of materialism will likely persist.

Death of the Self

One of the most disturbing consequences of the materialist position is that the notion of the Self dissolves. In the spirit of Nietzsche, *The Self is Dead!*, and materialism killed it. Essentially, this view is commensurate with a Buddhist or Humean view of the self—there is none, only sensations and impressions impinging on the senses in a fleeting moment. For Hume, there is no "I" directing mentation. There is only the theater of the mind where thoughts are cast by natural laws and where self-reflection is only second-order perceptions. The self is merely an illusion. Thus, free will and any sense of personal identity is non-existent. In Dennett's (1991) words, we "*spin a self*," or as Skinner would contend, we are only operantly conditioned to believe in a self. The "I" is just a social construction or invention of language: we are a collection of dynamic mental properties and perceptions in flux, that's all.

Whether one conceives of the self in the tradition of Descartes' *cogito* as the "I" that resides behind the cognizer, or the Kantian transcendental unity of apperception as the nominal, enduring, unified unifier, or Hegel's notion of subjective spirit (*Geist*), or Sartre's notion of the self as radical freedom, to the Freudian ego (*Ich*) as a self-directed synthesizing agent—the distinctive *psychical* processes and properties of consciousness, not to mention the unconscious, are dismissed from the materialist framework. Although a physical system can be dynamically organized and functionally sophisticated, in the end, the organism is doing the thinking and behaving, not the self. Materialists would contend, however, that the organism is the self. But it is precisely this definitional issue that becomes problematic. The notion of the self plays a great role in human value practices and should not be conceived merely as a physical entity. Human experience, personal identity, character formation, and selfhood simply cannot be reduced to atoms and sub-atomic particles without losing the integrity of freedom and an ontologically transcendental self-posit or act.

Furthermore, if you are looking for the possibility of a personal afterlife, materialism offers very little comfort. Not only are free will and the self eliminated, but materialism is also consequentially a fundamental atheism. Spiritual transcendence of the soul or personality, or the possibility of an afterlife, are not tenable within the materialist framework. If the mind or psyche is nothing more than its material substrate (i.e., merely active particles), then this substance would cease to exist upon its physical death. The soul as psychical substance could not exist in disembodied form; hence death of the organism is death of the soul. As Graham (1993) tells us, if "the soul is something mental and the soul survives bodily death, whereas the brain fails to survive, then there is no such thing as a soul" (p. 129). Unless by some miraculous means, such as the possibility that physical decomposition could be reconstituted in another physical medium—the likelihood of which is close to nil, the soul would not exist. It would be virtually impossible to rebuild and reconnect the millions of neural pathways destroyed by physical decay, such as in the case of brain trauma or dementia. And if this were possible, such as in some *Star Trek* episode, the question of sustained personal identity would remain equivocal. Reconstituted matter by definition would no longer be identical to itself. A duplicated or redesigned self would not be the same self. For materialists, all natural phenomena eventually pass out of existence and return to an eternal, primordial material ground in an eternal transformation of matter, so wave "good bye" to a personal afterlife. Simply put, spiritualism, supernaturalism, immaterialism, disembodiment, transcendentalism, transpersonal realms, and any appeal to mystical experience, revelation, or faith are untenable hypotheses.

There is something so counterintuitive to this claim, that human consciousness, or the self, personal identity, or soul (either theologically or non-theologically conceived) is not a transcendental agent with psychic properties and attributes. Materialism assumes that what is real is only what appears and that it can be objectively verified as tangible fact. But the whole notion of the spiritual is by definition that which cannot be empirically measured or quantified. It is by virtue of the fact that we have no direct epistemic access to the transcendental properties of the mind that we *must* posit its ontological status. In fact for Hegel (1991), there is nothing which we are more certain of than the spiritual by virtue of the fact that we posit it.

Even if we were to concede that the mind ceases to exist upon the moment of physical death, this would not rule out in toto the presence of Self, teleology, agency, free will, choice, and the spiritual dimensions of the human condition. The phenomenology of the lived experience—extending to all facets of human motivation, desire, emotion, and rational thought—cannot be adequately captured by the rigidly reductive language and ontological pronouncements that characterize some branches of natural science. Philosophical, historical, cultural, aesthetic, and psychological hermeneutics, to name just a few, allow for a plurality of interpretations to resonate among privileged discourse on the nature of selfhood. Materialism simply does not address the human aspect as a dynamic self-articulated totality or *complexio oppositorum*.

It appears that materialists must anchor ontology to something physical or tangible as a verification of their quest for certainty. Nagel (1974) nicely makes the point that materialists have a penchant for describing mental phenomena in physical terms as operating in the service of objectivity. Yet by espousing this viewpoint in the name of objectivity, it takes us further away from the real nature of consciousness (the subjective lived experience) rather than bringing us closer to it. One does not need to be reminded that the object of "objectivity" is always interpreted through the "mind's eye," that of the subject. Kant (1781) also reminds us of the limits to the possibility of epistemic certainty: we can never know the *noumena* directly, only through the translation of our senses mediated by rational understanding. Thus, materialism deceives itself by espousing a "God's eye" view of the universe in its attempt to logically account for all phenomena. Within this framework of natural science, such presumption about reality becomes manifested in the belief that if one can account for every particle, one can (at least in principle) accurately control and predict the world. Science *appears* as the touchstone of Truth, when in fact, science is just one appearance among many appearances. For Kant (1781), any physicalist attempt to make ontological claims about the "thing-in-itself" (*Ding an sich*) is fallacious: by definition this is unknowable, simply unverifiable, an unprovable tenet, hence an open indeterminate question—the very claim in contemporary physics (see Primas, 1993, 1994; Rössler, 1994).

Value Judgments Concerning Social Practices

Because materialism is over-identified with a scientific epistemology, there is a tacit prejudice that the human being is a biological machine one can control, predict, and manipulate. While science and medicine have provided and continue to provide humanity with knowledge and technology that drastically improves the quality of life, there is an inherent danger in the tendency to view the human being *only* as a biological organism. Within this context, there is a medicalization or objectification of the human subject. The hazard in this treatment of the subject as an object is that it may lead to social, political, and scientific practices that fail to account for the dynamic psychological complexity of mental life and the existential human needs inherent to conscious experience. This biased naturalistic view may condone various professional practices in medicine, psychiatry, the social sciences, artificial intelligence (AI), and posthuman eco-technological discourse. We have already seen how the medical model of psychiatry has usurped psychological approaches to the treatment of certain types of mental illnesses. For example, Prozac or its psychotropic equivalent is the salient choice mode of intervention for depression over psychotherapy—assuming that all forms of depression have a biological correlate, which is confused with etiology, hence are physically caused. This is simply erroneous.[4] The danger to such medical practices is that people get the message that all they need to do is take a pill and they will be happy. Physical interventions and psycho-pharmacological treatments may be appropriate for some medical or psychiatric conditions, but certainly not all. Such objectification of the human being may potentially justify myriad ethically dubious practices (e.g., fetal tissue and stem-cell research, bioengineering, euthanasia, physician-assisted suicide, genetic and human cloning). The reduction of the phenomenology of consciousness could further lead to an invalidation of uniquely subjective lived existential experience. The human being is not just an organism to be manipulated by science, rather is a person to be acknowledged and valued. The medicalization and clinical depiction of the human being seems to lack a degree of empathy, concernful solicitude, and careful insight into the array of human experiences that cannot be reduced or explained away with technical jargon or physicalist nomenclature.

In his refutation of modern scientific materialism, Alfred North Whitehead (1925) charges physicalist accounts of mind and nature with the Fallacy of Simple Location or Misplaced Concreteness; that is, the error of objectifying a high-order abstraction as a concrete entity. Whitehead points out the confusion and misguided conclusions that occur when levels of abstraction are reduced to simply located quantitative properties of matter. This attitude is essentially the belief that what comprises the basic elements of the real is the simply located particle. This also echoes the offense of committing a mereological error where a complex whole is reduced to the sum of its parts. In quoting a poem from Wordsworth, Whitehead shows that the antiseptic language of science can never capture the *feeling* of nature that is encountered in the lived experience:

> We forget how strained and paradoxical is the view of nature which modern science imposes on our thoughts. Wordsworth, to the height of genius, expresses the concrete facts of our apprehension, facts which are distorted in the scientific analysis. Is it not possible that the standardised concepts of science are only valid within narrow limitations, perhaps too narrow for science itself? (1925, p. 84)

If we were to ask a botanist to describe the essence of a flower, he/she would in all likelihood discuss its physical and chemical composition such as its reproductive organs, its petals, sepals, pistil, stamens, and its anther and filament. But if we were to consult a poet such as Wordsworth: "And 'tis my faith that every flower, / Enjoys the air it breathes" ("Lines Written in Early Spring," lines 11-12; see Kraus, 1998, p. 25), we are forced to confront a different perspective of reality. Are we to assume that science holds a privileged depiction of nature, such as the nature of a flower? Which one is more real? As useful as it may be in certain contexts, materialist explanations may only offer a limited glimpse into understanding the essence of mind. The aesthetic, the moral, the feelings that comprise the quality of lived experience are perspectives of being that can never be adequately explained by reductive science.

Another potentially dehumanizing aspect of the materialist agenda is to advocate a change in linguistic communication practices that emphasize physical description. For example, Paul Churchland proposes that we adopt a new language to describe brain states rather than conscious experiences. This is further echoed by Smart (1962) who states "it would make sense to talk of an experience in terms appropriate to physical processes" (p.173). Why? Why do we need a conceptual and social change in language and communication practices? What pragmatic usefulness would it have for people to talk about and communicate their complex cognitive, emotive, and psychological experiences in physically descriptive language? This seems to be the fantasy of the logical positivist in order to clear away any discourse that does not neatly fit into a materialist paradigm. How could it facilitate arriving at a more accurate picture of inner reality? Instead of saying, "I love you," we would say, "My neurons are firing in sector 14.2 of my left frontal lobe." Is love really like a heatwave (see Levin, 1986)? Churchland (1981) even goes so far to propose that we eliminate current social language practices and replace them with an alternative language that would require monumental social and educational reform, not to mention experimental surgery on human beings. He suggests we could "construct a new system of verbal communication entirely distinct from natural language" (p. 220). Such a proposal would require global changes in the way the world thinks, communicates, and operates, as if the metaphorical, aesthetic, and mythopoetic mind can be jettisoned by wishful expediency and grandiose denial of the feeling soul and need for subjective self-expression unconstrained by logocentrism and sterile science. Such a proposition violates human nature and displaces the varieties of culture with the vulgar reification of social collectives treated as manipulative objects in a thought experiment. In addition, Churchland proposes placing a "transducer for implantation at some site in the brain" (p. 221), arguably a precursor to the transhuman technology movement that has piqued futurists, AI designers, and the nanoengineering industry alike, as if the human race is to be converted into robots or cognitively enhanced machines.

To me this is clearly an unethical proposal and probably motivated out of the need to generate controversy in the service of personal narcissism or ideology. Experimentation on humans?—as if everyone would be a willing participant. The ramifications of such a practice would result in a complete alteration in the way people think, talk, and perceive reality; thus personality, identity, and one's sense of self would be radically mutated. In essence, people would no longer be who they previously were: it would be tantamount to turning people into automatons or appliances.

In his essay, "Quining Qualia," Dennett (1988) also wants to get rid of the word *qualia* and redefine the theory of consciousness within a materialist framework. He claims because subjective states have "ineffable" properties, they are only accessible from the first-person viewpoint and therefore cannot be detected by physical strategies. While he allows for conscious experience, he is denying any special attributes of qualia as lived experience; the only thing experienced is alterations in brain states. The phenomenon of conscious subjectivity that we know as our experience of the world is only the brain undergoing various neurochemical changes, which cannot be directly observed or communicated by the subject. While Dennett is arguing against essentialism, his position appears to be essentially reductive. If we are nothing but brain states, then we have a fixed essence in the form of physical organization despite dynamic complexities in its transformation and evolution. Once again, consciousness has no ontological status apart from its substance.

The materialist platform appears to ignore the very qualities of individuality and the phenomenology of experience, if not deny the social and psychological motivations behind our language practices. As societies, we strive for pluralism not singularity. Language practices are rich in diversity and multiplicity and cannot be made to conform to rigid and narrowly minded practices characteristic of oversimplification. Part of the very nature of human psychology is to resist such restrictions on human expression: the creative, aesthetic, and generative powers of imagination and human desire would be sacrificed to an antiseptic oppressive regime characteristic of a totalitarian state. What would we do with a language that would require intensive specialized training tantamount to thought control? And how would this be implemented and enforced? Not only is such a proposal ridiculously impractical, it would do nothing but stifle the diversity and idiosyncrasy of human experience. We have the responsibility to apply science in a humanistic fashion, not pass value judgments on authentic ways of being as lacking purpose, meaning, and value.

Materialism poses further problems surrounding the nature of value inquiry. How could values and ideals (as well as the broader transcendental dimensions of consciousness) be reduced merely to biology, or even in some more extreme cases, physical particles alone that, if properly measured through empirical means, inform us how we ought to think and reason? This is particularly imperative when addressing the question of morality. Can moral responsibility be boiled down to biology? Kim (1994) also questions whether "ethical expressions are definable, or reducible... in terms of 'descriptive' or 'naturalistic' expressions" (p. 242). How can moral behavior and ethical responsibility be reduced to matter? Behavior genetics is a highly controversial and problematic science for it attempts to explain human psychological functioning from the standpoint of evolutionary biology. Despite our discovery of increased genetic detail that has greatly enriched our understanding of human biology and evolution, it has done nothing to resolve the questions concerning differences between human values and social practices (Shipman, 1994). Dreyfus and Nelkin (1992) have gone so far to attribute "genetic essentialism" to criminality. Imagine this legal defense: "I couldn't help it, my genes made me do it!" If this were the case, social, legal, and political-congregational systems would be confronted with a diffusion of personal responsibility that places the locus of control on factors independent of the self. While I am not concerned that materialism offers any threat to the moral responsibility and actions of human beings, I am concerned that the metaphysical integrity of freedom, selfhood, and the principle of morality itself could become sullied.

Toward Psychic Holism

Throughout this chapter, I have attempted to delineate five dangers of materialism characteristic of the naturalistic and physically reductive paradigms within the cognitive sciences and the philosophy of mind today. Perhaps the main motive of materialism is simply this: If you say all mental events are just physical events, then you do not have a mystery—the mind-body conundrum is solved. Searle (1994) summarizes this position: "The famous mind-body problem...has a simple solution...Here it is: mental phenomena are caused by neurophysiological processes in the brain and are themselves features of the brain" (p. 277). This is reductionism at its finest.

The claim that the mind is nothing but the brain is a dogmatic assertion that attributes ontological primacy to physical states over mental processes and properties. In short, the materialist holds a fallacious and simplistic view of causality, denies free agency of the self, and increasingly portrays the human being as a clinical object. The ethical implications of such approaches in medical and social-political practices may potentially threaten the integrity of individuality and collective identity, which may further lead to an invalidation or empathic impasse regarding human difference and understanding.

Furthermore, within this context, the transcendental features of psychic reality—emotive, aesthetic, spiritual, moral, and religious experience—are trivialized. Not only is the quality of the lived experience truncated, materialism consequently neglects the function and role the concept of self assumes for human value. The value and concept of our sense of self serves a fundamental structural and functional role in identity, ethical responsibility, and self-representation. The transcendental qualities of experience and selfhood are in danger of becoming displaced if we are to view the human condition solely from naturalistic paradigms. While the boon of materialism is scientific, medical, technological, and consequently social advancement, the bane is the demise of the self and greater social collective forces as the amalgamation and expression of complexifications derived from a diverse yet unintegrated whole.

Compatiblist interpretations may offer a promissory reconciliation of the mind-body problem through the unification of material and psychic embodiment. One such champion of compatiblism is Alfred North Whitehead who, in his endeavor to bridge the Cartesian rift between *res extensa* and *res cognitans*, offers a speculative metaphysics that unifies physical and mental realities. For Whitehead (1929), the universe is comprised of incalculable "societies" of "actual entities" or "actual occasions" that are interconnected "drops of experience, complex and interdependent" (p. 18). In the tradition of German Idealism that conceives of *Geist* as pure activity, Whitehead sees mind as the interpenetration of *events* constituting psychic reality. Although Whitehead characterizes the "dipolar" constitution of the mind in terms of its physicality and mentality, which permits him to avoid the "bifurcation of nature," the polarities of the psyche are ontologically undifferentiated, thus allowing for the unification of the mind and the body as a cohesive whole. Following Heraclitus' dictum: "Everything flows" (*panta hrei*), Hegel's dialectic of Spirit, or Whitehead's process reality, mind is a process of becoming.

Psychic holism constitutes the belief in the multifarious existence and interdependence of the intrapsychic, mental, somatic, and materialistic processes that comprise the individual's relation to the world and life. This philosophical position is exemplified by Carl Jung's notion of the *unus mundus* as "one unitary world." Adopted from various schools of Gnosticism, neo-Platonism, and medieval philosophy,

> the idea of the *unus mundus* is founded on the assumption that the multiplicity of the empirical world rests on an underlying unity...; everything divided and different belongs to one and the same world...That even the psychic world, which is so extraordinarily different from the physical world, does not have its roots outside the one cosmos is evident from the undeniable fact that causal connections exist between the psyche and the body which point to their underlying unitary nature...The background of our empirical world thus appears to be in fact a *unus mundus*.
>
> (Jung, 1970, p. 538)

Although problematic and not without its own set of metaphysical conundrums, something I cannot claim to resolve, the emphasis on psychical holism allows for the multiplicity of psychological, material, spiritual, aesthetic, mystical, transcendental, and transpersonal conceptions of mind to flourish as potentially equally viable ways of articulating the dynamic structures, experiences, and processes that underlie mental life, although fallible. Within holistic and compatibilist paradigms, the nature of the Self, freedom, choice, personal autonomy, and responsibility are sheltered from the blight of physical reduction. Here psychic reality becomes a *unus mundus*; and like the mandala, signifies and symbolizes the unity and integrated wholeness of differentiated features within a monistic ontology we know as mind.

Notes

1 There is a spectrum of doctrines that call themselves realists ranging from: naive realism, direct realism, intuitive realism, natural realism, critical realism, blind realism, scientific realism, metaphysical realism, epistemic realism, medieval

realism, radical realism, Platonic realism, semantic realism, internal realism, realism with a capital R and realism with a small r, sophisticated realism, commonsense realism, pragmatic realism, ontological realism, and revisionary realism (see Bitsakis, 1993 for a review). Traditionally, the issue of realism is a metaphysical question. If we are to assume the historical position in the tradition of Aristotle, then realism is the belief that objects in the material world exist independent of consciousness and do not require thought to sustain their existence. In other words, they would exist despite whether they could be thought or perceived. Some materialists would qualify their claim by arguing that metaphysical realism is unverifiable, thus a meaningless proposition. Instead they may adopt a critical realist position, assuming that there must be something behind the appearance of natural objects of investigation, or else they adopt phenomenalism: reality is only that which appears.

2 The chief difference between behaviorism and materialism is that behaviorism does not posit complex intervening mental structures, processes, or strategies that govern or mediate one's responses to stimuli, while materialism does. Contemporary materialism offers a more sophisticated physicalist theory that does not explain cognition and behavior in solely mechanistic or environmentally conditioned terms.

3 Davidson is following Quine's thesis of indeterminacy of translation, which claims that ascriptions of propositional attitudes are relative to schemes of translation. See Quine's (1969b) *Ontological Relativity* and Levin (1979) for discussion.

4 There is a great body of literature, primarily in psychoanalysis and cognitive-behavioral psychology, that denotes the psychological etiology of various forms of depression ranging from bereavement; responses to loss, death, separation, and divorce; insecure attachments; emotional detachment and abandonment from love objects; inverted aggression; persecutory and self-punitive admonitions, to characterological forms of depression commensurate with a structurally depleted self (Arieti & Bemporad, 1978; Freud, 1917; Kohut, 1977).

References

Anderson, P.W., & Stein, D.L. (1987). Broken symmetry, emergent properties, dissipative structures, life: Are they related? In F. E. Yates (Ed.), *Self-organizing systems: The emergence of order*, 445–457. New York: Plenum Press.

Arieti, S., & Bemporad, J. (1978). *Severe and mild depression*. New York: Basic Books.

Armstrong, D.M. (1968). *A materialist theory of mind*. London: Routledge, Kegan & Paul.

Atmanspacher, H. (1997). Cartesian cut, Heisenberg cut, and the concept of complexity. *World Futures*, 49, 321–343.

Atmanspacher, H., Amann, A., & Müller-Herold, U. (Eds.) (1999). *On quanta, mind, and matter: Hans Primas in context.* Dordrecht, Netherlands: Kluwer Academic Publishers.

Atmanspacher, H. & Kronz, F. (1999). Relative onticity. In H. Atmanspacher, A. Amann, & U. Müller-Herold (Eds.), *On quanta, mind, and matter: Hans Primas in context,* 203–216. Dordrecht, Netherlands: Kluwer Academic Publishers.

Ayala, F.J. (1987). Biological reductionism: The problems and some answers. In F. E. Yates (Ed.), *Self-organizing systems: The emergence of order,* 315–324. New York: Plenum Press.

Bechtel, W. (1988). *Philosophy of mind: An overview for cognitive science.* Hillsdale, NJ: Erlbaum.

Bickle, J. (1998). *Psychoneural reduction: The new wave.* Cambridge, MA: Bradford Books/MIT Press.

Bitsakis, E. (1993). Scientific realism. *Science and Society,* 57 (2), 160–193.

Churchland, P.M. (1981). Eliminative materialism and the propositional attitudes. *The Journal of Philosophy,* 78, 67–90.

Dancy, J. & Sosa, E. (1992). *A companion to epistemology.* Oxford, England: Blackwell.

Davidson, D. (1980). *Essays on actions and events.* Oxford, England: Clarendon Press.

Dennett, D.C. (1981). True believers: The intentional strategy and why its works. In A.F. Heath (Ed.), *Scientific explanation: Papers based on Herbert Spencer lectures given in the University of Oxford,* 37–61. Oxford, England: Oxford University Press.

Dennett, D.C. (1984). *Elbow room.* Cambridge, MA: The MIT Press.

Dennett, D.C. (1988). Quining qualia. In A. Marcel and E. Bisiach (Eds.), *Consciousness in contemporary science,* 42–77. Oxford, England: Oxford University Press.

Dennett, D.C. (1991). *Consciousness explained.* Boston: Little, Brown and Company.

Descartes, R. (1984). Meditations on first philosophy. In J. Cottingham, R. Stoothoff, & D. Murdoch (Trans.), *The philosophical writings of Descartes, Vol. II,* 1–62. New York: Cambridge University Press. Original work published in 1641.

Dretske, F. (1988). *Explaining behaviour: Reasons in a world of causes.* Cambridge, MA: MIT Press.

Dretske, F. (1995). *Naturalizing the mind.* Cambridge, MA: Bradford Books/MIT Press.

Dreyfus, R.C. & Nelkin, D. (1992). The jurisprudence of genetics. *Vanderbilt Law Review*, 45 (2), 313–348.

Flew, A. (1984). *A dictionary of philosophy: Revised second edition*. New York: St. Martin's Press.

Fodor, J. (1974). Special sciences, or the disunity of science as a working hypothesis. *Synthese*, 28, 97–115.

Fodor, J. (1987). *Psychosematics: The problem of meaning in the philosophy of mind*. Cambridge, MA: Bradford Books/MIT Press.

Fodor, J. (1998). *In Critical condition: Polemical essays on cognitive science and the philosophy of mind*. Cambridge, MA: Bradford Books/MIT Press.

Freud, S. (1900). The Interpretation of dreams. In James Strachey (Ed. & Trans.), *The standard edition of the complete psychological works of Sigmund Freud*, Vol. 5. London: Hogarth Press.

Freud, S. (1916–1917). Introductory lectures on psycho-analysis. In James Strachey (Ed. & Trans.), *The standard edition of the complete psychological works of Sigmund Freud*, Vol. 15. London: Hogarth Press.

Freud, S. (1917). Mourning and melancholia. In James Strachey (Ed. & Trans.), *The standard edition of the complete psychological works of Sigmund Freud*, Vol. 14. London: Hogarth Press.

Graham, G. (1993). *Philosophy of mind: An introduction*. Oxford, England: Blackwell.

Gustafson, K. (1999). The geometry of quantum probabilities. In H. Atmanspacher, A. Amann, & U. Müller-Herold (Eds.), *On quanta, mind, and matter: Hans Primas in context*, 54–77. Dordrecht, Netherlands: Kluwer Academic Publishers.

Hanly, C. (1979). *Existentialism and psychoanalysis*. New York: International Universities Press.

Hegel, G.W.F. (1991). *The encyclopaedia logic, Vol.1 of the Encyclopaedia of the philosophical sciences*. T.F. Geraets, W.A. Suchting, & H.S. Harris (Trans.). (Indianapolis: Hackett Publishing Company). Original work published in 1830.

Horgan, T. (1994). Nonreductive materialism. In R. Warner and T. Szubka (Eds), *The mind-body problem*, 190–207. Oxford, England: Blackwell.

Hume, D. (1961). An Enquiry Concerning Human Understanding. In R. Taylor (Ed.), *The empiricists*, 307–430. Garden City, NY: Dolphin Books. Original work published in 1748.

Jackson, F. (1982). Epiphenomenal qualia. *Philosophical Quarterly*, 32, 127–136.

Jung, C.G. (1970). Mysterium Coniunctionis. In H. Read, M. Fordham, & G. Adler (Eds.); R.F.C. Hull (Trans.), *Collected Works of C.G. Jung*, Vol. 14. London: Routledge & Kagan Paul; Princeton: Princeton University Press. Original work published in 1956.

Kant, I. (1781). *Critique of Pure Reason*. N.K. Smith (Trans.). New York: St. Martin's Press. Original work published in 1781.

Kim, J. (1994). The myth of nonreductive materialism. In R. Warner and T. Szubka (Eds.), *The mind-body problem*, 208–222. Oxford, England: Blackwell.

Kohut, H. (1977). *The restoration of the self*. New York: International Universities Press.

Kraus, E.M. (1998). *The metaphysics of experience*. New York: Fordham University Press.

Levin, J. (1986). Could love be like a heatwave? Physicalism and the subjective character of experience. *Philosophical Studies*, 49(2), 245–261.

Levin, M.E. (1979). *Metaphysics and the mind-body problem*. Oxford, England: Clarendon Press.

Lewis, D. (1966). An argument for the identity theory. *Journal of Philosophy*, 63, 17–25.

Nagel, T. (1974). What is it like to be a bat? *The Philosophical Review*, LXXXIII(4), 435–450.

Penrose, R. (1989). *The emperor's new mind: Concerning computers, minds, and the laws of physics*. Oxford, England: Oxford University Press.

Place, U.T. (1956). Is consciousness a brain process? *The British Journal of Psychology*, 47, 42–51.

Post, J.F. (1987). *The faces of existence: An essay in nonreductive metaphysics*. New York: Cornell University Press.

Post, J.F. (1991). *Metaphysics*. New York: Paragon.

Post, J.F. (1995). "Global" supervenient determination: Too permissive? In Elias Savellos & Mit Yalcin (Eds.), *Essays on supervenience*. 73–100. Cambridge, MA: Cambridge University Press.

Primas, H. (1993). The Cartesian cut, the Heisenberg cut, and disentangled observers. In K.V. Laurikainen & C. Montonen (Eds.), *Symposium on the Foundations of Modern Physics 1992: The Copenhagen Interpretation and Wolfgang Pauli*, 31–56. Sinapore: World Scientific.

Primas, H. (1994). Endo- and exotheories of matter. In H. Atmanspacher & G.J. Dalenoort (Eds.), *Inside versus Outside*, 23–49. Berlin: Springer-Verlag.

Putnam, H. (1967). Psychological predicates. In W.H. Capitan and D.D. Merrill (Eds.), *Art, mind, and religion*, 156–170. Pittsburgh: University of Pittsburgh Press.

Putnam, H. (1975). The nature of mental states. In *Philosophical papers, vol. 2, mind, language, and reality*. Cambridge, England: Cambridge University Press.

Putnam, H. (1983). Why reason can't be naturalized. In P.K. Moser & A. Vandernat (Eds.), *Human knowledge*, 355–365, 1987. Oxford, England: Oxford University Press.

Quine, W.V. (1969a). Epistemology naturalized. In *Ontological relativity and other essays*. New York: Columbia University Press.

Quine, W.V. (1969b). Ontological relativity. In *Ontological relativity and other essays*. New York: Columbia University Press.

Rössler, O.E. (1994). Endophysics — Descartes taken seriously. In H. Atmanspacher & G.J. Dalenoort (Eds.), *Inside versus Outside*, 50–64. Berlin: Springer-Verlag.

Searle, J. (1994). What's wrong with the philosophy of mind? In R. Warner and T. Szubka (Eds.), *The mind-body problem*, 290–311. Oxford, England: Blackwell.

Shimony, A. (1999). Holism. In H. Atmanspacher, A. Amann, & U. Müller-Herold (Eds.), *On quanta, mind, and matter: Hans Primas in context*, 86–99. Dordrecht, Netherlands: Kluwer Academic Publishers.

Shipman, P. (1994). *The evolution of racism*. New York: Simon & Schuster.

Smart, J.J.C. (1962). Sensations and brain processes. In V.C. Chappell (Ed.), *The Philosophy of mind*, 19–36. Englewood Cliffs: Prentice-Hall.

Sober, E. (1985). Putting the function back into functionalism. *Synthese*, 64(2), 165–193.

Stich, S.P. (1994). What is a theory of mental representation? In R. Warner and T. Szubka (Eds.), *The mind-body problem*, 321–341. Oxford: Blackwell.

Sudarshan, E.C.G. (1999). Probability and quantum dynamics. In H. Atmanspacher, A. Amann, & U. Müller-Herold (Eds.), *On quanta, mind, and matter: Hans Primas in context*, 176–191. Dordrecht, Netherlands: Kluwer Academic Publishers.

Teller, P. (1983). A poor man's guide to supervenience and determination. *Southern Journal of Philosophy*, 22, Supplement, 147.

Thalberg, I. (1983). *Misconceptions of mind and freedom*. Lanham, MD: University Press of America.

Vendler, Zeno (1994). The ineffable soul. In R. Warner and T. Szubka (Eds.), *The mind-body problem*, 197–214. Oxford, England: Blackwell.

Vollmer, G. (1975). *Evolutionary epistemology*. Stuttgart: Hirzel.

Warner, R. (1994). In defense of dualism. In R. Warner and T. Szubka (Eds.), *The mind-body problem*, 215–229. Oxford, Engalnd: Blackwell.

Whitehead, A.N. (1925). *Science and the modern world.* New York: Free Press.

Whitehead, A.N. (1929). *Process and reality,* Corrected Edition, D.R. Griffin & D.W. Sherburne (Eds). New York: Free Press.

Wuketits, F. (1990). *Evolutionary epistemology.* New York: SUNY Press.

Yates, F. E. (Ed.) (1987). *Self-organizing systems: The emergence of order.* New York: Plenum Press.

Chapter 2

Notes toward the Psychoanalytic Critique of Mind-Body Dualism [1]

Barnaby B. Barratt [2]

Mind-body: The question lies in the hyphen (or in the slash, mind/ body). Obviously. But in what sense is it a question? A problem? A conundrum? I will suggest how this is primarily, *not* an epistemological conundrum, but an ethical and ontological issue, as well as a political, aesthetic and cultural one. That is, both one that takes us out of the hegemonic notion that epistemology must be, or can be, our 'first philosophy,' and one that empowers us to rediscover psychoanalysis (Barratt, 2013b, 2016, 2019b). I will then briefly contest the way in which much contemporary 'neuropsychoanalysis' (mis)uses the notion of dual-aspect monism, and finally, as a sort of interim 'concluding note,' I will argue for a reinstatement of the notion of psychic energy as pervasively both/and yet neither/nor in the sense of possible relations of ontological (non)identicality. This situates psychoanalysis, defined as the radical commitment to free-associative speaking and listening, as a uniquely *ontoethical* discipline.

Unless one relaxes the definition of 'psychoanalysis' to embrace any professionally conducted conversation that concerns the patient's thoughts, feelings, wishes, and fantasies, then the definition must, directly or indirectly, be anchored on the implications of Sigmund Freud's discoveries specifically that of the free-associative method. Freud's writings have thematic continuities, but also inconsistencies and, as has been argued by André Green (e.g., 2002) and others, a 'cesura' both stylistic and substantive, around 1914 or 1915. Much of his earlier writing was tightly associated with his revolutionary discovery of the method. Subsequently he became increasingly preoccupied with speculative theorizing, elaborating the objectivistic

DOI: 10.4324/9781003090755-3

edifices of metapsychological conceptualization, and less concerned with the question why he considered free-associative discourse to be the *sine qua non* of this discipline (a point he continued to assert even after the cesura). Here I will argue that, even while Freud could not himself see the implications of his methodical discovery, free-associative *praxis* indicts the dominant assumption that psychoanalysis is first and foremost epistemological—an enterprise in knowing. Rather, it is more authentically appreciated as an *ontoethical adventure* in being-as-becoming, a spiritual-existential science of healing. Thus, it is a mistake to consider this discipline as having an objectivistic theory of subjectivity, which is applied instrumentally in the treatment situation as 'technique.' Praxis entails a radically different notion of 'method' in relation to conceptual theorizing (Barratt, 2013b, 2016, 2019b).

As is well known, there are two macroscopic ways of reading the significance of Freud's *oeuvre* within the general trajectory of—European—intellectual history, and these lead us to fundamentally divergent ways of addressing the hyphen/slash in question. In one frame, Freud's thinking is the culmination of the European Enlightenment. It stands at the zenith of the analytico-referential episteme of the so-called modern era (Reiss, 1988). In this vein, Freud is foremost a scientist (in the restrictive sense of this term), innovative yet passionately following the epistemologically dominative visions of men (*sic*) from Robert Boyle and Isaac Newton to such as Carl Rokitansky and Hermann Helmholtz. He is the inaugurative 'biologist of the mind.' This prevalent way of reading Freud, he would almost certainly have endorsed (with some intermittent ambivalence). However, in another frame (involving dimensions somewhat more veiled in the publication of his thinking, and probably less recognized by Freud himself), his praxis implodes the presumptions characteristic of the very episteme of which it might be understood as the culmination. It is the harbinger of 'postmodern' impulses, profoundly challenging a tradition of 'science' characterized by dichotomies such as reason/passion, rational/irrational, objectivity/subjectivity, real/imagined, knowable/unimaginable, conscious/unconscious, agential/subaltern or systemic, male/female, and hetero/homo (Barratt, 1993/2016). It is in this vein that we must ask not only in what sense, or senses, Freud subverts the dichotomous treatment of body/mind, calling into question the venerable binary of the material and the immaterial (even while not rendering such distinctions meaningless). As indicated earlier, there are three sets of argument to be sketched here.

A Note on the Ontoethical Subversion

To immerse oneself in the flow of free-associative discourse, as patient and as psychoanalyst, is—I would suggest and as I have previously discussed in several publications—to engage a way of experiencing our being-in-the-world, our psychic reality, as an incessant process of *becoming,* being-as-becoming (the 'subject-in-process,' as some post-Lacanian commentators phrase it). Ontoethical praxis and philosophy, as brilliantly expounded by Elizabeth Grosz (2017), involve ways of experiencing not just the world as it is, but how it could be, how it may be opened to change (transformative or transmutative), and, above all, the 'becomings' that may occur.[3] It thus challenges the hegemony of epistemology as 'first philosophy'—the dominant mode of reason represented in dualism (and rationalism) that threads Platonism, Cartesian, Hegelianism, and much contemporary psychology.

The project of knowing and the production of knowledge requires presumptions about the being that is to be known (whether subjectivistically, objectivistically, or hermeneutically). Epistemology requires ontological presuppositions, which are, in turn, ethical and political (as well as aesthetic and cultural). The ontology entailed by the epistemological project and production of knowledge (of whatever representational form) addresses what *is,* rather that taking-off from an ontology and an ethical determination to address *becoming,* or what might be—a determination to open discourse to that which is otherwise than the rules and regulations of meaningfulness within that discourse (cf. Barratt, 2017a). That is, epistemological enterprises require suppositions that prioritize being over being-as-becoming. They tend to obscure their own ontological foundations or presuppositions and admit to the possibility of knowing only that which can be known in terms of their own discourse. Through the course of the modern era (i.e., the past three to five centuries in North Atlantic cultures), ontology has increasingly ceded to the hegemony of epistemological philosophies. Claims about what *is* (or could become) are determined by the evaluation of what we know or think we can know. Value in epistemology becomes a matter of considering ideological and moral prescriptions (as contrasted here with the ethicality of ontology) and political coda. These are like afterthoughts, pertaining to the knowledge that has already been constructed or is, for technological reasons, about to be used constructively.

In *The Incorporeal: Ontology, Ethics, and the Limits of Materialism,* Grosz traces a counterhistory or genealogy of a radically different lineage of philosophy from that which ends up mired by its prioritization of epistemology as 'first.' These are philosophies that explore the links between ontology, ethics and politics—from the pre-Socratics and Stoics, via Baruch Spinoza and Gottfried Leibniz, to such contemporaries of Freud as Friedrich Nietzsche and Henri Bergson, and then to Gilles Deleuze and others. This is a complex and multifarious thread that Grosz tracks using Michel Foucault's notion of 'incoporeal materialism' (e.g., Foucault, 1969–1971). The notion of the *incorporeal* signals "the subsistence and immanence of the ideal in the material and the material in ideality…it is an 'extramaterialism' in that it asserts the inherence of ideality, conceptuality, meaning, or orientation that persists in relation to and within materiality as its immaterial or incorporeal conditions" and this is because matter itself "requires extramaterial conditions by which it is framed and through which it can be thought or spoken about" (Grosz, 2017, pp. 5–6). This comprises an ethical orientation to the ontology of being-as-becoming that thus assigns a central role to ideality without subordinating it to materiality (cf. Coole & Frost, 2010).

The pertinence to psychoanalytic praxis of this way of thinking about our being-in-the-world becomes clearer as soon as we consider the limitations of epistemology (whether subjectivistic or phenomenological, objectivistic or empirical-experimental, or hermeneutic in the 19th-century tradition). As Grosz (2017, p. 3) expresses it, "When epistemology questions itself and its own conditions of knowledge, its own lacunae and places of nonknowledge, there is a residue or remainder of ontological issues and concerns that are untouched by epistemology and that may not always be submitted to existing schemas of knowledge, existing forms of grammar … or representation" (the law and order of syntax and morphology, including inflections, phonology, semantics, pragmatics, and perhaps even mathematics). My contention is that it is precisely the deconstructive power of free-associative discourse that addresses for us, invites from within us, this "residue or remainder" of what *is* (cf. Barratt, 1984/2016, 1993/2016). The processive momentum of this praxis is unique in its negatively dialectical and deconstructive impact upon our existing forms of thinking, feeling, wishing, and fantasizing, such that whatever is the "residue or remainder" of our being-as-becoming is mobilized. It is invited, so to speak, to "join in the conversation" (to borrow Freud's wording for Elizabeth von R's communications from the pains in her legs), even if this 'joining' is profoundly disruptive, unsettling the *status quo* of our being-in-the-world. In this sense, psychoanalysis offers us an ontoethical 'reach' (an openness to whatever is) behind, beneath, and beyond what extant epistemologies provide us (with the assumption that epistemology should be elevated to 'first philosophy'). That is, a process of inviting whatever is excluded or precluded from interpretive comprehension (whether, as Bertrand Russell expressed it in 1910, following the hermeneutic and neo-Kantian distinction between explanation and understanding, as 'knowledge by description' or 'knowledge by acquaintance').

The brevity of these notes prohibits even an outline of Grosz's sophisticated thesis. For example: her discussion of the way the Stoics held the universe to be animated by a fiery pneumatic force (a universal momentum of 'breathing') as the subsisting condition of all existence; her discussion of Nietzsche's privileging the energetic forces of our embodiment, giving primary emphasis to the question of orientation, the directionality of the future as the 'becomingness' of being, and the way in which he holds the universe to subsist as force fields that are primarily chaotic, conflictual, contradictory and open-ended; and her discussion of Gilles Deleuze along with the psychoanalyst Félix Guattari (and their links with the Surrealists, Georges Bataille, Roger Caillois, Jacques Derrida, and Luce Irigaray), who contest notions of transcendent or teleological organization with a dissertation on a 'plane of immanence.' The latter is also described as the plane of expression, which is the plane of breath or life that suffuses all entities (Deleuze & Guattari, 1987, 1991). Here I am postponing both Grosz's important introduction to Spinoza until I come to my critique of the way in which so many writers, who subscribe to the enterprise of 'neuropsychoanalysis,' use his philosophy in ways that are problematic or even intellectually guileful.

Sadly, Grosz does not mention Freud specifically nor psychoanalysis generally, nor does she touch on those Asian philosophies that connect so well with her thesis (cf. Coutinho, 2013; Ganeri, 2006; Raju, 1985). But studying the lineage of ontoethical thinking that she traces opens for us, as psychoanalysts, a 'take' on Freud's notion of psychic energy in relation to the hyphen/slash problem. As I can demonstrate, at least at certain junctures of his thinking, he holds this energy to suffuse animatively both 'body' and 'mind' yet to be identical with neither, thus requiring free-associative praxis to be appreciated as an ontoethical discipline. In the final section of these brief notes, I will outline the project of exploring the topic that Grosz does not address—namely, the possibility of appreciating Freud's notion of 'psychic energy' as the intimation of a unique 'take' on the hyphen/slash 'question.'

Toward a Critique of Dual-Aspect Monism as Misused in Neuropsychoanalysis

Grosz's thesis operates most valuably in relation to dual-aspect (or dual-attribute) monism as providing a refreshing alternative to Cartesian dualism, and as articulated foremost in Spinoza's complex—at times seemingly paradoxical and even convoluted—masterpiece, *Ethics* (1677). The latter has become a focus of increased philosophical interest, especially in France during the past three decades, with an impressive range of published debate and commentary. This is arguably of great significance in considering what psychoanalysis implies about the hyphen/slash 'problem.' Spinoza is, in so many ways, *the* philosopher of immanence, emphasizing—so to speak—the 'in-ness' of a *substance* that is universally operative within all that exists and that is the force of all its becoming. With Spinoza's dual-aspect monism, the materiality of things (including the neural circuitries of our brain) and the immaterial ideality of representations (imagistic, enactive, and verbal; i.e., the thoughts, feelings, wishes and fantasies that comprise our psychic life) are both ontologically different *aspects* or *attributes* of a singular *substance* that expresses itself in these (related but incompatibly divergent from an ontological standpoint) modes of discourse. Brain and mind are ontologically divergent aspects or attributes of this 'substance,' and the essence of this substance lies in its expression in these aspects or modes.

Substance is "not only the totality of all infinite things but also the uncaused causal force that makes each thing, and each kind of thing, able to exist" (Grosz, 2017, p. 60). In relation to psychoanalysis, it is important here to note three points.

First, Spinoza does not discount the possibility that *substance* could express itself in the discourse of other attributes besides, or in addition to, the materiality of things and the immateriality of ideas. The duality of body and mind is simply the two aspects that we know. I will return to this shortly, because it is as relevant to Freud's intimations about psychic energy, as it was to Spinoza's intuitions about the divine.

Second, Spinoza insists that the attributes of substance are its expressions, but *not* in the sense of properties or predicative formations (cf. Macherey, 1997). This is particularly relevant to the tendentious misuse of Spinoza's philosophy in contemporary neuropsychoanalysis wherein—all too often and despite the liberal and democratic rhetoric of "neither objectivity nor subjectivity is to be privileged one over the other"—the mind, as consciousness, is treated as the property or predicate of neuronal operations, and it is then erroneously imagined that, because both brain and mind depend upon a singularly underlying substance, the operations of one attribute are logically translatable into those of the other (a mistake which essentially ignores the duality of Spinoza's philosophy and reverts it to some species of monism or emergentism). Regularly, in their zeal, neuropsychoanalysts write as if data from neuroscience should be able to predict and prescribe the conduct of lived-experience, but not, of course, *vice versa* or rarely so (I will discuss the fallacy and falsity of this position in a moment).

Third, Spinoza holds substance to be not only universally ubiquitous, but also not divisible into calculable orders or fields of force (indeed, he mocks those who might speak of it as if it were finite). He argues both that it is an energy whose qualitatively intensive nature must be understood, and that it is mischaracterized or misunderstood if it is taken as merely mathematical (so, for example, he criticizes Descartes for defining matter as extension, arguing that it is an expression of substance rather than substance itself). This not only implies that *substance* cannot be reduced to, or comprehended in terms of, either the material discourse of the brain's operations or the immaterial discourse of the mind's representationality. It also means that Spinoza disallows the notion that substance might involve modes that are, in some sense, *contrariwise*. Like God, 'substance' is assumed to be, so to speak, auto-affective and inherently harmonious or monolithic. This prompts Deleuze and Guattari to refer to substance as a 'plane of composition,' since it seems not to accommodate the possibility that the expressions of substance could, in some sense, be inherently conflictual or contradictory—constituted, so to speak, with intrinsic ruptures, cuts and cracks. This is a point that seems to me profoundly relevant to the psychoanalytic notion of life as endemically ruptured (and so I will return to this shortly).

With radical modifications like those initiated by Deleuze and others, Spinoza's dual-aspect monism may be profoundly useful as a point of engagement in our further understanding of psychoanalytic discourse. However, the way in which this dual-aspect or dual-attribute philosophy is spuriously recruited or referenced, as if to legitimate some of the flawed yet flamboyantly overambitious claims of contemporary neuropsychoanalysis must be addressed, for they actually damage the future of psychoanalysis.

Here I am going to pass briefly over the 'neuro-archaeological' or 'psycho-ethological' enterprise, which comes within the province of neuropsychoanalysis. This is the program which brings together three types of data from the investigation of brain functions in young mammals (notably rats), from other studies of 'instinctive behaviors' (i.e., of modular action patterns and their innate releaser mechanisms), and from brain scanning (neuroimaging such as CT, MRI, and PET imaging). The putative convergence of these data inspires the conclusion that there are seven innate affective circuits or systems ('instincts') in the mammalian brainstem, which motivationally instigate and govern all observable behavior (including our 'subjectivity'). It is then suggested that this conclusion should guide the interpretation of psychotherapeutic 'data' (and other matters). That is, the lived-experience of psychoanalysis, which led to our ideas about the fundamental resourcefulness of libidinality (and its attendant aggressivity), should be discarded (or modified and augmented) in favor of the 'discovery' that there are 'in fact' seven basic motivations. Neuroscience now dictates how the lived-experience of psychoanalysis is to be undertaken. This is entirely wrong-headed. I am not going further with the multiple fallacies of this particular program, because I have initiated such a critique elsewhere (Barratt, 2015b, 2015c). However, it serves to illustrate the damage that is being done to psychoanalysis when dual-aspect monism is seriously misunderstood (yet invoked as 'justification' for the enterprise).

There have been several strong essays on the "trouble with neurobiological explanations of mind" (e.g., Brothers, 2002) and accordingly in defense of the disciplinary autonomy of psychoanalysis. These are cogent theses standing against the—illegitimate yet hegemonic—prescriptivity of neuroscience (e.g., Blass & Carmeli, 2007, 2015; Carmeli & Blass, 2013; Joannidis, 2017). Not inappropriately, the latter has been dubbed 'neuroism,' biologism, or even neuroscientific imperialism. I am more or less in accord with these efforts to rebut the presumption that "neuroscientific findings are relevant and important for the development and justification of psychoanalytic theory and practice" (Blass & Carmeli, 2007, p. 19). However, approaching this rebuttal with an ontoethical emphasis—rather than a traditionally epistemological one, with its acquiescence to the importance of distinctions such as objectivity/subjectivity and theory/technique—leads to a critique of neuropsychoanalysis that diverges from the more familiar one.

Whenever a psychoanalyst addresses the fundamental problems of the fashion for neuropsychoanalysis, it seems *de rigueur* to begin by stating our gratitude to neurological medicine and our appreciative interest in the truly fascinating discoveries that neuroscience has made (especially with the advances in artificial intelligence and neuroimaging techniques). Also, how admittedly useful it might be for any psychological practitioner to know whether a patient has neurological deficit or deterioration before addressing his or her psychic life. But none of this licenses neuroscience to make pronouncements about the content and quality of lived-experience and the method of its healing. Such pronouncements are a fundamentally inappropriate ethical and existential infringement. Nothing coming from neuroscience can legitimately require us, as psychoanalysts, to alter the method of our discipline. It might, however, inspire a rethinking of certain aspects of the metapsychological edifices that psychoanalysis has historically generated (e.g., Solms, 2013). There is also an argument by Clarici (2015) that neuroscience could affect 'technique' with brain injured patients, but not the fundamental psychoanalytic 'method.' I cannot delve into these arguments herein.

Occasionally, neuroscience provides data that would seem to *parallel* what those who have engaged in psychoanalytic praxis already knew. The most conspicuous example of this is the tomographic evidence that "the feeling of what happens" precedes the cognition of what is happening (e.g., Damasio, 1999, 2003, 2012; Solms, 2015), although experimental studies of cognition had already seemed to prove this important thesis (e.g., Zajonc, 1984). The crucial point here is that *in no way does the documentation of such parallels 'justify' or 'validate' psychoanalysis.* However academically interesting such parallels may be, to twist them in this way is not only entirely illegitimate, from the standpoint of the dual-aspect monism that neuropsychoanalysts purport to espouse, it is also a rampant example of how the specious hegemony of neuroscience over the healing science of lived-experience (i.e., psychoanalysis) is wrongly asserted or enacted, and its seductiveness should be eschewed.

It is indeed abstractly interesting to know that my nucleus accumbens and ventral pallidum are activated when I listen to Mozart's 11th concerto, but the knowledge neither adds to nor alters in any way my pleasurable experience as such. Moreover, if some hubristically nefarious scientist were to artificially excite these structures (by electrical or chemical intervention on my synapses and my neural circuitry), I might experience pleasure, but I surely would not experience Mozart's 11th. The point is that in line with the rigor of Spinoza's dual-aspect monism, the discourse of neuroscientific data and the discourse of lived-experience might seem to have *parallels*, but they are not, and cannot ever be, intertranslatable (this is precisely because they are dual, ontologically different attributes, albeit both expressions of an underlying substance that is ineffable).

I do not want to overdo this point, but it is the central one that is exceedingly often ignored in the fashionable frenzy to make disingenuous or even guileful (mis)use of the advances of neuroscience. So I will give another example: That it can be predicted I will hallucinate having ingested lysergic acid diethylamide, or that my frequency of inapposite remarks is likely to increase with too much alcohol, and that it can be objectively demonstrated that these drugs have this or that synaptic effects, *cannot* be taken to imply—predict or prescribe—that, if those synaptic systems are similarly activated, I will or should have *this* rather than *that* hallucination or that I will make *this* rather than *that* clumsy remark.

Again, the fundamental precept of dual-aspect monism is precisely that discourses concerning the two main attributes, about which we can know something (i.e., the material world including the brain as one attribute of substance, and the immateriality of what we call 'mind' as the other attribute), are not, and cannot be, inter-translatable. If they were, then Spinoza's efforts to write about *substance* as underlying and pervading both would be vacuous.

A fundamental misunderstanding of the issue of reductionism seems at stake here (cf. Boden, 1970, 1972/2010). If we concede that the representationality of psychic life is housed in the neural circuitries of the brain's anatomical structures (i.e., if we forego the theological or cosmological notion of souls that do not require embodiment), then we must indeed accept the tenets of *empirical reductionism*. At least for our present purposes let us accept that minds do not operate without the operations of brains and, from the philosophy of dual-aspect monism, we hold that both must be dependent on an underlying *substance* (or immanent plane of energy). However, the precepts of dual-aspect monism fundamentally entail the intransigent refutation of *logical reductionism*. The latter implies intertranslatability of the two attributes, which is not a tenable stance, given that they are different modes of discourse.[4] Events that occur within the ontologically same mode of discourse (aspect or attribute of substance or energy) are potentially intertranslatable to greater or lesser extent (as are Portuguese and Punjabi). But events occurring in ontologically different modes of discourse (aspect or attribute) are definitely not. Thus, materiality (e.g., the electro-chemical 'thingness' of synaptic connections) is not translatable into the ideality of representationality; just as the composition of a rock has a history, but this composition does not translate into a historiographic articulation of this history. In this context, slogans such as "you are your synapses" are as flashily "unarguable" as they are delusional (cf. Ledoux, 2003, 2019).

In terms of the issue of parallel effects (such-and-such events occur in the brain at the same time that so-and-so events occur in psychic reality), some neuroscientists restrict themselves responsibly to terms such as 'correlation' or 'concomitancy' (an example would be the way in which Ritchie Davidson usually speaks and writes about altered states in meditation). However, the allure of 'hard science' in our culture is such that talk of correlation and concomitancy readily slides into the language of causality, as does the currently fashionable but slippery term 'consilience' (which is used as if it could license translatability between the events of 'brain' and 'mind'). This is not a logical slide (in fact, dual-aspect monism decisively debars it). Rather, it is argument by analogy—or allegory—that is seductive but illicit. It is as I have argued previously an act of myth-making (Barratt, 2013b, 2015a). Catherine Malabou has demonstrated compellingly *both* the extent to which neuroscientists insist on affirming (as an act of faith) a perfect or seamless continuity between neuronal operations and the representationality of thoughts, feelings, wishes or fantasies, *and* the extent to which neuroscientists, even while admitting that this continuity is not yet testable, fail to realize that this faith in its seamlessness could *never* be testable (Johnston & Malabou, 2013; Malabou, 2004, 2007).

Thus, we have influential neuropsychoanalysts beguiling us with stories about how an ensemble of neural devises *maps* the body, the external world and the brain's own functioning, and then how this 'proto-self' *permits* the formation of a 'core-self' which, in turn, *allows* the creation of the 'autobiographical-self' or reflective or narratolo-gical consciousness. A lovely tale. But the problem of the hyphen/slash is precisely concealed in the verb(iage) of *maps, permits, allows,* and so forth. This sort of myth-making is perfectly acceptable, *except* that its proponents do not concede that this is indeed its status. Additionally, it is nowadays buttressed not only by rather slippery uses of the notion of 'consciousness' that would is incongruent with psychoanalytic method (e.g., a confusion between it merely implying being alive versus dead, and what Gerald Edelman called 'secondary' or reflective consciousness) and of the notion of 'subjectivity' (e.g., "there can be no objects…without a subject…'being there' to ex-perience them," which would seem to imply that slugs and computers have equivalent 'subjectivity' to that of humans, about which many philosophers would take issue).[5] It is also buttressed by very sophis-ticated mathematical models (Karl Friston's 'free energy principle,' about which more later, along with 'Markov Blankets') which purport to exhibit the possible 'top-down' and 'bottom-up' informational interactions within the brain by 'prediction error minimization.' In relation to this neuroscientifically interesting theorizing, it must be noted both that the model assumes a certain sort of seamlessness (which, I am going to suggest, is fundamentally at odds with the lived-experience of psychoanalysis) and that, neuroscientifically plausible as it may be, there is not a shred of empirical evidence for its truth (cf. Holmes, 2020).

In sum, neuropsychoanalysis, which claims to be a subfield of both psychoanalysis and neuroscience, proves to be a seductive and scientistic myth-making ideology without substance. Under dual-aspect monism, neuroscience cannot claim to predict or prescribe lived-experience, which is the existential domain that is precisely the focus of psychoanalytic praxis as an ontoethical science of healing. Moreover, neither neuroscience nor its 'neuropsychoanalytic' spin-off has anything more than myth-making to engage our understanding of the hyphen/slash 'problem.' It neither enlightens nor offers us a horizon-expanding understanding of the human condition.

Interim 'Concluding Note'—Psychic Energy and Nonidenticality

Contrary to a culturally prevalent understanding of 'hard science,' myth-making may actually be integral to any exploration of the human condition. For psychoanalysis—defined as free-associative praxis—the adventure of its discourse cannot entirely escape from mythematics (Kolakowski, 1972), just as it cannot entirely avoid the interim 'staging-post' of interpretative moments (cf. Fink, 2014a, 2014b; Nobus & Quinn, 2005). However, unlike other disciplines, it never 'arrives,' but rather is committed to the ongoing free-associative interrogation of any position of understanding at which it appears to arrive. This is what takes psychoanalysis 'beyond psychotherapy' (Barratt, 2018, 2019a, 2021a, 2021b).

By way of an 'interim conclusion,' I want to suggest that Freud's praxis might illuminate, complexify, and in a certain specific sense contribute to the mysticality of Spinoza's dual-aspect monism (much of what follows is indebted to Deleuze and Guattari, although I believe significantly different from their thesis, in ways that may or may not be evident).

Freud was no fool. He did, however, not infrequently propound ideas incongruent—or potentially incongruent—with his ambition to be a scientist in the narrowly epistemological sense, to be the 'biologist of the mind.' With almost two decades of experience with free-associative discourse (and his lifetime conviction that this method is the *sine qua non* of his discipline), he argued in 1913 that "we cannot avoid the term *Trieb* as a boundary notion for what ubiquitously mediates the psychological and the biological ... as a concept on the frontier between psychology and biology" (my translation; GW, p. 410; SE, p. 181). The awkwardness of this passage is palpable, especially coming as it does in a paper that aims to explain psychoanalytic claims to be of—'scientific'—interest, and that involves an explicit "effort to prevent biological terminology and considerations from dominating psychoanalysis" (*ibid*). As I have argued elsewhere, the notion of *Trieb* is best translated as 'desire,' libidinality, or psychic *energy* (cf. Quindeau, 2013). Freud knew about Spinoza and certainly would have given considerable thought to the problematics of Cartesian dualism; but he did not dwell on the mythical challenges of the pineal gland, but rather seemed to favor the notion that traces of a subtle energy are distributed throughout the 'bodymind.' I use this term not as a flashy 'new age' way to expunge the hyphen/slash issue, but rather to emphasize the possibility that traces of subtle energy might be ubiquitously distributed (cf. Barratt, 2013a, 2013b, 2014, 2018, 2019b).

What can it have meant to Freud (and now to us) to write of "boundary notions" or "concepts on the frontier" (*Grenzbegriff*), to assert that there is something that "mediates" (*ausgiebige Vermittlung*) the immaterial of representationality and the materiality of neural operations, or of a "concept on the frontier" of these two 'aspects,' about which we have knowledge? Freud believed he had learned (inferred or intuited) from free-associative praxis was not only the rupture of psychic life, via repression (*Verdrängung*), which he defined as a "failure in translation" (1896, p. 235), and at various times contrasted with "gradations in the clarity of consciousness" (*Deutlichkeitsskala der Bewusstheit*) resulting from processes of suppression (*Unterdrückung*), condemnation (*Verurteilung*), and the detours of selective inattention (*Unaufmerksamkeit*). In addition to the repressiveness-of-consciousness, he believed he was compelled to infer the operations of libidinality or psychic energy as the force expressing itself in repression and other dynamics (Barratt, 2015a, 2016). Significantly, this 'discovery' came alongside the realization of the crucial role of the incest taboo in the establishment of the 'repression-barrier' (Barratt, 2019c). My thesis is that this 'energy' has as ontological force that either subverts the duality of dual-aspect monism or intimates subtle energy as Spinoza's *substance*. This is *both* because psychic energy is evidently an exuberant excess in relation to its investment (*Besetzung*) in representationality (and the *demand* for transformation that it makes such that one representation transforms into another by condensation, displacement, etc.), *and* because, as in the notion of *Anlehnung*, psychic energy may seem to lean-on, be propped-upon or follow-from biological operations but is not, and cannot be, identical with them. The former is clearly demonstrated in the 1900 *Interpretation of Dreams*, along with its metapsychological elaboration in the set of three 1915 papers. The latter is inherent in Freud's early writings, but well explicated by Jean Laplanche, *Triebe* are not purely biological, but develop out or and depend upon neural circuitries, including those initiated by innate *Instinkte,* such as modular action patterns with their innate releaser mechanisms (cf. Laplanche, 1992–1993, 1992–1998, 2000–2006). That is, the subtle pervasive force of psychic energy is both 'in but not of' neuronal operations and 'in but not of' representational operations; neither/nor yet invested or divested both/and. This is—I propose— Freud's most daring contribution to the issue of the hyphen/slash conundrum.

The use of the term 'energy' can be confusing here, because of both the enthusiasm for neuropsychoanalysis and the conventions of neuroscientific terminology. There is surely room for skepticism around the potentially facile way in which much contemporary science has—since Claude Shannon's pioneering paper of 1948— equated information with energy. The 'free energy principle'—as first promulgated by Friston and his colleagues in 2006—is a mathematical model about informational exchanges. This is basically a variational Bayesian mathematics explaining how living and non-living systems maintain themselves in nonequilibrium steady-states by self-restrictive procedures that are effected by loops of active inference, or 'predictive error minimization.' As appropriated for what purports to be 'psychoanalytic theorizing' (e.g., Solms & Friston, 2018; Solms, 2017, 2019), this mathematics can be applied to the top-down predictions and bottom-up input that characterizes the brain's hierarchical functioning within and between its various cortical and sub-cortical systems (although the math was initially developed for other applications). More specifically, associated with this principle is the notion of Markov Blankets (chains, processes, boundaries), which essentially offers statistical functions that utilize a subset of variables to distinguish which variables are useful and which are not, and can therefore be omitted from future calculation (these statistical functions were so named by Judea Pearl in 1988 in honor of the famous Russian mathematician, Andrey Markov, who was best known for his work on stochastic processes). Now it may seem highly plausible that—at least in some measure—the brain's operations conform neuronally to these sorts of mathematical models (the free energy principle, Markov blankets, and prediction error minimization), but the point here is that this is merely a mathematical model, an allegory for relations between 'brain' and 'mind'—that has no empirical proof, nor is it empirically testable, *and* is of an entirely different ontological status from most notions of 'energy' that science has promulgated.

In her 2015 exploration of the notion of energy, Jennifer Coopersmith emphasizes the elusiveness of the definition. She concludes her serious scholarship almost whimsically, writing that energy is "the ceaseless jiggling motion, the endless straining at the leash, even in apparently empty space, the rest mass and the radiation, the curvature of spacetime, the foreground activity, the background hum, the *sine qua non*" (Coopersmith, 2015, p. 362). The open tone of this 'definition' is certainly pertinent to the way we consider Freud's free-associative 'discovery' of psychic energy.

Surely we must entertain the possibility that, whereas Spinoza intuited *substance* as God, Freud had intimations of psychic energy as a subtle system that pervades the material and the immaterial world? That is, as substance itself or as a third attribute of substance, leading us to a 'triple-aspect monism' (which previously I, rather clumsily, called a trifold ontology). In either case, psychic energy could not be purely endogenous (as Freud believed in alignment with his Helmholtzian loyalties). Every known indigenous culture has held that the entire universe, both material and immaterial entities and events, is permeated with subtle energies of which we can have only intimations (or perhaps intuitions, as a sort of awareness outside of representational consciousness). *Prāṇa* and *ch'i* are those notions that have, in the past hundred years, gradually entered the mainstream of North Atlantic cultures. It is only because Freud's discoveries have been read almost exclusively within the values of the analytico-referential episteme of the so-called modern era in these Eurocentric cultures that the ontoethical implications of his notion of psychic energy have been so grievously overlooked.

Are we so sure that in what would seem to be an instance of North Atlantic and modernist arrogance, we should discount all ancient indigenous insights into subtle energy systems? Does it make sense to do so merely in the name of ostensibility, evidentiality, and parsimony? Freud was no fool, even if he often discounted the significance of what were his own intimations of a different sort of subtle energy system that he called 'psychic energy'—often even discarding such. Today we live in an era in which the notion of energies seems increasingly elusive and enigmatic the more we learn about them. Indeed, it would now seem foolhardy to discount—recklessly in the name of 'science'—the notion that subtleties of psychic energy animate our lives.

Psychic energy is akin to what Deleuze and Guattari discuss as the plane of expressionism or immanence (a plane of breath, lifelfulness, and deathfulness suffusing all entities and events), which underlies, pervades, and animates the realities that we are able to grasp epistemologically. Freud's discoveries through free-associative discourse do not allow us to consider this as entirely equivalent to Spinoza's plane of composition or *substance*, which is assumed to be auto-affective and inherently harmonious or monolithic. That is, 'God' as the godhead source of all being-becoming (like the Supreme *Ahaṁ Brahmāsmi,* which is celebrated in the *mahāvākyāni,* the sayings of the *Upaniṣad*s, and elsewhere). Although psychic energy is the source of the rhythms of the lifelulness and deathfulness of life itself (similar to Freud's 1920 notions of *Lebenstrieb* and *Todestrieb,* or Deleuze's discussion of the explicative and implicative rhythms of the plane of immanence), it does not distribute itself equally in all its aspects or attributes, nor is it, so to speak, meaningless. Rather, it is akin to fields of force that seem fundamentally chaotic, contradictory, and open-ended. This contrariness or contradictoriness of the plane of psychic energies requires an ontoethical praxis that listens to that which is otherwise. It is also the unique way in which free-associative praxis both attends even to the unfathomable 'navel' of each re-presentational event and addresses the conjunction, the hyphen/slash, of mind and body.

Notes

1 This paper is referred to as 'notes,' because the requirements of brevity demand that I merely sketch much of the argumentation and omit much of the referencing to a sizeable literature that would seem to support these arguments.
2 I am grateful to many colleagues variously for their candid criticisms, supportive comments, and thoughtful counterarguments on this and associated topics. These especially include Drs. Jerry Gargiulo, Elizabeth Grosz, Jeremy Holmes, Jill Gentile, and Jerry Piven.
3 The significance of my distinction between procedures of *transformation* (in which one item or set of items changes into another that is within the same mode of discourse) and processes of *transmutation* (in which a change in one mode of discourse inspires or demands a change in a different mode of discourse) will become clear as these notes proceed. The distinction is also discussed in Barratt (2017a, 2017b, 2021a).
4 There are several sophisticated and specialist discussions of this point. Jane Flax (1993/2013) provides an accessible introduction to some of these issues about divergent about modes of discourse.
5 These are topics urgently in need of clarification and a fuller psychoanalytic critique than can be given herein. For a discussion of "senses of the subject," Judith Butler's writings are extremely helpful (e.g., Butler, 1997, 2005, 2015).

References

Barratt, B. B. (1984/2016). *Psychic reality and psychoanalytic knowing.* Hillsdale, NJ: Analytic Press. [Republished by Routledge in 2016.]

Barratt, B. B. (1993/2016). *Psychoanalysis and the postmodern impulse: Knowing and being since Freud's psychology.* Baltimore, MD: Johns Hopkins University Press. [Republished by Routledge in 2016.]

Barratt, B. B. (2013a) Free-associating with the bodymind. *International Forum of Psychoanalysis, 22*, 161–175.

Barratt, B. B. (2013b). *What is psychoanalysis? 100 years after Freud's 'Secret Committee.'* London, UK: Routledge.

Barratt, B. B. (2014). A practitioner's notes on free-associative method as existential praxis. *International Forum of Psychoanalysis, 23*, 185–208.

Barratt, B. B. (2015a). On the mythematic reality of libidinality as a subtle energy system: Notes on vitalism, mechanism, and emergence in psychoanalytic thinking. *Psychoanalytic Psychology, 32*, 626–644.

Barratt, B. B. (2015b). Critical notes on the 'neuro-evolutionary archaeology of affective systems'. *Psychoanalytic Review, 102*, 183–208.

Barratt, B. B. (2015c). Rejoinder to Mark Solms' response to critical notes on the 'neuro-evolutionary archaeology of affective systems'. *Psychoanalytic Review, 102*, 221–227.

Barratt, B. B. (2016). *Radical psychoanalysis: An essay on free-associative praxis*. London, UK: Routledge.

Barratt, B. B. (2017a). Opening to the otherwise: The discipline of listening and the necessity of free-association for psychoanalytic praxis. *International Journal of Psychoanalysis, 98*(1), 39–45.

Barratt, B. B. (2017b). On the otherwise energies of the human spirit: A contemporary comparison of Freudian and Jungian approaches to 'Spirit.' In R. S. Brown (ed.) *Re-Encountering Jung: Analytical Psychology and Contemporary Psychoanalysis*. London, UK: Routledge, pp. 47–67.

Barratt, B. B. (2018). On the unique power of free-associative discourse: Notes on the contributions of Henry Lothane and Christopher Bollas. *Psychoanalytic Inquiry, 38*(6), 478–487.

Barratt, B. B. (2019a). *Beyond psychotherapy: On becoming a (radical) psychoanalyst*. London, UK: Routledge.

Barratt, B. B. (2019b). Sexuality, esoteric energies, and the subtleties of transmutation versus transformation. *International Journal of Transpersonal Studies, 38*(1), 1–19.

Barratt, B. B. (2019c). Oedipality and oedipal complexes reconsidered: On the incest taboo as a key to the universality of the human condition. *International Journal of Psychoanalysis, 100*(1), 7–31.

Barratt, B. B. (2021a). On difference and the 'Beyond Psychotherapy' of psychoanalytic method: The pivotal issue of free-associative discourse as de-repressive praxis. *American Journal of Psychoanalysis, 81*(1), 27–50.

Barratt, B. B. (2021b). Überlegungen zu einem frei assoziierenden Zuhören: 'Ich bin hier selbst ein Fremder.' *Jahrbuch der Psychoanalyse, 82*, 45–72.

Blass, R. & Carmeli, Z. (2007). The case against neuropsychoanalysis: On fallacies underlying psychoanalysis' latest scientific trend and its negative impact on psychoanalytic discourse. *International Journal of Psychoanalysis, 88*(1), 19–40.

Blass, R. & Carmeli, Z. (2015). Further evidence for the case against neu-ropsychoanalysis: How Yovell, Solms, and Fotopoulou's response to our critique confirms the irrelevance and harmfulness to psychoanalysis of the contemporary neuroscientific trend. *International Journal of Psychoanalysis*, *96*(6), 1555–1573.

Boden, M. A. (1970). Intentionality and physical systems. *Philosophy of Science*, *37*, 200–214.

Boden, M. A. (1972/2010). *Purposive explanation in psychology*. Cambridge, MA: Harvard University Press.

Brothers, L. (2002). The trouble with neurobiological explanations of mind. *Psychoanalytic Inquiry*, *22*(5), 857–870.

Butler, J. P. (1997). *The psychic life of power: Theories in subjection*. Palo Alto, CA: Stanford University Press.

Butler, J. P. (2005). *Giving an account of oneself* (4th edition). New York, NY: Fordham University Press.

Butler, J. P. (2015). *Senses of the subject*. New York, NY: Fordham University Press.

Carmeli, Z. & Blass, R. (2013). The case against neuroplastic analysis: A further illustration of the irrelevance of neuroscience to psychoanalysis through a critique of Doidge's 'The Brain That Changes Itself.' *International Journal of Psychoanalysis*, *94*(2), 391–410.

Clarici, A. (2015). Neuropsychoanalysis has an influence on psychoanalytic technique but not on the psychoanalytic method. *Neuropsychoanalysis*, *17*, 39–51.

Coole, D. & Frost, S. (eds., 2010). *New materialisms: Ontology, agency, and politics*. Durham, NC: Duke University Press.

Coopersmith, J. (2015). *Energy, the subtle concept: The discovery of Feynman's blocks from Leibniz to Einstein* (revised edition). Oxford, UK: Oxford University Press.

Coutinho, S. (2013). *An introduction to Daoist philosophies*. New York, NY: Columbia University Press.

Damasio, A. R. (1999). *The feeling of what happens*. San Diego, CA: Harcourt.

Damasio, A. R. (2003). *Looking for Spinoza: Joy, sorrow, and the feeling brain*. Boston, MA: Mariner.

Damasio, A. R. (2012). *Self comes to mind: Constructing the conscious brain*. New York, NY: Vintage.

Deleuze, G. & Guattari, F. (1987). *A thousand plateaus: Capitalism and schi-zophrenia* (translated by B. Massumi). London, UK: Athlone Press, 1988.

Deleuze, G. & Guattari, F. (1991). *What is philosophy?* (translated by H. Tomlinson & G. Burchill). New York, NY: Columbia University Press, 1994.

Fink, B. (2014a). *Against understanding, volume 1: Commentary and critique in a Lacanian key.* London, UK: Routledge.

Fink, B. (2014b). *Against understanding, volume 2: Cases and commentary in a Lacanian key.* London, UK: Routledge.

Flax, J. (1993/2013). *Disputed subjects: Essays on psychoanalysis, politics and philosophy.* Abingdon, UK: Routledge.

Foucault, M. (1969–1971). *The archeology of knowledge* (translated by A. M. Sheridan Smith). New York, NY: Pantheon, 1972.

Freud, S. (1896). Letter 52 from 'Extracts from the Fleiss Papers.' *Standard Edition, 1,* 233–239.

Freud, S. (1900). Die Traumdeutung. *Gesammelte Werke, 2–3,* 1–642. [Translated as: The interpretation of dreams. *Standard Edition, 4–5,* 1–627.]

Freud, S. (1915a). Trieb und Triebschicksale. *Gesammelte Werke, 10,* 210–232. [Translated as: Instincts and their vicissitudes. *Standard Edition, 14,* 109–140.]

Freud, S. (1915b). Die Verdrängung. *Gesammelte Werke, 10,* 248–261. [Translated as: Repression. *Standard Edition, 14,* 146–158.]

Freud, S. (1915c). Das Unbewusste. *Gesammelte Werke, 10,* 264–303. [Translated as: The unconscious. *Standard Edition, 14,* 166–204.]

Friston, K., Kilner, J. & Harrison, L. (2006). A free energy principle for the brain. *Journal of Physiology, 100*(1–3), 70–87.

Ganeri, J. (2006). *Artha – meaning: Testimony and the theory of meaning in Indian philosophical analysis.* Oxford, UK: Oxford University Press.

Green, A. (2002). *Time in psychoanalysis: Some contradictory aspects* (translated by A. Weller). London, UK: Free Association Books.

Grosz, E. (2017). *The incorporeal: Ontology, ethics, and the limits of materialism.* New York, NY: Columbia University Press.

Holmes, J. (2020). *The brain has a mind of its own.* Woodbrieg, UK: Confer.

Joannidis, C. (2017). Conversing does not constitute need: The case of psychoanalysis and its relationship to neuroscience. *Free Associations: Psychoanalysis and Culture, Media, Groups, Politics, 70,* 118–128.

Johnston, A. & Malabou, C. (2013). *Self and emotional life: Philosophy, psychoanalysis, and neuroscience.* New York, NY: Columbia University Press.

Kolakowski, L. (1972). *The presence of myth* (translated by A. Czerniawski). Chicago, IL: University of Chicago Press, 1989.

Laplanche, J. (1992–1993). *Essays on otherness* (edited by J. Fletcher). Abingdon, UK: Routledge, 1999.

Laplanche, J. (1992–1998). *Between seduction and inspiration: Man* (translated by J. Mehlman). New York, NY: The Unconscious in Translation, 2015.

Laplanche, J. (2000–2006). *Freud and the 'Sexual'—Essays 2000–2006* (translated by J. Fletcher, J. House & N. Ray). New York, NY: International Psychoanalytic Books, 2011.

LeDoux, J. E. (2003). *The synaptic self: How our brains become who we are* (2nd edition). New York, NY: Penguin.

LeDoux, J. E.(2019). *The deep history of ourselves: The four-billion-year story of how we got conscious brains.* London, UK: Penguin.

Macherey, P. (1997). The problem of attributes. In: W. Monag & T. Stolze (eds.), *The new Spinoza.* Minneapolis, MN: University of Minnesota Press, pp. 65–95.

Malabou, C. (2004). *What should we do with our brain?* (translated by S. Rand). New York, NY: Fordham University Press, 2008.

Malabou, C. (2007). *The new wounded: From neurosis to brain damage* (translated by S. Miller). New York, NY: Fordham University Press, 2012.

Nobus, D. & Quinn, M. (2005). *Knowing nothing, staying stupid: Elements for a psychoanalytic epistemology.* London, UK: Routledge.

Quindeau, I. (2013). *Seduction and desire: The psychoanalytic theory of sexuality since Freud* (translated by J. Bendix). London, UK: Karnac.

Raju, P. T. (1985). *Structural depths of Indian thought.* Delhi, India: South Asian Publishers.

Reiss, T. J. (1988). *The uncertainty of analysis: Problems in truth, meaning, and culture.* Ithaca, NY: Cornell University Press.

Russell, B. A. W. (1910). Knowledge by acquaintance and knowledge by description. *Proceedings of the Aristotelian, 11*, 108–128.

Shannon, C. E. (1948). A mathematical theory of communication. *Bell System Technical Journal, 27*(3), 379–423.

Solms, M. L. (2013). The conscious Id. *Neuropsychoanalysis, 15*(1), 5–19.

Solms, M. L. (2015). *The feeling brain: Selected papers on neuropsychoanalysis.* London, UK: Karnac.

Solms, M. L. (2017). The neurobiological underpinnings of psychoanalytic theory and therapy. *Frontiers in Behavioral Neuroscience, 12*, article 294.

Solms, M. L. (2019). The hard problem of consciousness and the free energy principle. *Frontiers in Psychology, 9*, article 2714.

Solms, M. L. & Friston, K. (2018). How and why consciousness arises: Some considerations from physics and physiology. *Journal of Consciousness Studies, 25*(5–6), 202–238.

Spinoza, B. (1677). *Ethics: Treatise on the emendation of the intellect and selected letters* (translated by S. Shirley; edited by S. Feldman. Indianapolis, IN: Hackett, 1992.

Zajonc, R. B. (1984). On the primacy of affect. *American Psychologist, 39*(2), 117–123.

Chapter 3

Freud's Views on Mental Causation

Claudia Passos-Ferreira[1]

According to psychoanalysis, mental conflict divides the mind into conscious and unconscious parts (Freud, 1900). Mental conflicts are mental events composed of conflicting representations, or contradictory narratives that clash because of opposing demands in the subject's mind. Mental conflict causes the activation of defense mechanisms, such as repression (Laplanche & Pontalis, 2002).

The notion of mental conflict has been present since the beginning of psychoanalysis, when Freud observed hysterical patients resisting pathogenic memories, and interpreted this resistance as a defense mechanism against irreconcilable representations. For mental conflict to play this role, there must be *mental causation*: a causal role for mental states in causing other mental states. Mental causation lies at the center of Freud's theory of the mind. He constructed numerous hypotheses about mental causation, with mental events playing a number of different roles in causing changes in mental states (Passos-Ferreira, 2005, 2006, 2011).

Both assumptions – the division of the mind and mental causation – are relevant for explaining irrational acts and mental conflicts. Freud created a picture of human life in which our actions are caused by unconscious mental states. The Freudian theory of mind expanded the list of rational mental phenomena, identifying mental expressions such as phobias, Freudian slips, and dreams as justifiable intentional acts. When explaining human behavior, he gave rational justifications the status of scientific explanations: they are causal explanations that allow for experimental control and prediction.

DOI: 10.4324/9781003090755-4

How can we reconcile mental causation with a scientific view of the world? Freud's starting point is that the mind is a mechanism whose functioning is determined by causes. He holds that a scientific theory of the mind should adopt causal determinism that is incompatible with chance. This determinism of the mind is grounded in the belief that all vital phenomena, including the mental, can be explained by a causal theory.

However, Freud's view of mental causation encounters theoretical challenges. Critics such as Ludwig Wittgenstein (1966, 1977) hold that the causal role of mental phenomena is not mechanistic or deterministic, and is not subject to scientific laws. Faced with the impasse of the problem of how the mind interacts with the body, Freud creates a two-dimensional picture of mental causality, with one dimension involving a mechanistic (arational) cause and the other involving an intentional cause.

To understand Freud's view of mental causation better, I will analyze three moments in his work. In his first topography, Freud uses a hybrid vocabulary, describing the mind in terms of both mechanistic causes and intentional causes. In his second topography, the mind increasingly assumes an intentional description. The third moment is Freud's revised theory of anxiety, in which the arational cause of the unconscious drives, initially presented as a motor of the mind, gives rise to anxiety as an affective state that forces the self to find a solution for its mental conflicts.

My central thesis is that over these three moments, Freud moves from a mechanistic to a more purely intentional picture of mental causation. Freud's ultimate view of mental causation, and the most coherent view that he develops, describes mental causes as intentional causes using psychological vocabulary.

Mental Causation and Causal Determinism

Wittgenstein criticizes Freud's causal determinism by distinguishing between causes and reasons (Wittgenstein, 1966, 1977; Bouveresse, 1991). He argues that mental events should be described in terms of reasons and justifications that don't obey causal laws. For Wittgenstein, it is a category mistake to equate motives and causes, because there isn't a causal explanation that respects the accidental and random aspect of human actions.

Underlying this criticism is the idea that it is not possible to find nomological laws that govern mental events. By treating psychoanalytical interpretations as scientific causal explanations, Freud seems to conflate two explanatory frameworks. The first framework affirms that "each mental event is caused." The second affirms that "each mental event is caused by laws." Stating that "a mental event is caused by another mental event" is not the same as stating that every cause or determination in the mental domain is subject to scientific generalization. Standard scientific explanations propose that "for every group of causes of type X, there occurs a group of effects of type Y." In psychoanalytical theory, however, this principle is not justified. While in some cases Freud seeks psychophysical and psychological laws that apply to the mind, in other instances, he points to the unpredictable nature of cause and effect implied in the explanation of a mental event.

The accidental and unpredictable nature of mental events is compatible with the idea that mental events are caused, but it is hard to reconcile with the idea that mental events fall under deterministic scientific laws. In the mental realm, causes are always unique. Each case is unique in its causal explanation and there is no *general type* that always obeys the same law of causality and that allows one to always predict the same effects. Instead, we might consider the generalizations of psychoanalysis – like the universality of the Oedipus complex – not as a deterministic and universal scientific theory, but as a hypothesis that works like a mythical cause offering a new repertoire for causal explanations to justify why we perform certain actions.

Psychoanalysis works with an explanatory model based on reasons that explain intentional actions motivated by the agent's beliefs and desires. This model separates psychoanalysis from the field of physical sciences that work with nomological causes, and defines it as a discipline in which reasons occupy an explanatory role. Historically, when opponents such as Adolf Grünbaum (1984) criticized the scientific status of psychoanalysis, the reaction was to construe psychoanalysis as an extension of folk psychology, removing it from the realm of scientific theories. This approach can be found in psychoanalytic philosophers such as Richard Wollheim, Jonathan Lear, and Marcia Cavell. Cavell (1993), for example, argues that psychoanalysis is an interpretative discipline, in which interpretations play a causal role. For Cavell, the task of psychoanalysis is to build a metapsychology in which unconscious motives figure as the cause of the conflict and subsequently of the agent's actions. In opposition to this interpretative turn, neuropsychoanalysts, such as Mark Solms and Linda Brakel, have tried to resume Freud's naturalist project. They have argued that psychoanalysis intervenes in the mind at a physical level, and have defended a physicalist ontology of the mind in light of neuroscientific evidence about the dynamic biological unconscious (Brakel, 2013) and neuroaffective consciousness (Solms, 2013). The naturalist turn certainly brought a more updated and coherent view of the brain and neurophysiological processes. However, it has its own problems, in explaining the connections between physical events and mental events and subjective experiences.

In my view, the best way to understand Freud's project is by adopting a nonreductive approach, such as Donald Davidson's anomalous monism, which claims that psychology cannot be reduced to physics, but nonetheless is grounded in a physical ontology. Davidson's theory of anomalous monism is a classic defense of non-nomological mental causation (Davidson, 1992, 1995). Davidson presumes an identity between physical and mental events. The events can be described in either a physicalist or a mentalist vocabulary. In the physicalist description, the events allow for the formulation of laws that explain the causal interaction of events. In the psychological vocabulary, there are no strict laws, but rather generalizations valid on a case-by-case basis. There are recurring patterns of cause and effect that apply to one individual and one event at a time. Even if the pattern repeats itself in similar cases, the uniqueness of each event prevents its interpretation as the occurrence of a strict law or general function, valid for all cases.

On Davidson's picture, the events conceptualized in the intentional vocabulary are not in themselves undetermined or unpredictable. On the contrary, the vocabulary of folk psychology is capable of producing generalizations with a reasonable predictive capacity, although it does not allow regimentation into laws. This is the causality of the anomalism of the mental. Psychological facts cannot be described by *type-type* relations but rather by *token-token* relations. For example, we can't say that "every person who is humiliated by someone else will react with rage, with hurt, with the desire to pay back the humiliation or with repression, depression or the desire to commit suicide." But, given a specific person X, we can say that when that person is humiliated, she will typically respond with fear and the desire to cry.

According to Davidson (1995), reasons can be causes. The ordinary use of the notion of cause shows that there is a set of possible motives to justify an action, but only *one* is the actual cause of the action. The notion of intentional action already supports the idea that actions are caused by the agent's beliefs and desires. Every intentional action is something done by the agent to satisfy a desire, based on certain beliefs about the world, and about how to achieve the object of desire. What explains intentional actions is the agent's desire and a belief connecting the desire with the action to be explained.

One of Freud's challenges is explaining apparent irrational and aberrant actions using an intentional vocabulary. The intentional vocabulary is constrained by coherence and rationality; our motives to act are rationally connected to our actions. Freud's solution is to create a mental framework in which motivational structure has causal effects. As Davidson argues, the unconscious motivations proposed by Freud are causes that don't sustain a logical and rational connection to the action.

As Davidson (1982) points out for a mental event to cause another mental event without being a reason for it, cause and effect have to be properly separated as with the Humean notion of causality; cause and effect need to occur in different parts of the mind. The Freudian mind is divided into semi-autonomous structures, with non-logical relations between the parts, allowing us to explain how an unconscious desire can cause another thought or desire with which it maintains an arational relationship – acting as a mental cause that is not a reason for the mental state it causes. Each subdivision of the mind presents a set of beliefs, goals, and affects that characterize the events as intentional. These notions justify the mix that Freud makes of rational explanations with causal explanations in which reasons don't occupy the normal normative and rational role.

However, by describing mental phenomena in the vocabulary of causal laws, Freud creates a *hybrid theory* that oscillates between two analogies: the mechanical (a-rational), which involves an impersonal and scientific approach to the phenomenon, and the anthropomorphic, which is based on intentional explanations. On the one hand, the unconscious is an agent, which behaves in mechanical ways; on the other hand, it is primarily cognitive and illogical, composed of desires and using language. The mechanical description removes the unconscious from the intentional realm in which reasons occupy an explicative role.

By affirming the causal role of reasons in human behavior, Freud is not denying physicalist explanations in terms of the nervous system. On the contrary, Freud's metapsychology is an attempt to find a solution to the mind-body problem. The mind-body problem is the problem of how mental processes correlate with brain processes. For Freud, unconscious mental events can have an effect on the brain and the body (e.g., conversion hysteria and compulsive actions) and on the mind (e.g., phobias, fantasies, and dreams). Without neurophysiological processes, reasons could never be causes and have effects. As Solomon (1974) points out, neural functioning is the paradigm of Freud's work. But accepting underlying neural mechanisms does not entail replacing motivational explanations with non-motivational ones, because that would mean accepting that the mind can be reduced to neurophysiological processes – like Solomon's neurode – and giving up the psychological vocabulary of intentional actions, in which beliefs and desire take up a central causal role.

It is difficult to place Freud's conceptions within the vocabulary of mind-body theories, as this is a vast area that lends itself to numerous controversies and interpretations. As pointed out by Solomon (1974), Freud is a materialist with dualist tendencies. He advocates a psychophysical monism by trying to derive the theory of the mind from the neurophysiological theory, and, at the same time, rejecting the thesis of the identity between the physical and the mental, because the identity established is not between events, aspects or descriptions, but between the functions of the mental apparatus and the neurophysiological processes.

My question is how Freud relates mental causation to neurophysiological causation. One of his central contributions is formulating neurophysiological processes in an intentional vocabulary. Over his career, he moved from an emphasis on neurophysiological causation to an emphasis on intentional causation. Once we see how the various stages of his picture integrate both sorts of causation, we can better see how he preserves a picture in which we are intentional agents acting in a natural world.

The Hybrid Topography: Between Mechanism and Intentionality

In formulating his first topography, Freud already has a causal theory of the mind, in which the notion of mental conflict is presented as a causal explanation for mental events. A conflict between antagonistic representations causes a defensive response and a psychological symptom. To this causal explanation, Freud adds his drive theory. The mental conflict is preceded by the instinctual conflict between opposing drives. From this idea, Freud creates a hybrid topography, where the different parts of the mind instantiate both levels of causes, describing the mind in terms of both arational causes and intentional causes. It is this hybrid topography and its problems that I discuss now.

In Freud's first theory of mind, the explanation of mental conflict is derived from the conjunction of the hypotheses of dual drives and of the mind as systems of representations (Freud, 1915a, 1915b, 1915c). The mental apparatus consists of two opposing systems: the Unconscious and the Preconscious. The ego is identified with the Preconscious system, which is related to the functions of consciousness, censorship, and the reality-testing. The ego is the defensive pole of the mind, which examines representations and censors those that produce conflict. The conflict is described as the opposition to the Unconscious and Preconscious systems, separated by repression: what is displeasure for the Preconscious is pleasure for the Unconscious.

Mental conflicts are fueled by constant instinctual energy, coming from sources internal to the organism, which incites it to carry out actions to discharge the unpleasant excitation. In the first topography, drive dualism is expressed by two opposing drives: the drives of the ego (instincts of self-preservation), regulated by the principle of reality; and the sexual drives, regulated by the pleasure principle (Freud, 1915a). The sexual representations and representations of the ego are animated by those opposing drives that seek to associate themselves with representations capable of promoting instinctual satisfaction. The drive hypothesis introduces a new link in the causal chain: symptoms are caused by a conflict between representations, which are representatives of the clash between drives that seek antagonistic satisfactions – self-preservation and sexual satisfaction. The intensity of the excitement causes unpleasant effects in the mental apparatus and creates a mental representation that serves to produce behaviors to satisfy the instinctual source.

In this first picture, the mental is reduced to neurophysiological processes, with causal patterns of physical and biological processes, associated with a system of representations with intentions and fantasies. The mind is conceived as a neural system with circulating energy through connected veins, whose function of censorship is carried out by a repressing mechanism. The ego functions as a neural mechanism that physically registers the increase of excitation. The overflow of instinctual energy provokes effects in the mind, at first felt and translated into alterations in one's state of pleasure or displeasure. The drives are the psychosomatic intermediary required to explain how the energy of the biological body transforms into feelings, intentions, fantasies, and actions.

With the concept of drive, Freud tries to solve one aspect of the mind-body interaction: how do unconscious mental events affect mental and physical states? In Freudian theory, the drives play two roles: it serves as an intermediary to connect the biological body and the mind; and as the force that explains the alterations of the system. As Solomon (1974) shows, the notion of energy is paradigmatic to Freud's work and fulfills the *causal role* in the interaction between neuronal processes and psychological processes.

Freud's definition of drive preserves a residual Cartesian mind-body dualism (Flanagan, 1991), which requires third-party intermediaries that connect two different ontological realities, and promotes the alteration in a mental state. It is this theoretical void that the notion of drive fills. The mental apparatus is conceived as a mind connected to a body, whose functioning involves a constant interaction capable of producing effects both in the body and in the mind.

Both the drive artifice and the energetic mechanism that support it can be seen as an attempt to overcome Cartesian dualism. Freud tries to develop a spatial functional mental apparatus, avoiding localizationistic and reductionist neuroanatomical concepts, in which the instinctual energy promotes the causal interaction between the mental and the neurophysiological processes. In the absence of a causal notion along the lines of Davidson (1992), Freud tries to appeal to two distinct explanations. He doesn't see them as descriptions of the same event, but as *two types* of events – a physical event and a mental event – that interact causally.

This assumption results in a theoretical oscillation in Freud's explanation of the functioning of the mental apparatus. This oscillation starts in the *Project* (Freud 1895). On the one hand, the mental apparatus is a machine that executes functions, moved by energetic circuits, ruled by arational physical causality. On the other hand, the mind is an intentional system, in which motives from folk psychology are rational causes for alterations in mental states.

Within this oscillation — between rational and physical causes — the Freudian ego is conceived. The ego is formulated as an intermediary between the internal and external world, with the task of avoiding displeasure. In *Repression* (Freud, 1915b), the repressive structure functions as a censor of sexuality, reacting every time a possible sexual satisfaction becomes incompatible with the ego's survival demands. In the mechanistic description, the ego functions as a neural mechanism that is automatically activated, whenever the energy reaches elevated levels. It is a neural mechanism sensitive to energetic oscillations, capable of distinguishing and avoiding intense stimuli by recognizing the signs. The *neural ego* reacts to syntactic similarities, with rules for identifying patterns, recognizing similar syntactic signs between events (see Costa, 1995).

However, the arational explanation proves to be insufficient in explaining the pathological conditions found in the clinic. How can a mechanism like the neural-ego explain how a symptom can be caused by an incestuous fantasy? To solve the impasse, Freud connects his psychological account of the etiology of neurosis, which explains the mental causality of the symptom, to his instinct theory, which explains the symptomatic origin, appealing to a physicalist vocabulary. He adapts concepts such as *repression* and *unconscious* to the vocabulary of instinctual energy. In order to sustain the hypothesis of conflicting mental systems resulting from the arational power of the instinctual energy, Freud adds representation to the drive. So unconscious fantasies represent sexual desires, which reflect the instinctual sexual energy.

But how can a neural mechanism recognize the threat of displeasure in a sexual fantasy? How can the neural-ego repress a substitutive representation that was associated with a traumatic event? Freud created a mechanism capable of recognizing the energetic oscillation, not by using physicalist criteria, but by using semantic criteria – *a semantic machinery*. Attributing the capacity of semantic recognition to the machine is attributing beliefs and desires to the system. The neural-ego responds to syntactic similarities, but also to semantic similarities.

The ego is also described as a system of representations that makes complex evaluations in which it compares different representations, establishes relationships between recent and past representations, and anticipates future dangers. It is an *anticipatory system* that helps to predict future situations. The idea of an anticipatory system is central to the assumption of a *rational agency* that defends itself from the conflict between the different parts. The rational agency evaluates both the conflict between its own autobiographical history and experiences, and the conflict between conflicting desires or representations. To avoid the displeasure of the conflict, one must have had a first experience classified as displeasure that serves as a criterion for evaluating new experiences and allows some sort of prediction, so the system can recognize the danger and avoid it. If the ego could not discriminate it, then it would always be like the first time. Conceiving a mind that classifies experiences by using semantic criteria is describing it as an intentional system – with beliefs and desires, with a rationality that motivates its behaviors.

In Freud's first view of repression, the maintenance of a hybrid grammar tends to dismiss beliefs and desires as part of causal history, weakening the notion of a *mental cause* and attributing arational causes as the origin of conflicts. The second topography puts more emphasis on psychological terminology and doesn't refer explicitly to neural interaction.

The Intentional Topography

In the articles after 1920, Freud reformulates his theory of the mind and redesigns its mental structures. Freud's second theory of mind (1923), the second topography, undoes the opposition between the

Unconscious and the ego. The ego assumes the function of self-criticism, deducted from the unconscious feeling of guilt. If feelings of guilt are unconscious, then a part of the ego is unconscious. By attributing an unconscious property to the ego, Freud recovers the descriptive sense of the concept of unconscious and creates a new mental division: *id, ego, and superego.*

In the new topography, Freud establishes links of approximation between the new and old mental structures. The id is classified as unconscious and it is attributed most of the characteristics of the Unconscious System. The organization of the ego is also described from its relation to the repressing agency of the first topography. This attempt to frame the second topography in the previous theoretical framework causes the new structures of the ego and the id, to present similar descriptive oscillation, at times mechanistic, at times intentional. If Freud maintains the mechanistic description, he would need to explain how the neural-ego recognizes certain representations, and is able to identify the meanings they carry. Once again, when faced with this problem, Freud changes his explanatory model, describing the ego as a system of representations, governed by rational causality. Throughout the text, Freud (1923) increasingly dispenses with the notion of neural-ego and focuses his arguments on an intentional conception of the ego. The causal ambiguity ends up being restricted to the id as a structure driven by excitations.

Mechanistic explanations are also insufficient to explain how unconscious feelings of guilt arise. Unconscious feelings of guilt can only arise in a mind with beliefs and desires that is capable of understanding the meaning of words such as authority, duty, and social values. It is not possible to describe the superego as a mechanism nor the feeling of guilt as an energetic excitation. The superego is an intentional structure, which, when in conflict with the ego, produces unconscious feelings of guilt. The second topography describes a system in which intentional causes rather than mechanistic causes do the most important work.

The mind is described as a superstructure of intentional systems driven by displaceable energy that functions as an engine for the mind. There is an instinctual tension between life and death instincts, configured by distinct energy circuits that aim to bind and disunity by principles of binding and destruction (Freud, 1923). The drive tension causes a conflict between the structures of the mind. Mental conflict is also responsible for energy changes. The a-rational causality is restricted to the energy alterations of the drives that inflame the excitatory process of the id. The id is defined both as a *reservoir of instinctual energy* and as a *collection of phylogenetically acquired contents*, such as innate fantasies. Each innate fantasy structure works as an intentional system ruled by rational causality.

The ego is a collection of representations incorporated by perceptual experiences, responsible for censorship and control of the tendencies of the id, and affective and bodily control. For each newly incorporated representation, it occurs a rearrangement of the ego's configuration. The ego is sensitive to internal and external modifications caused by the body-environment interaction. From the conflict between the ego, the representative of the world, and the id, representative of the instincts, emerges the structure of the superego. Pressured by the instinctual sexual drive, the id invests in the first love objects. When becoming conscious of the id's sexual investments in the love object, the ego may try to repress them. By abandoning the sexual object, it occurs the "installation" of this object in the interior of the ego, which will constitute the *superego* – a set of identifications with the beloved renounced objects that form the ideal image of the ego. Once the superego is in place, some impulses of the id are repressed because they harm the ideal narcissistic image of the ego.

Despite partly functioning as an intentional system, the id is not a deliberative structure. If there is no deliberation, how do the id's desires interact causally with the other structures? This can't be determined a priori. There is a contingent component: causal interactions, internal or external to the organism, which, depending on the circumstances, mobilize different aspects of the mind. Once the process has started, unconscious desires of the id behave as a mental cause that tends to produce effects on the ego and superego. The superego evaluates and decides if the id's desires are pertinent to the beliefs and desires of the complex ego-superego. The moral demands of the superego function as a second-order principle, expressed in the dual aspect of the ideal: "we ought to be like" and "we ought not to do." If the unconscious desire is contrary to these principles, the superego responds with criticism of the ego. The superego is the deliberative structure that approves or disapproves of possible actions of the ego, but is not capable of carrying out the action. Any unconscious desire of the id that contradicts this second-order principle, the superego will censor. The censorship causes an effect that is felt by the ego as a feeling of guilt.

The ego interacts causally with the superego, the id, and the external world. In situations in which the desires are in conflict, the ego evaluates its options for action and decides based on the principle of "avoiding annihilation of the ego," "avoiding the threat of castration." Any time an action involves a desire that threatens these principles, the ego will respond in a way to avoid the action. The ego creates defenses against the id's desires and the attacks from the superego and the world. The ego, whether conscious or not, controls the bodily movements and deliberates about the execution of a voluntary act.

In the second topography, Freud develops an explanation where unconscious desires are the cause of mental events, which can rationally explain the agent's actions, its bodily behaviors, and symptoms. This is central to our conception of ourselves as agents. But the connection between physical processes and mental processes is still described by the hybrid theory: unconscious desires are expressions of instinctual drives that have causal powers as mind-body intermediaries. Next, I will discuss how Freud's notion of anxiety can help to explain the connection between physical processes and mental processes without these intermediaries.

Anxiety as a Mental Cause

The third movement is Freud's second theory of anxiety (Freud, 1926). In my view, Freud's thesis that the affective state of anxiety alters the ego's will is closely related to the idea of anxiety as a mental cause that plays a causal role in mental conflicts.

In Freud's first formulation, anxiety was the accumulated undischarged sexual excitation – understood as purely physiological process without any psychological components. In this picture, anxiety is reduced to physical processes and it is not clear how it could cause any mental effect.

In the first topography (1915b, 1915c), anxiety is conceived as a discharge resulting from defensive mechanisms, or rather, as a quantitative effect caused automatically by repression – the automatic anxiety. The action of repression, by separating the affect from a pathogenic representation, resulted in an accumulated undischarged sexual excitation that was transformed into anxiety – a subjective manifestation of a quantity of energy that wasn't mastered mentally or physically. Anxiety is the transformation of an inhibited sexual excitation (in Freud's terms, libidinal instinctual impulses) in a psychological effect. In this picture, Freud's notion of anxiety seems compatible with a physicalist reductionist view of the mind, where psychological facts are described by *type-type relations*, generating psycho-physical laws connecting the physical to the mental. That is, given a subject undergoing an event of repressing a desire, there will always be a transformation of the energy into anxiety. This reductionist idea raises at least two problems. First is the failure of determinism: repression of a desire does not always cause anxiety. Second, the psychological state of anxiety seems to play no causal role; it is the inhibited energy that seems to be causally efficacious.

In Freud's revised theory of affect (Freud, 1926), anxiety is conceived as a psychological reaction to situations of danger – anxiety is an affective state, an unpleasant feeling, which is a signal of danger. In the revised notion, anxiety is a mental state with physical correlates. This affective state is accompanied by physical sensations connected to particular organs of the body: respiratory organs, heart and motor innervations (Freud, 1926, 132). It is a state with "(1) a specific character of unpleasure, (2) acts of discharge and (3) perception of those acts" (Freud, 1926, 133).

In the revised theory of anxiety, Freud reverses the causal mechanism of anxiety and introduces the notion of *signal anxiety*. The *signal anxiety* (anxiety as signal) is an affective state associated with memory – what Freud calls a *mnemonic symbol* (Freud, 1926). The signal anxiety is the affect felt by the ego that evaluates situations of danger and carries the intention of protecting the mind from the potential threat of suffering. It is a mental reaction of an intentional system, capable of evaluating situations based on its set of beliefs and desires. This implies classifying anxiety as a mental reaction – a signal – and no longer as a brute force that modifies mental states. Automatic anxiety, understood as the involuntary externalization of the accumulation of tension, works as a prototype experience for signal anxiety which is the mental cause of mental conflicts. The prototype experience Freud has in mind is the traumatic experience of "the primal anxiety of birth" when the first separation of the newborn from the mother occurs.

In the second topography, Freud limits the a-rational causality of quantitative factors, both to early states of the mind and to situations in which the ego is exposed to causes with no associative connections to its set of beliefs and desires. Freud pictures the early stages of an organism as a stage of biological and mental *helplessness*, extremely dependent on other people. Exposed to a situation in which tension increases, the ego responds with automatic anxiety – a state of intense excitement that results from situations that increase the circulating energy. The ego displays discriminative awareness, a sort of reflexive capacity to react with crying and innate bodily movements to any increase in excitement, caused by an inflow of excitations, from external or internal origins.

However, based on what criteria does the ego define a situation as potentially dangerous? Freud's hypothesis is that the initial *state of helplessness* in which the newborn infant finds itself is an original moment in which there is no ego narrative yet. In the early stages, the rudimentary ego passively experiences the first traumatic experiences of helplessness that leave a mark (a memory trait), to be used as a sign that identifies the threat of danger. With each new experience, the ego reconfigures and expands its repertoire of situations identified as traumatic. The rudimentary ego functions as an intentional system of low complexity, which is in a constant state of reformulating and editing new experiences. With the emergence of the ability of conceptual thoughts, the ego acquires the pattern of rationality that is capable of anticipating, with increasing certainty and sophistication, the situations that present the threat of danger and it gradually develops as an intentional ego. The anticipatory capacity of the ego is ensured by the capacity of the reaction. When it identifies danger, the ego emits the signal of anxiety.

In my view, in creating the concept of signal anxiety as an affect in response to danger, Freud develops a completely intentional explanation for mental conflicts which makes the mechanism of the neural-ego dispensable. The maintenance of the notion of neural-ego is problematic because it proves insufficient to explain human behavior in the face of the sophistication that intentional topography offers us. We can conceive of an intentional ego that largely dispenses with the arational aspect of the concept of automatic anxiety. The intentional ego is an anticipatory system that reacts to any situation, dangerous or not, with some kind of affective state. On occasions when there is no danger, the ego reacts with joy or serenity. In situations where the ego recognizes a threat of danger, it reacts with the affective state of signal anxiety. In situations of effective danger, and where there has been no warning sign, the ego is taken by surprise and reacts with fear, panic and dread feelings typical of post-traumatic reactions. There are also situations in which the ego recognizes danger or triggers anxiety, which is followed by a failure of the ego defense, leading to an uninterrupted triggering of anxiety, causing outbreaks of despair and anxiety outbreaks.

Freud defines anxiety as an affective state of displeasure, which is characterized by its relationship with motor discharge. From an intentional point of view, a motor discharge is nothing more than a physicalist description of an intentional action. By defining anxiety as an affective state of the ego, Freud connects it to actions of the ego. The ego is responsible for controlling the processes of discharge and for executing intentional actions, and its affective states alter its deliberative processes and its intentional actions.

If the ego controls the access to bodily movement and exercises its own will, how should one explain an ego that complains about the limitations in exercising its will? Freud relates the limitations to the bonds of dependency that the ego maintains with the external world, the id and the superego. The task of the ego is to orchestrate the heterogeneous interests so that these result in a single will. On the one hand, the ego is powerful and can exercise its will, because of its connections with the perceptive system and the external world. This forces the ego to submit the mental processes to the reality test. It is in the repression that the ego proves the power of its organization. Through the bonds that it maintains with the id, the ego transforms many desires of the id into identifications of the ego. On the other hand, the bonds weaken the ego and make it feel threatened by the possibility of a rupture or instability. The threats are experienced as situations of danger, to which the ego responds with anxiety. The anxiety interferes with the volitional function of the ego.

Before carrying out an unconscious desire, the ego evaluates if giving in to the desire will lead to the danger of castration. In case of a negative evaluation, the ego reacts with anxiety in order to repress the processes of the id. Anxiety is the cause, of which the defensive processes are the effect. But, how is this process associated with symptoms formation?

The unconscious desire affected by repression functions as a cause of symptomatic formation. If the ego represses the unconscious desire, there is no knowledge of anything. If the repression fails, the unconscious desire finds a disfigured substitute, whose destiny may be the symptom. The formation of the symptom impedes the threatening process of the id and eliminates the situation of danger. Suffering from anxiety, the ego can develop other defenses such as splitting of the ego, denial of reality, and changes in the character of the ego (e.g., reaction formations). Sometimes anxiety provokes the weakening of the will of the ego. The ego deliberates that it should behave like X, but as a result of the feeling of anxiety, it behaves like Y. Not always does anxiety provoke an akratic act. It may provoke a bodily change, such as conversive symptoms, or an alteration of the will, such as compulsive actions. An intense and lasting anxiety is capable of changing the set of beliefs and desires of the ego, changing its deliberations and intentional choices. The ego doesn't act anymore against "its best judgment," because it has changed its best judgment. This pattern of behavior can be identified in subjects whose symptomatic behavior doesn't cause any strangeness. They are ego-syntonic.

In Freud's theory of affect, anxiety is the mental cause which modifies the intentional actions of the ego. This role for anxiety offers a description of ourselves that includes the distinctiveness of the vocabulary of agency and of mind-body causation, dismissing third-party intermediaries between the body and mind. At this point, Freud finally offers a fully intentional picture of mental causation.

Conclusion

The idea that the mind causes our behavior is crucial for our view of ourselves as agents. It is also at the heart of the mind-body problem. In my view, following Davidson, the best way to understand mental causation in Freud is by adopting a non-reductive physicalist approach. This conclusion is supported by an analysis of the development of Freud's views of mental causation. I have reviewed three moments in Freud's theory of mind: the first topography, the second topography, and the revised theory of anxiety. I have argued that Freud's view gradually moves from a reductionist view of the mind-body problem on which mental causation is understood in terms of physical mechanisms, to a non-reductionist view where the mental becomes causally efficacious in its own right. In effect, Freud moves from a *type-type* relation between mental and physical processes (anxiety and compulsive actions, say) to a *token-token* relation. On this *token-token* picture, different people may respond to anxiety in entirely different ways. Psychological causation is not reduced to the deterministic process of physical causation. In this way, Freud's picture makes room for a nonreductive picture of mental causation.

Note

1   This chapter is the result of the ideas developed from my book *Freud's Semantic Machine* published in 2011 in Portuguese. I thank Jurandir Freire Costa and David Chalmers for their helpful comments on earlier versions of this chapter.

References

Bouveresse J, (1991). *Philosophie, mythologie et pseudoscience, Wittgenstein lecteur de Freud*, Paris, l'Éclat.

Brakel L, (2013). *The Ontology of Psychology: Questioning Foundations in the Philosophy of, Mind*, Routledge.

Cavell M, (1993). *The psychoanalytic mind: from Freud to philosophy*, Boston, Harvard University Press.

Costa J, (1995). *A face e o verso: estudos sobre o homoerotismo II*, Rio de Janeiro, Escuta.

Davidson D, (1992). *Mente, mundo y acción: claves para una interpretación*, Buenos Aires, Paidós.

Davidson D, (1982). "Paradoxes of Irrationality", in Wollheim R & Hopkins J, *Philosophical, essays on Freud*, Cambridge, Cambridge University Press, pp. 289–305.

Davidson D, (1995). "Thinking Causes", in Heil J & Mele A, *Mental Causation*, Oxford, Clarendon Press, p. 3–17.

Flanagan O, (1991). *The science of the mind*, Massachusetts, Institute of Technology.

Freud S, (1895). Project for a Scientific Psychology. *The Standard Edition of the Complete, Psychological Works of Sigmund Freud*, 1 281–391, (1950).

Freud S, (1900). The Interpretation of Dreams (Second Part) and On Dreams. *The Standard, Edition of the Complete Psychological Works of Sigmund Freud*, 5 (1953).

Freud S, (1915a). Instincts and their Vicissitudes, *The Standard Edition of the Complete, Psychological Works of Sigmund Freud*, 14 109–140, (1957).

Freud S, (1915b). Repression. *The Standard Edition of the Complete Psychological Works of, Sigmund Freud*, 14 141–158, (1957).

Freud S, (1915c). The Unconscious. *The Standard Edition of the Complete Psychological Works of, Sigmund Freud*, 14 159–216.

Freud S, (1923). The Ego and the Id and Other Works. *The Standard Edition of the Complete, Psychological Works of Sigmund Freud*, 19 1–68, (1961).

Freud S, (1926). Inhibitions, Symptoms and Anxiety. *The Standard Edition of the Complete, Psychological Works of Sigmund Freud*, 20 75–176, (1959).

Grünbaum A, (1984). *The Foundations of Psychoanalysis: A Philosophical Critique*. Berkeley, CA: University of California Press.

Laplanche J & Pontalis J-B, (2002). *Vocabulaire de psychanalyse*, Paris, Quadrige/PUF.

Passos-Ferreira C, (2005). "Causalité Psychique: La Machine Sémantique de Freud," in: *Le Corps, et L'Esprit. Concepts. Revue Semestrielle de Philosophie*, 9 108–127.

Passos-Ferreira C, (2006). "Conflit Psychique," in *Dictionnaire du Corps*. Paris, CNRS Editions, 2006, pp. 98–99.

Passos-Ferreira C, (2011). *A máquina semântica de Freud: do mecanismo à intencionalidade*. São, Paulo, Annablume.

Solms M, (2013). The Conscious ID, *Neuropsychoanalysis*, 15 (1) 5.

Solomon R, (1974). "Freud's Neurological Theory of Mind", in Wollheim R, *Freud: a collection of, critical essays*, New York, Anchor Books, pp. 25–52.

Wittgenstein, L, (1966). *Lectures & conversations on aesthetics, psychology and, religious belief*. Berkeley and Los Angeles: Blackwell.

Wittgenstein, L, (1977). *Culture and value*. Chicago: University of Chicago Press.

Chapter 4

Developing a Metaphysical Foundation for Analytical Psychology

Erik Goodwyn

> A circle existing in nature and the idea of the existing circle, which is also in God, are one and the same thing...therefore, whether we conceive nature under the attribute of Extension, or under the attribute of Thought...we shall find one and the same order, or one and the same connection of causes.
>
> —Spinoza (1677/1985, Part 2, Prop. 7, scholium)

Introduction

From early on, Carl Jung faced skepticism regarding two important concepts in his overall theory of the psyche: the collective unconscious and the archetype. Briefly, the collective unconscious was initially forwarded by Jung as a part of the psyche, which was unrepressed but contained unconscious and innate contents:

> Just as the body has an anatomical prehistory of millions of years, so also does the psychic system. And just as the human body today represents in each of its parts the result of this evolution, and everywhere still shows traces of its earlier stages— so the same may be said of the psyche...The psyche of the child [is] equipped with all specifically human instincts, as well as with the a priori foundations of the higher functions.
>
> (Jung, 1961, p. 348)

Similarly, Jung proposed that the contents of this structure, the archetypes, were described as innate predisposition to formulate certain cross-culturally appearing narratives and images that differed in

DOI: 10.4324/9781003090755-5

surface details but were identical in underlying structure. Jung started his theorizing of these concepts by proposing that they were simply related to our human instincts (discussed later). But Jung did not stop there. Later in his career, Jung ventured into metaphysical ground, even though he himself expressed distaste for metaphysics, and tried to claim that he wasn't doing such a thing. But as we will see further in the chapter, he did in fact make metaphysical claims and implications, particularly when he discussed synchronicity.

It is easy to see, however, that the plausibility of such statements depend greatly upon one's metaphysical assumptions. Unfortunately, since such assumptions are often unstated or unexamined, the reaction one often observes to analytical psychology (hereafter AP) is often a visceral one: either one appears to "get it," or one doesn't. Put another way, a physicalist (conscious or otherwise) might dismiss AP as pure dime-store hokum since it is "obvious" that mental contents can only come from brains, which have individual experiences and do not connect on any fundamental level with any other brains except through the usual mundane channels of verbal communication. Therefore concepts like synchronicity, visions of the future or cosmic/ heavenly landscapes, near-death experiences, and so on, all of which Jung commented on throughout his works, are highly suspect because they are assumed to be metaphysically impossible.

Thus, Jung's theory, perhaps more than any other psychodynamic theory, asks the most of metaphysics, and requires that we examine our metaphysical assumptions more than any other psychological theory does *because* Jung himself felt AP had metaphysical implications. But asking psychology to ground metaphysics results in an unconvincing line of reasoning—psychology is not equipped to do that. Instead let us ask which metaphysical positions might ground and integrate best with AP, so that when AP ventures into metaphysical matters, we can assess whether or not they are defensible with metaphysical, rather than psychological argument.

The reason this matters most for AP is because physicalism is probably the most popular metaphysical position, but Jung's late theory of archetypes is incompatible with physicalism. Because Jung opened up the metaphysical "can of worms" (whereas many psychological theories do not), we must do additional homework to make sense of it in light of the discipline of metaphysics of mind.

The Early Biological Theory of Archetypes

Jung began describing the archetype as an innate process that guides development of the individual psyche, such that certain kinds of expressions (i.e., mythic story structures, mother- and father-images, etc.) become much more likely than others to spontaneously emerge from the unconscious regardless of personal history. Similarly, Jung proposed that the collection of these innate processes, because they are unconscious, should be grouped into a concept he termed the collective (rather than personal) unconscious. Therefore, in what we may call "Early-AP," archetypes were derivative from biological principles. If we stay within Early-AP, since it has biological derivation, no additional metaphysical work is really needed. At this simpler level, AP can be straightforwardly integrated into evolutionary neurogenetics (e.g., Goodwyn, 2013, 2020b), for example, without needing to defend any metaphysical claims.

But later in his career, Jung asked what might be behind the biology, and so his explorations into synchronicity and particularly through his correspondence with Wolfgang Pauli, Jung expanded his theory into territory that requires a more thorough metaphysical treatment. After his intense correspondence with physicists Wolfgang Pauli and Markus Fierz, Jung began to suspect that the archetypes were actually prior to biology, not derivative from it:

> Since psyche and matter are contained in one and the same world, and moreover are in continuous contact with one another and ultimately rest on irrepresentable, transcendental factors, it is not only possible but fairly probable, even, that psyche and matter are two different aspects of one and the same thing.
>
> (Jung, 1954, para 418)

Elsewhere, he states:

> The idea of the *unus mundus* [the single, holistic ontological reality] is founded on the assumption that the multiplicity of the empirical world rests on an underlying unity...everything divided and different belongs to one and the same world.
>
> (Jung, 1955, para 767)

With statements like these, Jung began to propose that the collective unconscious and the archetypes might be more foundational that mere biology and that the archetypes were somehow embedded in the fabric of the universe in a way that is quite incompatible with physicalism (we will see why later). We may call this theory Late-AP.

In other words, Early-AP could be compatible with physicalism, but Late-AP cannot be. But incompatibility with physicalism is insufficient to throw out Late-AP, since physicalism is not the only plausible metaphysical framework that philosophers take seriously, though at present, it is the most popular. In fact, the popularity of physicalism is likely why Jung has faced resistance in some scientific communities due to unexamined physicalist assumptions, and an insufficient consideration of the other alternatives that *are* perfectly compatible with it.

In this chapter, we will review the most commonly discussed objection to physicalism—the explanatory gap problem—and this will lead us to the alternative metaphysical positions that might compare more favorably with Late-AP, building on the already highly significant work of Harald Atmanspacher and colleagues (Atmanspacher & Fach, 2013; Atmanspacher, 2014). Since unlike Early-AP, Late-AP requires us to take a metaphysical stand, this chapter will show which position makes the most sense with it.

The Pauli-Jung Conjecture

Late-AP can be distinguished by its incompatibility with physicalism. Rather, it is far more compatible with *neutral monism*, the idea that both mental and physical phenomena arise from a non-directly observable neutral substance. Neutral monism, apart from being championed by modern philosophers such as Spinoza and Schopenhauer, has also been pursued by physicists and psychologists, including David Bohm, Bernard d'Espagnat, and Hans Primas, among others (Atmanspacher, 2012). Though rarely explicitly stated, Jung's deeper explorations of the concepts of archetypes and the collective unconscious required a move away from physicalism into neutral monism.

Only the effects of *ordering* influences on to conscious contents can be detected. The study of these effects leads to the peculiar fact that they emerge from an unconscious objective reality which, however, at the same time appears to be subjective and conscious. This way, the reality underlying the effects of the unconscious comprises also the observing subject and is therefore of unimaginable constitution. It is in fact both most intimately subjective and most universally true, something that does not apply to conscious contents of personalistic nature. The elusiveness, capriciousness, haziness and uniqueness, with which the layperson connects the conception of the psyche, only applies to consciousness, but not to the absolute unconscious. The efficacious elements of the unconscious, to be defined not quantitatively but only qualitatively, the so-called *archetypes, can therefore not with certainty be designated as psychic.*

(Jung, 1969, para 439)

This difficult paragraph appears to mark the transition from Jung's proposal that archetypes are composed of biological, instinctive unconscious entities into transcendental metaphysical principles, and it appears to have occurred in the last 11 years of his life (Atmanspacher & Fach, 2013, p. 226), placing the transcendental principles into the realm of what he termed the *psychoid*. The archetypes as catalogued by Jung and his followers appear, in this system, to have varying "depth," meaning largely composed of individual trappings and experiences, such as the archetypal core of the shadow and the anima/us complexes, on "down" to the Self, number, and other more fundamental and universal archetypes. These latter archetypes belong to the psychophysically neutral domain of the psychoid, which Jung likens to the Unus Mundus idea of 16th-century alchemist Gerard Dorn.

He privately expressed this idea in a letter to physicist Wolfgang Pauli: "In reality…there is no dissected world: for a unified individual there is one 'unus mundus.' He must discriminate this one world in order to be capable of conceiving it, but he must not forget that what he discriminates is always the one world, and discrimination is a presupposition of consciousness" (Von Meyenn, 2001, p. 800). For his part, Pauli, with Jung, called for an understanding of psyche and matter that therefore transcended both via the phenomenon of *meaning*, "and, thus, entirely outside the natural sciences of his time and also, more or less, of today" (Atmanspacher & Fach, 2013, p. 230). Of course, *meaning* is a notoriously difficult term to pin down. In the present context, as outlined by Jung, meaning is not a formal relationship between signifier and signified, which suffers from the ability to be consciously manipulated and arbitrary, but rather as a *qualitative feature of experience*—a "what-it's-likeness." Focusing as Jung does on this sense of the word "meaning" frees it from arbitrariness and roots it in unconscious preconditions. Archetypes, therefore in Late-AP, constellate synchronistic events and because of their qualia, they cannot simply be attributed any arbitrary meaning.

Under Late-AP, synchronistic phenomena (i.e., events that are not connected via efficient causation but appear connected via meaning) are the result not of mental events causing physical events or vice-versa, but the result of mental and physical events being epistemic split pieces of an underlying unitary phenomenon that is not directly observable. Two events are synchronistic only if one is intrapsychic and one is externally perceived, and there is no conceivable (efficient) causal connection between them but they nevertheless have a common apparent symbolic meaning. Despite the term, however, the two events do not actually have to be simultaneous. Jung and Pauli felt that such meaningful correspondences had an acausal archetypal ordering to them, using the concept of Aristotelian final causality rather than efficient causality as a way to understand the causal connection between them. Atmanspacher considers "meaningful" as ordered toward a final cause via an archetype as one end of a spectrum with stochastically accidental events on the other end as meaning-less. In this sense, the experienced intentionality as a qualia of a synchronistic event is "inflicted upon the experiencing subject" (Atmanspacher & Fach, 2013, p. 233) as a primary datum, rather than an arbitrarily assigned ratiocination.

Pauli and Jung found that the principle of quantum holism or non-locality, along with the psychological concept of the unus mundus, formed the basic underlying neutral reality from which mind and matter must derive. Accordingly, matter and mind are generated by decomposition of the whole, which is in opposition to the *derivation* of mind via the composition of more basic plural elements.[1]

The Explanatory Gap

Abandoning physicalism should not be done lightly, or because it is not compatible with Late-AP. Rather, if we're going to do that, it should be for metaphysical reasons rather than psychological, since metaphysics is more fundamental. As it turns out, there are well-known challenges to physicalism that remain within the field of metaphysics that we need to know about before we look at what metaphysics might be more compatible with the Jung-Pauli conjecture. Rather than its incompatibility with late-AP, the main reason to consider other frameworks than physicalism is that it has a classic challenge known as the *explanatory gap* problem. It goes as follows: how is it that isolated cells do not appear to display any experiential properties, yet large aggregates of them, interacting in just the proper way, apparently miraculously *acquire* phenomenal experience—something so manifestly different from the properties of humble cells in isolation. Where do these properties come from, and at what point in their assembly? Do they appear ex nihilo, and if so, how is this possible? This disparity between the physical and the phenomenal is the root of the so-called explanatory gap argument against the idea that mental properties actually *derive* from the physical components of the body—the central tenet of all physicalisms—rather than having some other sort of relation between mind and matter. Phenomenal properties, like the taste of cold beer, or the characteristic qualitative sound of guitar chords, so the argument goes, are so alien to the properties of isolated bits of matter (e.g., mass, charge, velocity, etc.) that it appears incoherent to suggest the former somehow derive from the latter.

These "other sorts" of relations, often prompted by an aversion to the explanatory gap problem, range from proposals that the mind is actually of a different substance entirely from matter (substance dualisms), to the reverse situation of matter actually being derivative of mind (idealist monisms), to both mind and matter being themselves derivative of a pluripotent, not directly observable prior substance (neutral monisms or multi-aspect monisms).

All of these proposals are attempts to answer the (in)famous Mind-Body Problem (MBP): *how does the mental relate to the physical?* As I hope to show, even composing what sort of answer one might generate to this problem contains many conceptual difficulties. This is because, even before considerations of substance is concerned, the MBP is really getting at the following question: are "mind" and "matter" completely separate, similar, related, or identical categories? Before we try to answer this question with one of the metaphysical frameworks, we need to postulate as precise a definition of the characteristics of these categories as we can that is itself free of suppositions of substance, since the suppositions of substance are what we are evaluating. Only from there can we establish what sort of relationship these categories may or may not have to each other in terms of substance.

Postulate 1. Phenomenal Experience (Mind) Exists

This may be the most indisputable element of this whole discussion and is defended very nicely by Goff (2017) and was defended by Jung throughout his work. That phenomenal experience *in itself* exists, there can be no reasonable dispute (though see further in the chapter). Sure, the universe I see may be a hallucination, but I cannot deny that I am hallucinating *something*. In any case, this experience is what we mean when we say "mind" or "consciousness." But this phenomenal experience also has certain characteristics that we must remain cognizant of: that is, this phenomenal experience typically is of *coherent and unified* phenomena, often accompanied by a con-comitant phenomenal impression of "separateness" between the ex-periencer and that which is experienced (hallucinatory or not). Note the scare quotes are essential, in order to remain free of metaphysical assertion prematurely, as this *impression* of separateness may or may not reflect true metaphysical distinction.

Postulate 2. The *Concept* of "Matter" Exists

Of the continuous stream of experiences, *some* phenomenal experi-ences will carry with them a strong impression, sense, or quality that they are somehow "external to" or even "independent of" our general phenomenal experience as a whole. In other words, we all have the impression that some experiences feel like they correspond with en-tities that are "outside" of our coherent phenomenal experience, and can exist independently of it. Again, I have to include all the scare quotes here because these impressions cannot be taken as foundationally required for the definition. For example: if it turns out that mind and matter are in essence the same substance (as might be the case if neutral monism were true), then the experiencer and the experienced are not truly separate in our metaphysics; rather, they are only separate in our experience.

Given postulates 1 and 2, then, the MBP naturally emerges from several simple observations: namely, that aggregates of matter, as defined earlier, sometimes and under the right conditions, seem to "acquire" general phenomenal experience that suggests similarity with our own where it previously did not appear to have any—that we cannot a priori explain how this happens is the explanatory gap problem. Note, however, that the explanatory gap problem is *dependent* upon our subsequent framing of the aforementioned two postulates. This is because each proposed metaphysics actually adds *more conditions and parameters* to the aforementioned postulates that inform our proposed solution to the MBP.

Physicalisms

what we perceive as "matter" is not merely a concept or experience, rather it has ontological status and is in fact the most fundamental substance in the universe. Furthermore, phenomenal experience is derived from this fundamental substance (different physicalisms vary on how this happens, and to what degree they consider phenomenal experience to be "real"); bits of matter, when organized into just the right way, give rise to phenomenal experience, and these phenomenal experiences are entirely dependent upon the matter giving rise to them, and this includes (essentially recursive) phenomenal experiences of matter, which may or may not correspond to how matter actually is—hence phenomenal experience is highly suspect in this metaphysics. Physicalisms have the most "classic" explanatory gap problems concerning exactly how phenomenal experiences arise from bits of matter. Late-AP is not compatible with physicalism because archetypes, being mental contents, would have to be fully derivative from matter, and in Late-AP, this is explicitly denied.

Idealist Monisms

Matter is a mental entity, but does not have ontological status. That is, it is only a concept and nothing more. Matterlike experiences appear the way that they do (i.e., as strongly suggesting that they continue to exist independently of an experiencer) as a result of it being mental contents of a universal experiencer such as God. Late-AP is compatible with idealist monism; however, there are other positions which fit it better, as we will see. In any case, this metaphysics has no apparent explanatory gap problem since everything is considered to be phenomenal experience with no non-phenomenal originators; however, it has another problem discussed below.

Substance Dualisms

both matter and experience are separate substances, each with a separate source. Both have ontological status as real. Matter is not merely a concept but a foundational substance that is fully extant regardless of whether or not there is an experiencer, and mental substance can also exist independently of matter. Dualisms also do not have an explanatory gap problem since phenomenal experience is not claimed to derive from matter as in the case of physicalism, yet it has an *interaction problem*, which concerns explaining how these entirely separate substances can influence with one another. In any case, substance dualism is not compatible with Late-AP because of the latter's insistence on the ultimate *identity* between matter and psyche.

Neutral/Multi-aspect Monisms

phenomenal experience and matter-like experiences are both secondary to a more fundamental substance that cannot be directly experienced but only inferred. Like physicalism, phenomenal experience is derivative, but unlike physicalism, so is matter. Only the neutral substance has foundational ontological status; mind and matter are derivative of it. This neutral substance is in a sense "mind independent"—since it is the stuff from which mind derives rather than the other way around—but it is also "matter independent" for the same reason. All material objects in this metaphysics have intrinsic phenomenal qualities (however dimly realized) associated with them that do not derive from the matter in itself, but from the not-directly-observable neutral substance of which it is constituted. Phenomenal experiences likewise have (possibly multiple) intrinsic material qualities to them (however strangely arranged). Since the phenomenal is taken to be foundationally co-derivative along with matter, there is no explanatory gap problem with respect to matter "creating" the phenomenal. Instead, in this case, there are other explanatory problems that depend upon how we think phenomenal experience arises. If we assume, in the manner of panpsychism, that bits of phenomenal experience possessed by bits of matter build up into larger scale experiences, then we have an explanatory gap problem concerning explaining how this occurs (i.e., the so-called combination problem).[2] Note that this problem exists *only if* we assume that phenomenal experience does indeed "build up" from bits of proto-experience—that is, the mental parts are prior to the mental whole. If, rather, we assume that phenomenal experience starts with the whole, for example, the entire universe (i.e., cosmopsychism—see Goff, 2017 for a brilliant defense of this model), then phenomenal experience appears the way it does in humans and other animals because we are small *parts* of the greater whole universe—that is, the wholes are prior to the parts rather than the other way around. In this case, we have a kind of reverse explanatory gap problem—the so-called *de-combination problem*: when the universe (or any other larger whole) is broken down, why do such systems *lose* their larger phenomenal qualities? If they are not derived from matter, as asserted by neutral/multi-aspect monisms, where do such qualities disappear to? As we will see, Late-AP integrates best with a specific version of this *kind* of metaphysics known as *cosmopsychism*.

Heaps and Syllables

As mentioned, one quick way out of the problem is to claim that matter does not exist as a separate category of experienced entities that have their own separate ontological status—idealist monism. In this system, "matter" is simply a class of mental experiences, and in the case of no immediate experiencer, we can always resort to God/universal consciousness/and so forth as the mind in which it appears. But even in that case, there is a problem: the regularity with which phenomenal experiences—in particular matter-like experiences—occur. We will get more into it later, but it must seem curious to the idealist that *certain* collections of matter-like experiences appear to be the *only* ones that correlate with phenomenal experiences to the degree that they do. Within the framework of idealism, there is no easy way to account for this regularity.

In any case, for purposes of this chapter, we will set aside the interaction problem of dualism and the regularity problem of idealism in favor of the explanatory gap and reverse explanatory gap problems that relate to physicalisms and neutral monisms, as only these relate to the mereological issue that I think underlies them, and are most applicable to Late-AP. This proposal stems from the interesting empirical fact that it seems *integrated wholes* are the only ones that appear capable of presenting phenomenal experience-like behavior as we understand it (note that I do not feel qualified to discuss "phenomenal experience as we *don't* understand it" so I will avoid that subject). As Aristotle pointed out, an integrated whole is "that which is compounded out of something so that the whole is one—not like a heap, but like a syllable" (1984, p. 1644). Only syllables appear capable of bearing phenomenal properties, as far as we can tell. Why is this? Note that while idealism has no way to attack this question, the others do not necessarily fare much better, and they necessarily import mereological analysis into the problem, since the property of being an integrated whole appears to be a necessary (though not sufficient) condition that must obtain in order to allow for the possibility of phenomenal experience. This seems intuitively plausible (if not inevitably following) because phenomenal experience is *itself* an integrated whole—however; it relates to other kinds of integrated wholes (like human organisms), this at least seems to make sense. In any case, since only integrated wholes appear capable of displaying behavior that is consistent with the existence of phenomenal qualities, it means that whereas all entities with phenomenal experience correlate with, or have properties of, integrated systems of matter-like "stuff" (whatever we think that is), it is not the case that all integrated systems correlate with phenomenal experience. More on this later. For now, let us consider some of the attempts to resolve the explanatory gap and see why they fall short of their goal.

Attempts to Span the Gap

As mentioned, there are two broad types of explanatory gap problems: for physicalisms, we have the so-called hard problem of neuroscience (Chalmers, 2012), and for panpsychist neutral monisms, we have the so-called combination problem (Chalmers, 2016). All of these problems entail the same basic issue: entities that appear to have independent separateness that are free of their own phenomenal experiences (like cells or biomolecules) sometimes *obtain* phenomenal experience *as an integrated whole* once they are combined in *thus-and-such* a manner (like during human development), and this appearance has no obvious explanation. For physicalism, it's the "hard problem of neuroscience": how do neurons buzzing in just-so a manner acquire the properties of phenomenal experience? For certain kinds of neutral/multi-aspect monisms like panpsychism, it's the combination problem: if we grant that all bits of matter have corresponding bits of (proto) phenomenal experience to go with them, how is it that combining them just-so gives us a unified phenomenal experience that spans the new integrated whole? Though physicalism and panpsychism employ very different metaphysics, they both share a similar explanatory gap problem related to parts and integrated wholes.

Notice also that the gap with respect to phenomenal experience appears to be a *special kind* of explanatory gap. Few are puzzled as to how 2H-and-1O-molecule-units acquire watery properties when they are arranged just so, and yet taking a handful of biological molecules that have no (apparent) phenomenal awareness and joining *them* in a particular way can result in an integrated whole that speaks of experiences of pain, love, the taste of chocolate, and even things like perception, memory, consciousness, identity, selfhood, abstract concepts, and so forth. The gap here seems of a different quality altogether than the above water one (though it may not be—we will get to this later).

Nevertheless, there have been a number of attempts at getting around this problem, and these fall into a few broad categories: elimination, identity, and emergence/supervenience. As we will see, all of these attempts fall short in a number of serious ways. We will look at the first three before getting to emergence and its close ally, supervenience.

Elimination and Identity

Elimination is a physicalist argument that phenomenal experiences are illusory, "convenient fictions," and so on, and are therefore not real, thus we need not concern ourselves with how they are generated. No explanatory gap must be surmounted in this case: problem solved. Examples include Churchland (1996), Kim (1992) and Dennett (1988, 1992). But the objection to this maneuver is fairly simple: asserting that phenomenal experiences are illusory simply shifts the problem rather than solve it. The trick comes in when we claim that unified, coherent, phenomenal experiences are "illusions." Since we cannot dispute that they *happen,* as that would be absurd, we must instead be proposing that what these experiences *represent* is actually what is not real. That is, while we may *feel* like we are having a coherent, unified experience of conscious awareness or pain, we are in our inner workings actually *not* coherent or unified or "in pain," and so there is nothing that needs to be explained. Under physicalism, the phenomenal experiences are secondary to matter, but when they are recursive experiences that refer to the matter from which they are derived, they can take any form and can clearly be wildly mistaken. Examples are typically given of folk psychology ideas that don't match up to what we learn from neuroscience; hence, the phenomenal impressions we are trying to explain—since they are faulty—need no explanation.

But this approach does not take care of the explanatory gap; it sidesteps it. It does not make any difference whether the experience accurately represents anything. Rather, the problem is that the experience—whatever it is—is *in itself* coherent, unified, and full of phenomenal quality and flavor as experienced. Even if we grant that the brain creates this illusion to help us cope with life, we cannot explain *how* the brain does it, which is what the MBP is really about. Thus, hiding the explanatory gap problem behind what phenomenal experience is "representing" doesn't get us out of trouble. We have to explain not what the image represents, but the image itself.

Identity theory seeks to resolve the MBP by stating that the component parts are "exactly equivalent" to the integrated whole experiences they give rise to and hence there is no explanatory gap. In other words, the systems of material parts (i.e., neural networks) and the phenomenal experiences that correspond to them have identical referents—it is merely a matter of semantics, and so the distinction is a false one (e.g., see: Smart, 1959), and phenomenal qualities are merely shorthand, folk-psychology terms for the more rigorously defined neural states that they actually are. The situation is analogous to the evening and morning stars: two names for experiences that appear different, but actually refer to the same underlying reality: the planet Venus.

But this again sidesteps the issue rather than explain it. Claiming that phenomenal impressions are fully reducible to neural systems (etc.) does not explain the key issue we are interested in: if they are identical, why don't they *look* identical? To use Thomas Nagel's example of sound and aural networks (1974), to claim that the subjective human viewpoint "simply is the same thing as" such-and-such neural networks engaging with pressure waves is to assert that the former reduces to the latter, but without any actual reductive mechanisms given. Furthermore, to claim that they are analogous to the evening and morning star experiences doesn't work either, ironically, unless you are operating within a neutral monist framework, where both are derivative of the "real" thing: Venus (i.e., the neutral substance). Hence, mind-brain identity doesn't really escape the explanatory gap, since it doesn't even bother to address the actual gap itself: why such-and-such a system should appear the way it does in phenomenal experience. To state that they are simply identical buts up against the simple fact that they appear fully distinct, begging for the identification to be made, and semantics doesn't help. To justify it, we would need to assert with the eliminativists that the phenomenal experience is an illusion, shorthand, "fiction," and so on therefore again begging the question of how and why the *illusion* appears the way it does.

Emergence and Supervenience

Finally, sometimes the concept of emergence is used to leap across the explanatory gap while still remaining within a physicalist framework. Emergence works in this manner: certain systems, upon reaching a certain level of complexity and integration, show the emergence of irreducible system-wide qualities that themselves can have causal top-down efficacy. The concept of emergence is one which dates back to Aristotle, but found new life among the British emergentists in the early 20th century, only to fall out of analytical philosophy until the 1990s when it resurfaced. Kim (2010) is illustrative, showing that two apparently key features of emergence are *supervenience and irreducibility*. Supervenience is defined in emergent terms and has been invoked on many occasions to try to sort out problems in the philosophy of mind; it consists of the following:

> If property M *emerges* from properties N(1)...N(n), then we can say that M "supervenes" on N(1...n). Put another way, any time something has N(1...n), it necessarily has M.

Kim points out that mind-body supervenience is commonly assumed in theories of the mind-body relation—type physicalism, functionalism, epiphenomenalism, emergentism, and dual-aspect theory commonly assume or are consistent with supervenience. Kim, however, shows how that fact does not tell us very much, and in considering emergentism of mind/phenomena, we really just wind up back at square one, in which phenomena are emergent but fully irreducible in principle.

> *The demands of emergentism make the supervenience relation involved in emergence necessarily unexplainable; we cannot know what kind of dependence grounds and explains the supervenience relation involved in emergence.*
>
> (Kim, 2010, p. 556, emphasis original)

This is precisely our old friend the explanatory gap. Kim shows that emergentism gives us a rather anemic explanatory structure: while we may know all the details about the mechanisms behind pressure wave interactions with auditory centers in the brain, to say that the subjective qualia of the sound "emerges from" this complex interaction is to simply describe the situation rather than explain it. If emergence is to stay true to its definition, it really cannot do more than frame emergent properties as brute unanalyzable facts, so while emergence works well as a *description* of how complex systems work, but it does not provide the needed *reduction* to explain phenomenal qualia—it simply asserts that while phenomenal experiences may supervene on neural substrates they are not reducible to them, period. Right back to the explanatory gap. If phenomenal experience cannot in principle be reduced to neural systems, then it is easy to see why there is an explanatory gap: to explain across the gap is an incoherent and contradictory attempt to reduce that which is *in principle* irreducible. Furthermore, it renders emergence an essentially negatively defined relation: "irreducibility" is as useful as the quality of something being "non-red"—a nonzero quality, but only barely.

Kim also shows that another issue emergentism faces is downward causation, and this is a consequence of accepting the supervenience relation with respect to emergent properties. If substrate P consistently gives rise to M, a novel property, M must have some kind of causal power to produce P*, otherwise it becomes a superfluous quality—why not simply explain the change to P* in terms of P?

A Mereological Problem

We saw earlier that one thing is consistently observed: the only entities that appear to possess or be capable of acquiring phenomenal experience where there previously appeared to be none are systems of elements that are working together in a highly complex and integrated manner. Only syllables can be conscious—not heaps. As mentioned earlier, this curious fact, provided it holds throughout the universe, opens up the possibility that the MBP may be a special case of a more general part-whole problem, and as such part-whole issues may apply to it.

Thus, whereas the various approaches to the MBP involve attempting to define whether or not mind and body are the same or different *substances*, it is less often looked at from the point of view of various mereological relations; that is, viewing the mind and body not as separate or equal substances but as part (matter) and whole (mind), and then subsequently asking *which* mereological system may address the MBP complexities best. The central observation here is that since only systems of matter-like "particles" integrated into a coherent whole appear to be capable of possessing phenomenal qualities, whereas unintegrated heaps of the exact same particles are apparently not capable of it, it may be that the quality of being-an-integrated-whole is a necessary (but not sufficient) condition to allow for the possibility of phenomenal experience. In other words, minds belong only to a certain subclass of integrated wholes and nothing else, therefore the manner in which parts relate to wholes may inform us to some degree as to the way in which matter relates to mind.

If we are to think of the MBP as a kind of whole-part problem, however, we must consider the various possible ways of proposing this configuration. Coming at the MBP from the perspective of mereological pluralism (parts are prior to wholes, and the particles of physics are the most fundamental objects) creates a very different set of possible answers than coming at it from the perspective of mereological monism (parts are derivative from wholes and the cosmos is the most fundamental object). Jonathan Schaffer (2010) outlines the difference between these two positions nicely: under the system of pluralism, parts are seen as *metaphysically prior* to wholes—that is, that wholes are derivative of parts. Physicalism, then, can be seen as a special kind of mereological pluralism. Mereological monism, on the other hand, proposes the opposite. Despite the prominence of mereological monism throughout the history of ideas, in more recent analytical philosophy, monism has fallen out of favor since Bertrand Russel, but Schaffer offers a number of well-argued reasons for reconsidering it. The present essay offers an additional reason: it appears that under a framework of mereological monism, significant progress on the MBP can be made, whereas frameworks that pre-suppose mereological pluralism, such as physicalism and some kinds of panpsychism, are fatally blocked by their pluralistic assumptions. More on Schaffer's treatment, and his later article of 2017, is given next.

The Inherent Pluralism in Common Approaches to the MBP

Various approaches to the MBP typically cluster around a relatively small number of offered possibility types (Chalmers, 2012): physicalisms (which include eliminativism, mysterianism, type physicalism and functionalism), substance dualism (and its cohort epiphenomenalism), idealism, and various substance monisms (e.g., dual-aspect and neutral substance monism—not to be confused with mereological monism). What many of these systems share is a presupposition of pluralism:

that the parts (bits of substance—however defined—with or without proto-mind properties) are *prior to* the whole (mind, consciousness, phenomenal qualia, etc.). In all types of physicalism, pluralism is presupposed: mind, through whatever mechanisms, is fully dependent upon and therefore derivative from the matter which gives rise to it. But even in some types of substance monism (except perhaps idealism), proto-consciousness is seen as inhering on some basic level with the fundamental parts of the universe, and so upon their organization into bodies and brains, mind also arises in a dependent and ontologically posterior fashion in this framework.

The substance monism described earlier is not to be confused with the mereological monism I am discussing here. Substance monism, as an approach to the MBP, proposes that mind and matter are essentially of the same substance. Mereological monism, however, proposes that there is only one basic object—the cosmos—and all other parts of that basic object are *derivative* and ontologically posterior to it. Hence, these concepts are overlapping but non-identical.

Monism, Pluralism, and the Explanatory Gap

How then might we apply this mereological concept to the MBP? The primary assumption operating in a mereological monist framework is that composition is not identity (but see Baxter, 1998 for a rebuttal against this claim), since in that case, pluralism and monism would not be opposing views in general, but more importantly because—with respect to the MBP—starting with this assumption helps to avoid the problems encountered with the identity theory attempts to resolve the MBP discussed earlier. Furthermore, the monist approach to the MBP assumes with Aristotle a frame of metaphysical foundationalism, that is, that there is some sort of ground of being rather than metaphysical infinitism or circular dependence, and that there is a priority ordering among parts and wholes. For both monism and pluralism, the cosmos exists and is made of proper parts. The difference is that in monism, the whole is prior and in pluralism the parts are prior (Schaffer, 2010).

Schaffer observes that common sense, empirical facts about quantum entanglement (about which we will have more to say), relativistic quantum theory, and other considerations actually favor monism over pluralism (2010, pp. 50–56), but for our purposes, it is the treatment of supervenience that obtains the most relevance, which we will explore more below. For now, assuming that the MBP can be viewed as a whole-part problem can be justified because of the empirical observation that phenomenal experiences seem to *only* be associated with being a kind of integrated *whole*, as opposed to, say, objects that are within a certain mass range, or going within a certain velocity range. In other words, parts that have no phenomenal experiences can apparently contribute to the acquisition of phenomenal experiences once those previously non-experiencing parts are *arranged just so*. There is nothing else we can do with such parts that does the trick. Thus, it makes sense to ask what whole-part dynamics may tell us about the MBP. Let's look at approaches to part-whole dynamics in general first, then look at the special case of *integrated* wholes.

As mentioned earlier, there are two broad approaches to whole-part questions (mental or not): *pluralism*, in which the isolated parts are prior to any wholes constituted by them, up to the universe, and *monism* where the universe is prior to any proper parts of it considered in isolation. In pluralism, wholes are derivative and posterior, and in monism, parts are derivative and posterior. If we view the MBP as a special instance of these general relations, it means that the properties of isolated human cells and properties of human beings (as integrated wholes) still function in the same manner, with the caveat that only integrated wholes have the possibility of experiencing phenomenal events (an additional characteristic we will deal with in a moment), whatever other properties they may have.

Therefore, under mereological pluralism, human phenomenal experience (as a property of integrated whole human beings) *must be derivative of* the properties of isolated human cells. On the other hand, under mereological monism, human phenomenal experience is prior, and the properties of isolated parts of a human being (like the brain, or isolated neurons or other cells) will instead be *derivative of* that integrated whole. Assembly and integration, then, is *not a process full of novel properties popping up ex nihilo via some mysterious efficient causes, but rather it is a process of obtaining greater closeness to integration via a kind of final causality.*

Earlier we clarified that of the metaphysical frameworks that attempt to tackle the MBP, we would only concern ourselves with physicalism and multi-aspect monism. Now we can see how these line up in accordance with the two mereological systems in question: all physicalisms are pluralist, since they propose that minds derive from bits of interacting matter. Multi-aspect monism, however, can come in two varieties: the pluralist form of this framework would be *panpsychism:* the idea that all bits of matter have some kind of proto-phenomenal experience or proto-consciousness associated with them. One monistic form of this framework, however, is *cosmopsychism:* one where the universe is itself conscious, and all other consciousnesses are derivative of the cosmic consciousness. This maximal phenomenal experience would be prior to all the parts observed composing it, so the only concern would be the reverse explanatory gap.

Each of these frameworks has its own (reverse) explanatory gap with respect to the MBP, but as mentioned, the interesting thing to notice is that both physicalism and pluralist panpsychism have a very similar explanatory gap: in both cases, it is caused by the pluralism underlying each of them. The explanatory gap in panpsychism is called the "combination problem," but it's the same problem physicalism has, only with different parts. In physicalism, we are trying to explain how phenomenal experience derives from bits of matter. In panpsychism, we are trying to explain how phenomenal experience derives from bits of proto-phenomenal experience. In both cases, however, we are trying to explain how properties of an integrated whole arise from the properties of the isolated parts before integration. Both could be subject to the same analysis Kim provides and we would wind up with the problems he notes with respect to supervenience, emergence, and downward causation. This is because the issues Kim raises with respect to emergence are consequences of the pluralist framework that is assumed. In other words, the problems of emergentism arise *because* emergentism assumes that wholes are derivative from parts, which then require that there be an explanatory apparatus in place to explain how the derivation works. This derivation, however, must propose that in-principle irreducible qualities emerge from more fundamental substrates in a way that is consistent with supervenience relations but nevertheless must completely prohibit any possibility of reduction. From there, downward causation becomes another issue in that it becomes superfluous, which is at the very least counterintuitive.

Schaffer (2017) explores how mereology can inform the MBP with respect to the explanatory gap. Like myself, he argues that the explanatory gap with respect to mind and matter is really no different than the explanatory gap with respect to wholes and parts. As such, he argues against the idea that the mind-matter explanatory gap is "special" and fundamentally different from other explanatory gaps such as the "2H+O somehow → watery stuff" explanatory gap. Thus, *any* property of a whole will have an explanatory gap with respect to the properties of the isolated parts that compose them. Schaffer's (2017) solution is to propose that the ordering principles that determine the emergence of holistic properties (e.g., phenomenal experience) be called "grounding conditions" and that they simply be assumed as brute facts—but no different in principle from the brute facts the order the emergence of watery properties from the arrangement of H and O molecules *just so*. Thus, it stands, and with the downward causation issue raised by Kim essentially remaining to be dealt with. As Chalmers points out (2016), panpsychism faces essentially the same issue, just replacing bits of matter with bits of experience.

But what if we view it the other way—from the perspective of mereological-monism-as-applied-to-mind? We will see how the Jung-Pauli formulation of metaphysics developed by Atmanspacher et al. takes this approach given ahead. In this case, since we have an underlayment of merological monism, it is not necessary to explain how properties of wholes derive from properties of parts, since that is not how the relation flows no matter how you slice it. Rather, properties of parts derive from properties of the wholes from which they are partitioned, and for our purposes that means properties of isolated human cells derive from the properties of the wholes from which they were separated. In this case, the explanatory gap issues described earlier dissolve, but another problem takes its place: the reverse explanatory gap issue known as the "de-combination problem": how can we explain why isolated human cells *don't* have phenomenal experience? Mereologically, the underlayment of this question is: why does partitioning an integrated whole cause it to lose properties? Why *aren't* isolated neurons (or electrons for that matter) as conscious and aware as the wholes from which they were derived? Even in the case of cosmopsychism, the reverse-explanatory gap becomes: why is human phenomenal experience limited compared to what must be the phenomenal experience possessed by the cosmos (disregarding visionary/paranormal reports)? More on this momentarily.

Mind-Body Relations and Whole-Part Relations

This kind of thinking about the MBP as a special kind of whole-part problem is not new. There is a longstanding tradition that views many of the aforementioned conceptual troubles of the MBP as related to whole-part concepts. This approach dates back to Aristotle, wherein it is proposed that questions such as "what is the relation between mind and brain?" cannot actually be answered because they involve category errors, unless the "relation" discussed here is that of part to whole.

Smit and Hacker argue that their underlying metaphysics, neo-Aristotelian monism, allows us to avoid the aforementioned conceptual quagmires and incoherencies by framing psychological attributes (e.g., having experiences or qualia) as attributes of the experiencing creature as a whole *only* rather than trying to pinpoint some area of the body or brain, or even some abstraction of its total experience like "the mind" as its origin. The aforementioned quandaries regarding reduction, the HPN, BP, and CP with respect to qualia as well as the issues of emergence and downward causation, are all caused by assumptions that import pluralism and (crypto-) Cartesian dualism, sometimes without apparently knowing it. As they put it:

> Monism clarifies why psychological attributes are attributes of an animal as a whole. It is not the mind...that is for example in pain...but the living organism...to have a mind, and to have a body, is not to stand *in a relation* to anything—it is to have and to exercise a range of powers and to have an array of somatic attributes.
>
> (Smit & Hacker, 2014: 1087)

Applying this approach to the current issues raised in this chapter, and its corollary problems involving emergence and supervenience, reveals that under a monist framework (neo-Aristotelian or not), it seems the explanatory gap becomes a pseudo-problem caused by conceptual incoherencies. Thus, phenomenal experiences are simply brute properties displayed by the whole before it is partitioned into bits of matter (or whatever). Thus, the explanatory gap is not a problem for this system—but there is another problem.

This other problem comes from that odd fact noted earlier that only *certain* parts of the whole person appear to be necessarily healthy and functional for that person to remain conscious: a missing leg, or even a missing cerebellum, does not interrupt a whole person's phenomenal experience, whereas damage or variable functioning in the frontal cortex of the brain often does. The aforementioned authors would argue, however, that it is not the frontal cortex that is conscious, only the whole person is, but in this case, it remains something of a mystery why one part is essential and another is not for maintaining phenomenal experience in a person. What mysterious characteristic does the frontal cortex possess that gives it this power over the person's overall conscious experience? Our first guess is that it is in itself and integrated whole.

The Decomposition Problem

Monism with respect to the MBP leaves only a reverse explanatory gap or "decombination problem." But I do not believe the reverse explanatory gap is nearly as intimidating as the explanatory gap. The reason the explanatory intransigence does not go both ways equally has to do with asymmetries in supervenience and downward causation.

First of all, supervenience, Schaffer (2010) observes, has an asymmetry to it in terms of metaphysical possibility, insofar as where proper parts must supervene upon their whole, wholes need not supervene on their proper parts. This has direct consequences for emergence, since this asymmetry in supervenience translates into an asymmetry in emergence. That is, wholes can display emergent properties when proper parts are arranged in a particular way, but the opposite, what Schaffer calls "submergence," cannot happen. In submergence, when proper parts are arranged in such-and-such a way, their intrinsic properties would disappear. Since this isn't even metaphysically possible (Schaffer, 2010, p. 57), much less observed, mereological monism is the only view that can give a complete inventory of the universe. The asymmetry of supervenience and emergence make it impossible for any pluralist account to provide such an inventory.

We can apply these principles to the MBP: we know that arranging neurons in such-and-such a way and having them behave in such-and-such a way (as revealed by continually improving neuroscience) correlates with the organism "gaining" the properties of mind, qualia, consciousness, and so on (emergence), though more accurately—from the perspective of monism—we should say they *re-gain* such properties due to their coalescing into a configuration that is closer to the most comprehensive integrated whole possible—whatever that might be. Separating the neurons in neural tissue, however, does not give us emergent properties—it only takes previously present ones away.

Hence, providing a complete account of the mind as it relates to the brain and body is only possible within a monist framework due to the possibility of emergence and the asymmetrical manner in which it manifests. In other words, since the pluralist requires that wholes derive from parts, the possibility of irreducible emergence makes it impossible to explain *how* it is done. This is precisely the character and shape of the problems thus fielded so far with respect to the MBP: it is the asymmetrical possibility of emergence that appears to stymy a pluralist account of how the trick is done because it begins with the presupposition that neurons (or atoms, etc.) are prior to the wholes they compose.

Monism, however, does not have this problem because it is assumed that the data of neuroscience, which involves looking at isolated parts of the whole (i.e., behaviors of neural networks, brain scans, EEG measurements, etc.), gives us at best only a partial view of the entire functioning inventory of a person or other animal that is derivative of that whole. We do not require an explanation of how such neural networks "produce" subjective mental experiences because such mental experiences are not derivative from those networks, but rather our scientific observations of those networks are derivative from the whole in the precise way that our experimental design isolates the functioning parts.

Where we ultimately wind up in this journey is a kind of tentative cosmopsychism. Ultimately what I am proposing is that the explanatory gap objection to physicalism can be answered by making the following assumptions:

1 Mereological monism is true and the properties of parts derive from the properties of the wholes they came from, and the first whole object is the cosmos itself.
2 The property of phenomenal experience is of special kind that belongs to wholes of a particular type, and that is *integrated* wholes.
3 Since humans and other animals possess consciousness, these subsets of the universe have the required level of integration to qualify.
4 Larger systems such as ecosystems and biomes, or even galaxies, may also possess the required level of integration—this will require further inquiry.

Viewing the MBP in this manner eliminates problems related to emergence, supervenience, and downward causation, and leaves no explanatory gap. In exchange for this gain, we acquire the reverse-explanatory gap problem, which may be far more manageable in the end.

Toward an Integrated Framework for Late-AP

Physicalism cannot make sense of Late-AP. Under its assumptions, the idea of metaphysical archetypes, synchronicity, and so on must at best be illusions conjured up by an individual mind. Moreover, Late-AP cannot defend itself from such assumptions because any such psychological argument will meet the same objection. What the aforementioned text shows, however, is that physicalism itself has metaphysical objections that threaten to undermine it. As such, it seems significant that Late-AP makes so much sense under the aforementioned kinds of holistic neutral monism. By working from the ground up, we can see how Late-AP phenomena that cannot be explained under physicalism *can* be explained by our tentatively cosmopsychist but firmly holistic neutral monist framework. As an added bonus, this framework is also compatible with quantum theory, and in fact many of the protagonists of the holistic perspective in metaphysics have their roots in quantum physics.

For example, for Pauli and Jung, the primordial whole cannot be derived from its parts (Atmanspacher, 2014, p. 252)—essential to holistic metaphysics. Moreover, in the Pauli-Jung schema, this primordial unity, termed in Late-AP the *unus mundus*, can be viewed as the collective unconscious from the point of view of consciousness, and the phenomenon of quantum non-locality from the point of view of externally perceived objects (Atmanspacher, 2014, p. 253). As we have seen, the epistemic decomposition of the primordial unity provides correlations relatively "for free," though they do entail a decomposition problem.

Nevertheless, this epistemic split should not be conceived as a rigid boundary, however, but a progression of levels of unity from consciousness to the underlying neutral reality, the unus mundus, which is in itself all-encompassing and distinction free:

> A viable idea in this regard is a picture with increasing degrees of generality: the unus mundus at bottom, the mental and physical on top, and intermediate levels in between would make more sense...ontological relativity or, in another parlance, relative onticity. The key motif behind this notion is to allow ontological significance for any level, from elementary particles to ice-cubes, bricks, and tables—and all the same for elements of the mental... [these can all] be seen epistemic relative to the *unus mundus*.
>
> (Atmanspacher, 2014, pp. 244–255)

Other thinkers have similar schemes such as "The Real" of Bernard d'Espagnat (2006), and the "implicate order" of David Bohm (1980). For Late-AP, Atmanspacher points out that *meaning* is expressed in the content of constellated/activated archetypes, which are not arbitrary but subject to the ordering principle of the archetype itself. As Pauli puts it:

> The *ordering* and *regulating* factors must be placed beyond the distinction of the "physical" and "psychic"—as Plato's "ideas" share the notion of a concept and of a force of nature (they *create* actions out of themselves). I am very much in favor of referring to the "*ordering*" and "*regulating*" factors in terms of "archetypes"; but then it would be inadmissible to define them as contents of

the psyche. The mentioned inner images ("dominant features of the collective unconscious" after Jung) are rather psychic *mani-festations* of the archetypes which, however, would also have to *put forth, create,* and *condition* anything lawlike in the behavior of the corporeal world.—Wolfgang Pauli in a letter to Markus Fierz in 1948.

(von Meyenn, 1993, p. 496, italics added by Atmanspacher)

Atmanspacher therefore argues not for a simple boundary between ontic and epistemic, but rather a complex system of relative onticity, with the most basic level being that of the distinctionless whole,

a whole spectrum of boundaries, each one indicating the transition to a more comprehensive level of wholeness until (ultimately) a totally distinction-free domain is approached *in the limit*…the Pauli-Jung conjecture [proposes] archetypal levels with increasing degrees of generality: the undivided world at bottom, the mental and physical on top, and intermediate levels in between…[if] archetypes are understood as *epistemic or ontic relative to* other archetypal levels, this opens up a way to epistemic access.

(Atmanspacher, 2014, p. 287)

Interestingly enough, Fach (2011, see also Belz & Fach, 2012) provides empirical evidence that this so-called Pauli-Jung conjecture holds up to predictive validity, and cognitivist Steven Horst observes that a decompositional monistic view of substance agrees well with Jung's version of mind-matter metaphysics and he also detects the Neoplatonism within it (Atmanspacher, 2014, p. 281).

Archetypes as Metaphysical Ordering Principles

Where does this leave us in terms of archetype? Atmanspacher observes that the Early-AP way of defining archetypes as inner images of the psyche is actually inappropriate within a dual-aspect framework of thinking (Atmanspacher, 2014, p. 284, n. 6). Rather, the Late-AP way of conceptualizing archetypes is that they are external elements of the greater unity operating and manifesting on both psyche and matter, but only in the manner of formal causes, *not* efficient causes, with more fundamental ontic entities operating in such a way upon entities at less fundamental ontic levels. Atmanspacher suggests a system of archetypes as possessing relative onticity that break symmetry in a systematic manner.

This framing of the metaphysics of Late-AP curiously finds us in a system highly reminiscent of the Neoplatonists, who proposed a metaphysical framework very similar to it as far back as the 3rd century CE. Jung himself referenced the Neoplatonists and so was aware of them, though it is difficult to say just how much he felt to be influenced by them (MacLennan, 2005). In any case, Neoplatonic metaphysical systems such as that of Plotinus, for example, start with the most fundamental entity in the cosmos: the One (for some, "God"), which is completely devoid of distinction and at the root of all, prior, and from which through decomposition all other things are derived. From there, Neoplatonists proposed a variety of ways in which the One can be epistemically split into decompositional systems. Such decompositions (called "emanations" by some) could easily be compared to the archetype as defined in the manner of Atmanspacher. For example, Plotinus begins his analysis with the One, then postulates decompositions involving Nous (Rationality, analogous to the Demiurge), from which derives at the next level the *anima mundi* (world soul, itself containing distinctions of upper and lower), which decomposes into Nature, from which are derived "intermediaries" of the Divine Beings, down to humans, down to matter, which has the least level of ontic status. Other Neoplatonists break it down differently in terms of exact categories and ontic levels, but the process remains the same. Proclus, for example, makes even finer-grained ontic-level distinctions. In any case, revisiting these texts with the modern thought reviewed here, however, may lead the way for newer, more precise systems to be developed that continue the preliminary system Jung and Pauli worked on to place the archetypes and collective unconscious into a defensible metaphysical framework.

Notes

1 Seager (2014) remarks that an advantage of the Pauli-Jung approach is the link to holistic quantum states, also mentioned by philosopher Jonathan Schaffer (2010) in his defense of mereological monism. Quantum theory suggests the whole takes ontological priority and the parts are derivative (Seager, 2014, p. 276), but has

reservations about using quantum theory as a direct analogy to the mind-body problem (See Atmanspacher, 2014, p. 284–286 for reply, however).

2 The binding problem of neuroscience is an empirical variant of the combination problem.

References

Aristotle. (1984). *The Complete Works of Aristotle, vol. 2*, ed. Jonathan Barnes, 1552–1728. Princeton, NJ: Princeton University Press.

Atmanspacher, H. (2012). Dual-aspect monism a la Pauli and Jung. *Journal of Consciousness Studies* 19 9/10: 96–120.

Atmanspacher, H. (2014). 20th century variants of dual-aspect thinking. *Mind and Matter* 12(2): 245–288.

Atmanspacher, H., and Fach, W. (2013). A structural-phenomenological typology of mind-matter correlations. *Journal of Analytical Psychology* 58: 219–244.

Baxter, D. (1998). Many-one identity. *Philosophical Papers* 17: 193–216.

Bohm, D. (1980). *Wholeness and the Implicate Order*. New York: Routledge.

Belz, M. and Fach, W. (2012). Theoretical reflections on counseling and therapy for individuals reporting ExE [exceptional experiences]. In W. H. Kramer, E. Bauer and G. H. Hövelmann (Eds.) *Perspectives of Clinical Parapsychology*, Bunnik: Stichting Het Johan Borgman Fonds, 168–189.

Chalmers, D. J. (2012). Consciousness and its Place in Nature. In D. J. Chalmers (Ed.), *Philosophy of Mind: Classical and Contemporary Readings*. New York: Oxford University Press.

Chalmers, D. J. (2016). The Combination Problem for panpsychism. In D. J. Chalmers (Ed.), *Panpsychism*. Cambridge: Oxford University Press, 179–215.

Churchland, P. (1996). The rediscovery of light. *Journal of Philosophy* 93: 211–228.

d'Espagnat, B. (2006). *On Physics and Philosophy*. Princeton, NJ: Princeton University Press.

Dennett, D. C. (1988). Quining qualia. In A. Marcel and E. Bisiach (Eds.) *Consciousness in Contemporary Science*. New York: Oxford University Press.

Dennett, D. C. (1992). *Consciousness Explained*. New York: Back Bay Books.

Fach, W. (2011). Phenomenological aspects of complementarity and entanglement in exceptional human experiences. *Axiomathes* 21: 233–247.

Goff, P. (2017). *Consciousness and Fundamental Reality*. Oxford: Oxford University Press.

Goodwyn, E. (2020b). Archetypes and the 'impoverished genome' argument: updates from neurogenetics. *Journal of Analytical Psychology.* November. doi:10.1111/1468-5922.12642

Jung, C. G.. [1954] 1985. *The Practice of Psychotherapy.* Princeton: Princeton University Press.

Jung, C. G.. [1955]. *Mysterium Coniunctionis.* Princeton: Princeton University Press.

Jung, C. G. (1961). *Memories, Dreams, Reflections.* New York: Vintage Books.

Jung, C. G. (1969). On the nature of the psyche. CW 8, pp. 67–135.

Kim, J. (1992). Multiple realization and the metaphysics of reduction. *Philosophy and Phenomenological Research* 52: 1–26.

Kim, J. (2010). *Philosophy of Mind: Third Edition.* New York: Routledge.

MacLennan, B. (2005). Evolution, Jung and Theurgy: their role in modern Neoplatonism. In J. F. Finamore and R. M. Berchman (Eds.) *History of Platonism.* Plato Redivivus: University Press of the South, pp. 305–322.

Schaffer, J. (2010). Monism: the priority of the whole. *Philosophical Review* 119: 31–76.

Schaffer, J. (2017). The ground between the gaps. *Philosopher's Imprint* 17(11): 1–26.

Smart, J. J. C. (1959). Sensations and brain processes. *Philosophical Review* 68: 141–156.

Spinoza, B. (1677/1985). Ethics. In E. Curley (Ed.) The Collected Works of Spinoza. Princeton, NJ: Princeton University Press.

Von Meyenn, K. (Ed.). (2001). *Wolfgang Pauli. Wissenschaftlicher Briefwechsel, Band IV, Teil III.* Berlin: Springer. 1955–1956

Chapter 5

Lacan on Mind and Body

Shlomit Yadlin-Gadot

Whereas Freud's work can be seen as a brave attempt at bridging mind and body, Lacan's work offers to deconstruct this binary and examine its significance in his notion of the subject, articulated in three orders: the Symbolic, the Imaginary, and the Real. This subject negotiates endlessly the paradoxes and the tensions of belonging simultaneously to the natural and to the linguistic, while modulating the desires and the demands of both himself and his Other. The Lacanian body expresses itself in multiple dimensions such as organism, personal and social identity. It is explored here in its simultaneous relations with both mind and other, as fragmented and seeking cohesion, as a speaking unconscious and an instrument of jouissance, always resisting the signifying functions that constituted it.

Introduction

Lacan was a self-proclaimed Freudian advocating a "return to Freud" (Lacan [1955] 1977:116) in the psychoanalytic field of his times. Despite this proclaimed loyalty and consistent use of Freudian concepts, Lacan's rereading of Freud under the influence of the postmodern zeitgeist gradually created a unique school of thought, veiled by enigmatic, often obtuse, writing. Lacan's take on the mind-body problem will be discussed here in the context of the Lacanian effort to both retain and reformulate the Freudian subject in anti-essentialist terms.

Freud was a modernist, an aspiring scientist. Discovering the ties between psychic etiology and the cure of the hysterical, bodily

DOI: 10.4324/9781003090755-6

symptom, he established the inextricable ties of body and mind as the basis of his evolving scientific psychoanalysis. Deep into his late writings, Freud remained convinced that only a properly scientific Weltanschauung must, and can, account for the vicissitudes of the human instincts in pathology and health. In the context of this worldview, Freud marked the body as the origin of all psychic and social life.

Inspired by scientific discoveries of his time, Freud described the body-psyche as a hydraulic mechanism of sorts, powered by innate drives that perpetually create tensions. Drive was defined as a concept on the frontier between the mental and the somatic, originating from within the organism and presenting the mind with a demand for work in consequence of its connection with the body. The pleasure principle that governs psycho-somatic functioning defined the mechanism's tendency towards homeostasis and the pleasure experienced when drive tension is released. In the service of self-preservation, the reality principle is gradually formed, ensuring that the ultimate objective of pleasurable drive satisfaction doesn't endanger the organism in its entirety. The interplay of the pleasure and reality principles comes to be represented in the dialectic of id and ego. The ego, originating from within the id and in the service of its demands, gradually gains strength and dominance, and eventually masters its progenitor.

The bodily drive is not only the source of psychic structure, it is also the basic determinant of social relations. The Freudian object satisfies the drives and allows their phylogenetically programmed development. This object manifests differently across different stages of development – the oral, the anal, the phallic, and the Oedipal stages. The resolution of the Oedipal complex marks the maturation of the drives from polymorphous partiality to genital cohesion and the move from autoeroticism to object love. The superego, heir to the Oedipal complex, is both the consequence and the driving force of civilized life and completes the Freudian tripartite model of the psyche.

For Freud, then, everything begins with the body. The drives are innate as is their programmed development. The mind is formed in lieu of the drive's demands, and throughout life, they remain its driving force. The body gives rise to the psyche and its development, yet this very same psyche is predicated upon the mastering and taming of the body. Proper development is achieved when reality trumps pleasure and ego takes over the id. This of course comes at a price, with an array of defenses giving rise to diverse symptoms. By basing sanity on rationality and social norms, Freud, who started as a modernist revolutionary, transformed into a conservative representative of the Cartesian subject, with its divisions of mind and body, self and other.

Lacan began his psychoanalytic writing in the wake of the catastrophic failure of rationalism during World War II. He was steeped in the thought that construed the extreme horrors of World War II as violent ramifications of Western metaphysical philosophy and its modern formulations. In fact, Lacan is considered by many as a key figure in the critique of the gravitational force of binary metaphysics. Ethical conviction may be seen as driving his undeclared endeavor to re-write the modern, essentialist psychoanalytic subject.

Using Freudian vocabulary, yet constantly and subtly shifting its meanings and references, Lacan recreated the psychoanalytic subject as deeply contextual, always-already given in webs of culture, language, and significations. A derivative of this recreation was a drastic revision of mind-body relations. This revision began by a deconstruction of the basic mind-body binary, turning towards a highly influential and irreducible third element – *the other*, in its double capacity as significant person (with a small "o") and cultural order (with a capital "O"). This other infiltrates body, mind, and their relations.

In Freudian theory of development, the body is the absolute beginning, the prime determinant of the psyche. The psyche is borne of the body in the gradual unfolding of the drive's phylogenetic, innate program of development. An "other" is required for this development and is defined by his ability to serve as the drive's means of satisfaction. By distinction, for Lacan, the other is not a derivative of the drive. (S)he is the essential, constitutional maker of the subject. *(S)he is the primordial given:* both mind and body are constituted through this other's effects and influences.

In the following sections, I will describe mind-body relations in the context of Lacan's developmental account. For Lacan, there are two logical moments in the formation of psychic life: the mirror stage and the Oedipal stage as he conceives of it. Both are predicated upon an other, transforming the binary system of body-mind into a triangulation of *other*-mind-body. This triangulation essentially changes the causal relations of body and mind, their dynamics of development and interrelations. It explains differently the experience of body and the mind, the formation and resolution of symptoms, and the body's positioning in this process. Throughout, I will show how Lacan weaves his new account of the subject, retaining many Freudian concepts and progressively assigning them new meanings.

The Logics of Lacanian Development

Lacan did not present his ideas in the form of developmental theory, so as not to create a "normative" course of development defining a health-pathology binary. Nevertheless, he defined "logical" developmental moments without which we cannot account for the development of the subject. For the present discussion I present a fluid ordering of these moments to illuminate mind-body relations. Lacan, like Freud and Klein, emphasizes the premature birth of the human infant, which renders it totally reliant on others, both physically and mentally. The newborn is functionally helpless and mentally flooded with anxieties of annihilation and fragmentation. In this terrifying realm of disintegration and threatening death, the infant is offered the irresistible lure of his own mirror image. This image presents him with an integrated, coordinated totality. In a jubilant moment of "Aha!," the infant identifies himself with this promising imago, thus creating the Imaginary nucleus of his ego (Lacan, [1949] 1997).

The overcoming of helplessness accounts for the lure of the mirror image, but it is not the only motivation for identifying with it. Before the infant's encounter with this image, he experiences himself as a bundle of fluid and fragmented sensations and impulses. He has no conception of a "me," as an identified unit that encompasses and contains his experience. In as much as the mirror stage "is a drama whose internal thrust is precipitated from insufficiency to anticipation" (ibid.:4), it is this experience of an identity in its primordial form that accounts for the infant's jubilant response. The upright imago is the infant's first opportunity to position himself in relation to the question of identity: who am I? In Lacan's developmental account, this question is both the point of departure and a point of closure, as we shall see further.

This first experience of mental permanence is not achieved by a direct experience of the *body*, but rather by creating a body *image*. This has a major mental effect, Lacan notes, because the infant's recognition of himself in his mirror-image is an absurd "misrecognition" that involves deep alienation. Alienation is, firstly, the consequence of the gulf that lies between the unified imago and the infant's authentic fragmented bodily experiencing. Second, this imago is steeped in the discourse of the Other; it is suffused with desires and narratives of others as they encourage the child to recognize herself in the mirror ("What a strong boy!," "You're going to be beautiful, just like Mommy," etc.). Thus, from the start, the child's developing ego is immersed in the desires of speaking others.

This description brings forth Lacan's basic anti-essentialist stand. The initial "I" is created by *detaching* from a body *that we know little of*. This body and its drives are no longer understood as giving rise to psychic structure. Indeed, the Lacanian subject does not exist without an initial *break* from the body; he is *predicated upon* this break, a precondition for the response, recognition, and affirmation of the other. Instead of an essential kernel, a bodily or "true" self, Lacan presents body image, alias ego, as giving rise to the first image of identity. The experience of the body as organism is not an integral part of the subject's life: indeed, subject and organism may be described as existing on different sides of a seemingly unbreachable divide. The demand of the other causes this divide, leaving the infant forevermore cleaved and un-identical to himself.

In Lacan's formulation of the mirror stage, we can identify the workings of an implicit human drive – the drive towards identity. There is no essentialist starting point for identity, but the need for it is a strong force, delineating its own axis of development. Its first satisfactions are given in a tragic-comic point – a misrecognition, a mistake. But there is no substitute for it. Lacan's logic is such, that all identity necessarily begins in this form of deep alienation. The mirror-born ego is a hoax, a fraud, presenting unity, coherence, and boundaries in accordance with, and for the sake of, the other's recognition. It is imaginary in the sense that it holds no truth or validity in relation to the infant's psychosomatic experiencing. The unified imago adopted as ego is the paradigmatic representative of Lacan's Imaginary order.

The Imaginary order is an order of visual, specular representation. In ways resonating Kant's realm of phenomena, the Imaginary consists of images ordered, made whole and distinct by mental operations. Their relation to things-in-themselves resonates the ego's relation to the un-known fragmented body. Despite being illusory, the Imaginary positions the developing subject in relation to himself and to a world that accords with the need for stability and certainties. The relations with the specular other of this order mirror the child's relations with his own imago. This perfect, coherent image of himself arouses envy in the child, and he seeks to own it and put himself in its place. Simultaneously, the child feels that the image is there to usurp him, to further alienate and deplete his ex-perience of self. In cycles of introjection and projection, a basic paranoid positioning is created, boiling down to the binary choice: "It's me or you." These intense relations of love, hate, and narcissistic rivalry remain a paradigmatic dimension in all future interpersonal relations. They are tempered in later development by the dimension of Symbolic relating, formed after the resolution of the Oedipal complex.

The second phase in the subject's development is the entry into the Symbolic order, via the Oedipal complex. The Lacanian Oedipal stage consists of three successive moments. At first, mother and child are given in a seemingly undifferentiated matrix held together by the mother's desire. To maintain this, the child seeks to be able to satisfy his mother's desire, namely "to be or not to be" (Lacan, 1957–1958: 22.1.1958) the object of her desire. The mother's desire in this first moment delivers us, as some Lacanian passages do, to a classic Freudian formulation, which serves as a point of departure for the formulation of diverging ideas.

Freud (1925), discussing anatomical distinctions, described how sexual orientation is determined during the Oedipal stage. With the young boy, the story is relatively simple. The mother is his primary attachment figure both before and after the Oedipal stage, albeit in transformed forms of affection, erotic elements dutifully repressed. The little girl's story is more complex, as her affections need to be transferred from mother to father in conformity with the heterosexual scheme. Freud attributes this move to the little girl's deep disappointment with her mother. The mother, recognized as damaged (with no penis), has inexcusably created the girl in her own image. The resentful, angry little girl turns to her better-equipped father, hoping that someday he will supply her with a baby, standing in for the longed-for penis.

In the first moment of the Lacanian Oedipal complex, we re-meet this girl, finally fulfilled. She has received her penis-baby, her all. The child, born lacking, is made whole and safe by her desire. But for Lacan, the lack of the infant is oblivious of sex. *All* infants are lacking and their lack is inherent, organ-free and due to primal helplessness and fluid formlessness. The ticket to survival is given in an imaginary reunion with the mother and her body. The infant aspires to be as close and inseparable from her as possible. It is here that we meet the first meaning of the Lacanian credo – desire is for the other's desire. Being the ultimate object of mother's desire secures for the infant her devotion and ongoing presence. The child presents himself as *being* the mother's longed-for phallus, resonating the perfection he had found in his mirror image.

With the desire of both mother and infant seemingly satisfied, an imaginary wholeness is created and no lack exists. Mother and infant here are given in what other psychoanalytic languages describe as symbiosis, an autonomous unit fulfilling wholly its own needs, the elements constituting it neither quite dead nor alive when apart. The experience here is boundless, touching on the Freudian "oceanic," an intermixture of pleasure and pain, life, and death. In Lacanian parlance, mother and child dwell here in the positive real(m) of jouissance.

In the second moment of the Oedipal phase, seemingly in line with the Freudian construal, the father appears as prohibition and forbids endless jouissance between mother and child. But for Lacan, this imaginary father and his threat of castration are not the crux of the matter, nor what set the wheels of development going. For this imaginary father to be effective in his prohibition, a representation of the Symbolic order must already be internalized within the mother. Incest prohibition is imaginary, Lacan explains, because sheer inability ensures its impossibility. On a deeper level, the game is not of organs or genitality. The one and truly fatal game is the one of desire, and in the second moment of the Oedipal drama, it is acted out between mother, child and the Symbolic with which she identifies.

In this second moment, as the child becomes increasingly aware of the mother's absences, he realizes that she has desires that he cannot satisfy. Narcissistic injury and renewed threat of fragmentation pose the question that will haunt the subject throughout his life as he continues to seek the other's desire: "what does she want?" (Lacan, [1960]1977):312). Also, a new danger presents itself with the new image of the mother. If she desires, if she is lacking and hungry, the infant may become nothing more for her than an object of consumption. Having formerly solved the problem of lack by *being* the object of mother's desire, the infant now seeks to satisfy the mother by means of something (s)he *owns*.

The existential question the child now faces changes from "to be or not to be" to "to have or not to have?" the object of mother's desire. The child now needs to figure out where he might obtain it, who is the one who "has" that which governs the mother's desire? *He* must be more than an imaginary creature, otherwise his value does not exceed that of the child. He must be a representative of something *other* that governs the system in its entirety and exceeds its known satisfactions. The father can function as that object that locates and names the mother's desire only as representative of this other order. Thus, the imaginary prohibiting father is superseded by the *name* of the father, by the father as abstract, impersonal, *lawfulness* itself. Indeed, this fa/ o-ther" can be anything that acts as the object of mother's desire – her work or ambition, her love of books or yoga; anything that marks *her* as being of a different order, apart from the imaginary unit she and her child constitute.

In the third moment of the Oedipal phase, the child recognizes the larger possibilities of ownership, like those of *vicarious* owning. If the (name of the) father enables the mother to "have" the phallus, it can also do this to the child. Thus, he can both hold on to the illusion that he may satisfy the mother's desire and be saved from the terror of being lost with it. "Having it" constitutes the father as an ego-ideal, an ideal that begins a play of identification with what was formerly the ideal (mirror-image) ego. The willing interiorization of the ego-ideal marks the entry of the signifier into the psychic world of the child, the resolution of the Oedipal complex and the transformation of the dyadic mother-child space into a triadic one. Effectively, this marks the entry of the child into the Symbolic order of language and law.

Lacan termed the maternal object of desire the phallus. This phallus is *not* equivalent to the Freudian desired penis. It may signify *any* desire of the mother, other than her desire for her child. Lacan marks the phallus with the signifier Φ, ironically (and in line with Kojeve's construal of desire as lack) used in mathematics to designate an empty group. Interiorizing the name of the father (S1) brings on the repression of this primitive signifier of mother's desire alongside with this desire itself, thus creating the Lacanian unconscious. It transforms the subject from desired object to *desiring subject* in the father's mode, namely, in the realm of ideas, culture, and society. It modulates the aggressivity of Imaginary relations and the immediacy of experience, allowing linguistic mediation to represent the subject and identify himself to another subject. Yet, these positive developments come at a price. Language does not arise from the individual. It precedes him, blurs, and distorts his physical *needs* as they transform into *demand* and *desire*. The signifier curtails symbiotic jouissance with the mother and irrevocably tears the subject from animal existence. Reiterating and elaborating the alienating effect of visual representation, the primal existence of a human being is further truncated. From now on, all man desires will be mediated by the (de) forms and the pre-given structures of the Symbolic order.

This dual effect of alienation and identity formation is encompassed in Lacan's re-rendering of the Freudian notion of castration. In Freud's formulation, the penis plays a nodal part in Oedipal castration. He describes the boy as having already seen the "lack" in girls and experienced the loss of body-parts (the mother's breast and his own stool). Here, the threat of castration is portrayed in anatomical terms, and narcissistic wholeness is secured by repudiating incestual wishes. Similarly, the small girl experiences herself as already castrated, and driven by penis envy, she is redeemed by heterosexual positioning in relation to her father and all men. For Lacan, at best, this is a completely Imaginary drama. As he sees it, castration is not defined in relation to the penis. It is defined in relation to the signifier. All soon-to-be-subjects undergo castration, as a two-tiered affair. The first is the separation from the mother. The second is alienation in language. All psychic structures – the psychotic, the neurotic and the perverse, like the subject herself – are determined in relation to the signifier. These processes are gender indifferent.

For Freud, the penis is the protagonist of castration, while for Lacan, the signifier is the critical element. This shift from organ to signifier again exemplifies Lacan's deconstructive reading of Freud and his re-definition of the body's functions in the constitution of mind and psyche. Here, like in the mirror stage, Lacan dissociates development from its inextricable ties with anatomy. Development is predicated first and foremost on the other. It is driven by desire to-wards this other and towards a sense of identity that cannot be achieved without the other.

Graduating from Oedipal development, the Lacanian subject is a tripartite entity, spanning across the three orders that function in parallel, with complex synchronizations. He exists as subject of the unconscious in the Symbolic order comprising signifiers, answering to the law, to linguistic and cultural rules, social roles, and norms. In the Imaginary order, the subject exists as "ego," namely, as a conscious self, defined by interpersonal relations with specific specular others. The subject of the Real exists as that part of experience that evades all representation, meaning and signification, both Imaginary and Symbolic. The Real is experienced as uncanny, traumatic, un-controllable, and ineffable. It is indicated by such experiences as trauma, intense pleasure (jouissance), and the collapse of the sense of self in the subject's innermost core. The Real is also the cause and driving force of signification. It may also be conceived as a mythical existence predating the signifier; a primordial strata that holds and resonates primal sensation, contingent markings of the body, and the turbulence and fragmentation of partial, polymorphic drives.

From Otherly Tamed Body to Self-Determined Mind

Having traced the Lacanian de-anatomization of development, we are left with the question of the Lacanian body and its relation to subjecthood as given along the dimensionality of the three orders. The Imaginary body is the body formation that satisfies the need for envelope and container, and fills the functions of what is often de-scribed in psychoanalytic writing as the skin-ego, delineating "inside" from "outside," insulating, protecting, and leaving behind the ori-ginal experienced fragmentation and open-endedness of the body. The Symbolic body is tamed and dominated by the Other as culture, language, and law. It is a "socialized" body, programmed, and structured by cultural practices, disciplines, ideals, and norms in ways that resonate Foucault's "discipline" and Bordieu's "habitus." The body of the Real is unknown, akin to the lost, fragmented body. It is revealed only when its Imaginary or Symbolic coordinates are thrown into question. When something of unknown origin appears on the skin or in a person's posture, we are immediately transported to the uncanny, beyond the body's normally perceived signification. Injury may bring about such a "de-symbolization" of the body, making it feel alien. Ironically, only in its foreignness the cultivated body may become organic to the subject.

The body of the Real is given also in the organismic experiencing of jouissance: a tension, a mode of pleasure that exists at a level in which pain begins to appear. This mode entails approaching the limits of exploit, like the experience of oceanic merger with the primordial mother. While assuming identity in Imaginary and Symbolic dimensions, primordial jouissance is evacuated to the margins of the body, creating the classical Freudian erotogenic zones: oral, anal, and genital. Whereas Freud understood their formation as part of the epigenetically programmed development of the drive, Lacan sees them as vestiges of jouissance, disciplined in accordance with the other's demand. Moreover, Freud's drive is innate, while Lacan's motivational force is borne from the subject's search for what he had re-lost when re-losing his primal connection with the mother. Freud's drive may find a satisfaction in the drive's object. Lacan's drive forever circuits around its object, sustaining desire and leaving this object's status of "lostness" unchanged.[1]

Until seminar 20, "Encore," Lacan's construal of jouissance remained relatively straight forward. It was seen as lost in castration with the subject's entry into the Symbolic: "so that it can be reached on the inverted ladder of the Law of desire" (Lacan, (1966) 1970:324). Desire, lying in the realm of Symbolic representation, is a negativity created when the positivity of jouissance is renounced and involves the imposition of law upon the Real of jouissance. The law limits jouissance and marks the strictly regulated paths of its partial achievement.

In the 1970s, Lacan began to unravel the many forms of jouissance, describing its different modes and reconsidering their various relations with subjecthood. After seminar 20, three modalities of jouissance may be clearly marked: *Phallic* jouissance is defined in relation to the name of the father. It is found in speech, and remains within the laws of the Symbolic. Prior to phallic jouissance, Lacan speaks about a mythic, retroactively experienced jouissance, phantasmatically created moment it is lost. This is the pre-Symbolic jouissance related to the mother's body, to her desire and to being its object. The third jouissance, feminine jouissance, lies *beyond* the signifier. Given in the terms of topological set theory, it exceeds the rules and regulations of Symbolic law. Extending beyond the phallus, it signals the possibilities of replacing the name of the father as an anchorage of a lawful order with one's own name. This mode of jouissance is "not-all in the Other, not wholly governed by the phallic, social order" (Lacan, 1972: 57). Consistent with Lacan's de-anatomized stance, both his feminine and his masculine are not defined by bodily properties. The phallic is limited by Oedipal imperatives, by a law that is always arbitrary, always defined by, and in relation to, an other. The feminine exceeds this law, progressively freeing itself from the reign of Symbolic meanings and constraints. It incarnates an additional realm of existence that leaves conformity behind and delves into unknown bodily, mystic, and radically original experiencing.

The character of feminine jouissance can be illuminated by two additional binaries: truth and knowledge, thinking and being. Lacan's initial emphasis on the Symbolic and his construal of the Symbolically constituted subject, set great store on knowledge, thought, and, generally, rule-governed media. Progressively throughout his writings, Lacanian *truth* becomes *a mode of being,* divorced from knowledge and thought. Both are increasingly integrated into the Real, and the flashes of their manifestation become highly particular. The feminine, diverging from the law of the Other, anchors truth and being in a radically different way of thinking, knowing, and existing. This particularization is Lacan's way of wresting the subject from complete subjection to the Other, the signifier, and the law.

What cannot be fully inscribed in the realm of the law and the signifier and lies beyond it is "the path of ek-sistence," characterized by a "jouissance one experiences and yet knows nothing about" (ibid.: 77). Thus, a link is formed between the feminine, being, and a mode of bodily sensation (jouissance), all highly particular and not encompassed in the law. This triad is positioned in the Real, that "can only be inscribed on the basis of an impasse of formalization" (ibid.: 93). Lacan creates here a link between the twilight zone of the pre-Symbolic and what lies beyond it, and in both areas, the unknown body and its experience of jouissance become increasingly important.

Alongside the new formulations of jouissance, a new dimension of the unconscious is articulated. The Lacanian unconscious is formed when the paternal signifier replaces earlier maternal significations and brings about their repression. For Lacan, the process of repression determines the structure of the repressed. This allowed him to describe the unconscious in linguistic terms, as *the discourse of the other* and as being *structured like a language*. In seminar 20, Lacan offers a new definition of this unconscious, or alternatively, grants it an additional dimension: "The Real, I will say, is the mystery of the speaking body, the mystery of the unconscious" (ibid: 131). The "mystery of the speaking body" is jouissance, the mode in which the body experiences itself, and this mode becomes increasingly related to the unconscious. As the linguistic aspect of the unconscious begins to give way to jouissance, the Other – as an anchorage of identity – gives way to the body. Until now the subject we knew had twice divorced his bodily experiencing; first when identifying with the mirror image and secondly when subjecting to the distortions of Symbolic demand. We come now to re-find a particular and highly unmodified bodily dimension in the innermost being of the subject.

In seminar 23, Lacan continues to elaborate the Real dimension of the unconscious, conceived as "a short circuit passing by way of meaning," constituted "from the copulation of language with our own body" (Lacan, 1974–1975:18.11.75). This "copulation" is an event of the body given and recorded in the corporeal hieroglyphics of jouissance. It is a primal encounter between language and bodies, an accidental meeting between bodily substance and vocalization – the sound, the rhythm, the lallation of the other's speech – on a level apart from the logic of both (Imaginary) fantasy and (Symbolic) language. "Lalangue" is Lacan's term for this melodious vocalization.

This second unconscious is a "knowledge articulated by dint of *lalangue,* the body that speaks there only being held together by the Real it enjoys" (Lacan, 1975: 189 in Prieto 2012: 175). Here we find a formulation of the body held together not by the mirror imago and not by socialization, but rather by the "Real" it enjoys, by jouissance. If formerly we knew of this jouissance only in the primal totality and merger of the infant-mother desire, we now find it as an effect of "lalangue," the phrasing, rhyming, and breathing that accompany the parents' discourse, on the delineated body. This jouissance affects the body in ways devoid of meaning. The contingent, unique encounter between speaking and spoken-to bodies creates particular patterns of jouissance that are distinctive to the particular body. The knowledge of these patterns, different from that of the signifier, is inscribed in the Real unconscious.

Lalangue precedes both meaning and the distinction of signifier/signified. Its elements are not meaningful signifiers; they are letters that inscribe the way the subject was affected by the sounds and rhythms of language and bears their imprint. As difference precedes sense, these "ones" precede the chains of signifiers and signification. They do not join up and create chains. Each letter remains autistic and self-referential, a "thing" rather than a representation, enjoyed in and for itself as an object of jouissance. Carrying no meaning, these letters remain *outside* the chain of signification, in enigmatic coalescence with jouissance.

The letter holds and anchors jouissance that is enjoyed by the body in ways that resonate Freud's articulation of the symptom as a deep mode of satisfaction. Letters emerge in dreams and slips of the tongue. They also inhabit the irreducible kernel of the symptom that carries no sense. In Lacan's phrasing, the symptom is "the way every one may find jouissance in his or her unconscious" (Lacan, 1974–1975:18.2.1975). The kernel of the symptom holds a unique knowledge-without-a-subject, a particular operational knowledge of the ways in which jouissance needs to be handled.

Jouissance, experienced on the level of the speaking (and spoken-to) body, is what may re-animate, when found, the Real body as organism. *Just as the signifier had denaturalized the anatomical body, the jouissance of the body evokes the dissolution of the bond with the other.* This bodily dimension of subjectivity undermines the bond with the other as the main determinant of identity. While the *Symbolic subject* of the unconscious is constituted without a body and metonymically shifts along a signifying chain, *the speaking-being* is inseparable from a body impregnated by a letter that moors and holds jouissance.

As the letter stands in relation to the signifier, so the sinthome, the "equivalent of the Real" (Lacan, 1974–1975:10.12.1974), stands in relation to the symptom. For Lacan, the symptom holds, as a receptacle, the portions of desire and jouissance, which did not find a culturally acceptable way of expression. A Lacanian analyst does not place himself in opposition to the symptom. Quite the opposite: he views the symptom as a reservoir of authentic, unedited potential life force, one that the patient seeks to express and yet is afraid to own. Allying himself with the symptom, the analyst tries to understand what Symbolic prohibitions have denied the desire's expression, what prices the patient was loath to pay in lieu of their realization.

For Lacan, the task of the analytic process is to free captured and stunted desires, but it can never completely eliminate the symptom. In every symptom, the unrelenting "kernel" remains and is acknowledged as a reservoir of pleasure and pain that does not answer to meaning and signification. This kernel holds the letter, the bodily inscription, of the way a particular mother's language affected the particular enjoying and pained body of her child. Acknowledging this "pure" part of the symptom and acquiring the "know-how" of its assimilation into the subject's life is effectually mastering the knowledge of the real unconscious. It heralds the final phase of analysis. Henceforth, its acceptance signals the subject's singularity, implying the assimilation of the parts of himself that will forever retain their alterity in relation to the Symbolic.

In Lacanian thought, the subject of analysis is presented with a choice. Whereas formerly he had sought his identity and formulated it in terms of the Symbolic – namely, of conforming with the Other – he is now given the choice of identifying himself in terms of the *body* as Other, in terms of the bodily contingency that is wholly his own, in the terms of his particular economy of jouissance. Identification with the kernel of jouissance given in the symptom creates the "sinthome," which heretofore provides the binding and conjunction of the three orders (Symbolic, Imaginary, and Real). Always involving the organism, it allows the subject to discover and formulate his secret, private name.

One of Lacan's final conclusions was that there is no subject without a symptom. The symptom serves not only to identify a subject; it marks the possibility of this subject to redefine himself in terms of bodily being, and thus receives a new meaning in relation to the goal of analysis. As an inscription given in the body, it enables the subject an anchorage in the Real, instead of in the Other. It demonstrates the jouissance of the bodily subject and holds a singularity that doesn't conform.

Formulating the Bond of Body and Mind

The Freudian body is the source of all psychic life and defines its relational objects. Mind develops from body, gradually mastering its progenitor. Lacan's project can be described *as destabilizing both the primacy of the body and the binary relations between body and mind.* For Lacan, the primal beginning is the o/Other. Identity is predicated on the desire of an other and involves an inevitable alienation from bodily experiencing. The infant, long before he speaks, is submerged in a world of law and language. He is given shape, name, and identity in the language of an Other, and by means of an Other. What is seemingly his, belongs to others.

The Freudian subject begins with his body but is expected to conform to the credo of "Where id was there ego shall be."(Freud 1933:79) Development is effectually a perfecting of sublimation that is attuned to, indeed defined by, norms of social acceptability. The Lacanian subject, both as ego of the Imaginary and as subject of the Symbolic, is first and foremost a social creation of the other. He "has" a body but is not *in* it or *borne of* it. He is alienated from bodily experiencing, encased in Imaginary envelope and Symbolic bearings. His organismic experiencing is unknown to him, and yet potentially holds, in the realm of jouissance, the anchorage for his distinctive subjectivity. If in the fifties jouissance was paired with the death of the Symbolic subject, in the seventies, it was seen as a vehicle for *transcending the limits of the Symbolic* into the potentialities of a unique individuality. The Symbolic subject (of the mind) finds his *being, his truth and ek-sistence* by assimilating the Real of bodily experiencing. In terms of sexuation (Lacan's term for gender), the subject is born into the phallic, but is given the possibility of feminization. This is a process of reaching beyond known meanings into an existence guided by a highly particular jouissance.

Whereas Freud moves from the body as a first given to the rational and social, Lacan begins with the o/Other and poses the possibility of a return to the body. But Lacanian thought rarely dwells in binaries and this has direct implications for the discussion of body and mind. Neither body nor mind can exist without the concept of the other. But whereas Imaginary and Symbolic o/Others carry a program of desire that molds the subject and his body, the other of lalangue provides an experience unmediated by desire. She provides the music that will "impregnate" the mind but doesn't control the encounter by means of particular significations and meanings. Much of its effect will be determined by the unpredicted and particular responses of the spoken-to body. The other, by dint of his lalangue, exists in the subject's core, providing the material for primal bodily inscription, but this inscription is contingent and bodily-determined, unmediated by the other's demand or desire.

Throughout Lacan's writing, the triangle of mind-body-other remains, yet the interrelations between these elements shift throughout the processes of subjectification, as do their relative dominance. The early Lacan states that the (Other's) word kills the Thing. The late Lacan seizes the moment of encounter between word and bodily thing. The contingent and particular nature of this encounter, inscribed in letters of jouissance, this portion of the unconscious that is Real and exceeds the Symbolic, offers the subject a possibility of wresting himself from subjection to the Other.

In the process of analysis, subjectification and the sinthome remain in the context of the body-mind-other triangulation. But this other is no longer the Other of the Symbolic or Imaginary. He is the articulator of lalangue, the supplier of that element of the Symbolic made Real by the effect of language's melody upon the body-as-organism. As such he no longer determines or defines meaning or meaningful living. By turning the symptom into a sinthome the relationship between Other and body reverses: the Other, who formerly granted the subject identity at the cost of alienating the body, becomes alienated himself, while the subject weds his particular bodily jouissance and thus encounters novel possibilities in the organizations of mind. If for Freud the body is the primal beginning, for Lacan, it offers the end of an otherly-determined existence and an entry into the realm of bodily-based, self-determined subjectivity.

Note

1 This deems sexual relations impossible. The subject will always search in his sexual other for what he lacks and will never refind: the lost jouissance borne of the merger he had known in his mythic past.

References

Freud, S. (1933). New Introductory Lectures On Psycho-Analysis. *The Standard Edition of the Complete Psychological Works of Sigmund Freud*, 22, 1–182.

Freud, S. (1925). Some Psychical Consequences of the Anatomical Distinction between the Sexes. In *The Standard Edition of the Complete Psychological Works of Sigmund Freud, Volume XIX (1923–1925): The Ego and the Id and Other Works*, London: The Hogarth Press and the Institute of Psychoanalysis. pp. 241–258.

Lacan, J. ([1949] 1997). The Mirror Stage as Formative of the Function of the I as Revealed in Psychoanalytic Experience. In *Ecrits: A Selection*. Translated by A. Sheridan. London: Tavistock. pp. 1–7.

Lacan, J. ([1955] 1977). The Freudian Thing, or the Meaning of the Return to Freud in Psychoanalysis. In *Ecrits: A Selection*. Translated by A. Sheridan. London: Tavistock. pp. 115–145.

Lacan, J. (1957–1958). The seminar of Jacques Lacan, Book V: *The Formations of the Unconscious*, Translated by C. Gallagher. Retrieved from: The-seminar-of-jacques-lacan-v_formations_de_l_in.pdf.

Lacan, J. ([1960] 1977). The Subversion of the Subject and the Dialectic of Desire in the Freudian Unconscious. In *Ecrits: A Selection*. Translated by A. Sheridan. London: Tavistock. pp. 292–325.

Lacan, J. ([1972] 1998). *The Seminar of Jacques Lacan, Book 20: Encore*. Translated by B. Fink. New York: Norton & Company.

Lacan, J. (1974–1975). *The seminar of Jacques Lacan. Book XXIII: R.S.I.* Translated by C. Gallagher. Retrieved from: http://hdl.handle.net/10788/179.

Lacan, J. (1975). La troisième. In Lettres de l'École freudienne, n°no 16, p. 189. In G. Prieto (2011) Writing the Subject's Knot. Translated by K. Valendinova. In *Research in Psychoanalysis*, Vol. 12, issue 2, July 2011, 169–179.

Lacan, J. (1975–1976). *Seminar XXIII: Le Sinthome*. J. A. Miller (Ed.). Translated by L. Thurston. Retrieved from: http://www.lacanonline.com/index/wp-content/uploads/2014/11/Seminar-XXIII-The-Sinthome-Jacques-Lacan-Thurston-translation.pdf

Chapter 6

Self and the Experience of Interiority

Jurandir Freire Costa

Self is the noun form of the reflexive pronoun "se" in Portuguese, and is likewise used reflexively in English as the object of an action. Self has approximately the same meaning as the term "I," namely, subjective identity. However, to speak of "identity" implies alluding to the idea of sameness. And yet, what remains identical in the subject if we know that we are never the same over the course of our personal history? The theories alternate on this issue. Identity invariably is defined alternatingly as the body's physical and mental expression.[1] In the former case, the anatomical-physiological or genetic particularities lend the unique touch to each self's mental life; in the latter, psychological events such as fantasies, the unconscious, desires, or cognitive devices are considered the constant element of subjectivity.

From the Individual to the Relation with the Environment

Nevertheless, other theories find such conceptions of identity insufficient. Among these, I cite phenomenology and ecological psychology. Both are holistic descriptions of subjectivity, that is, they view the *individual organism's relationship to the environment* as identity's invariable factor. Still, while phenomenology emphasizes the organism's physical and mental intentionality, ecology emphasizes the environment's *affordances*. In other words, phenomenologists preferably describe the holism from the organism's perspective, while ecologists describe it from the environmental components' point of view. For phenomenologists, a creature's identity coincides

DOI: 10.4324/9781003090755-7

with its typical way of dealing with the environment as a function of its *inherited physical legacy* and *acquired physical-mental habits*; for ecologists, identity obviously depends on the organism's range of intentionalities but also on the surrounding elements' unintentional or extra-subjective attributes. Ecologists say we are what our bodies allow us to be and what the environment, based on its own characteristics, calls on us to be. The environment's situations and objects condition the body's expressive possibilities in both the physical and mental dimensions. The referent of the self's "sameness" is not an exclusive attribute of the body's physical or mental expressions. The affordances, due to their properties as irreducible to the organism's intent, are likewise decisive in the identity's formation.

From Sentient Self to Agent-Self

Still, holistic theories of the self are not limited to shifting the individual factor's theoretical weight to the organism-environment relations vis-à-vis construction of the identity. They also shift the importance of *feeling* to *acting*, which is essential for understanding the idea of interiority.

The sentient self's identity is defined as a precipitate of representations resulting from the organism's physical-mental "reactions" to environmental imperatives. Representations are mnesic traces of (a) images and descriptions of affectively relevant objects, (b) physical sensations and feelings associated with them, and (c) narratives of oneself, constructed by the subject based on the discourse of the other. In short, the sentient self's identity is the mental response to the actions that objects, persons, and situations exert on the subject. In other words, it is a historical residual of the subject's passivity toward external physical or mental stimuli.

The agent-self is different. In this case, the environment is the sum of the specific resources – the affordances – that an originally active agent appropriates to perform acts that favor him. The agent-self is both normative and evaluative. For agent-self, the environment is not primordially a source of affectation or traumatism; it is a terrain of *opportunities for actions* that unfold in various phases. The self initially explores the surroundings, projecting his real or possible actions on them. Next, upon encountering resistance from the circumstances, agent-self modifies his action strategies to surmount the obstacles to his intent.

Identity's two faces emerge from this clash. The first, *physical identity*, emerges in parallel to the creation of the universe of "needs" and "objects for satisfaction of needs." "Needs" are alterations to bodily states, which once rebalanced, bring satisfaction to the subjective organism. To satisfy needs thus means to use *acquired physical habits* efficiently *to achieve adjustments to the environment* (Todes, ibid.).

The agent-self, by using the environmental affordances that satisfy his needs, simultaneously demarcates the borders of his body from the other surrounding bodies (Henry, 2001[1965]; Todes, 2001; Cassam, 2003). *Thus, discriminating the profile of needs and the corresponding objects means demarcating the contour of one's own body.* The more effective the organism's fit to the environment, the more the agent-self reinforces his physical self-perception. This is the first face of identity.

The second face is a complexification of the first. After acquiring language, the agent-self radically changes his way of dealing with the environment. Linguistic ability allows him both to fabricate tools that enhance his innate biological devices and to *imagine future adjustments to unprecedented situations, based on experience with previous successful adjustments.* We are in the area of what we call symbolic activities or *mental habits.* In this area, the tendency to adjust beliefs, desires, and judgments to changes in the environment can take two courses: (1) either they *repeat, symptomatically,* previous adjustment mechanisms with no consideration for the potential benefits or harms resulting from them, or (2) *they creatively innovate the repertoire for management of the environment.* In any case, what matters for the time being is that this collection of *mental habits* is what we call the agent's *subjective identity.* Subjective identity is a synonym for the *memory* of habits from past actions and the use we make of such habits for prospecting or predicting real or virtual (known or unusual) future acts. This is the face of identity that we call the "internal" part or the self's "inner life."

At first glance, the observation seems trivial. However, when we take a closer look, the current conception of "interiority" raises at least two questions. The first concerns the term's *meaning*: what does "interior," "internal," or "inner" mean? The second concerns its *function* in mental life: what is the role of the experience of "interiority"?

Such questions are at the core of psychoanalytical theory and practice, and there have been numerous attempts to solve them. One such attempt consists of underlining a curious characteristic in the use of the words "interior" and "interiority." The vernacular meaning of internal, interior, and interiority consists of (1) an inconsistent cognitive attitude and (2) a functionally indispensable emotional attitude. That is, we use the words in a *theoretically unfounded but psychologically justified* way. The arguments that legitimize the use of the terms *interior* or *internal* are usually invalid, circular, or incoherent. Meanwhile, the psychological reasons that lead us to use them are emotionally justifiable and legitimate, *as long as they are conceptually re-described.*

We thus employ the term *interior* in an epistemologically loose and psychologically rigorous way. The issue is thus to theoretically justify the use of the word "interiority" in the psychological field, without however validating the commonsense arguments on its nature. In other words, I suggest two things. First, I suggest that the commonplace idea of "interior" as an imaginary space or continent, peopled by private mental processes unverifiable by empirical observation, is unsustainable. This idea can be replaced usefully by the idea of interiority as a relational public phenomenon, founded on physical embodiment and on which we can make testable empirical affirmations. I will discuss this topic through a brief review of the logical equivocations permeating the term's routine use. Based on some theorists, I will attempt to show that the *mental predicates* called "interior" are the description of human organisms' "external" activities, made of a particular perspective. Interior and exterior are phenomenic forms of the self's concrete and material relations with the world.

Second, I suggest that the "interiorization" of these predicates is a necessary (but not sufficient) condition for us to stabilize the meaning of self or identity. The feeling of continuity of existence depends on the internalizations of the agent-self's external expression on the environment. Without the internalization of the flow of exchanges between the inner and outer worlds, there can be no satisfactory life. The balance between the two universes of physical-mental processes is the necessary condition for emotional stability.

On the Meaning of the *Inner World or Internal Mental Reality*

When speaking of internal reality, we generally know what it is about. Except in psychological disorders, initial stages of mental development, and similar phenomena, we are all capable of distinguishing inner world from outer world. Inner world is formed by bodily self-perception, by the representations of objects and environmental situations, and by the first-person narratives of ourselves. Outer world is formed by objects and events whose existences or realities are independent of particular perceptions by particular subjects.

As we see, the description avoids but does not untie the Gordian knot of defining the word interiority. Exactly what does "interior" mean? To which empirical sediment does this word refer? Furthermore, if we accept that "interior" is a relational term, then thoughts, feelings, emotions, and sensations are "interior" to what? Can we say that such states, processes, or events are "inside" something, as we say that a table is inside a room, a heart is inside the body, or molten rock is inside the Earth? If we can, what authorizes us to do so?

Ryle was one of the first thinkers to tackle this difficulty in his canonic discussion of the concept of "mind" (Ryle, 2002[1949]). The target of his critique is the notion of interiority as the equivalent of private *events, known immediately and indubitably by introspection.* In his view, such is the ordinary notion of mind or inner world. Ryle, however, objects that there is no such thing as the "mind," if we understand it as a self-subsisting entity, apart from individuals' bodily expressions in interaction with the environment. What we call mind or inner world are heterogeneous activities such as thinking, feeling, speaking, making calculations, mourning, dreaming, desiring, and so forth, summarized by ordinary language under the heading "mental." Ryle does not refuse to employ the term *mind* or *mental*, but he refutes the idea that all acts labeled as mental possess a same common quality lent to them by an undefinable and evanescent mind. This idea, he says, is the inertial byproduct of idealist philosophical conceptions and unthinking speech habits.

But if the mind is only a word that stems from poor linguistic and philosophical habits, what leads us to maintain such habits? Ryle says that the mistaken understanding of the mind's nature is born of a *category mistake* by speakers who ignore the logical infraction they have committed. The error consists of treating the member of a class of phenomena X as belonging to the class of phenomena Y. To illustrate this hypothesis, he uses the famous example of the university. Someone whom we invite to visit university Z, after visiting the buildings, faculty and students, laboratories, library, classrooms, snack bars, bookshop, and patios or gardens, asks, "But where is the university?" After all, Ryle says, "university" is not a thing or event belonging to a logical type that subsumes things and events like laboratories, faculty, or classrooms. University is a noun, whose extent and meaning encompass material equipment, people, symbolic rules of coexistence and purposes, integrated in the network of higher learning and research and graduate studies courses. Something similar occurs in the ordinary use of the word *mind* or *interiority*. Individuals take these words as if they were members of the *class of empirical psychological manifestations*, when in fact they are convenient abbreviations used to speak of the similarity in the family that exists in such manifestations.

These errors are sustained mainly by three beliefs that make the idea of interiority plausible as an autonomous and transcendent property of mental acts. The first is the belief in a sort of lay soul, the mind, purportedly subdivided into faculties such as intellect, memory, consciousness, or sensitivity (Ryle, 1979:52). The second is the naïve or fallacious belief in a parallel that there must be between the machine and human nature. On this belief, Ryle says that just as we explain physical movements by mechanical causes, we tend to explain psychological phenomena as the effect of supposed mental causes (Ryle, 2002[1949]).

The third is the belief that makes us confuse a *meaningful description* of external, visible, and material facts with a *meaningless description* of internal, invisible, "made-in-mind" facts. The naming of emotions is a typical example of this confusion. In linguistic commonsense, when speaking of feelings or states of spirit, we believe we are describing events occurred in an ineffable or fantastic region of the brain inhabited by *internal psychological entities*. In fact, Ryle notes, to recognize or speak of emotions is to assign meaning to behavioral manifestations that can emerge on unique occasions. For example, when we say we are ashamed, afraid, or moved, we are identifying *physical expressions, circumstances,* and *causal reasons* associated with conducts of shame, fear, or commotion. We first learn to recognize such conducts by perceiving how they are used by others, later using them ourselves after correcting the deviations and incorrections in their use. Before emotions become private, they are public, and before they are internalized, they are externalized, available for subjects' observation and learning.

To have access to inner emotions means to know how to identify certain conducts in the actual situations in which they appear. Emotions are visible signals, signs, or evidence of objective reactions, reproducible in certain circumstances. To feel afraid, ashamed, or moved means to experience and display conducts *that make the connection intelligible between them and the environmental situations that caused their emergence.* On this point, I recall that what makes a conduct "intelligible" is that which makes it effective as a means of communication with others or as a tool for altering the reality we wish to change. Therefore, to know inner mental occurrences, states, and processes is not to have access (via introspection) to immediate, indubitable mental occurrences, processes, and states that are inaccessible to third-person observation and description. It is to assign meaning to certain *physical sensations, dispositions to act, and complex conducts* that emerge in certain contexts.

Merleau-Ponty, with another terminology, defends similar points of view. For him, emotions are collective habits shared by subjects belonging to a certain cultural tradition. In his opinion, however, to define emotional habits as simple conducts or behaviors, as Ryle does, is insufficient. To be moved, to feel an emotion, is more than to display expressive gestures appropriately in certain situations. To be moved means to perceive things, events, and persons different from we would perceive them if we were not experiencing the emotion in question. Emotions are ways of being-in-the-world; to value certain things rather than others, to shine light on angles of reality that would remain dark if we were not "moved" (Crossley, 2001:85). However, to be willing to act in the world or to perceive it from the emotional perspective is not the same as to affirm the existence of inner emotional realities accessible only to the person that feels them. Emotional events are not facts hidden in the basement of consciousness. As Merleau-Ponty (2002) says:

Faced with an angry or threatening gesture, I have no need, in order to understand it, to recall the feelings that I experienced when I used these gestures myself. I know very little, from inside, of the mime of anger, so that a decisive factor is missing for any association by resemblance or reasoning by analogy, and besides, I do not perceive the anger or the threat as a psychological fact hidden behind the gesture, I read the anger in the gesture. The gesture does not make me think of anger, it is the anger itself. ([1945]:215)

Emotion is thus a public way of being-in-the-world. We first learn to feel emotion by recognizing the emotion of others or receiving from them the "emotional" meaning of our own gestures. We later become competent users of the emotional expressions by being capable of producing the correct gesture according to the cultural rule, with the correct interlocutors, and at the correct moments and on correct occasions.

The explanations by Merleau-Ponty and Ryle are certainly convincing. But they avoid the nodal problem: why do we insist on making logical and metaphysical mistakes, dissociating outside from inside or the gesture from its supposed hidden intentional matrix? After all, the explanation for the mistake does not eliminate its phenomenic density. Understanding why we use the idea of interior in a logically inadequate way does not make us fail to experience the difference that exists between interiority and exteriority. Everyone knows, for example, what it is to think "to oneself," to imagine nonexistent scenes, to recall past events, or to hum songs "in one's head." The enigma thus returns: what are the proper qualities of the phenomenon we call "interior"?

Two criteria can be used to distinguish inner from outer facts. The first concerns the purported immateriality of internal events; the second, their purported imaginary location. Both refer to human action's potential, but in slightly different ways. Let us analyze the first criterion. It is Ryle who undertakes to solve it. When we think to ourselves; engage in an imaginary dialogue; or evoke a song, landscape, or mythological animal, we are facing phenomena that we describe as "internal." However, Ryle says that thinking to oneself, for example, is not to enter into the magical zone of ethereal and mysterious facts; it is *to manifest embodied dispositions to mobilize vocal mechanisms, without concluding the action.* Silent dialogues or soliloquies are subvocalizations of speech behaviors interrupted before they are expressed out loud as dialogues or discourses. Meanwhile, evoking an image or landscape is the disposition to see images and landscapes, inhibited by the inexistence of material referents. Likewise, hearing or humming a song "to oneself" is a preparation for the act of singing or listening, which is not carried out fully and originally. Finally, to revisit past scenes in one's imagination or to remember smells or tastes means to outline gestures or sensations maintained in the rudimentary state of execution by the absence of the material reality that would reactivate them fully or by the intention of deactivating, in the middle of the road, the preparation to act, which had been triggered (Crossley, 2001:58). We can thus activate sensory-motor habits without actually executing them, which is what we call inner phenomena.

The second criterion is phenomenological, in the strict sense of the term. As the model, let us take Straus' theory of sensation as a form of communication (Straus, 2000). In the author's analysis of the nature of "feeling" or "sensation," he also challenges the idea of interiority as the set of facts that possess an *in-extension* or *imaginary extension,* void of the substrate of physical realities. In fact, says Straus, if rather than taking psychological facts as an example of inner facts, we analyze the application of the term *interior* to observable behavioral realities, much of the philosophical and psychological perplexity vanishes.

From this angle, Straus says, we say that we are "inside" something when we suffer limitations on our *possibilities for relating* to the rest of the environment. Interior and exterior do not point to symmetrical and opposite positions in geographic spaces, neutral and indifferent to the surroundings. The two terms indicate the particular position of a human individual in the *totality of the world.*

Still, Straus notes, the idea of limitation only makes sense because we are beings that "move," "act," "desire," and have an awareness of these potentialities. If we were incapable of performing such movements as revolution and rotation and thus of altering our current position in the world, we would have no reason to feel "limitations" to our mobility. The word interior thus *concerns the field of action and the relation with the world's totality.* We often use the word to speak of inanimate things or nonhuman events. In such cases, however, we are using it inadvertently, in a logically imprecise way. By an anthropomorphic extrapolation, we impute to things and events the same kind of constraint that we would experience if we ourselves were in the position of the things and events.

For example, to understand a phrase like "the chair is inside the room" implies assuming that the mere physical distance between the object "chair" and the environment "room" does not suffice for us to establish "the relation between something inside and something outside." We understand such a phrase easily because we know what it means "to be inside a room" for a moving and acting being. Likewise, we understand an enunciate like "the chair is outside the house" because we have the experience of "being deprived of the possibility of entering a house that we would like to enter." Finally, we understand the meaning of a statement like "the jewel is inside the safe" for similar reasons. "Being inside," in the aforementioned example, means "to be totally or partially immune to the other's action," just as we feel totally or partially protected from external demands when we are inside our own rooms, homes, workplaces, or any other shelters.

In short, interior has nothing to do with mental contents *confined to an imaginary geometric space.*[2] This topic is a construction *after the fact*, conceived to adjust to the idea of mind as an *abstract continent that encompasses mysterious facts.Interior* is a term belonging to the grammar of action and communication. "To be inside something" is to occupy a position in which the relation with the whole world is hindered or impeded (a) by the limits of our biological performances or (b) by the intention of segregating ourselves from things or events, due to a wide range of reasons or purposes: the search for protection against dangers and aggressions, the search for tranquility, the search for concentration, or the desire for solitude. The inner world expresses a relation with the environment, in which *subjects see themselves as limiting their action or imposing action on the other.* Based on these notions of interiority, I will attempt to address the problem of its *function* in mental life.

The Function of Interiority in the Life of the Self

The analysis by Straus, applied to mental interiority, reveals two reasons by which the use of the term does justice to psychological experience. The first refers to the idea of the *action's limit*. We call some mental events "inner" because they prove inaccessible or less accessible by the means we have at our disposal to act. By way of illustration, we have the case of emotions characterized by impulsiveness or compulsiveness. If we concede that psychological life is divided, in broad strokes, into cognitive, volitional, and affective aspects, we will say that the realm of affects – sensations, feelings – escapes almost entirely from cognitive or volitional control, that it is the driver of autonomous action. The emotions I refer to are defined as "inner" mental events over which we do not spontaneously have any voluntary command. To be moved, as described, is a physical-mental experience whose form of contact with the world's totality tends to inhibit the expression of cognitive-volitional skills that are the anchor of the subject's free action.

Obviously, not all emotions are factors inhibiting one's autonomous action in relation to the world's totality. Many emotions facilitate or reinforce the dispositions to expand the range of action by the self. Yet they only acquire this feature as part of the action designed or performed. The emotion integrating the agent-self's intentional arc acquires the very nature of this event, that is, opening oneself to the diversification of the multiple possible links to the world. In opposition to this kind of emotion, impulsive or compulsive emotion competes with the action and immobilizes the self in passive suffering, which is not translated as intervention in the outer world.

The second reason by which the word *interiority* is faithful to our psychological experience of it does not originate in the limitations on action imposed by factors alien to one's will and the subject's cognitive efforts. Its source is the self-limitation that aims to reinforce the individual's independence from the environment's intrusions. This aspect is highly attractive to psychoanalytical practice and concerns the imaginative zone of the secret.

Numerous authors call attention to the meta-psychological value of the *secret* in the self's life. To keep a secret is what prevents the agent's intent to become public and to be protected in his sensitive, delicate points. There are several reasons that lead us to keep a secret. For Margolis, the capacity to keep a secret is not simply to hide this or that particular fact. It is a mandatory clause for the emergence of the feeling of identity (Margolis, 1976:131–157). The author understands that to preserve the sphere of inner facts from others is to create a barrier against occasional unwanted influences on self's desire and pleasure, thereby increasing the margin of sovereignty for oneself.

Aulagnier revisited the question of the perspective of indispensable requirements for the subject to be able to think (Castoriadis-Aulagnier, 1976: 141–157). The author addresses secret thought, not via the pleasure that one may extract from its occasional erotic or aggressive contents, but by the pleasure that comes from the selfsame exercise of thinking. To feel deprived of one's enjoyment of thinking can represent a serious assault on mental equilibrium. Secret information, ever since the child discovers that he may keep information from the adults, shows that self learns to defend himself from the other's omnipotence by concealing that which, in him, no one can take without his consent and cooperation. To dissimulate, to lie, to pretend, to omit, or simply to refuse to display what one wants to guard from the public gaze and scrutiny is a privileged way of experiencing freedom in one's relation with the world.

Winnicott, in turn, approached the topic in two decisive articles, "The Capacity to Be Alone" (in Winnicott 2018*[1965]:29–36)* and "Communicating and Not Communicating Leading *to a* Study of Certain Opposites" (in Winnicott 2018*[1965]:179–192)*. In the first article, the capacity *to be alone* assumes the trust placed in a favorable environment, thanks to sufficiently good maternal care. In addition, due to this same trust, the self acquires the competence to live states of non-integration, which are the basis for a creative life. In non-integration, the self can exist without being concerned with intrusions from the environment or with the efficacy of immediate action. These are moments of repose in which the feeling of self-reality can sometimes achieve the intensity of what Winnicott called the "orgasm of self."

In the article on communication, the role and value of inner life are appreciated somewhat differently. Winnicott's point of departure is the notion of maternal *constancy* and *inconstancy* to speak of the meaning that *communication* and *non-communication* can assume in psychological dynamics. While the child doubts the constancy of inputs from the mother-environment, he relies on explicit communication to have his needs and demands met. By trusting in the predictability of maternal care, the child begins to feel that *to communicate is simply to exist.* That is, trust leads the child to perceive that his presence is sufficient for the mother to know what he needs. The child thus learns to value moments of *isolation without withdrawal,* moments in which he remains tied to the subjective objects that are substitutes for maternal attitudes.

Silent communication with the subjective objects is at the root of the *feeling of being real,* which is the opposite of the feeling of falsehood, coming from relations based on obedience to the other. For Winnicott, the satisfaction that comes from permanence in this inner state is necessary for the self *to feel in life,* another way of defining the feeling of self-reality. Non-communication means that the self enjoys the fact of *being in life, which contrary to what one might think, is not the antonym of* "not being dead," but that of "not having existed until the moment of birth." Birth, not death, is what prevents the self from recognizing that "being alive is everything."

Winnicott's nuances need to be understood. As he himself calls attention in article "Dreaming, Fantasying and Living: A Case-History Describing a Primary Dissociation" (in Winnicott, 2005[1971]:35–50), the enjoyment of non-communication, of immersion in the inner world, does not always result in the feeling of being alive. We are able to not communicate or to refrain from communicating two types of psychological production: (a) *dreams and imaginative activities* and (b) *fantasies and daydreams.*[3] Only in the former case of dreams and imagination do we maintain psychologically productive ties with the real world's objects. In the latter case, of fantasies and daydreams, thoughts and feelings display the traces of impulsiveness and compulsiveness mentioned earlier. Non-communication here represents a dissociation of the self that results in a break with the objective world. Thus, the inner experience capable of spawning the feeling of reality or of being in life is what makes non-communication a stage in the path or movement of *creation.* Any inner experience, deprived of this latter time, that of action on outer reality, becomes a *feeling of impotence* rather than *creative omnipotence.* It is what happens with fantasies and daydreams. These psychological formations are symptoms of dissociation of the self who, through the effect of various orders of traumas, learns to submit to the environment while yielding to the enjoyment of fantasies incapable of being transformed into projects for action.

After discarding the philosophical and psychological traps and dualisms and taking the aforementioned analysts' contributions into account, we can then return to our initial question: Why does it make sense to continue to speak of interiority, despite the epistemic disadvantages created by the ordinary use of the notion? I would answer briefly: because the immediacy of sensory experience and the efficiency of action are not sufficient for the self to feel the reality of his existence or the pleasure of existing. We continue to speak of "interior" because the word's referent is the world of memory itself, that is, the only world that can ensure the self of the feeling that life is worth living.

The activity of remembering is the part of mental reality that has the specific property of positioning the self in the universe of *contingency*, a *sine qua non* condition for life's enjoyment. When the self feels and acts, it exhausts the intention that moves itself at the very exact moment in which the intended act is performed. Sensation and action are what they are, that is, they only exist when manifested, and by manifesting themselves, they can never be anything else except that in which they enacted themselves. The conditional "if it had been or could have been" does not belong to the domain of that which merely "is or is not," or "was or was not."

Meanwhile, in evocation, we can situate sensory actions or reactions in the *conditional*. Remembering, as an outline of what or may not come to be, allows us to hesitate, to waiver, to come-and-go in imagined decisions. It is life in transit, in movement, before and after acting and feeling. It is the rehearsal that makes us conceive the possibilities and probabilities before and after the certainties. This prospective or retrospective illusion is an attribute of the inner world, and only it can renew our permanent interest in life. Without the inner sphere's perspectivism, conditionality, and contingency, we would be prisoners of the instantaneous, of that which exhausts itself even as it materializes. As we can easily see, this imprisonment in immediacy would never allow the fruition of experiences that make us continue to desire, to feel, and to act. Love and hate, fear and fearlessness, prudence and foolhardiness, enthusiasm and dismay, hope and despair, compassion and indifference, in short, good and evil would be empty words without the possibility that everything could turn out differently.

Self, the feeling of identity with oneself, can thus not be found in the repetition of the same or in the absolute unprecedentedness of what is unknown as such. Self is the effect of the constant effort by human beings to unify the dissimilar, to predict the unpredictable, to reproduce what satisfies us, and to explore what we do not know. This set of physical-mental activities is what we call creativity, and which finds its dwelling place in "inner life." If we truly convinced ourselves that our life was, is, and always will be the same, and that nothing new could happen, we would lose the feeling of continuity of existence and the attraction to the task of living. The activity of re-membering releases action and sensations from fusion with the pre-sent and transposes them to the inner domain, where they can color life with memories of the past, in turn, capable of becoming promises for a new beginning.

Notes

1 On the notion of the body's physical and mental expression, see Costa (2004).

2 This idea can be reinforced by Bergson's critique of the ordinary notion of space. For Bergson, to perceive the diversity of objects and events is not the same as locating them in a "homogeneous, empty, and indifferent space.".The concept of space or of spatial localization is an "act of the spirit" (Bergson, 2001:70); a "scheme of our possible action on things" (Bergson, 1996:158). Space is time contracted or dilated as a function of the interests and possibilities of the body's action on objects. From this perspective, "interior" or "exterior" is what can be more or less transformed by the means available to action. Space, in short, is what "provides us immediately with the scheme for our near future" (Bergson, 1999:160) and expresses, as Philonenko said, our expectations for survival or satisfaction (Philonenko, 1994:182).

3 Winnicott employs the terms *dream, imagination, fantasy,* and *daydream* idio-syncratically in relation to the psychoanalytical terminology established by Freud and by the majority of psychoanalysts. I do not intend to dwell on this matter in this chapter, although I think that on this particular aspect, Winnicottian theory is subject to criticism. I contend that dreams, daydreams, and fantasies are phe-nomena that belong to the class of imaginative manifestations, and that it makes little sense to order them the way he does. At any rate, what matters is to char-acterize the difference between the inner facts described, highlighting each one's role in the appearance of the feeling of being alive.

References

Bergson, Henri. *L'évolution créatrice*. Paris: PUF. 1996. 7ª ed.

Bergson, Henri. *Matière et mémoire*. Paris: PUF. 1999. 6ª ed.

Bergson, Henri. *Essai sur les données immédiates de la conscience*. Paris: PUF. 2001. 7ª ed.

Cassam, Quassim. Representing bodies. In: *The philosophy of the body*. Ed. Mike Proudfoot. Malden, USA & Oxford, UK: Blackwell Publishers. 2003:1–20.

Castoriadis-Aulagnier, Piera. Le droit au secret: condition pour pouvoir penser. In: *Nouvelle revue de psychanalyse*. Paris: Gallimard. Numéro 14. Automne. 1976: 141:157.

Costa, Jurandir Freire. O *vestígio e a aura – corpo e consumismo na moral do espetáculo*. Rio: Garamond. 2004.

Crossley, Nick. *The social body – Habit, identity and desire*. London/ Thousand Oaks, California/New Delhi: Sage Publications. 2001.

Henry, Michel. *Philosophie et phénoménologie du corps*. Paris: PUF. 2001[1965]. 4ª ed.

Margolis, Gerald J. Identité et secret. In: *Nouvelle revue de psychanalyse*. Paris: Gallimard. Numéro 14. Automne. 1976: 131–140.

Merleau-Ponty. *Phénoménologie de la perception*. Paris: Gallimard. 2002 [1945].

Philonenko, Aléxis. *Bergson, ou de la philosophie comme science rigoureuse*. Paris: Les éditions du Cerf. 1994.

Ryle, Gilbert. *The concept of mind*. Chicago: University of Chicago Press. 2002 *[1949]*.

Ryle, Gilbert. *On thinking*. London: Basil Blackwell. 1979.

Straus, Erwin. *Du sens des sens – Contribution à l'étude des fondements de la psychologie*. Grenoble: Éditions Jérôme Millon. 2000.

Todes, Samuel. *Body and World*. Introduction by Hubert L. Dreyfus and Piotr Hoffman. Cambridge, MA and London, England: The MIT Press. 2001.

Winnicott, D. W. *The maturational processes and the facilitating environment*. New York: Routledge. 2018 [1965].

Winnicott, D. W. *Playing and reality*. New York: Routledge. 2005 [1971].

Chapter 7

The 'Hard Problem' of Consciousness[1]

Mark Solms

Introduction

In this chapter, I apply a psychoanalytic insight to a philosophical problem. James Strachey (1962, p. 62) described the insight in question as one of 'the most fundamental of the theoretical notions on which all [Freud's] later work rested.' This theoretical notion was introduced in 'The Neuro-Psychoses of Defence' (Freud, 1894):

> In mental functions something is to be distinguished – a quota of affect or sum of excitation – which possesses all the characteristics of a quantity (though we have no means of measuring it), which is capable of increase, diminution, displacement and discharge, and which is spread over the memory-traces of ideas somewhat as an electrical charge is spread over the surface of a body.
>
> (p. 60)

The larger point of the paper in which this sentence appeared was that the 'quota of affect' which activates the 'memory trace of an idea' – that is, the activation that renders the idea conscious (enables the subject to 'feel' it) – can become detached from the idea, and thereby render it unconscious. This was an early formulation of 're-pression' – a term which, at that time, Freud used synonymously with 'defence' (e.g., the affect may become displaced onto memory-traces of neighbouring ideas.)

Freud elaborated and developed this theoretical notion in many directions, but the aspect I want to focus upon is that he conceptualised

DOI: 10.4324/9781003090755-8

'memory-traces of ideas' as relatively enduring *structures* and 'quotas of affect' as transient *states* of those structures. I am not going to trace the myriad vicissitudes of Freud's thinking about consciousness. What matters here is that he held steadfastly throughout his scientific life to the view that *there is no such thing as an unconscious feeling*. For example, in his metapsychological paper on 'The Unconscious' (1915a), Freud wrote:

> It is surely of the essence of an emotion that we should be aware of it, i.e., that it should become known to consciousness. Thus the possibility of the attribute of unconsciousness would be completely excluded as far as emotions, feelings and affects are concerned.
>
> (p. 177)

He explained:

> In comparison with unconscious ideas there is the important difference that unconscious ideas continue to exist after repression as actual structures in the system *Ucs.*, whereas all that corresponds in that system to unconscious affects is a potential beginning which is prevented from developing.
>
> (ibid., p. 178)

I am aware that many people (even psychoanalysts) dispute this notion of Freud's, and claim that unconscious emotions do indeed exist. In doing so, they typically cite the 'unconscious sense of guilt,' which, ironically, was precisely the example that Freud used in the metapsychological paper just cited. He explained that what the term 'unconscious sense of guilt' denotes, properly speaking, is a process whereby guilt becomes *displaced*, not repressed.

Be that as it may, let me be clear from the outset what *I* mean by the word 'affect.' I mean *feeling*. If some of my colleagues want to claim that 'unconscious emotions' exist, so be it; but if they do, they are talking about something different from what I am talking about in this chapter. I am talking about simple, raw feelings. And a feeling is not a feeling if you do not feel it. 'Unconscious feeling' is an oxymoron.

The argument set out further in the chapter does not rest upon a semantic point, however, nor does it rest upon an appeal to Freud's authority. As I will show, converging lines of neuroscientific evidence, accumulated gradually over the past 70 years, demonstrate that affect (and not cognition) is the fundamental vehicle of consciousness. I begin my argument by setting out the 'hard problem' of consciousness, as formulated by Chalmers (1995).

The 'Hard Problem' Concerns the Functional *Mechanism* of Consciousness

The physicist Paul Davies (2019) writes:

> Among life's many baffling properties, the phenomenon of consciousness leaps out as especially striking. Its origin is arguably the hardest problem facing science today and the only one that remains almost impenetrable even after two and a half millennia of deliberation … Consciousness is the number-one problem of science, of existence even.
>
> (pp. 184, 207)

I could quote many similar statements by other scientists. The 'hard problem' (as it is reverentially abbreviated) asks why and how you – 'your joys and your sorrows, your memories and your ambitions, your sense of personal identity and free will' (Crick, 1994, p. 3), in short, your experience of existence – could possibly spring from the physiological processes that occur in brain cells. These cells are not fundamentally different from those that constitute other bodily organs. So, how do they bring 'you' into being?

The question is hardly new; it is probably the most ancient and heartfelt of all human mysteries. In past times, it took the form 'How does my soul come to reside in my body?' But it was posed in its current form in 1995 by Chalmers. Let me quote his celebrated formulation of it:

> It is undeniable that some organisms are subjects of experience. But the question of how it is that these systems are subjects of experience is perplexing. Why is it that when our cognitive systems engage in visual and auditory information processing, we have visual or auditory experience: the quality of deep blue,

the sensation of middle C? How can we explain why there is *something it is like* to entertain a mental image, or to experience an emotion? It is widely agreed that experience arises from a physical basis, but we have no good explanation of why and how it so arises. Why should physical processing give rise to a rich inner life at all? It seems objectively unreasonable that it should, and yet it does.

(p. 201, my emphasis)

Chalmers's formulation owes a large debt to an earlier paper by Thomas Nagel (1974), who emphasised the *something-it-is-like-ness* of subjective experience. He pointed out: 'An organism has conscious mental states if and only if there is something it is like to *be* that organism – something it is like *for* the organism.' He added: 'If we acknowledge that a physical theory of mind must account for the subjective character of experience, we must admit that no presently available conception gives us *a clue* about how this could be done' (my emphasis). Nagel concluded: 'It seems unlikely that any physical theory of mind can be contemplated until more thought has been given to the general problem of subjective and objective.'

I agree. What I would like to provide in this chapter is 'a clue' of the kind that Nagel lacked. However, let us be clear about the terms of the problem we are dealing with, because its defenders have an unfortunate tendency to shift the goalposts (see Havlík, Kozáková & Horáče, 2017). When Karl Friston and I first published our proposed solution to the problem (Solms & Friston, 2018), one of the anonymous re-viewers for the *Journal of Consciousness Studies*[2] wrote: 'The hard problem (following Chalmers) is a metaphysical problem and as such it is not open to being "solved".' Friston wrote to me afterwards: 'I get the impression that the hard problem is not there to be solved; it is there to be revered' (letter of December 23, 2017). Not everyone who follows Chalmers, it seems, has read the paper in which he formulated the problem. Here is the closing sentence of that paper: 'The hard problem is a hard problem, but there is no reason to believe that it will remain permanently unsolved.' So, let's be clear what the problem is that we're trying to solve. According to the quotation from Nagel just cited, the 'hard problem' is this: Why (and how) is there something it is like to *be* an organism – something it is like *for* the organism?

But there is more. Specifically, according to Chalmers, the hard problem of consciousness cannot be solved by *mechanistic* explanations:

> The easy problems are easy precisely because they concern the explanation of cognitive abilities and functions. To explain a cognitive function, we need only specify a mechanism that can perform the function.[3] The methods of cognitive science are well-suited for this sort of explanation, and so are well-suited to the easy problems of consciousness. By contrast, the hard problem is hard precisely because it is not a problem about the performance of functions. The problem persists even when the performance of all the relevant functions is explained ... What makes the hard problem hard and almost unique is that it goes *beyond* problems about the performance of functions. To see this, note that even when we have explained the performance of all the cognitive and behavioural functions in the vicinity of experience ... there may still remain a further unanswered question: *Why is the performance of these functions accompanied by experience?* A simple explanation of the functions leaves this question open ... Why doesn't all this information processing go on 'in the dark', free of any inner feel?
>
> (1995, pp. 202–3)

To understand the gravity of the problem identified here, consider the 'knowledge argument' – first articulated by another philosopher, Frank Jackson (1982). It goes something like this:[4] Imagine a congenitally blind neuroscientist named Mary who knows everything there is to know about the *functional mechanism* of vision. Although she can explain all the mechanistic facts of visual information processing – right down to the cellular level, including the impact of light waves on the photosensitive rods and cones, and how these waves are converted into nerve impulses, and how those impulses are propagated via the lateral geniculate body to the cortex, and how they are further processed there by neatly arranged columns of neurons, organised in vast numbers into a variety of information-processing modules spread far and wide throughout the cortical mantle, the multiple specialised visual processing streams of which are well understood – still she would not know *what it is like* to experience vision. Being blind since birth, she would know nothing about the experienced qualities of redness and blueness – for example – which are, after all, the actual stuff of conscious seeing. This is not only because she herself has never experienced such qualities but also because nothing in her anatomical and physiological *knowledge* about the functional mechanism of vision explains what it is like to see. If she were to suddenly acquire the gift of sight, she would learn something utterly new about vision – something that none of her mechanistic understanding prepared her for. *Her mechanistic understanding does not explain why and how there is something it is like to see.* It only explains why and how the brain decodes visual information: how *it* sees, not how *you* see. This supposed irreducibility of what philosophers call 'qualia' – the something-it-is-like-ness of subjective experience – to functional mechanisms is the hard problem.

So, again, we must be clear about the problem we are trying to solve. According to the second quotation from Chalmers, just cited: Why is the performance of these mechanistic functions accompanied by experience? Why doesn't all this information-processing go on 'in the dark,' free of any inner feel? At the end of this chapter, you must ask yourself whether I have answered these questions.

Before proceeding, however, let me clarify what I mean by 'functional mechanism.' I mean the interacting forces and processes that *cause* observable phenomena. Here, I am invoking the level of explanation that Freud called 'metapsychology': a term which denotes 'that which lies behind (meta-) the phenomena of consciousness (-psychology).' Importantly, as I see it (Solms, 1997), following Freud, the causal mechanism we are seeking can be inferred from *two* sets of observable phenomena: subjective mental events *and* objective brain events. These are the 'dual aspects' of being, which, according to Freud (1940), are registered on the inner and outer surfaces of our consciousness. They provide us with two observational perspectives upon one and the same thing: the 'mental apparatus.' Thus, the *subjective* feeling of fear (for example) can be observed also *objectively* (using optogenetics) as an activated tissue of neurons. Combining these two data sets, within their wider context, we can infer the function of the abstraction called 'fear' – and its mechanism must *explain* them both. So, functional mechanisms are not observed as such, but rather *abstracted* from observation. People who criticize neuropsychoanalysis as a reductionist exercise fail to appreciate this point. For me, like Freud, the mind *in itself* is not the brain; it is a functional apparatus the mechanism of which explains why there is 'something it is like' to be a brain.

Consciousness Is Not a *Cognitive* Function

I said that my intention is to apply a theoretical insight of Freud's to the 'hard problem.' I was referring (in part) to Freud's discovery that *cognition is mostly unconscious*. This is no longer a uniquely Freudian notion. Although he is not always given credit for it, Freud's notion that cognition is mostly unconscious is widely – perhaps even unanimously – accepted in cognitive neuroscience today. The title of a famous review of the relevant research by the cognitive scientist John Kihlstrom (1996) says it all: there is indeed 'Perception Without Awareness of What is Perceived, Learning Without Awareness of What is Learned.' Another well-known review article by Bargh *et al.*, 1999 summarises our current understanding under a more poetic title, 'The Unbearable Automaticity of Being':

> Most of moment-to-moment psychological life must occur through non-conscious means if it is to occur at all ... To consciously and wilfully regulate one's own behaviour, evalua-tions, decisions, and emotional states requires considerable effort and is relatively slow. Moreover, it appears to require a limited resource that is quickly used up, so conscious self-regulatory acts can only occur sparingly and for a short time. On the other hand, the non-conscious or automatic [psychological processes ... are unintended, effortless, very fast, and many of them can operate at any given time. Most important, they are effortless, continually in gear guiding the individual safely through the day.
>
> (p. 476)

The reason why Freud is not credited with the discovery that most 'moment-to-moment psychological life' occurs unconsciously is that it was independently *rediscovered* by cognitive neuroscientists, using entirely different methods from those that Freud used. What these methods revealed initially is that only *cortical* (as opposed to sub-cortical) cognition is conscious. But tachistoscopic studies – which flash visual information for just a few milliseconds – have since shown that even cortical processing is not intrinsically conscious. I have space for just one example (see McKeever, 1986). Negative and positive words were flashed very briefly to research participants, so briefly that the subjects were unaware of having seen anything at all. Their subsequent behaviour was clearly influenced by the words they claimed not to have seen: for example, after negative words like 'rapist' were flashed in association with a photograph of face A and positive ones like 'philanthropist' with face B, the research partici- pants subsequently showed a preference for face B, when shown it consciously, notwithstanding the fact they did not know *why* they preferred it. This shows that the faces must have been seen and re- membered, and that the negative and positive words must have been seen, read, understood, and remembered, and that the remembered words must have been associated with the remembered faces, all of it *unconsciously*. Since face recognition and reading with comprehension are exclusively cortical functions – functions of precisely the kind that cognitive psychologists have considered quintessentially 'mental' – we must conclude that even the highest cognitive functions (even ex- clusively human and exclusively cortical ones, like reading) are not inherently conscious.

This is the generally accepted view today: the part of the brain that performs conscious cognitive functions – the cortex – can perform *the very same functions* in the absence of conscious experience.

This brings us back to Chalmers's problem: if most moment-to- moment psychological life carries on without conscious experience, then why does it *ever* involve conscious experience? Why doesn't all this information processing go on non-consciously? As the 'knowl- edge problem' shows, consciousness seems to be *extraneous* to the functional mechanisms of vision, and indeed of all cognition.

My provisional conclusion is the following. I agree with Chalmers, but only because neuroscientists seeking the neural correlates of consciousness in functions like cortical visual processing – which is the model example used by cognitive neuroscientists – *have been looking in the wrong place*. Why? Because cortical vision is not in- trinsically conscious. It is therefore perfectly reasonably to ask, with Chalmers: Why is the performance of these functions accompanied by experience? Why doesn't all this information processing go on 'in the dark,' free of any inner feel? But is it equally reasonable to ask this question of *feeling*? Can the performance of the function of feeling go on in the dark, free of any inner feel?

Consciousness Is an Function

Classical neurology, building on empiricist philosophy (which was based in common sense), taught that the contents of consciousness are derived from sensory experience, which lays down 'memory-traces of ideas' in the cerebral cortex. It therefore came as a great surprise when, in 1949, two neurophysiologists named Giuseppe Moruzzi and Horace Magoun discovered that consciousness is obliterated completely by tiny lesions which disconnect the cortex from the reticulate (net-like) core of the brainstem. This revealed that cortical consciousness is *dependent* upon arousal of the cortex by this group of primitive nuclei located in the core of the brainstem (now called the reticular activating system). This was in cats, but the same applies to humans: naturally occurring lesions as small as 2 mm^3 in this part of the brain in us humans reliably causes coma (Fischer et al., 2016).

The way that neuroscientists (Moruzzi and Magoun included) dealt with this unexpected discovery, and thereby saved the cortical theory of consciousness, was to draw a new distinction between its 'contents' and its 'level,' and to claim that what the brainstem provides is only the latter aspect of consciousness: the level. This distinction coincides with the qualitative and quantitative dimensions of consciousness: the cortex supplies the 'qualia' (the philosophical term for something-it-is-like-ness) while the brainstem supplies the on/off switch or volume control. Still today, most neuroscientists distinguish between 'consciousness as the waking state' and 'consciousness as experience' (Zeman, 2001). Coenen (2007, p. 88, my emphasis) elaborates: 'Consciousness in the first meaning (consciousness of the waking state) is in this view a *necessary condition* for consciousness in the second sense (consciousness of experience or phenomenal consciousness).'

On this view, consciousness as the waking state (i.e., the 'level' of consciousness) is like the power supply of a television set, which nevertheless provides the actual 'contents' of the programming: consciousness as experience. Although an intact power source is a necessary *prerequisite* for generating televisual content, it is absurd to claim that power supply is the actual grounding *medium* of television.

The good thing about neuroscience is that its methods enable us to *test* hypotheses like this experimentally. If the reticular activating system supplies a purely quantitative form of consciousness (the waking state) while the cortex supplies its qualitative contents (experience), then one may confidently predict that, if the cortex is removed, *blank wakefulness* will ensue. This condition does actually exist. Neurologists call it the 'vegetative state,' also known as 'nonresponsive wakefulness.'

Does surgical removal of the cortex (a procedure called 'decortication') produce the vegetative state? Obviously, such experimental procedures cannot be performed on humans, but they have often been performed (all too often) in other mammal species, including in newborn dogs, cats and rats. The outcome is always the same: by the behavioural criteria that we normally use to measure responsive consciousness in neurology (e.g. the Glasgow coma scale), it is *preserved*. The post-operative behaviour of these animals cannot by any stretch of the definition be described as 'vegetative' (let alone 'comatose'). The neuroscientist Bjorn Merker (2007) writes that decorticate animals show 'no gross abnormalities in behaviour that would allow a casual observer to identify them as impaired.' Antonio Damasio concurs: 'Decorticated mammals exhibit a remarkable persistence of coherent, goal-oriented behaviour that is consistent with feelings and consciousness' (Damasio & Carvalho, 2013, p. 147). The emphasis on feelings is important. What these animals display is a full range of *instinctual* emotional behaviours. Rats decorticated at birth, for example, stand, rear, climb, hang from bars and sleep with normal postures. They groom, play, swim, eat and defend themselves. Either sex is capable of mating successfully when paired with normal cage mates. When they grow up, the females show the essentials of maternal care, which, though deficient in some respects, allow them to raise pups to maturity.

In many respects, decorticate mammals are in fact *more* active and emotionally responsive than normal ones. Jaak Panksepp (1998) regularly asked his graduate students to choose between two groups of rats, to determine from their behaviour which group had been operated upon. The students typically selected the *normal* ones, reasoning that the other group (really decorticate) was 'more lively.'

These are rats. What about human beings? Some human children are born without a cortex due to the pathological condition called hydranencephaly (see Figure 7.1). Like the decorticate rats, these children show emotionally responsive and goal-directed behaviours. Consider, for example, the response of the hydranencephalic girl pictured in Figure 7.2, when her baby brother is placed in her lap.[5] Similar things happen in other emotional situations: she shows situationally appropriate responses to a wide range of emotional stimuli, and spontaneously initiates emotional behaviours of her own. Merker (2007) has studied a large number of such children. He (like Shewmon et al., 1999, before him) observed these children expressing pleasure by smiling and laughter, and aversion by fussing, arching their backs and crying, 'their faces being animated by these emotional states.' He observed familiar adults enlisting their responsiveness to build up play sequences,

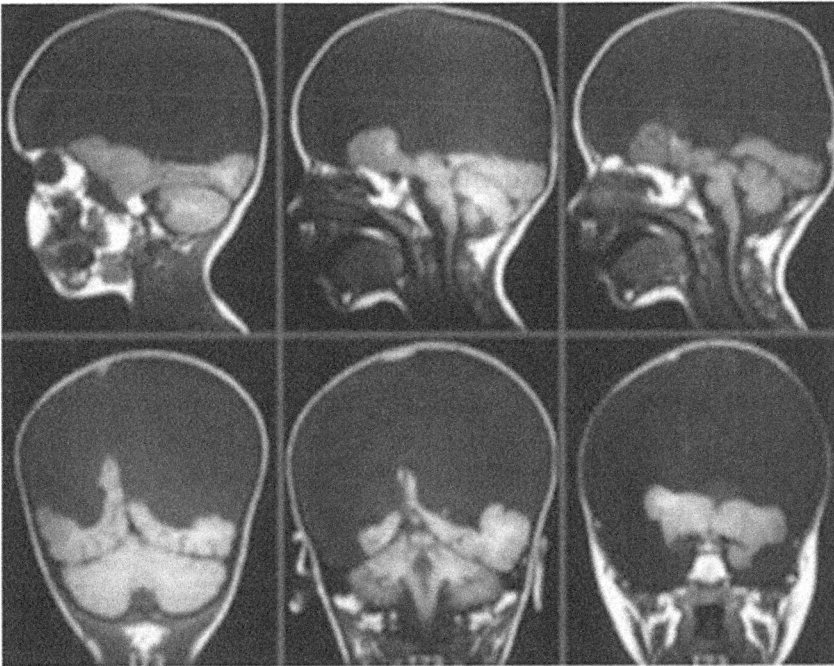

Figure 7.1 MRI brain scans of a child with hydranencephaly.

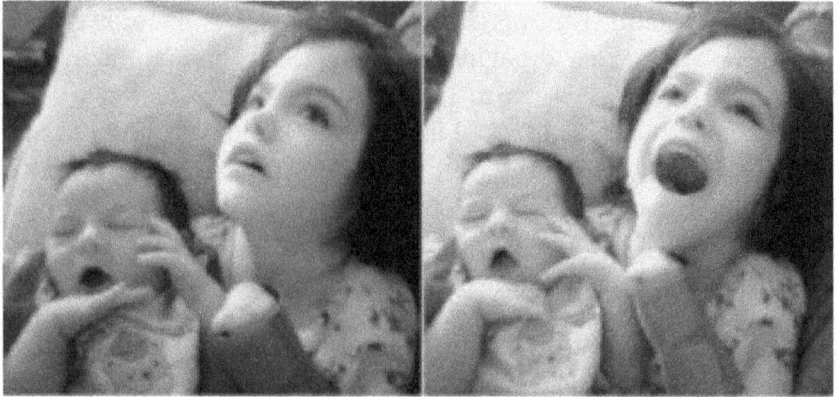

Figure 7.2 Emotional response of a child with hydranencephaly when her baby brother is placed in her lap.

predictably progressing from smiling, through giggling, to laughter and great excitement on the part of the children. They responded most vigorously to the voices and actions of their parents and other people they were familiar with, and they showed preferences for certain situations over others. For example, they appeared to enjoy specific toys, tunes or videos, and they even came to expect the regular presence of such things in the course of daily routines. Though behaviour varied from child to child, some of them clearly showed initiative (within the limitations of their motor disabilities), for example, by kicking noise-making trinkets hanging in a special frame constructed for the purpose, or by activating favourite toys using switches. Such behaviours were accompanied by situationally appropriate signs of pleasure or excitement on the part of the child.

These children clearly cannot be described as 'vegetative.' The evidence just summarised suggests that they are, at a minimum, capable of experiencing feelings and responding accordingly, even if – like the tachistoscopic research subjects – they have no idea (no conscious *knowledge*) as to where their feelings come from. In other words, to paraphrase Freud (1894), they experience 'quotas of affect' in the absence of any possibility of them activating 'memory-traces of ideas.'

But can we be sure that these children possess 'consciousness as [affective] experience'? The philosophical problem of other minds dictates that we can never know such things for certain, since the mind is something subjective; we can only ever observe *directly* our own mental qualia. Experiences can never be observed objectively, from without, *as experiences.* Hydranencephalic children could therefore be 'philosophical zombies'; that is, they might appear to have feelings but actually don't.

Fortunately, in science, we do not aspire to absolute certainty; we rely instead upon binding *inferences* derived from testable predictions, which yield converging lines of evidence, using multiple experimental methods.

For example, using *deep brain stimulation*, the hypothesis that affects are generated in the reticular activating system can be tested by placing electrodes into its nuclei, in conscious human patients, and then asking them to describe the subjective consequences. If the theory that the brainstem controls only a quantitative 'level' of consciousness (what Zeman calls 'consciousness as the waking state'), then stimulating it electrically should not affect its qualitative 'contents' (what Zeman calls 'consciousness as experience'). In other words, we would predict that deep brain stimulation of reticular activating nuclei should attenuate only the global level of consciousness, 'wakefulness,' and perhaps switch it on and off, as occurs with sleep.

Yet, an electrode implanted in the reticular brainstem of a 65-year-old woman (for treatment of Parkinson's disease) reliably evoked this remarkable response:

> The patient's face expressed profound sadness within five seconds ... Although still alert, the patient leaned to the right, started to cry, and verbally communicated feelings of sadness, guilt, uselessness, and hopelessness, such as 'I'm falling down in my head, I no longer wish to live, to see anything, hear anything, feel anything ...' When asked why she was crying and if she felt pain, she responded: 'No, I'm fed up with life, I've had enough ... I don't want to live any more, I'm disgusted with life ... Everything is useless, always feeling worthless, I'm scared in this world.' When asked why she was sad, she replied: 'I'm tired. I want to hide in a corner ... I'm crying over myself, of course... I'm hopeless, why am I bothering you?' ... The depression disappeared less than 90 seconds after stimulation was stopped. For the next five minutes the patient was in a slightly hypomanic state, and she laughed and joked with the

examiner, playfully pulling his tie. She recalled the entire episode. Stimulation [at another brain site, which was the actual target of the electrode] did not elicit this psychiatric response.

(Blomstedt et al., 2008)

This patient had no previous history of psychiatric symptoms of any kind. The nucleus that was stimulated was the substantia nigra (see Figure 7.4).

The reticular activating system contains the source nuclei for a whole host of neurochemicals that are responsible for the 'level' of consciousness. This enables us to utilise another method to investigate the hypothesis that the level of consciousness has no qualitative 'content.' If that were true, then we could confidently predict that by stimulating and blocking the outputs of the reticular activating system *pharmacologically*, we would elicit only global shifts in 'wakefulness.'

But that is not what happens. Antidepressants – serotonin boosters – act on neurons whose cell bodies are located in the raphe nuclei of the reticular activating system (see Figure 7.4). Antipsychotics – dopamine blockers – act on neurons sourced in another part of the reticular activating system: the ventral tegmental area. The same applies to anti-anxiety drugs – many of which block a chemical called noradrenaline,

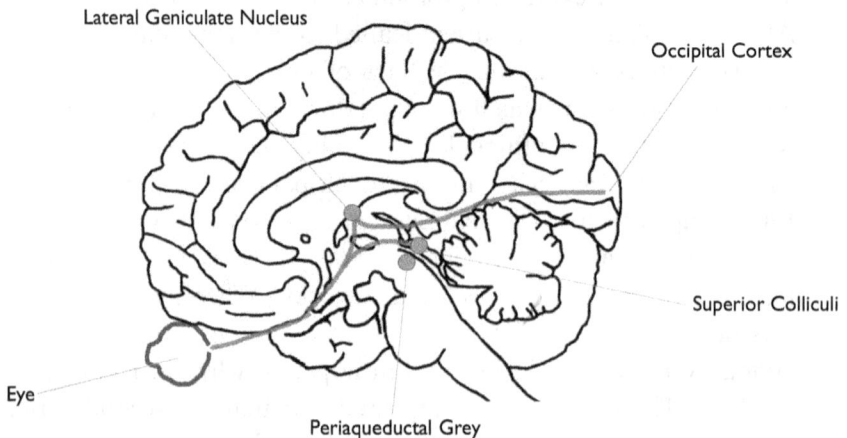

Figure 7.3 Pathways from the eye to the visual cortex and superior colliculi.

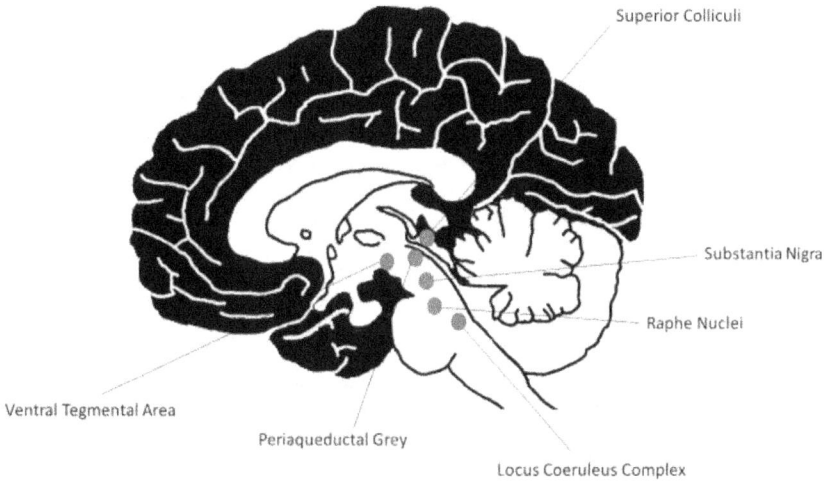

Figure 7.4 Location of some nuclei of the reticular activating system, in relation to the periaqueductal grey and superior colliculi.

which is produced by neurons sourced in the locus coeruleus complex, yet another part of the reticular activating system. All these neurons are clumped together in the core of the brainstem. Psychiatrists wouldn't tinker with this region of the brain if it merely switched consciousness on and off. If that were what it did, it would interest only anaesthetists.

Another experimental method, *functional neuroimaging* of the brain in emotional states, points to the same conclusion. Positron emission tomography of human beings in states of grief, joy, rage and fear, for example, show that the highest metabolic activity occurs in their brainstems (and other subcortical regions; see Figure 7.5) while the cortex shows *de*activation (Damasio et al., 2000). Functional magnetic imaging during orgasm reveals the same: the increased haemodynamic brain activity that correlates with this intensely af- fective state is almost exclusively subcortical (Holstege et al., 2003).

Lesion studies, deep brain stimulation, pharmacological manipula- tion and functional neuroimaging research all point to the same con- clusion: the reticulate core of the brainstem generates *affect*. Apparently, therefore, the part of the brain that we know is necessary for arousing consciousness *as a whole* has an equally powerful influence over *feeling*. In short, the grounding medium of 'consciousness as

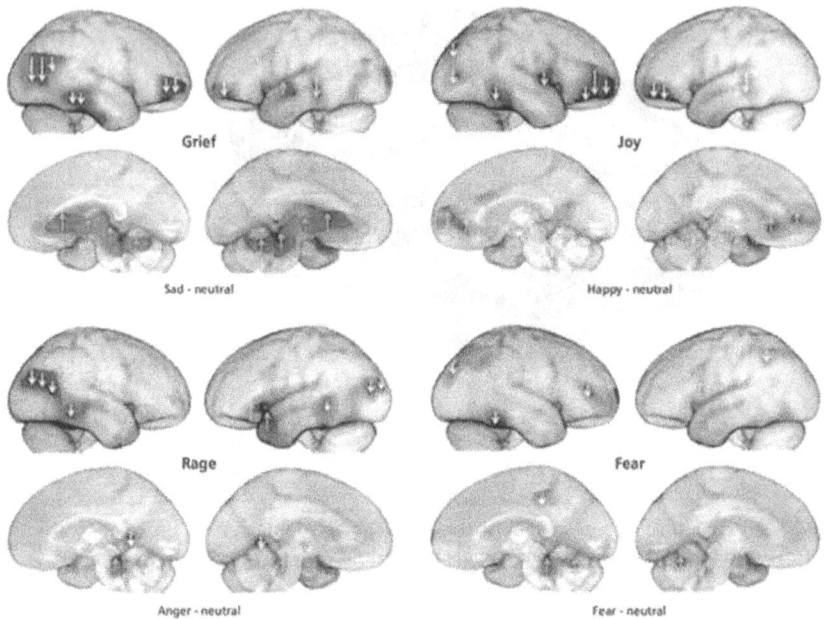

Figure 7.5 Positron emission tomography of the human brain in states of grief, joy, rage and fear.

experience' – its prerequisite – *is* feeling. The sentient subject is literally constituted by feeling.

The Functional Mechanism of Affect

Freud (1911) took the view that affect is the most basic form of consciousness: it registers 'oscillations in the tension of drive needs [... which] become conscious as feelings in the pleasure-unpleasure series' (Freud, 1940, p. 198).[6] 'Drive,' in turn, was defined by him as 'a measure of the demand made upon the mind for work in consequence of its connection with the body' (Freud, 1915b, pp. 121–2). According to Freud, increasing drive demand is felt as unpleasure and decreasing drive demand as pleasure. For this reason, Damasio (1999) remarked that 'Freud's insights on the nature of affect are consonant with the most advanced contemporary neuroscience views' (p. 38).

The contemporary view – which Damasio shares with many others – is that affective valence registers the *degree* and *direction* of homeostatic deviations from our biologically viable states. These deviations are known as 'error signals.' The differential *quality* of each affect registers, in addition to its valence, the category of error in question; so that hunger feels different from thirst and sleepiness, and fear feels different from lust and rage. These examples are given to indicate the fact that all affects, whether they be bodily or emotional ones, are governed by *homeostasis*. The homeostatic mechanism of affect is not very complicated (see Figure 7.6).

The easiest way to explain the difference between the simple forms of homeostasis that regulate vegetative functions and the more complex ones that regulates voluntary behaviour is to describe the transition from the one to the other. Let's take respiratory control, for example. Respiration is normally automatic: so long as the levels of oxygen and carbon dioxide in your blood stay within their homeostatic bounds (the 'settling point' in Figure 7.6), you don't have to be aware of your breathing in order to breathe. When blood gases exceed these limits, however, respiratory control intrudes upon consciousness in the form of an acute feeling called 'air hunger.' Unbalanced blood gas values are an indication that *action is required*. It is urgently necessary to remove an airway obstruction or to get out of a carbon-dioxide filled room. At this point, respiratory control

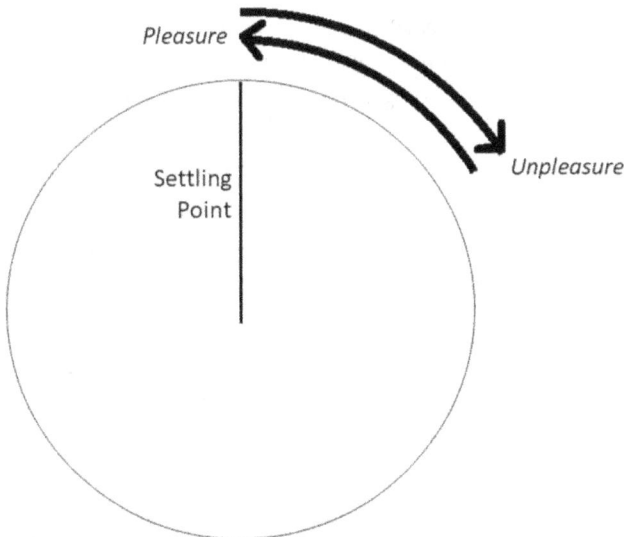

Figure 7.6 Feeling in relation to homeostasis.

enters your consciousness, via an inner warning system that we experience as *alarm* – specifically, in this case, suffocation alarm.

The simplest forms of feeling – hunger, thirst, sleepiness, muscle fatigue, nausea, coldness, urinary urgency, the need to defecate and the like – might not seem like affects, but that is what they are. What distinguishes affective states from other mental states is that they are hedonically *valenced*: they feel 'good' or 'bad.' This is how affects like hunger and thirst differ from sensations like vision and hearing. Sight and sound do not possess intrinsic value – but feeling does.

The goodness or badness of a feeling tells you something about the state of the biological *need* that lies behind it. Thus, thirst feels bad and quenching it feels good, because it is necessary to maintain hydration within the bounds that are viable for survival. The same applies to the unpleasant feeling of hunger in relation to the pleasurable relief that is brought about by eating. In short, pleasure and unpleasure tell you *how you are doing* in relation to your biological needs. Valence reflects the value system underwriting all biological life, namely that it is 'good' to survive and to reproduce and 'bad' not to do so.

What motivates each individual is not these biological values directly, but rather the subjective feelings they give rise to – even if we have no inkling of what the underlying biological values are, and even if we do not intellectually endorse them. For example, we eat sweet things because they taste good, not because they have high energy content, which is the biological reason why they taste good. The same applies to lust: we have sex (in our various ways) because it feels good, not because we are trying to perform our biological reproductive duty. Affects tell long evolutionary stories of which we are completely unaware. We are aware only of the feelings.

The reason I use Freud's word 'unpleasure' rather than 'pain' is that there are many different types of unpleasure and pleasure in the brain. This is the categorical (qualitative) aspect of affect mentioned earlier. Hunger feels bad, and it feels good to relieve it by eating; a distended bowel feels bad, and it feels good to relieve it by defecating; pain feels bad, and it feels good to withdraw from the source of it. These are bodily affects but the same applies to emotional ones. Separation distress feels bad and we respond to it by seeking reunion. Fear feels bad and we escape it by fleeing the danger. Suffocation alarm and hunger and sleepiness and fear all feel bad, but they feel bad in different ways. Getting rid of them, by contrast, feels good, also in different ways.

The different feelings signal different situations of biological significance, and each one compels us to *do* something different: urinating cannot satisfy hunger and eating cannot relieve a full bladder. Recall what I told you about decorticate rats and hydranencephalic children: they register feelings of hunger, thirst, and separation distress, and so on, *and behave accordingly*. To do otherwise proves fatal.

Feelings make creatures like us do something *necessary*. In that sense, they are measures of demands for work. With air hunger, the required work must rebalance your blood gases. With hypothermia, the work must return us to a viable temperature range. With separation distress, it must reunite us with a caregiver and so on. In the jargon of computational neuroscience, as mentioned earlier, blood-gas imbalances, temperature undershoots, missing caregivers and approaching predators are 'error signals,' and the actions they give rise to are meant to *correct* the errors. The resolution of affect through something like satiation means that an error has been successfully corrected, whereafter it disappears from the radar of consciousness. This is 'Nirvana.'

Now you see how closely affects are tied to drives; they are their subjective manifestation. Affects are *how we become aware of our drives*; they tell us how well or badly things are going in relation to the specific needs they measure.

This is what affects are for: they convey *which* biological things are going well or badly for us, and they arouse us to do something about them. In this respect, affects are very different from perceptions. John Locke was exercised by the possibility of what is nowadays called 'qualia inversion.' How do I know that the red I see is the same as the red you see? Mightn't my red look blue to you? The problem of other minds suggests that we can never know, because you and I would both point to the same objects in the world and call them 'red.' But what is true of visual perception is not true of affective experience. Redness does not *cause* anything different from blueness, so you can arbitrarily swap them around without any physical consequences. The same does not apply to feelings like hunger in relation to urinary urgency, or fear in relation to separation distress. For example, one feeling (fear) impels you to escape something; another one (separation distress) impels you to search for someone. The feeling is inextricable from the bodily state it entrains.[7] If you swapped them around, you would feel an irresistible urge to escape from a missing caregiver and you would tearfully search for a stalking predator. If you swapped subjective redness with blueness, there would be no consequences, but if you swapped the feeling of fear with separation distress (or hunger with urinary urgency), it would kill you.

The second thing to notice about feelings is that *it makes a difference whether a need is felt or not.* Not all homeostatic need-regulating mechanisms are conscious. Your water-to-salt ratio may be sliding all the time, in the background, but when you feel it, you want to drink. You might objectively be in danger without noticing it, but when you feel it, you look for ways to escape.

Different things call for different names, and the difference between felt and unfelt needs makes it necessary to introduce a terminological distinction: 'needs' are different from 'affects.' Bodily needs can be registered and regulated *autonomically*, as in the examples of cardiovascular and respiratory control, thermoregulation and glucose metabolism. These are called 'vegetative' functions, and with a good reason: there is nothing conscious about them. Hence, the term autonomic 'reflex.' Consciousness enters the equation only when needs are felt. This is when they make demands on *you* for work. Please note: drives measure demands made upon *the mind* for work; some needs never arouse voluntary action and therefore never become conscious. Blood pressure is a clinically notorious example; you know nothing about the under and overshoots until it is too late.

Emotional needs, too, can be managed automatically, by means of behavioural stereotypes such as 'instincts' (inborn survival and reproductive strategies, which Freud equated with 'primal phantasies' and placed at the centre of his conception of the unconscious [see endnote 5]). But emotional needs are more difficult to satisfy than bodily ones, because they involve other mental *agents* with needs of their own, not mere *substances* like food and drink. That is why emotional feelings are typically more sustained than bodily ones. A feeling disappears from consciousness only when the need it announces has been met.

The third thing to notice about feelings is that felt needs are *prioritised* over unfelt ones. We are constantly beset by *multiple* needs. Vegetative functions like energy balance, respiratory control, digestion, thermoregulation and the like are going on constantly; and so are stereotyped behaviours of various kinds. You could not possibly feel all these things simultaneously, not least because you can only *do* one thing (or very few things) at a time. A selection must be made. This is done on a *contextual* basis. Priorities are determined by the *relative* strengths of your needs (the size of the error signals) *in relation to* the range of opportunities afforded by your current circumstances. Here is a simple example. While giving a two-hour lecture, my bladder gradually distends, but I do not feel the increasing pressure until the lecture is over, at which point I suddenly need to pee. I *become aware* of the error signal because of the contextual change. At that point, sensing the opportunity, my bodily need becomes conscious as a feeling. (Urologists call this situation 'latch-key urgency.')

Prioritising needs in this way has major consequences. The most important one is that when you become aware of a need (when it is felt), *it governs your voluntary behaviour.*

What does 'voluntary' mean? It means the opposite of 'automatic.' It means subject to here-and-now *choices.* Choices can be made only if they are grounded in a value system – the thing that determines 'goodness' versus 'badness.' Otherwise, your responses to unfamiliar events would be random. This brings us full circle, back to the most fundamental feature of affect: its valence. You decide what to do and what not to do on the basis of *the felt consequences of your actions.*

Voluntary behaviour, guided by affect, bestows an enormous adaptive advantage over involuntary behaviour: it liberates us from the shackles of automaticity and enables us to survive in unpredicted situations. This is the mechanistic function of feeling.

The fact that voluntary behaviour must be conscious reveals the deepest biological function of feeling: it guides our behaviour in conditions of *uncertainty.* It enables us to determine in the heat of the moment whether one course of action is better or worse than another. In the example of air hunger, the regulation of your blood gases becomes conscious when you don't have a ready-made solution to maintain your physiologically viable bounds. In your rush to escape from the carbon-dioxide-filled room, for instance, how do you know where to turn? You have never been in this situation before (in any burning building, let alone this specific one) so you cannot possibly predict what to do. Now you must decide whether to go this way or that, up or down, and so on. You make such decisions by *feeling your way through the problem*: the feeling of suffocation waxes or wanes, depending upon whether you are going the right way or not – that is, depending upon whether the availability of oxygen increases or decreases. The same applies to emotional choices. Consciousness is *felt uncertainty*.

The conscious feeling of suffocation alarm involves different neural structures and chemicals from those responsible for unconscious respiratory control, just as the feeling of hunger recruits different brain systems from those responsible for autonomic regulation of energy balance. Science would never have discovered these things if it had continued to ignore feelings.

There is still a lot more to be said about feelings, such as how they enable *learning from experience* and how they relate to thinking, but the points I have just made, in a nutshell, explain *why* we feel. I have described what feeling adds to the repertoire of non-conscious mechanisms we living creatures use to stay alive and reproduce. This is what psychology contributes to biology. Natural selection determined these survival mechanisms, but once feelings evolved – that is, the unique ability we have as complex organisms to *register our own states* – something utterly new appeared in the universe: subjective experience.

These facts, in my opinion, answer the questions: Why is the performance of these functions accompanied by experience? Why doesn't all this information-processing go on 'in the dark,' free of any inner feel?

In his (1995) article, Chalmers wrote the following:

> This is not to say that experience *has* no function. Perhaps it will turn out to play an important cognitive role. But for any role it might play, there will be more to the explanation of experience than a simple explanation of the function. Perhaps it will even turn out that in the course of explaining a function, we will be led to the key insight that allows an explanation of experience. If this

happens, though, the discovery will be an *extra* explanatory reward. There is no cognitive function such that we can say in advance that explanation of that function will *automatically* explain experience. (pp. 203–4)

Note his word 'cognitive.' Could he have said such things if he had been talking about affective functions rather than cognitive ones? I can say in advance that explanation of the function of feeling will automatically explain experience. I do not see how an adequate scientific account of it can fail to do so.

The Relationship Between Affect and Cognition

To recap, why affects are generated is that they respond to endogenous demands made upon the mind to perform work. In this section, I argue that conscious cognition performs the mental work so demanded.

We have seen that drive demands arise from a multiplicity of 'error' signals which converge on the core of the brainstem. Most such signals are dealt with automatically and unconsciously; they demand consciousness only in situations where stereotyped responses cannot suffice. Where does this seemingly magical shift from automatic reflex (need) to volitional feeling (affect) occur?

The shift depends upon the integrity of a small, tightly packed knot of neurons surrounding the central canal of the midbrain, – the *periaqueductal grey* (PAG). This is where *all* the brain's homeostatic circuitry converges (see Figures 7.3 and 7.4). In this sense, the PAG can be described as the brain's 'meta-homeostat.'

We have seen what happens when the reticular activating system is damaged: coma. Damage to the PAG has a somewhat different effect:

Early studies in which lesioning electrodes were threaded from the fourth ventricle up the aqueduct to the caudal edge of the diencephalon yielded striking deficits in consciousness in cats and monkeys as operationalized by their *failure to exhibit any apparent intentional behavior* and their *global lack of responsivity to emotional stimuli*. While forms of damage to any other higher areas of the brain can damage the [cognitive] 'tools of consciousness', they typically do not impair the foundation of intentionality itself. PAG lesions do this with the smallest absolute destruction of brain tissue.

(Panksepp, 1998, my emphasis)

The state just described is not a 'coma' but rather a 'vegetative state' (the state that we would have expected in decorticate animals and hyndranencephalic children if the cortical theory of consciousness were correct). The main difference between the vegetative state and coma is the preservation of wakefulness. But the circadian sleep/wake cycle is just another autonomic function. That is why the vegetative state is also called '*unresponsive* wakefulness' – an apparent oxymoron which reveals the critical distinction between (vegetative) wakefulness and (affective) arousal – what Panksepp called 'intentionality' in the aforementioned quotation. Intentionality enables *voluntary action*. This is what the PAG adds to vegetative functioning.

How does it do this? The PAG is the final common path to affective output. Since all residual homeostatic error signals converge upon it at the end of each action cycle, the PAG must 'choose' what to do next. It does so by segueing the residual error signals that are relayed to it, with each error signal communicating its component need, and then *setting priorities* for the next action sequence. The gaggle of need-conveying error signals arriving at the PAG cannot all be felt at once, because you cannot *do* everything at once. This, then, is the nub of its prioritisation function: which of these error signals is the most salient, given current circumstances? *Which of my needs can be deferred (or handled automatically) and which must I feel my way through?*

These priorities cannot be determined by needs alone. Needs must be *contextualised* not only by each other but also by the prevailing opportunities.

Take the example of respiratory control, described previously. Consider first the inner context: if I register suffocation alarm and thirst at the same time, the suffocation alarm must be prioritised over the thirst, but thirst in comparison to sadness, say, might take priority. Secondly consider the outer context: if I experience suffocation alarm, the context will tell me whether I need – for example – to remove an airway obstruction or get out of a carbon-dioxide filled room. The outside context in which I am acting stays relevant as the events unfold and I decide over and again what to do next.

The requirement that current circumstances must be taken into account naturally requires some further apparatus. The PAG renders its verdict with the help of an adjacent midbrain structure, known as the *superior colliculi* (see Figures 7.3 and 7.4). This is located immediately behind the PAG and is divided into several layers, each of which provide simple mappings of the body's external surfaces. The deeper layers supply motor maps of the body, while the superficial layers are responsible for spatial-sensory ones. Together they assemble a massively compressed and integrated representation of the exteroceptive world, arriving partly from the cortex but also from subcortical sensory-motor regions such as the optic nerve (see Figure 7.3). The superior colliculi thus represent in distilled form the moment-by-moment state of the *external* (sensory and motor) body, in much the same way as the PAG monitors its *internal* (need) state. Merker (2007) calls this affective/sensory/motor interface between the PAG, the superior colliculi and the midbrain locomotor region the midbrain's 'decision triangle.' Panksepp (1998) called it the primal SELF, the very source of our sentient being.

Midbrain decisions about what to do next are therefore based upon feedback from the brain's homeostatic need circuits *together with* its sensory-motor maps, each of which updates us on different aspects of 'where things stand now.' Recall my example of suddenly becoming aware of my need to urinate at the end of a lecture. At that point, sensing the opportunity, my bodily need was felt and it became a volitional *drive*. In short, because the midbrain decision triangle takes both internal and external conditions into account, it prioritises behavioural options on the basis not only of current needs but also of current opportunities.

As mentioned in endnote 5, however, brainstem sensory-motor processing is entirely *unconscious*. The superior colliculi contain only a representation of the direction of target deviation – the target being the focus of each action cycle – producing gaze, attention and action orientation. White et al. (2017) call this a 'saliency' or 'priority' map.

Conscious perception of the world around us becomes possible only with the help of *suitably activated* cortex, which is what hydranencephalic children and decorticate animals lack. The superior colliculi provide condensed here-and-now mappings of potential targets, but the cortex provides in addition the detailed 'representations' that we use to guide each action sequence as it unfolds. Alongside these highly differentiated representations, there are in the subcortical forebrain many *unconscious* action programmes, which neuroscientists call non-declarative 'procedures' and 'responses.' These are encoded primarily in the *subcortical* basal ganglia, amygdala and cerebellum.

Memories are not mere records of the past. Biologically speaking, they are *about* the past but they are *for* the future. They are, all of them, in their essence, *predictions* aimed at meeting our needs.

The motor tendencies that are activated through midbrain affect-selection release simple reflexes and instincts – and that is all they do in babies, hydranencephalic children and many animals. But such automatic behaviours are brought under individualised control during development, through *learning from experience*. Stereotyped (id) responses are thereby supplemented by a more flexible repertoire of (ego) options. The behavioural sequence arising with each new action cycle unfolds upwards over these progressively expanding levels of forebrain control, from procedural 'responses' to representational 'memory images.' This generates what Merker (2007, p. 72) calls a 'fully articulated, panoramic, three-dimensional world composed of shaped solid objects: the world of our familiar phenomenal experience.'

Recall that long-term memories serve the future. Once the midbrain decision triangle has evaluated the compressed feedback flowing in from each previous action, what it activates is an expanded *feedforward* process which unfolds in the reverse direction, through the forebrain's memory systems, generating an *expected context* for the selected motor sequence. This is the product of all our learning. In other words, when a need propels us into the world, *we do not discover that world afresh with each new cycle*. It activates a set of predictions about the likely sensory consequences of our actions, based upon our past experience of how to meet the selected need in the prevailing circumstances.

Voluntary action then entails a process of testing our *expectations* against the *actual* consequences of our actions. (This is what Freud called 'reality testing.') The comparison produces an error signal, which we use to reassess our expectations as we go along, and adjust our action plans accordingly. This is what 'voluntary' behaviour is all about: deciding what to do in conditions of uncertainty, mediated by the consequences of each action. This involves both affectively felt and perceptually sensed consequences, which is why both affective and sensory-motor residual error signals converge on the midbrain decision triangle. I like Jakob Hohwy's (2013) term for the mental process that controls voluntary behaviour: 'predicting the present.'

Most people don't realise that our here-and-now perceptions are constantly guided by predictions, generated unconsciously from long-term memory. But, as every psychoanalyst knows, they are. That is why far fewer neurons propagate signals from the external sense organs to the internal memory systems than the other way around. For example, the ratio of incoming connections to outgoing ones in the lateral geniculate body (which relays information from the eyes to the visual cortex and vice-versa; see Figure 7.3) is about 1:10. The heavy lifting is done by the predictive signals that *meet* the sensory ones arriving from the periphery. This saves an enormous amount of information processing and therefore metabolic work. Considering that the brain consumes about 20 per cent of our total energy supplies, this is a valuable efficiency. Why treat everything in the world as if you'd never encountered it before? Instead, what the brain does is propagate inwards only that portion of the incoming information which does *not* match its expectations. That is why perception is nowadays sometimes described *by neuroscientists* as 'fantasy' and 'controlled hallucination'; it begins with an *expected* scenario which is then adjusted to accommodate the incoming signal (Hohwy, 2013; Clark, 2015).

We know by now that the fundamental form of consciousness is affect, which enables us to 'feel' our way through unpredicted situations. But how does affect become conscious external perception?

Panksepp (1998) suggests that an evolutionary bridge between these two aspects of experience was forged by what he called 'sensory affects' (e.g., pain, disgust and surprise). 'Sensory affects' are simultaneously internal feelings *and* external perceptions; they are inherently valenced perceptions qualified by specific feelings. So, pain feels different from disgust, and you respond to them differently, withdrawing or retching, depending on which one you have. Over this evolutionary bridge, in Panksepp's view, internal consciousness became extended onto external perception, since it contextualises affect. After all, the external world acquires value for us only because we must meet our internal needs there; it acquires value *in relation to affect.*

So, my answer to the question as to why perception and cognition are ever felt at all is that *they are felt because they contextualise affect.* It's as if our perceptual experience says: 'I feel like this *about that.*' Perception is, as it were, *applied* uncertainty, which we use to feel our way through cognitive problems. (Recall that choices must be based in a value system.) This makes it reasonable to conclude that affective and perceptual consciousness utilise a common currency; they are different *kinds* of feeling, but they are feelings nonetheless. It is a small step further to infer that our five modalities of perceptual consciousness (sight, hearing, touch, taste and smell) evolved to qualify the different categories of external information that are registered by our sense organs, just as the qualities of affective consciousness qualify the different categories of emotional need.

But it is important to recall also that cortical perception involves *prediction.* What appear in consciousness are not the raw sensory signals transmitted from the periphery, but rather *inferences* derived from memory traces of previous such signals and their consequences. The fact that feeling is spread, as it were, over stabilised cortical inferences, to create what I call 'mental solids' (Solms, 2013) – the external world as it manifests in perception and cognition – accounts for the different phenomenal qualities of affective versus cognitive consciousness. Cognition *binds* affect. This is the basis of Freud's 'secondary process.' Secondary process (what neuroscientists call 'working memory') involves *delay*, which can also be dangerous. Hence, the imperative to automatise our predictions as much as possible.

Our predictive model is the map we use to navigate the world – indeed to *generate* an expected world. But we can't take all our predictions at face value. There are in fact two aspects to the 'expected context' that the internal model generates: on the one hand we have the actual content of our predictions, and on the other is our *level of confidence* about their accuracy. Since all predictions are probabilistic, the degree of *expected uncertainty* attaching to them must also be coded. The predictions themselves are furnished by the forebrain's long-term memory networks, which filter the present through the lens of the past. But the second dimension – the adjustment of confidence levels – is the essence of the work that is performed by the reticular activating system.

Adjusting confidence levels just means adjusting signal strengths. That's what the reticular activating system does: it sets signal strengths. Baseline strengths represent the *expected* context. However, as the actual (experienced) context unfolds, these 'precision weightings' (as they are called) must be adjusted. This is the mechanistic basis of *voluntary* action. It follows that increased confidence in an error signal necessarily implies decreased confidence in the prediction which led to the error. That is what happens in the midbrain decision triangle: the competing claims are assessed and a winner is declared. The outcome of this process is conveyed to the forebrain by the reticular activating system, which acts on the basis of your expectations and then – as the selected action unfolds – releases clouds of neuromodulators to fine tune the signals in your long-term memory networks, up-regulating the forebrain channels in which some predictions are stored and down-regulating others. This, in turn, leads to learning from experience. In this way, we keep improving our generative model of the world, by trial and error.

A clinical example is psychosis, which, in its essence, involves excessive confidence in predictions over errors.

Everything we do in the realm of uncertainty is guided by these fluctuating confidence levels. We think we know what will happen if we act in a certain way, but do we really? If our conviction drops below a certain threshold, we won't act, or we'll change tack. In the exteroceptive sphere, things are going well when they turn out as expected, and badly when uncertainty prevails. Accordingly, in conscious cognition: increasing confidence (in a prediction) is good, decreasing confidence is bad. So, we try to minimise uncertainty in our expectations.

Thus, perception and action are an ongoing process of *hypothesis-testing*, in which the brain constantly tries to suppress error signals and confirm its hypotheses. (Experimental science itself is just a systematised version of this everyday process: 'if hypothesis X is correct, then Y should happen when I do Z.') The more your hypotheses are confirmed, the more confident you are, and the less aroused – less cognitively conscious – you need to be. You can automatise your action sequences and drift off into default mode. But if you find yourself in an unexpected situation – one in which your predictive model appears to shed no reliable light – the consequences of your actions become highly salient. You switch out of autopilot and become hyper-aware: the decision triangle carefully adjusts your predictions as you feel your way through the consequences of your actions and make new choices.

Thinking entails the same process, in the *virtual* reality of imagination. (This is what Freud called 'experimental action.') It saves lives.

Feeling remains the common factor in all consciousness, both affective and cognitive. Its function is to evaluate the success or failure of our action programmes in their associated contexts, both real and imaginary.

Conclusion

That, on a mechanistic level, is how consciousness works. My account of it might not seem altogether satisfying. This is mainly because it is highly condensed; this topic really requires a book-length treatment (see Solms, 2021). Nevertheless, I hope you will agree that Freud's theoretical notion (that affect – registering 'oscillations in the tension of drive needs' – is the fundamental form of consciousness, and that cognition is mainly unconscious, except in situations of uncertainty) casts new light on Chalmers's hard problem and make it a little less hard. I, for one, believe that Freud's insight takes us some considerable distance towards answering the question: why (and how) is there something it is like to *be* an organism – something it is like *for* the organism? But recall that I promised only 'a clue.'

Notes

1   This chapter is based on an oral presentation to an Applied Section meeting of the British Psychoanalytical Society on January 14, 2021. It draws heavily upon Solms (2021) and paraphrases it in places. Readers interested in the deeper mechanistic details, especially as they relate to Freudian metapsychology, should consult Solms (2019, 2020, in press).
2   We submitted our paper to the *JCS* for the reason that that is where Chalmers (1995) published his original paper.

3 What does Chalmers mean by 'function'? He means this: 'Here "function" is not used in the narrow teleological sense of something that a system is designed to do, but in the broader sense of any causal role in the production of behaviour that a system might perform' (1995, p. 202–3).
4 I say 'something like' because I have simplified it here.
5 In case readers wonder how this can happen, I should point out that sensory information is transmitted from the eyes (and skin, etc.) directly to the brainstem, by-passing the cortex. This information is processed unconsciously, but it evokes an *affectively* conscious response. (See Figure 7.3)
6 In the *Revised Standard Edition*, I translate Freud's term *Trieb* as *drive* rather than *instinct*. Since the *RSE* has not yet appeared, however, I am retaining the *SE* pagination in my references.
7 For example, fear entrains rapid breathing, increased heart rate, redirection of blood from the gut to the skeletal musculature and, thereby, tonic alertness and readiness for escape. If the feeling of fear entrained slow breathing, reduced heart rate, redirection of blood from the skeletal musculature to the gut and, thereby, sluggish repose, *it would not be fear*. The embodied nature of affects is evident from whole-body thermal scans of the different emotions (see Nummenmaa et al., 2018). See also Niedenthal (2007).

References

Bargh, J. and Chartrand, T. (1999). The unbearable automaticity of being. *American Psychologist*, 54: 462–479.

Blomstedt, P., Hariz, M., Lees, A. et al. (2008). Acute severe depression induced by intraoperative stimulation of the substantia nigra: a case report. *Parkinsonism and Related Disorders*, 14: 253–256.

Chalmers, D. (1995). Facing up to the problem of consciousness. *Journal of Consciousness Studies*, 2: 200–219.

Clark, A. (2015). *Surfing Uncertainty: Prediction, Action, and the Embodied Mind*. New York: Oxford University Press.

Coenen, A. (2007). Consciousness without a cortex, but what kind of consciousness is this?. *Behavioral and Brain Sciences*, 30: 87–88.

Crick, F. (1994). *The Astonishing Hypothesis: The Scientific Search for the Soul*. New York: Charles Scribner's Sons.

Damasio, A. (1999). Commentary to J. Panksepp: Emotions as viewed by psychoanalysis and neuroscience. *Neuropsychoanalysis*, 1: 38–39.

Damasio, A. and Carvalho, G. (2013). The nature of feelings: evolutionary and neurobiological origins. *Nature Reviews Neuroscience*, 14: 143–152.

Damasio, A., Grabowski, T., Bechara, A. et al. (2000). Subcortical and cortical brain activity during the feeling of self-generated emotions. *Nature Neuroscience*, 3: 1049–1056.

Davies, P. (2019). *The Demon in the Machine: How Hidden Webs of Information are Solving the Mystery of Life*. London: Allen Lane.

Fischer, D., Boes, A., Demertzi, A. et al. (2016). A human brain network derived from coma-causing brainstem lesions. *Neurology*, 87: 2427–2434.

Freud, S. (1894). The neuro-psychoses of defence. *Standard Edition of the Complete Psychological Works of Sigmund Freud*, 3. London: Hogarth, pp. 45–61.

Freud, S. (1911). Formulations on the two principles of mental functioning. *Standard Edition of the Complete Psychological Works of Sigmund Freud*, 12. London: Hogarth, pp. 218–226.

Freud, S. (1915a). The unconscious. *Standard Edition of the Complete Psychological Works of Sigmund Freud*, 14. London: Hogarth, pp. 166–204.

Freud, S. (1915b). Instincts and their vicissitudes. *Standard Edition of the Complete Psychological Works of Sigmund Freud*, 14. London: Hogarth, pp. 117–140.

Freud, S. (1940). An outline of psycho-analysis. *Standard Edition of the Complete Psychological Works of Sigmund Freud*, 23. London: Hogarth, pp. 144–207.

Havlík, M., Kozáková, E. and Horáče, J. (2017). Why and how: the future of the central questions of consciousness. *Frontiers in Psychology*, 8: 1797, 10.3389/fpsyg.2017.01797.

Hohwy, J. (2013). *The Predictive Mind*. New York: Oxford University Press.

Holstege, G., Georgiadis, J., Paans, A. et al. (2003). Brain activation during human male ejaculation. *Journal of Neuroscience*, 23: 9185–9193.

Jackson, F. (1982). Epiphenomenal qualia. *Philosophical Quarterly*, 32: 127–136.

Kihlstrom, J. (1996). Perception without awareness of what is perceived, learning without awareness of what is learned. In M. Velmans (ed.), *The Science of Consciousness: Psychological, Neuropsychological and Clinical Reviews*. London: Routledge, pp. 23–46.

McKeever, W. (1986). Tachistoscopic methods in neuropsychology. In H. J. Hannay (ed.), *Experimental Techniques in Human Neuropsychology*. Oxford: Oxford University Press, pp. 167–211.

Merker, B. (2007). Consciousness without cerebral cortex: a challenge for neuroscience and medicine. *Behavioral and Brain Sciences*, 30: 63–68.

Moruzzi, G. and Magoun, H. (1949). Brain stem reticular formation and activation of the EEG. *Electroencephalography and Clinical Neurophysiology*, 1: 455–473.

Nagel, T. (1974). What is it like to be a bat? *Philosophical Review*, 83: 435–450.

Niedenthal, P. (2007). Embodying emotion. *Science*, 316: 1002–1005.

Nummenmaa, L., Hari, R., Hietanen, J. and Glerean, E. (2018). Maps of subjective feelings. *Proceedings of the National Academy of Sciences USA*, 115: 9198–9203.

Panksepp, J. (1998). *Affective Neuroscience: The Foundations of Human and Animal Emotions*. New York: Oxford University Press.

Shewmon, D., Holmes, G. and Byrne, P. (1999). Consciousness in congenitally decorticate children: developmental vegetative state as self-fulfilling prophecy. *Developmental Medicine and Child Neurology*, 41: 364–374.

Solms, M. (1997). What is consciousness? *Journal of the American Psychoanalytic Association*, 45: 681–778.

Solms, M. (2013). The conscious id. *Neuropsychoanalysis*, 14: 5–85.

Solms, M. (2019). The hard problem of consciousness and the Free Energy Principle. *Frontiers in Psychology*, 10: 2714, 10.3389/fpsyg.2018.02714.

Solms, M. (2020). New project for a scientific psychology: general scheme. *Neuropsychoanalysis*, 22: 10.1080/15294145.2020.1833361.

Solms, M. (2021). *The Hidden Spring: A Journey to the Source of Consciousness*. London: Profile Books.

Solms, M. (in press) Revision of drive theory. *Journal of the American Psychoanalytic Association*.

Solms, M. and Friston, K. (2018). How and why consciousness arises: some considerations from physics and physiology. *Journal of Consciousness Studies*, 25: 202–238.

Strachey, J. (1962). The emergence of Freud's fundamental hypotheses. *Standard Edition of the Complete Psychological Works of Sigmund Freud*, 3. London: Hogarth, pp. 62–68.

White, B., Berg, D., Kan, J. et al. (2017). Superior colliculus neurons encode a visual saliency map during free viewing of natural dynamic video. *Nature Communications*, 8: 14263, 10.1038/ncomms14263.

Zeman, A. (2001). Consciousness. *Brain*, 124: 1263–1289.

Chapter 8

Mentalizing from/to/with the Body

Elliot Jurist

In attributing primacy to sexuality in human life, Freud challenged the valorization of the rational mind that is central to modern Western philosophy, and thus could never be fairly accused of valuing the mental at the expense of the physical. Yet, over time, psychoanalysts, from the Upper West Side to Santa Monica, have drifted to become comfortable with normative, cultural assumptions about the superiority of "saying it in words" over "feeling it in the body."

Psychoanalysis has never been *not* about the body: as long as the unconscious and primary process are recognized and figure into the work, the physical realm intersects with, and is not excluded from the mental realm. Nevertheless, we have arrived at a moment when renewed attention is being given to the body and the mind/body relation (all the more so, as we endure the pandemic). Balsam (2019) offers a synopsis of our vexed history, with an acknowledgment of how confusing it remains to fathom psychoanalysts' current perspective on the body. Across several articles, Ricardo Lombardi (2018, 2019, 2020) raises the pressing question of "whatever happened to the body in psychoanalysis" and encourages us to observe patients' transferences to their own bodies and to help them to realize their capacity for bodily concern. Hartung and Steinbrecher (2018) propose the term "somatophilic" to capture the aim of helping patients to tune into their bodies.

A recent issue (first issue, 2019) of the *Journal of the American Psychoanalytic Association* was devoted to new perspectives on the body, and, in particular, stresses how new expressions of sexuality and gender must be recognized and addressed in psychoanalysis.

DOI: 10.4324/9781003090755-9

Lemma (2010, 2014) has led the way for the re-incorporation of the body in psychoanalysts, discussing cases of body modification, ranging across sexual reassignment surgery, breast augmentation/reduction, cosmetic surgery, self-mutilation, necro-philic fantasies, and more humdrum kinds of self-expression like piercing and tattooing. Encountering such phenomena in our practices has become frequent. In her most recent work, Lemma (2020) draws attention to a class of patients who are unattuned to their bodies and proposes that a way to advance work with such patients is often through analysts' attending to their own bodily states (also see Novack [2016] for an example, where a therapist utilizes her own bodily responses as a way to reach a patient with an feeding disorder who both denies and is obsessed with her body).

In an article in *Psychoanalytic Dialogues,* Levit (2018a) introduces a body-oriented treatment approach, "somatic experiencing," which he sees as opening up a case that was stalled, as the patient retreated into unreachable, dysregulated states. The patient is a woman struggling in her relationship with her husband and in her work life. She has a dramatic trauma history (a victim of a vicious sexual attack), and her as well as having a father who was quite punitive and both parents who failed to notice her anxiety. Levit encourages the patient to be aware of her body states in session, which helps her to stay with her emotions, and eventually to be able to place the memory of the trauma in the background. Based on this experience, Levit advocates a rapprochement between psychoanalysis and body-oriented treatment; more specifically, he proposes an "interweaving" of the two that stops short of the potential for integration.

Levit's article elicited an array of responses from the commentators, many of whom expressed concern about reading the body too literally and simplistically, and thus naively underestimating the complexity that a psychoanalytic approach demands. For example, Lombardi (2018) is critical of Levit's claim that somatic experiencing and psychoanalysis are compatible, asserting that what transpires in his case is merely that the patient becomes modulated, and also rejecting the facile use of neuroscientific language about allegedly eliciting changes in the brain. Ultimately, Lombardi discerns the absence of a mind/body dialogue between the analyst and patient that defines psychoanalysis.

In Levit's response to the commentary, he acknowledges that he did not focus enough on the transference, but he defends his effort to help the patient to work through her trauma as closer to the way that Lombardi works than Lombardi avers. While I believe that we ought to be open-minded and learn from body-oriented treatments, and I concur that asking patients to dwell on the specifics of bodily feelings can be productive, we need to be cautious not to construe body states in too literal a way (as the ultimate source of true emotions) and appreciate that they can be symbolic (that is, require interpretation and reinterpretation). To put the point somewhat ironically, it would be salutary for advocates of somatic experiencing to grapple with cases where their technique fails to be productive or even results in distortion or misreading. In the context of discussing mentalization, I will return to the question of how a more circumspect approach to neuroscience might inform our thinking about the mind/body relation.

There are multifarious ways of construing the mind/body relation in psychoanalysis. Tensions remain between views that promote the body as speaking in a literal way and those who wish to construe the body more symbolically. There also remains tension between approaches that value the body as a source of pleasure and meaning and those who focus mainly on the body as suffering and as a displacement of the mental. Perhaps, there is a dawning recognition across the differences that the body provides meaningful information that is desirable to process, and that it is too limiting to regard it merely as the repository for unwanted mental phenomena.

§ 1

In this chapter, I shall focus on a particular aspect of psychoanalytic theory and practice: mentalization and its current evolution which has become more concerned with the body. I describe my research on mentalized affectivity, a form of emotion regulation, which integrates cognition and emotion and sees autobiographical memory as playing a crucial role in the process. I then turn to discuss how this work has led my research group in the direction of heeding cultural differences having to do with positive emotions, expressing emotions, and somatization. Psychoanalysis can be understood as an effort to disentangle Western culture from the legacy of dualism; however, I shall argue that we ought to become more open to exploring cultural differences and register awareness of how the mind/body relation varies across cultures.

It is important to appreciate that mentalization was introduced as a term that had a close connection to the body. French psychosomatic thinkers in the 1950s described patients who chronically "dementalize," that is, rid themselves of feelings by attributing them to the body. Such patients are devoid of a fantasy life, tend to have impoverished relationship with others, and present with dulled affect. This perspective construed mentalizing as constituted by an awareness of and responsiveness to the body. Its foundation can be located in drives and emotions, and it primarily concerns an individual's relation to him/herself. This original connotation of the term has been obscured through its adoption in theory of mind and cognitive psychology.

Mentalization as a term became better known when it was embraced by psychologists in the 1970s. Influenced by philosophers who were intrigued by the problem of knowing other minds, psychologists undertook experiments about theory of mind, focusing on how we determine what others know in relation to what we know. So-called false-belief experiments, replicated many times, seemed to indicate that children over three to four years old were able to detect that someone held a false belief, based on inadequate knowledge, in contrast to themselves (who witnessed a change, when the confederate was out of the room). Children under that age failed to be able to discern that what they knew differed from what the confederate knew. Locating a shift from a more naïve to a more sophisticated theory of mind became widely accepted as a demarcation point. Yet, over time these experiments have been challenged, with the introduction of other experimental paradigms that do not rely on the use of language, resulting in debates about at what point mentalizing capacities first manifest themselves, and greater openness to the idea that such capacities might begin earlier in development. The source of mentalization remains controversial and need not concern us here. What is crucial to discern is the way that mentalizing migrated to be more cognitive, and also came to be presumed to be, generally speaking, accurate.

The originality of Fonagy and colleagues' work (2002) has been to bring these disparate aspects of mentalization together. In claiming it as a developmental construct, we understand that children mentalize when their caregivers mentalize about them, an affirmation of psychoanalytic and attachment theory. It adds an intersubjective aspect to the intrapsychic focus of the French psychosomatic perspective.[1] In this new account, mentalization can be about the self or about others; it is both cognitive and affective; and it can fluctuate and thus be a central factor in understanding psychopathology, especially severe personality disorders. Over time, mentalization theory has become rooted in social communication, focusing on epistemic trust and vigilance, capacities to depend upon learning from others and then eventually becoming able to weigh the value of that information (Jurist, 2018).

Mentalization Based Therapy has been developed as an evidence-based treatment approach, which, along with Kernberg's Transference Focused Psychotherapy, is contributing to keeping psychoanalysis represented in the larger realm of mental health. Some psychoanalysts have enthusiastically received mentalization theory and practice; others feel that it is a departure from psychoanalysis: that it minimizes the unconscious, that it is too cognitive, and that it ignores the body. In talks I have given, I regularly encounter the concern from psychoanalysts that while mentalization adds something valuable to our understanding of treatment, it also threatens to interfere with the challenge of working on a deeper level, like with dreams.

§ 2

Mentalization theory and practice has returned to focus on the body with the use of the term "embodied mentalization," borrowed, it would seem, from the literature on "embodied cognition" in theory of mind. Fonagy and Target (2007) took up the term "embodied cognition" as part of an argument that attachment theory has relied on a model of information processing, wherein the mind was the software run on the hardware of the brain, which has now been superseded by a model that acknowledges introspection and emotions, and utilizes ecological and new technological methods. The new "embodied cognition" model of cognitive science fits well, in Fonagy and Target's argument, with psychoanalysis, and thus represents a promising path to integrate attachment theory and mentalization theory. Although embodied cognition signifies a renewed interest in focusing on the body, the authors did not yet use the term "embodied mentalization."

Early uses of the term occurred in 2012 in Skärdeud and Fonagy's chapter on eating disorders in Bateman and Fonagy's edited volume (2012). In the glossary to this book, a definition of embodied mentalization is provided: "in which the body is used to fill in moments of mentalizing failure. The term is elaborated to cover mental states related to a person's physical being, including perceptions and cognitions about bodily function and sensorimotor perception" (p. 513). In the same year, Luyten and Van Houdenhove (2012) succinctly characterize embodied mentalization as "the ability to link bodily to mental states" (p. 18).

The interest in embodied mentalization coincides with the expansion of mentalization beyond Mentalization Based Therapy (MBT), primarily a treatment for borderline personality disorder, especially with the development of Interpersonal Dynamic Therapy (IDP) as a treatment for functional somatic disorders (FSD). In several articles, Luyten and Fonagy (Luyten & Fonagy, forthcoming; Luyten et al., 2017; Luyten & Fonagy, 2016; Luyten et al., 2012) emphasize a new aspect of embodied mentalizing as referring to the body as the seat of emotions. The deficit and treatment of FSD patients is understood in terms of recovering of mentalization. They draw attention to the attachment issues that often underlie FSD, and which result in reliance on pre-mentalizing modes, that are not adaptive in the long run. In a recent article by Ballespi et al. (2019), a study of adolescents' relation to emotions, mentalization is portrayed as functioning to serve as protection against somatizing.

A valuable perspective on embodied mentalization is offered in Fotopoulou and Tsakiris' *Mentalizing Homeostasis* (2017), where the authors define the term: "as the inferential brain process by which primary sensorimotor and multisensory signals are progressively integrated and schematized to form multiple, predictive models of our embodied states in given environments" (p. 8). They offer a neuroscientific perspective that places a special emphasis on the mind's capacity to be activated apart from online sensory experience (without discounting sensory experience that does come from the external world). What is crucial for embodied mentalization to thrive is interoceptive sensitivity, which fosters a sense of ownership of one's experience. Interoception denotes the perception of the physiological state(s) of the body, which involves things like "temperature, itch, pain, cardiac signals, respiration, hunger, thirst, pleasure from sensual touch, and other bodily feelings relating to homeostasis" (p. 14). In this account, interoception transcends the status of perception of the body from within; it monitors homeostasis.

While Fotopoulou and Tsakiris point to phenomenology as a source of embodied mentalization, where there is a pre-reflective sense of self that comes from the body, they ultimately argue that embodied mentalization is intersubjectively constituted, that is, it comes into being through interaction with other bodies. They wish to affirm how this manifests developmentally (between caregivers and infants), and socially (defined by the physical proximity and interaction among bodies). They do not attempt to differentiate the qualitative difference between attachment and more general social interaction. A hint of how they might address this occurs when they take up the question of interoceptive accuracy: we might presume that caregivers have an advantage in promoting accuracy over general social encounters, based on prior experience. Fotopoulou and Tsakiris' contribution follows other neuroscientific accounts, like Damasio, in challenging dualism by stressing how the brain is constantly monitoring the body and adjusting itself accordingly. Fotopoulou and Tsarkiris build on a developmental account, avoiding the reductionism of accounts that bypass subjective and intersubjective experience. Mentalization is given an early and large purpose in promoting humans to be able to function as individuals and in society. A developmental perspective is emphasized in Shai and Fonagy's (2014) work on "parental embodied mentalizing."

§ 3

It is worth keeping in mind that mentalization is a broad construct—one can mentalize ideas, beliefs, and values, not just emotions; moreover, it occurs in everyday life. My work has focused on the specific aspect of mentalization, mentalizing emotions, which is most germane to psychotherapy. This is fruitful way to ensure that mentalization is connected to the body, as emotions have their source in bodily experience (Critchley & Nagai, 2012). I have introduced the term "mentalized affectivity" to capture the experience of modulating emotions in a way that is mediated by autobiographical memory. In other words, we are best able to regulate emotions though being aware of how emotions were experienced in the past, in one's own, family and cultural history. There is a profound difference between models of emotion regulation in which cognitive appraisal is deemed to be crucial and my psychoanalytic model in which cognition and affect are integrated through the re-experiencing of emotion. This does not imply that we can or should try to regulate all emotions. Built into mentalized affectivity is that it functions retrospectively, and that it comes up against the unconscious, which limits and challenges all of our efforts to make emotions tractable.

Mentalized affectivity fosters better use of emotions. This includes some acceptance of how emotions can be confusing and difficult to identify. People frequently report what can be termed "aporetic emotions," emotions that are unclear and undifferentiated. The experience of knowing that you feel something but that it is elusive is universal, and ought to be distinguished from the phenomenon of alexithymia, in which there is a chronic inability to recognize emotions. Psychotherapy often entails the effort to render aporetic emotions intelligible and granular. Through mentalized affectivity, one might come to see that anger was not acknowledged in your family of origin; thus, that you tend to underestimate anger, and often end up becoming too angry because there is no room for anger to be expressed and communicated. Improving mentalized affectivity can allow us to have a wider palette of emotions, and to become more adept to shaping our emotions to exist in a way that fits what we deem to be appropriate. We become more flexible in our responses, in particular, being willing to revise and rethink our feelings in light of our own reflection or feedback from others.

In summary, mentalized affectivity offers an alternative way to conceptualize emotion regulation that is not based on a stimulus-response model of a single individual, where cognitive reappraisal is the crucial strategy. Mentalized affectivity is based on the notion that early childhood experience is formative, that autobiographical influences how anyone responds in the present, and that emotion regulation represents a challenge to utilize cognition without transcending or diminishing affect.

§ 4

So, mentalized affectivity is a form of emotion regulation that is mediated by reflection on one's past history (Jurist, 2018; Jurist, 2005; Fonagy et al., 2002). The Mentalized Affectivity Scale (MAS) was first introduced in Greenberg et al. (2017), and a brief 12-item measure of the MAS has been developed that will be especially useful in both research and clinical contexts. Mentalized affectivity theory posits that regulating an emotion, including managing, altering, or modulating an emotion, is reliant upon the individual's capacity for mentalization. Mentalized affectivity requires that individuals fathom their feelings, and, next, that they consider aspects of past and present that inform their experience of emotions.

Mentalized affectivity theory outlines three delineated aspects that are part of a concentric process of emotion regulation. First is *Identifying* emotions, which involves being curious about emotions, like naming basic emotions, and also involves trying to make sense of emotions in the context of one's personal history and exploring the meaning of emotions (globally or in the moment). Second is *Processing* emotions, which involves modulating, managing and tolerating emotions, including changing an emotion in duration or intensity. It can also involve more fully distinguishing among complex emotions, and, most importantly, it entails the effort to compare one's emotions in relation to one's ideal sense of agency, that is, how one wishes to be able to feel. Third is *Expressing* emotions, which involves the spectrum of communicating one's feelings outwardly, but also inwardly, a capacity that is typically cultivated in psychotherapy, where one allows oneself to fully experience emotions, without necessarily revealing them to others. Taken together, identifying emotions can be regarded as the inception of a sense of agency, while processing emotions entails the exercise of agency in reconciling one's beliefs and actions. Lastly, expressing emotions is a manifestation of agency, although it is important to acknowledge that it is mediated by cultural beliefs (Jurist & Perez Sosa, 2019).

My research team has begun to pursue questions about how culture impacts the expression of emotions. Our first results on the MAS concerning expressing emotions have been inconclusive, and feedback from translators (the MAS has now been translated into 11 languages) strongly suggests that a cultural aspect might be a factor that deserves further consideration. Our ethnocentric bias was to assume that expressing emotions would be construed positively (although we did mark a distinction between expressing emotions outwardly or inwardly). In East Asian cultures, this is not necessarily the case, as there is an expectation that others who are close to you will know what you are feeling, and so needing to come out and to tell them shades into having a negative valence. In a study of emotion regulation, Deng et al. (2019) claim that Chinese subjects value control over expression, and that they regard expression more negatively than European-Americans, using a measure of implicit emotion regulation. A widespread way of understanding this difference is to contrast individualistic cultures, where free expression is valued, with collectivist cultures, where there is a premium placed on preserving and not risking disruption to social harmony.

§ 5

In related research, studies by Ma et al. (2018) maintain that European Americans value positive emotions more highly than Asians: for the latter, positive emotions are regarded as unstable and hence as suspect. In other words, it is prudent to guard against indulging positive emotions, as this is a way to exhibit humility as well as a way to avoid disappointment, given that they are likely to evaporate. The implications are both fascinating and complicated to interpret. Studies of emotions ought to hesitate before the assumption that ideal human agency is defined by the dominance of positive emotion and the diminishing of negative emotions. Positive psychotherapy, in particular, ought to be especially vigilant about operating with an ethnocentric bias that overvalues positive emotions and undervalues negative ones.

In pursuing issues around the expression of emotions, we have delved into the expanding literature on culture, emotions, and the body. There was a literature from the 70s that contrasted Western culture as psychologizing emotions in contrast to East Asian culture in which they are somatized. A considerable body of research has endorsed the notion that Chinese subjects are more likely to describe depression in somatic terms. It is desirable to take account of fundamental differences about how to understand the mind/body relation and to entertain that somatizing can be a normative way to express emotions. Recent work has challenged the contrast between psychologizing and somatizing (Chentsova-Dutton et al., 2019; Kirmayer & Ryder, 2016), as it runs the risk of overgeneralizing, stereotyping, and pathologizing cultural differences. In addition, it has been argued that globalization is a factor that has impacted and mitigated these alleged differences, ushering in a time of "hyperdiversity" (Kirmayer & Ryder, 2016). Hyperdiversity points both to that historical cultural differences are lessening and that new hybrid forms of psychopathology are likely to arise.

Joseph K. So (2008) makes an argument that challenges our intuitive thinking in the West: proposing that somatization, in fact, is a universal phenomenon but is stigmatized due to the dualism that underlies Western bioscience. Laria and Lewis-Fernandez (2001) make a related claim: acknowledging that while somatization can be pathological, and often is a result of trauma, it also can be adaptive in contexts where stress cannot be otherwise resolved, inspiring social support. They discuss "ataque de nervios," where mainly women fall to the ground and enter dissociative states after a stressful event, which is found in some but not all Latinx cultures (in Puerto Rico, but not in Mexico). Such dissociative conduct is accepted and normative. Christian (2018) emphasizes the social and relational aspects of ataque de nervios, recalling that a student who was familiar with ataques responded to the question of whether they ever occur alone, by saying: why would anyone waste an ataque de nervious if she was by herself?

There is, indeed, a growing literature that questions whether somatization must be regarded as maladaptive. Clinically, it seems crucial to educate oneself to make sense of patients' cultural background. Here it is worth stressing that a culturally competent approach does not make inferences based on the external facts of patients' identity. Therapists need to know about patients' understanding of the culture from which they come and their (possibly non-static) relation to it. In a fascinating study, Choi et al. (2016), first asked Korean and American subjects to write distress narratives, using text analysis to assess whether Korean subjects used more somatic words, and second, asked Korean and American subjects to listen to distress narratives from others, hypothesizing that Korean subjects would respond more empathically. The results support the notion that Korean subjects preferred to express emotions through somatizing descriptions over verbalizing them. Not only is somatization an acceptable manner of expression, but also it is advantageous in producing greater empathic responses from others. This study concludes that, for Korean subjects, somatizing emotions is an estimable "communication strategy." The American subjects, on the contrary, preferred verbalizing emotions, so we are left with the impression of a strong contrast between the two cultures. The authors note the relevance of their findings to psychotherapy, where Western therapists can easily misread the somatic expression of emotions by Korean patients. They emphasize that psychotherapy, without attention to culture norms, can be alienating to such patients.

In an older study, Keyes and Ryff (2003) begin by claiming that somatization tends to be comorbid with mental illness in general and depression in particular, and they observe connections between somatizing and defenses like denial, repression, and suppression. Yet, in taking account of culture, Keyes and Ryff raise doubts about regarding somatization as maladaptive per se. They explicate this by exploring the distinction between tight and loose cultures, which strongly overlaps with the distinction between individualistic and collectivist cultures. Tight cultures value indirect expression, whereas loose cultures permit direct. Somatizing, in their account, has a different meaning in tight cultures: it can be "sociogenic." Indeed, they introduce an intriguing idea, that somatization can serve in those cultures as a kind of "sublimation," a psychoanalytic concept, although the authors do not recognize it as such, which engages rather than pushes away emotions.

In referencing various studies of emotions, somatization, and culture, it is our intention to expand the domain of psychoanalysis and psychotherapy to be better prepared and receptive to a wider range of patients. My intention supersedes this aim, though, in encouraging us to be more welcoming to the body, which is not just relevant to cultures in which somatizing has an accepted and valued place. We help patients to become better communicators, whether they tend to somatize or verbalize their feelings. Language is important, of course, although it can be deployed inauthentically or even deceptively. Immediate feelings from the body count, and they should never be ignored; however, the elaboration of their meaning through processing emotions is the most challenging and rewarding part of the work. In the next section, I will spell some of the clinical implications of my perspective.

§ 6

Psychoanalysts are becoming more welcoming to the body in their work with patients. In this chapter, I have proposed that mentalization and mentalized affectivity provide fruitful paths to work with the body, especially when and if we are sensitive to cultural differences. This ought to help psychoanalysts work better with all patients as well as to expand our appeal to a wider range of patients. In urging us in the direction of neuroscience and knowledge about culture, I am advocating a double perspective that is too often juxtaposed in terms of an either/or.

The notion that the purpose of mentalization is to monitor homeostasis implies universality: humans have evolved to have brains that function to know what is going on in one's own body and to be influenced by others' bodies as well. As a product of evolution, mentalization helps both to foster cooperation and to negotiate competition. Yet, improving mentalization, and especially mentalized affectivity, relies on sharpening interoceptive sensitivity and accuracy, and this effort must be mediated by not just those with whom we interact but cultural beliefs and practices as well.

My main argument here is to claim that the path to improving our knowledge about mentalized affectivity depends upon neuroscientific research that leaves room for the realm of subjective experience, as we saw in the case of Fotopoulou's work, and that is open to research about emotions, culture, and somatization, as reviewed in the studies reviewed in the last section. The mentalization literature has been more influenced by psychological science than by the study of culture, although this has started to change. Aival-Naveh et al. (2019) represent a first effort to examine mentalization from a cultural point of view, based on what we have learned about theory of mind, empathy, perspective-taking, alexithymia, and mindfulness. They acknowledge that research on perspective-taking would seem to support that Westerners are better at self-mentalizing and Easterners are better at other-mentalizing, but they also introduce evidence that complicates this. Wu et al. (2013) used a sophisticated time-series analysis, via eye tracking, to show that Chinese subjects initially show an egocentric response, but then suppress this as interference. In other words, it is less that Chinese subjects fail to do something, but that they do the same thing and more than American subjects. The authors thus affirm the complexity of grappling with generalizations about cultural phenomena.

My research team is currently carrying out a qualitative study of interviews with the researchers who have translated the MAS into other languages, seeking to find points of agreement, tension, and differences. Our hope to revise the MAS, thereby, to be a more sensitive clinical instrument. The most challenging aspect of mentalized affectivity is processing, where one attempts to modulate emotions, but that requires more than an upward or downward adjustment. Processing emotions entails an investment in seeing how one's emotions in the present reflect past history and experience. Ultimately, processing means that one compares one's present experience of emotions with how one would ideally like to respond, and this ideal must be mediated by cultural beliefs. Expressing, as we know, varies according to whether one's culture instructs someone to describe their emotions somatically or verbally.

Clinically speaking, it is desirable to encourage patients to tune into and work on improving interoceptive knowledge of emotions. This is a valuable first step with all patients, regardless of cultural expectations that govern how it ought to be manifested to others. Yet, interoceptive knowledge of emotions is a necessary, but insufficient condition for processing emotions, which requires a more active effort to make sense of and shape emotions. Although I have dwelled on ways that expressing emotions is influenced by culture, processing emotions is hardly immune to culture. When we help patients to realize their sense of agency, that ought to be construed not just in terms of individual choice, but cultural expectations that may or may not be deemed determinative. Psychoanalytic treatment offers patients an opportunity to practice communicating emotions, whether verbally or somatically expressed, as well as processing them.

In conclusion, I would like to emphasize that mentalized affectivity is not a retreat from primary process and the unconscious as long as it reckons with the body. The body is not a receptable for unwanted mental life; it informs and supports mental life. Yet, the body requires interpretation and cannot escape being infused with values and culture. The consequences are sizeable and bear on our understanding of well-being, which is less a matter of seeking positive emotions and retreating from negative emotions than it is a welcoming, and even a flowing dialogue between mind and body. The mind receives useful information from the body, and, of course, the mind is able to direct the body. When they are out of sync, there is a risk of psychopathology. The more they are in sync, the better. Our work with patients aims to foster communication both within as well as between self and others.

Note

1 Gubb (2013) distinguishes the Paris psychosomatic perspective and the attachment/mentalization perspective in terms of the former having an intrapsychic focus in contrast to the latter having an intersubjective focus. The former can be characterized in terms of "the speechless mind" and the latter "the speaking body." Arguably, however, the attachment/mentalization perspective, which has evolved to extend from a social communication paradigm, affirms the intersubjective aspect of mentalization without sacrificing the intrapsychic aspect. As we will see, it is consistent with contemporary neuroscience in a way that the French perspective is not. For contesting the either/or of intrapsychic and intersubjective, see Green (2000) and Loewald (1962).

References

Aival-Naveh, E., Rothschild-Yakar, L., & Kurman, J. (2019). Keeping culture in mind: A systematic review and initial conceptualization of mentalizing from a cross-cultural perspective. *Clinical Psychology: Science and Practice*. 26: e12300.

Ballespí, S., Vives, J., Alonso, N., Sharp, C., Ramírez, M. S., Fonagy, P., & Barrantes-Vidal, N. (2019). To know or not to know? Mentalization as protection from somatic complaints. *PLoS ONE*, 14(5), e0215308. 10.1371/journal.pone.0215308

Balsam, R. (2019). On the natal body and its confusing place in mental life. *Journal of the American Psychoanalytic Association.* 67(1): 15–36.

Chentsova-Dutton, Y. E., Gold, A., Gomes, A., & Ryder, A. G. (2019). Feelings in the body: Cultural variations in the somatic concomitants of affective experience. *Emotion.* Advance Online Publication. 10.1037/emo0000683

Choi, E., Chentsova-Dutton, Y. & Parrott, W. G. (2016). The effectiveness of somatization in communicating distress in Korean and American cultural contexts. *Frontiers in Psychology.* 7: 383. 10.3389/fpsyg.2016.00383

Christian, C. (2018). The analyst as interpreter: *Ataque de nervios,* Puerto Rican syndrome, and the inexact interpretation. In *Psychoanalysis in the Barrios: Race, Class, and the Unconscious.* Gherovici, P. & Christian, C. (Eds.). London: Routledge.

Critchley, H. & Nagai, Y. (2012). How emotions are shaped by bodily states. *Emotion Review.* 4(2): 163–168.

Deng, X., An, S., & Cheng, C. (2019). Cultural differences in the implicit and explicit attitudes toward emotion regulation. *Personality and Individual Differences.* 149: 220–222. 10.1016/j.paid.2019.05.057

Fonagy, P. & Target, M. (2007). The rooting of the mind in the body: New links between attachment theory and psychoanalytic thought. *Journal of the American Psychoanalytic Association.* 55: 411–456.

Fonagy, P., Gergely, G., Jurist, E. L., & Target, M. (2002). *Affect regulation, mentalization and the development of the self.* New York: Other Press.

Fotopoulou, A. & Tsakiris, M. (2017). Mentalizing homeostasis: The social origins of interoceptive inference. *Neuropsychoanalysis.* 19(1): 3–28.

Green, A. (2000). The intrapsychic and intersubjective in psychoanalysis. *Psychoanalytic Quarterly.* LXIX: 1–39.

Greenberg, D. M., Kolasi, J., Hegsted, C. P., Berkowitz, Y., & Jurist, E. L. (2017). Mentalized affectivity: A new model and assessment of emotion regulation. *PLoS ONE.* 12(10): e0185264.

Gubb, K. (2013). Psychosomatics today. *Psychoanalytic Review.* 100(1): 103–142.

Hartung, T. & Steinbrecher, M. (2018). From somatic pain to psychic pain: The body in the psychoanalytic field. *The International Journal of Psychoanalysis.* 99(1): 159–180, 10.1111/1745-8315.12651

Jurist, E. L. (2005). Mentalized affectivity. *Psychoanalytic Psychology.* 22(3): 426–444.

Jurist, E. (2018). *Minding emotions: Cultivating mentalization in psychotherapy.* New York, NY: Guilford Publications.

Jurist, E., & Perez Sosa, M. (2019). Commentary on mentalization and culture. *Clinical Psychology Science and Practice*, 10.1111/cpsp.12302

Keyes, C. & Ryff, C. (2003). Somatization and mental health: A comparative study of the idiom of distress hypothesis. *Social Science & Medicine*. 57: 1833–1845.

Kirmayer, L. & Ryder, A. (2016). Culture and Psychopathology. *Current Opinions in Psychology*. 8: 143–148.

Laria, A. & Lewis-Fernandez, R. (2001). The professional fragmentation of experience in the study of dissociation, somatization, and culture. *Journal of Trauma and Dissociation*. 2(3): 17–46.

Lemma, A. (2010). *Under the skin: A psychoanalytic study of body modification* London: Routledge.

Lemma, A. (2014). *Minding the body: The body in psychoanalysis and beyond*. London: Routledge.

Lemma, A. (2020). The aesthetic link: The patient's use of the analyst's body and the body of the consulting room. *Psychoanalytic Perspectives*. 17: 57–73.

Levit, D. (2018a). Somatic experiencing: In the realms of trauma and dissociation—What we can do, when what we do, is really not good enough. *Psychoanalytic Dialogues*. 28(5): 586–601.

Levit, D. (2018b). Continuing the dialogue between psychoanalysis and somatic experiencing: Reply to Bass, Leddick, Levine, Blakeslee, Sylvae, and Lombardi. *Psychoanalytic Dialogues*. 28(5): 640–645

Loewald, H. (1962). Internalization, separation, mourning, and the superego. In *Papers on Psychoanalysis*, pp. 257–276. New Haven: Yale.

Lombardi, R. (2008). The body in the analytic session: Focusing on the body-mind link. *International Journal of Psychoanalysis*. 89(1): 89–109. 10.1111/j.1745-8315.2007.00008.x. PMID: 18290793.

Lombardi, R. (2018). Beyond the psychosexual: The body–mind relationship discussion of 'somatic experiencing'. By: Lombardi, Riccardo. *Psychoanalytic Dialogues*. 28(5): 629–639.

Lombardi, R. (2019). Mysteries, abysses, and impasses in body-mind dissociation. *International Journal of Psychoanalysis*. Vol 100(6): 1371–1389.

Lombardi, R. (2020). Corona virus, social distancing, and the body in psychoanalysis. *Journal of the American Psychoanalytic Association*. 68(3): 455–462.

Luyten, P. & Fonagy, P. (submitted). Psychodynamic psychotherapy for patients with functional somatic disorders and the road to recovery. *American Journal of Psychotherapy*.

Luyten P. & Fonagy, P. (2016). An integrative, attachment-based approach to the management and treatment of patients with persistent somatic complaints. Hunter, J. & Maunder, R. (Eds.) *Improving Patient Treatment with Attachment Theory: A Guide for Primary Care Practitioners and Specialists.* Switzerland: Springer. 10.1007/978-3-319-23300-0_9

Luyten, P., De Meulemeester, C., & Fonagy, P. (2019). Psychodynamic therapy in patients with somatic symptom disorder. In *Contemporary Psychodynamic Psychotherapy: Evolving Clinical Practice* (pp. 191–206). Kealy, D. & Ogrodniczuk, J.S. (Eds.). Elsevier Academic Press. 10.1016/B978-0-12-813373-6.00013-1

Luyten, P., VanAssche, L., Kadriu,F., Krans, J., Claes, L., & Fonagy, P. (2017). Other disorders often associated with psychological trauma. In *APA Handbook of Trauma Psychology.* Gold, S. N. (Ed.). Vol. 1. Foundations in Knowledge. pp. 243–280.

Luyten, P., Van Houdenhove, B., Lemma, A., Target, M., & Fonagy, P. (2012). A mentalization-based approach to the understanding and treatment of functional somaticdisorders, *Psychoanalytic Psychotherapy.* 26(2): 121–140, 10.1080/02668734.2012.678061

Luyten, P. & Van Houdenhove, B. (2012). Common and specific factors in the psychotherapeutic treatment of patients suffering from chronic fatigue and pain. *Journal of Psychotherapy Integration.* 23(1): 14–27.

Ma, X., Tamir, M., & Miyamoto, Y. (2018). A socio-cultural instrumental approach to emotion regulation: Culture and the regulation of positive emotions. *Emotion.* 18(1): 138–152.

Novack, D. (2016). To know another inside and out: Linking psychic and somatic experience in eating disorders. *Journal of Infant, Child & Adolescent Psychotherapy.* 15(4): 278–288.

Shai, D. & Fonagy, P. (2014). Beyond words: Parental embodied mentalizing and the parent-infant dance. In *Mechanisms of Social Connection: From Brain to Group.* Mikulincer, M. & Shaver, P. (Eds.). Washington: American Psychological Association, pp. 185–203.

Skårderud, F. & Fonagy, P. (2012). Eating disorders. In *Handbook of Mentalizing in Mental Health Practice.* Bateman, A. & Fonagy, P. (Eds.). Washington: American Psychiatric Publishing.

Wu, S., Barr, D., Gann, T., & Keysar, B. (2013). How culture influences perspective taking: Differences in correction, not integration. *Frontiers in Human Neuroscience.* 7: 822.

Chapter 9

A Revised Psychoanalytic Model of Mind and Communication

Studies in Body-Mind Continuity

Anna Aragno

Background

> *For in the psychical field, the biological field does in fact play the part of the underlying bedrock.*
>
> *– S. Freud, 1937, p. 252*

Folded within Freud's ground breaking, 'The Interpretation of Dreams' (1900) is the layout of his first 'topographical' model of mind consisting of three systems, Unconscious (*Ucs*), Preconscious (*Pcs*), Conscious (*Cs*), straddled by the Primary and Secondary processes, his two modes of mental functioning. The Primary process (*Ucs*) operates via the most expedient path to wish-fulfilment with unbound, loose, and mobile energy; its expressions are idiosyncratic, free, impulsive, simultaneous, irrational, knowing no time, logic, negation, or reason. The Secondary process (*Pcs-Cs*) is linear, sequential, logical, operating with delay within reality and time constraints, accordingly, with 'bound' energy that makes use of verbal 'signs.' The former faces inward, the latter outward. The Ucs and Cs are divided by a 'repression barrier' creating a dynamic, conflictual psyche. Repression (of which there are two kinds; primary-*organic* and secondary-*dynamic*) and its many attendant psychical defences are gradually broken down and 'worked-through' via a complex interpretive dialogue, the 'psycho-analytic process,' through which unconscious 'meanings' are jointly understood.

Freud arrived at these landmark observations and *his scientific method* of interpretation through trial and error and a conceptual

DOI: 10.4324/9781003090755-10

synthesis of the biogenetic law; the unconscious as phylogenetically archaic; the primacy of early experience; the power of repression, fixation points, and formal regression in sleep; a process he called the 'dream-work' and, most importantly, the sharply dichotomized 'Primary' (impulsive) and 'Secondary' (inhibitory) processes, his two diverse modes of mental functioning. From his studies of conversion hysteria (with Breuer, 1895) Freud derived the etiological theory of pathogenic repression: from his study of the common dream, he uncovered deeper, universal, active wellsprings picturing impulses, affects, wishes, and thoughts, containing both primary (biological/organic) and secondarily repressed experiences.

For Freud, the dream was the entry point to viewing the development and evolution of the human mind as well as the deep unconscious where much of cognition occurs. He believed his dream book provided propositions from which "a number of inferences can be drawn that are bound to transform our psychological theories" (xxiv), holding enormous promise for future research. To the very end, Freud claimed that his unveiling of the two principles of mental functioning would lead to uncovering what is psychically innate in our species' archaic heritage, confident "that psycho-analysis would claim a high place among the sciences which are concerned with the reconstruction of the earliest and most obscure periods of the beginning of the human race" (Freud, 1900, 549).

An important feature of Freud's *Ucs-Pcs-Cs* model is its implicit epigenetic structure, the idea of 'regression' to earlier modes and fixation points detaching from 'reality' in psychosis, returning to an 'earlier mode of thought,' in dreams. Three forms of regression are identified (a) a *topographical,* a return to the 'primary process' mode of thought; (b) a *temporal,* a return to distant (unrepresented/repressed) past experiences, and; (c) a *formal,* a return to earlier more 'primitive' pictographic modes of *re*-presentation. These typically occur conjointly since what is older in time is more primitive in form and topographically lies closer to the perceptual end (Freud, 1900, 548). Topography is *not* to be taken literally, however, having nothing to do with anatomy but referring to "regions in the *mental apparatus* wherever they may be" (Freud, 1915, 175). It will be for Piaget to identify that the first sensory-motor (unrepresented) stage in cognitive development is indeed actualized and registered in the sensing-*moving body*.

Although Freud artfully interwove biological drive with mental representation through the motivational 'wish' as propulsive impulsion, and despite his great insight that the dream's pictographic imagery expresses 'ideas' and is merely 'another mode of thought,' the deterministic scientific paradigm in which he was embedded could not accommodate the subjective nature of his discoveries. 'Meaning,' whether conscious or unconscious, did not fit the prevailing physicalist paradigm based on causal forces. The fundamental underlying paradigm clash between a framework of *causal explanation* versus one of *interpretative understanding* was not mended, since meanings are not *caused* but *created*.

Freud's dynamic 'psychical apparatus' is divided by conflict with fundamental 'directional' excitatory and motivational qualities. Most problematically, these are accounted for by quantities of 'energy investments and expenditure' that change forms. Freud achieved meta-theoretical cohesion by redressing psychological processes in bio-energic ideas of a fictive 'energy' that changes form at different levels of organization during the transformation from unconscious to consciousness. His reaching for spatial, energic, and economic metaphors to depict formal and functional transpositions in psychical organization were ingenious constructs that he recommended should be revised as new knowledge was accrued. But the problematic concept of 'energy,' introduced provisionally, continued to haunt metapsychology, swelling to become a pivotal point of contention in Ego Psychology, especially in America, during the latter part of the past century. Battles between those *for* developing the natural science claims of Freudian Metapsychology (1915) and those for debunking it altogether tore apart the theoretical backbone and scientific aspirations of the Freudian framework. And as the great post-Freudian Ego psychologists passed away, amidst acrimonious disputes between arguing factions, the field split up into many schools each under the banner of a small piece of the very large discipline they inherited thereby splintering the whole. Without an updated unifying meta-theory accounting for the transformative action of its therapy, grounded in viable operative processes underlying its general theory of mind, Freud's 'Metapsychology' fell by the wayside, a term so rarely used nowadays as to have been forgotten. Where radical revision and updating was needed the field divided instead; a fragmented community much of its prime data sub-divided; a field stuck in a paradigm crisis.

Yet Freud's core passion and ambition, encapsulated in a series of five interconnected "Papers on Metapsychology," (1915) was to establish a core meta-theoretical explanatory base for his corpus of findings. Freud labored to create a somato-psychical framework in which the 'Unconscious' (Id) was also the 'core-self' of an organism governed by a nervous system that gradually develops to tame and socialize what is universally recognized as 'human nature.' His Darwinian investment in 'the mighty primordial melody of the instincts' reflected a need to create a psycho-biological metatheory accounting for human motives and behavior as universal as possible. The difficulty was incorporating into a unified metatheory what is instinctual and the compromises occurring during development, while also identifying the mechanisms involved in making the unconscious conscious through a dialogue. These difficulties were compounded by excluding the primary functional process of the human nervous system/brain in the mediation of action, emotion, and thought, through the socializing use of learned *signs*. Although several schools of semiosis circulated at that time, as a research-biologist turned neurologist, Freud may not have been exposed to them. When contrasting the "thing-presentation" of the unconscious versus the "word-presentation in consciousness" (1915), Freud touched on *semiotic* processes, just as he was adamant regarding the manifest/latent theory of dreams, also a semiotic structure. In fact, on closer look, the entire Freudian opus is tacitly steeped in semiotic processes and the developmental principles underlying them.

The interpolation of signs into human communication and thought, the gradual filtering of all experience through personal and cultural *signification*, leads inevitably to human meanings the natural soil of psychoanalysis. By 'human meanings', I refer specifically to *subjectively* generated and elaborated, emotionally tinged, complex meanings, as no other species can. To the end, he bitterly lamented that the *Weltanschauung* of his day could not provide adequate conceptual tools for his discoveries. The paradigm his life's work was pointing to would not materialize until the fifties along with advances in developmental studies, the neurosciences, semiotics, dialogics, and "cybernetics" (Weiner, 1948), a 'living' paradigm of pattern, form, and inter-Systemic *in*formation. Living systems could now be studied in terms of relationships, inter-actions and communication, in nonlinear recursive patterns of interface qualifying *meanings* according to their specific contextual frames of reference. With good reason, Gregory Bateson (1972), an epistemologist, remarked that Cybernetics was "the biggest bite out of the fruit of the tree of knowledge mankind has taken in the last 2000 years" (1972, 476). Arguably an even bigger bite was taken by von Bertalanfy's (1968) Systems Theory. Synthetic thinking evolved in reaction to hard determinism with the idea that a system's functioning must be understood through the changing organizations of its internal shifting parts in relation to other systems (Ackoff, 1975). What impacts and what is impacted upon, invoking Heisenberg, determines what we see; interactions have to be understood as a dialectic, in terms of recursivity. These innovative ways of looking at phenomena in the social sciences bare directly on psychoanalysis, once explanatory principles for our theory of mind and clinical process are identified and unified.

Most important regarding the early Freudian framework, and the centrality of the dream in it, is his insistence on incorporating the biological underlay into the principles of his 'metapsychology' (1915), so named to define "speculations about the origin, structure, function, etc., of the mind, and the relation between the mental and physical". For Freud, the organic/somatic underlay *was* the true unconscious; "The physiological substrate does not end once the psychical begins but rather creates a psycho-physical parallelism a 'dependent concomitant'" (1915, 207). For this reason, continuity with the body and epigenesis are emphasized as *core principles* in my revisions. The body's expressions continue to seep through words and actions, regardless of the semiotic level or medium, especially in art. And psychoanalysts are entrusted to feel/observe and interpret these subliminal meanings that reach us through multiple sensory channels in multiply coded forms. Nowhere is this continuity between biological and psychical more clearly expressed than in dreams which, straddling both, form a link from one to the other.

Freud's analysis of the dream's component 'mechanisms' yielded the following structure: "The dream-thoughts and dream-content are presented to us like two versions of the same subject-matter in two different languages, the dream-content seems like a transcript of the dream thoughts into another mode of expression" (1900, 277). This translation is effectuated by four 'Primary process' mechanisms: (i) Condensation, dreams are a mass of composite, multidetermined, polyvalent, images and elements: (ii) Displacement, a person or object is displaced onto, or taken to represent, another; for Freud this was in the service of camouflage due to super-ego 'censorship': (iii) Means of representation (considerations of representability), that is, idiosyncratic signs, universal symbols, *pars pro toto* (synecdoche), metonymy, analogy, reversals, all kinds of embodied, organic, dimensional, geological, geographical, meteorological, spatial, and architectural metaphors ('as if,' 'if then,' relations). In particular Freud mentions the "just as" relation of similarity or approximation in "dream formation" (320) stressing that "instances of 'just as' inherent in the dream-thoughts constitutes the "first foundations for the construction of a dream" (320), a point to which I will return: and (iv) Secondary Revision, the storying form or 'sense-and-sequence-making,' evinced in the linear narratizing processes of the 'Secondary Process,' linguistic mode of thought. Confusing manifest content with latent ideas would mean missing the entire process of the 'dream-work,' considered the *fundamental unconscious labour of mind,* referred to as the 'mind's work' elsewhere.

We would not presume the mind's 'work' to be an empty exercise! Yet the 'motive-force' for this phenomenon appears to *be its own operative process, re-presenting ideas from sensory-stimuli.* And a 'mode of thought' is not a force or a motive, but a *function* of how the human nervous system and brain 'work.' This, however, does not provide an explanatory answer for *why* we dream. Freud's recognition that the 'dream-work' is simply another mode of thought created a theoretical dilemma solved by introducing the 'wish' as explanatory spark. He had actually opened the door to an entirely new epistemology of 'meaning,' and of human semiotic processing that could not fit the causal conceptual paradigm of his day. What Freud named the 'dream-work' exhibits in *statu nascendi* proto-semiotic pictographic processes, later appropriated by language, within an overall *metaphorical* structure (Aragno, 2009) matching and condensing past with present, metabolizing and expressing emotions, fears, current desires, and dilemmas.

Since Freud (1900) identified the operative processes of the "dream-work" in creating "fresh parallels," (320); repeatedly pointed to mechanisms finding "similarity or consonance," the fundamental "just as" (320) of the dream *thoughts* in dream construction, and frequently implied a metaphorical structure, we wonder why he never referred to it by name? There are several possible answers: (i) in Freud's day, metaphor was firmly ensconced in a linguistic context as a figure of speech, a rhetorical or poetic devise. He was looking at nocturnal *pictographs,* unconscious processes, predominantly *non-linguistic* products. (ii) His observations were embedded in a deterministic paradigm requiring a *causal* basis for phenomena, a perspective conditioned by a need to account for the dream's *motive force.* And finally; (iii) as a pioneer in the uncharted terrain of the unconscious, Freud was himself immersed in metaphorical processes, naming new phenomenon as a conduit between the invisible and its first 'formulation' in which he was the first 'observer.' As interpreter of the unconscious, our master 'metaphorizer' of mind would not have recognized the pervasive workings of *metaphorical thought* underlying dream structure while focusing on its formal elements and purpose – to *fulfill a wish.*

The dream's compositional structure and primary-process mechanisms reveal emotive, multi-sensorimotor, source-points from which both presentational (image) and denotational (language) semiotic systems originate. Though expressed in pictographic form, these signifying mechanisms are precursors of linguistic tropes and other abstract semiotic systems, an embodied fabric out of which all signs and *meanings* in human cognition are represented and expressed. The dream's linguistic interpretation, negotiated contextually through associative trails leading to its 'core thoughts,' unveils this translation from primary to secondary process cognition, as unconscious meanings are transcribed into language and made conscious.

We now know that this cross-referencing of memories with current impressions from perceptual, sensory-motor, affective, and relational experience-elements is the cerebral activity of "dynamic schematization" (Werner & Kaplan, 1963) by means of which, from a flow of swiftly-passing sensory stimuli, some features are selected, matched, categorized, and funneled into idiosyncratic, newly integrated formulations (ideas). From an organismic perspective, this is precisely the bridging juncture between soma and psyche; where body originates mind through *signifying* – or *meaning-making* – activities. In our search for cohesion and comprehension, we *seek* pattern-matching finding common features and dynamic constellations in our experiences, especially those that are highly charged emotionally. When something is unfamiliar or as yet un-named, we summon a visual image, an 'embodied/idea,' to signify and represent that concept's meaning; this mental act *is metaphor*. The dream enables us to trace how the biological substrate is mediated by semiotic processes, body *into* mind, passing through a subjectively pictured gateway in dreams or, more socially, through language and other conventional signs. Supraordinate to this process is Symbolization – the dream as pictorial *signifier* for ideas it *signifies* – accompanied by its indispensable qualifying hand-maidens; metaphor – the transfer of the familiar onto the new; metonymy – a feature or attribute substituting for the 'thing' meant; synecdoche – a part for the whole; simile – corresponding to; and analogy – by comparison. Freud called this process the "dream- or mind's-work"; Piaget (1970) called it 'accommodation' the second step in assimilation; and in contemporary cognitive-science jargon, this unconscious activity of sensory integration and imagination is referred to as "conceptual blending" (Fauconnier & Turner, 2002).

When I entered the field, I realized the extraordinary potential in, and need for, updating Freud's *general* theory of mind, heralded in the Dream book (Freud, 1900). Freud's decoding the language of the deep Ucs as a Primary process form of cognition continues to be entry point for the study of the evolutionary development of the human mind and its implicit plasticity while the epigenetic composition of the topographical model provides important inroads through the study of dreams. Integrating a broad interdisciplinary pallet of current studies in paleo-anthropology; sociobiology; the philosophy of science and language; semiotics; narratology; contributions from important developmental theorists like Piaget (1969) and Vygotsky; Bakhtin's dialogics; and, from psychoanalysis, the invaluable studies of H. Werner and Kaplan (1963), Bowlby (1969,

1972, 1980), and Mahler et al. (1975) (to mention just a few) took me, over and over again, back to Freud, and to what he *specifically* pointed to advance the scientific base of the field; "**What characterizes psycho-analysis as a science is not the material which it handles but the technique with which it works.** What it... achieves is nothing other than the uncovering of what is unconscious in mental life." (Freud, 1917, 389)

The key question then was: *how does it work?* Since its method is a 'dialogue' (a 'conversation') the place to look was a developmental approach to the study of semiosis, language, and semantic reference in dialogues, with an eye to understanding the basic developmental principles underlying *all* sign and symbol systems. For this reason, I take *an organismic* perspective, preserving Freudian tenets like continuity with the body and epigenetic principles in the origins of mind and the achievement of conscious awareness. Psychoanalytic phenomena are pluralistic, multidimensional, each aspect contributing its own facet of inquiry, revealing its own developmental line, according to its own operative principles. And *meta*-theoretical principles are articulated at the highest levels of abstraction. So, my key question led to two guiding propositions: if the representational trajectory in the dream exhibits *natural* functional processes in a body/mind continuum, (i) it must have a traceable phylo- and onto-genetic line, which, (ii) would be applicable to development in a variety of semiotic media. This epistemological approach focuses on *functional* processes generating human meanings that can then be studied through linguistic dream analysis. In an organismic framework, epigenesis is manifest in a multistratal model of semiotic forms along a continuum that moves from hard-wired affect-signals, through indicative and denotive signs, to increasingly abstract forms of symbolization. Nowhere is this continuity between biological and psychical more clearly expressed than in the interpretation of dreams, a process forming a 'bridge' between what is still embodied through pictorial presentation and how these meanings may be transcribed and understood consciously through linguistic *re*-presentation.

The revision is part of a broader general paradigm shift in which the concept of 'energy' is replaced by functional semiotic and dialogical processes within dynamic, interactive, inter-penetrative fields of mutual influence. In these tilted interpretive dialogues, unconscious dynamisms run fluidly bidirectionally; hence, the importance of neutrality, opaqueness, and extreme vigilance, lest counter-transference or other projective inductions derail a delicate process composed of multiple levels of more and less-differentiated kinds of inter-action. On the other hand, due to this multilayered, polysemic array of communicative modes, it is also an optimal situation to investigate how one person's organism can 'attune' to the message/meanings (transmitted, projected, pictured, or uttered) that another is emitting spontaneously, if unconsciously. The technical directive is to 'meet the other' at their 'level' of interaction; an empathic stance that must be equipped to both reach-into and observe, to feel as well as listen.

Without Piaget's (1970) genetic-epistemology, arriving on the heels of Freud's death, or the integration of semiotic mediation, the fundamental continuity between body and mind, and therefore the translation from unconscious to conscious *modes of thought*, remained highly polarized and mired in physicalist metaphors describing, but not explaining, the functional/formal shifts in *organization* of a multilayered, polysemic, s*ign-infused* psyche. Built on the skeletal outline of Freud's tripartite topography, a more fleshed out multi-code developmental model of mind (Aragno, 1997/2016) composed of microgenetic stages in symbolization undergirds the phylo- and onto-genetic evolution of mind mirrored in the micro-genetic progressions in phases of psychoanalytic therapy, from embodied unconsciousness to verbalized conscious awareness.

The Revision

A Developmental Paradigm for a New General Model of Mind and Communication

> We must be prepared...to assume the existence...not only of a second unconscious, but of a third, fourth, perhaps of an unlimited number of states of consciousness, all unknown to us and to one another.
>
> – S. Freud, 1915, 170

The comprehensive revision of Freud's topographical model first presented in "Symbolization" (Aragno, 1997/2016) later incorporated and expanded in "Forms of Knowledge: A Study of Human Communication" (Aragno, 2008/2016) was undertaken to provide psychoanalysis with a viable, developmental, general theory of mind, based on operative processes of semiotic progression and discourse semantics. Such a model correlates with evolutionary and ontogenetic processes as well as those underlying progressions in conscious awareness in a unifying conceptual framework. This new bio-semiotic model, inclusive of non-conscious, unconscious, preconscious, and conscious (*Nc, Uc, Pcs, Cs*) modes of experience, thought, and communication, yields a seamless epigenetic six-stage continuum, crystallizing in hierarchic organization, detailing shifts in the phenomenological experience tied to each form (along the Ucs-Cs dimension).

The questions asked, and my constructivist/developmental approach, generated a vastly more detailed version of Freud's topography of mind. The key to this revision is symbolization, the unique faculty of the human mind at the root of all manifestations of our evolution and civilizations and the natural soil of psychoanalysis. Such a revision addresses the problems of our metatheory at their epistemological source. My goals at the outset were threefold: to reconceptualize the notion of convertibility of 'instinctual energy' as explanatory base for psychical transformation; to contextualize 'meaning' and subjective experience as operative, semiotic activities; and, in reconstructing a metatheory from new fundaments, to bring about a paradigm shift in how we view the nature of mind.

In 'Symbolization,' (Aragno, 1997/2016) the concept of a multi-layered, stratified, psyche is expressed along a developmental sequence of semiotic mediation moving from natural affect-signals, through acquired gestural/verbal signs to symbolic organization. The semiotic function is viewed as a hardwired inherited hominid trait gradually evolved to interweave with cerebral areas predisposed toward representing experience in ever more expedient ways, developing signs to record, represent, calculate, and language to name, point out, refer to, categorize, conceptualize, and communicate *complex meanings*, as no other species can. I make a clear distinction between the given biological affect – 'signal,' a natural mode of communicating through facial/motor expressions and sounds shared with higher primates and other species, and the discrete learned *systems* of signs and symbols, which, due to human cerebral architecture, provide semiotic means dominating communication, behavior, and experience, in many different ways.

Key essential points to understand regarding this model are: (i) each of these discrete semiotic functional-forms results in dramatic shifts in subjective experience, meaning, motives, thought, and psychological-organization; (ii) advances in semiotic functional organization during development are contingent on exposure as well as increased cognitive distinctions between reality and subjective experience/fantasy, implying *adequate* affect-modulation and intrapsychic separation and differentiation; (iii) several semiotic forms intermingle in everyday communication, experience, and thought; and (iv) pre- and proto-semiotic modes along the continuum, *particularly the least differentiated modes of regressed or psychotic states*, induce *powerful* bidirectional impact in human interactions.

The developmental continuum moves from a natural/biological anlage of *signals*, through *signs* (serving either indicative or denotive functions) to the formation of the symbol proper. These are not stages definitively arrived at but specific *functional forms* designating planes of mental organization that tend to crystallize favoring higher more efficient modes yet intermingle dynamically all the time and remain subject to various types of voluntary and involuntary regression. This is a highly simplified summary of what, in ontogenesis, are complex, interrelated, early separation-individuation and learning processes, tied to temperamental proclivities and environmental exposure. We would not expect language, our most universal and expedient yet complex semiotic system, to sprout fully hatched from its pre-linguistic egg! Precursors of verbal signification are hard wired, inherent in human dispositions for dynamic schematization and pattern-matching: seeds of signification are already germinating in visual processes of the perceptual apparatus, in expressive gestures and tonal sounds *long* before the first words are uttered. Although predisposition for language-acquisition is hard wired, it is conditioned by imitation and learning (environmental triggers) and subject to a time-sensitive window of exposure. Early language-use is governed by signal and sign-semiotic organization, a semantic still strongly tied to the senses and affects overlapping, but not yet firmly anchored in, the higher semiotic realm of stable symbolic thought. Verbal signs are by no means the only or even the best semantic through which to express *qualities* of human emotional experience for which nonverbal arts are far better suited (except for poetry, our music of the mind). Nevertheless, language is the semiotic system that provides denotive signs discrete, specific, and efficient enough, to enable us to communicate expediently and explicitly enough to lead to conscious awareness.

'Forms of Knowledge' (Aragno, 2008/2016) greatly expands this model's underlying principles through a comprehensive study of pre-, proto-semiotic, and dialogic phenomena aroused in these semantic fields. This included the *specific* semiotic/semantic-reference features of the specialized speech processes in psychoanalysis, correlating these with the gradual alterations in cerebral reorganization that we commonly refer to as 'structural change.' The ideas for this book came while participating in a two-year supervisory training program. One reaches this final lap of training seasoned by years of didactic and clinical experience only to discover a plethora of phenomena that theoretically speaking lie in uncharted terrain. This impressive area, that recapitulates many clinical and group processes, provides a wealth of valuable data to be experienced, studied, observed, and integrated into our metatheoretical framework. I was fortunate to be part of a comprehensive program in which in addition to readings, lengthy supervisory case discussions and the supervised practice of supervision itself also provided on-site observation opportunities. For two years, biweekly, we observed colleagues conducting supervisory sessions through a one-way mirror in a room nicknamed the 'fishbowl.' These observed sessions were followed immediately by group discussions.

On these occasions, which lent themselves perfectly for research purposes, I was struck by how vividly diverse unconscious transmissive and dynamic undercurrents became manifest. Amidst the heightened anxiety of the 'fishbowl' experience, in the vital presence of tense process-narratives and tentative educative interchanges between novice supervisors and novice therapists, minute nonverbal cues danced back and forth between interlocutors. These rich dialogues were replete with enactive, inductive, collusive, defensive, and parallel processes. A situation that provided such an array of new experiential data became my venue for research/observation. And while the entire supervisory framework generates fertile conditions for the investigation of unconscious communications and collusive blind spots, nowhere is the interrelationship between these and diverse forms of affect-induction and dynamic narrative-forms more vivid. My observations of the interactive phenomena within this triadic field and how I understood their implications for teaching the psychoanalytic attentional stance; understanding processes of clinical and supervisory dialogues; examining semiotic progressions in making the unconscious conscious; and, above all, adopting the psychoanalytic semantic as an epistemological window to identify the shifting morphology of human meanings is the essence of the book.

My first proposition was that the locus of inquiry must be what transpires *between* people, the *forms* of interactions themselves, examined from both sides, *in process,* and in terms of how interpretive transactions impact on psychical organization. Methodological use of the entire spectrum of human interactive-channels obliges us to recognize sensory-emotive registrations as important, valid, sources of in-formation in psychoanalytic research. An inter-penetrative paradigm of *in*-forming transformation enables one to avoid reifications, including the split between experiencing subject and observed object, as well as body/mind, by means of a reflexive method in which both subjects must collaborate in becoming their own objects of analysis and introspective interchange. The splitting of the 'ego' in the service of analytic observation is a key tool in the implementation of our 'method.' Cartesian divisions are explicitly undermined where full integration of the mind/body unity and the ability to *enter into* while observing the interactive field are not merely desirable, but essential. This adjustment of stance in relation to the *kinds* of meaning-phenomena under investigation (Freud's own) indicates a shift from a paradigm of causal explanation to one of compositional elements in mutually transforming interactions. Communication is therefore examined in process, bilaterally, observing how an interplay of diverse forms and modes of unconscious interaction and meanings are brought to consciousness in semantic fields that bring these shifts into sharp relief. Psychoanalytic situations are used here as research venues to observe and systematize various forms of interaction and to isolate the specific semiotic, referential, and dialogical, mediations by which the unconscious is made conscious.

The fundamental premise underlying this study then is that communication is reciprocally constructed between a communicant and an interpreter, implying a dialectic. The unit of study, therefore, must include the reciprocal interplay and respective contributions of both parties. What emerges from a developmental template is how human interactions are transformed by sign- and symbolic-mediation, and how the specific *contextual* features of semantic and discourse reference determine the meanings of what is spoken about. The study was designed to identify and differentiate various projective, enactive, inductive, and narrative forms, to trace their evolution ontogenetically, and then examine how they are recapitulated in analytic dialogues. Human communication in its *totality* becomes an empirical window into the many intrapsychic and interactive pre- and proto-semiotic processes we refer to under the broad term 'unconscious.'

Addressing all interactional phenomena bidirectionally and *in* process, and reconstituting semiotic activities that first capture, construct, and then crystallize into linguistically created realities exposed an emergent spectrum of transmissive, projective, replicative, and narrative modes, from deeply unconscious/enacted to conscious form-varieties. Pre-symbolic expressions shadow symbolic metaphoric articulation, while residues of earlier forms infiltrate and fuse into higher ones with language absorbing all that came before. Under the general rubric 'Morphic Sentience,' discrete intuitive or attuned unconscious forms are also posited and named. Although superseded by linguistic communication, these deep bio-psycho-social strata remain vitally active registering tonal nuances, intent, and unconscious dynamic/emotional dispositions subliminally, continuing to play a critical role in all interactions especially in groups.

I begin from eight primary affect-expressions (phylogenetically hard-wired) correlated with pervasive physiological changes as basic templates and prime motivators in humans. From these basic bodily states originate temperamentally preferred impulse/defense and adaptive or maladaptive compromises because in humans' impulses are rapidly overlaid by internalizations and *learning*, infused with *meanings* – and all *meanings* imply processes of *sign*ification. The early interpolation of the sign over the affect-signal is the basis for an entirely different way of understanding the developmental vicissitudes of the human psyche. Placing 'affects' at the fulcrum brings communication in line with organismic psychic/mental functioning and encompasses into one system of ideas principles of psychical integration generated by the speech processes of psychoanalysis in making conscious the unconscious. It thereby also integrates the practice of the method with its metatheoretical base.

Since many unconscious meanings are rooted in and expressed *through* the body, forms of human expression and communication examined from an organismic standpoint offer the best empirical viewing of 'psyche/mind.' The psychoanalytic study of *all* forms of communication becomes a vehicle for observing how humans register, transmit, and communicate, what is *in* and *on* their minds; what they project and induce unconsciously in others; the nature of internalization, transference, empathy, and the interweaving of enactment, and recall in the current presence of the past. Simply put: I was interested in what happens *between* interlocutors, in identifying and differentiating the *forms* of interactions themselves, especially unconscious ones, laying the groundwork for a systematic study of their logical forms. This was therefore a multidimensional study filtered through the unifying template of a revised bio-semiotic model of mind leading into the complex polysemic domain of meanings, forms of reference, and sources of 'gnosis' in the sense of knowing *prior* to the adoption of conventional signs. In psychical terms, semiotic *functional-forms* reveal *how* something is currently experienced or known: therefore, *transpositions in form lead to functional reorganization.* This, essentially, is the correlate of functional neuroplasticity, or structural change.

This functional role of form in the phenomenological organization of mind becomes apparent when considering the dynamic interaction of many elements in relation to a whole, like a composition. Interrelationships between function, form, and content, through time, provide a theoretical template for the gradual phase-progression in the psychoanalytic process. The analogy of a musical score helps envision the hierarchic nature of this model manifesting the multidetermined condensation of many levels of meaning-forms all expressed simultaneously in human communication. A free-associative verbal stream subsumes subliminal organic metaphors and unconscious dynamics enabling us to reach the core source-points of unconscious ideas, emotions, and meanings, peeling away by analysis surrounding layers of associations, as in the interpretation of dreams.

Psychoanalytic semantic fields are generated by a method embedded in an *interpenetrative epistemology*, a dialectical process that uncovers *how* we come to know. The yields of its inquiries bifurcate into branches each expanding human consciousness in different ways: one, via analysis of the personal unconscious, leads to therapeutic insight; the other displays microgenetic mediations in the transformation of *undifferentiated* experience into increasingly differentiated, verbally referenced ideation. The clinical task is to interpret unconscious meanings through an emergent contextual process: the theorists to identify, classify, and systematize their *forms*. From this perspective, my primary interest was to examine the reciprocal impact of different semiotic forms on how we receive and understand meanings issuing from these diversely coded or referenced modes. Their marked formal differences imply different organizations of experience and, most importantly, elicit radically different *kind*s of responses: *Natural Signals* alert to inner feelings; their transmission is immediate inducing a gut *reactive* response, unless inhibited; the referential distance between signal and signalizer is nil; hence, the expressive form and intensity of signaling behaviors *are* what they 'mean.' Due to their non-referential nature, signals incite *physical reaction*: feeling and action are their currency. *Signs*, on the other hand, are more differentiated; by their indicative or denotive reference, they point to, single out, and *signify*. But unlike the symbol, which is fully differentiated from that which it stands for, the sign-function still partakes in some way of that to which it points: its referential distance is greater than that of the signal but not sufficient to incite *conception*; signs point to their objects, symbols *conceive* of them (Langer, 1942). Only the *symbol* proper and *symbolic* referencing achieves abstract ideation, of the *mind*: the symbol frees experience from the senses becoming a vehicle and instrument of thought, representing 'ideas' contained within its referential orbit. It is this *complete* differentiation between verbal symbol and experience that lifts mental functioning to a higher plane. The symbol condenses within itself many possible meanings, and while symbolic functioning is expressed through different symbol-systems, only *linguistic* objectification leads to conscious awareness – an awareness of *being* aware.

With specialized speech patterns and an interpretive focus on *everything* unconscious, psychoanalytic situations generate a discourse-induced loosening, or temporary breakdown, of layers of semiotic organization and psychical defences, creating 'semantic fields,' or 'bio-semio-spheres,' of considerable multidirectional influence. Through a temporary situation-specific-regression, internalized interpersonal dynamics are transferred and projected into this 'unprejudicial space'; imagistic patterns and experiences are inductively transmitted; Ucs feelings, dreams, fantasies, and deeply repressed memories begin to reemerge permeating a fluid, porous situation and those in it. And the dream goes even deeper. Although superficially superseded by linguistic communication, less-differentiated bio-psycho-social strata remain vitally active, subliminally registering tonal nuances, intent, and unconscious dynamic/emotional dispositions, which, we infer, belong to phylogenetically earlier modes of human interaction

These profoundly organic phenomena are particularly manifest in the formation, cohesion, and unconscious convergence-dynamics of groups. Even with considerable semiotic overlay, layers of psychic defenses, and cultural norms, these deep bio-psycho-social strata, probably hard wired, continue to play a critical role in social behavior and group processes. And this fundamentally *interactive* consideration emphasizing the social role of communication is very important when speculating on the coevolution of language and mind in early groups and societies

Theoretical Summary and Conclusion

> *There is no need to be discouraged by these emendations. They are to be welcomed if they add something to our knowledge, and they are no disgrace to us as long as they enrich rather than invalidate our earlier views.*
>
> – S. Freud, 1926, 160

Freud was no stranger to modifications and revisions, and made many as he became better acquainted with his observations and more articulate in his theoretical conceptualizations. In fact, he encouraged those who would come after, to build on what he spearheaded, by updating and revising as new knowledge came about. My revision of the first topographical model of mind rather than a 'revision' is, more precisely, an updated version, and as N. Goodman (1984) so aptly put it, "A version is not so much made right by a world as a world is made right by a version" (127). A semiotic developmental model of mind does in fact better link body with mind, opening up further research hypotheses, and, in fact, has led to finding explanatory principles for phenomena first described in metaphors. In preserving its profoundly biological roots and expanding its amplitude of applicability, Freud's first general model of mind becomes a seamless biosemiotic continuum starting in biological affect/signals mediated by gestural, behavioral, and linguistic social-signs, which, through psychoanalytic 'working-through,' lead to higher symbolic organization. A preoccupation with feelings, meanings, and form threads through both books anchoring psychological manifestations in bodily/biological origins. In fact, this biosemiotic continuum is remarkable for its explanatory generativity: whether conceptualized as an epigenetic hierarchy or a developmental continuum of increasingly mediated organizations, this revised framework mirrors the evolutionary accretion of cerebral cortices layering over core brainstem and limbic systems enabling us to trace progressions in paths of conscious awareness in normal development; in microgenetic phases of treatment; in the disintegrative impact on metaphorical thought and the semiotic function by overwhelming anxiety; and in the dissolution of semiotic structuring in psychotic regression. Both works (Aragno, 1997/2016, 2008/2016) subsume key contributions from critical thinkers and major theorists from within the field spanning our 121 years of existence as well as inclusion of interdisciplinary research. From within psychoanalysis are integrated important studies on infant/childhood attachment and separation, growing into the full-fledged research of Mahler et al. (1975) and the compelling separation-individuation paradigm. Encapsulating an important phasic-process of interpersonal/intrapsychic differentiation, first in infancy then recapitulated in adolescence, this developmental passage has potentially momentous cognitive sequelae on the constitution and capacity of the symbolic function negotiated at these key psychobiological developmental stages. This crucial underlying developmental line adds an extremely important dimension to the already-multi-determining mix of elements contributing to mental/cognitive functioning and psychodynamic stability.

As biological gateways to an organism's internal state and our primary innate mode of communication, taking the modulation of natural affect-expressions by signs and the mediation of communication by language, continued the paradigm shift begun in 'Symbolization' (Aragno, 1997/2016) unifying within one system of ideas principles of psychical maturation with the mediating speech actions of the psychoanalytic process. The revision and analysis of the features of speech interactions in our discourse-process, then, subsume a paradigm shift: from transformations of energy to transpositions in *form,* an *in*-formation *Weltanschauung* looking at interactions between mutually impacting, evolving systems. Our focus over the past century shifted from a primary interest in *what* is known to *how* it is known, including the impact of the observer/knower; from content to an awareness of the functions of form. The invitation is to study the *forms* of interactions themselves, which telescope back bringing earlier layers in the dialectics of the formation of mind and the development of conscious awareness into view. An interpenetrative paradigm of *in*-forming transformation enables one to eliminate the split between experiencing subject and observed object, as well as body/mind, by means of a reflexive method in which both subjects must collaborate in becoming objects of their own analysis in introspective interchange.

Virtually *everything* that transpires in our semantic fields is taken as an index of unconscious meaning and many of these indices are expressed somatically, induced as moods, feelings, projected, pictured, conveyed metaphorically, enacted in contextual replays, or acted-out in life. This *interpenetrative epistemology* instrumentalizes human responsiveness *in its totality* because it generates a 'bio-semiosphere' of proto-semiotic forms of interaction that appear interspersed among narrative lines in manifestations that *exhibit, illustrate, relive, and reenact,* past personal experience. The only reliable 'data' of psychoanalytic situations, I believe, are these elements and features of the discourse process itself, and the only objectifiable phenomena are its forms and transformations. This model categorizes these stratifications and systematizes their forms uncovering the organizing principles of semiotic mediation in a preliminary vocabulary that identifies and refers to them. More importantly, it provides some internally consistent principles for how the recounting of experiences and events is *also*currently being reenacted *and* shown at that very moment, in another form. Unconscious meanings in communication emerge in interrelationships between form and content; 'content,' often a metaphorical commentary on experiential process, just as process often echoes narrative content.

The interdisciplinary sweep underlying these studies provides broad enough foundations to examine the full implications of our method, which, as Freud foresaw, reaches farther and deeper into the origins of mind than has been supposed. Examining the protocol and phases of our clinical dialogues through a semiotic and discourse analysis of their features, we find an *interpenetrative epistemology* undergirding a dialectical discourse that by its controlled regression *reactivates* earlier preverbal modes while simultaneously uncovering *how* we come to know. A developmental/epistemological approach reaches back both phylo- and ontogenetically, recalibrating psychoanalytic phenomena that may now be generalized in a unified metatheory of mind and therapeutic action. Placing affects at the core of human intercourse provides an organic base for a comprehensive analysis of the morphogenesis of human interactive modes (Aragno, 2008/2016) and communicative competencies in a continuum from non-discursive to discursive forms, possibly even the origins of 're-presentation' itself (Aragno, 2011).

These multidimensional studies are filtered through the template of a modernized model of mind, leading into the complex polysemic domain of meanings, forms of reference, and sources of knowledge. This includes an examination of the pre-semiotic and semiotic factors; narrative modes; analyses of speech forms and their functions, as well as the semantic and referential features involved in creating psychoanalytic semantic fields. Psychoanalytic dialogues are examined in terms of their predictable phases, modes of therapeutic impact, and emergent phenomena, with personally constructed meanings shifting and altering according to the level of symbolic organization in which experience is currently represented

In conclusion, the revised model of mind is corroborated by neuroscientific research (Damasio, 1999) on different levels and states of consciousness providing a neuro-epigenetic map inviting reconsideration of phenomena uncovered by the early Freud. The advantage of studying human modes of interacting through the morphology of their communicative forms is that this conceptual lens eliminates the inside/ outside dichotomy neither reifying nor distorting direct manifestations of 'mind.' Most importantly, because the processes in question are observable, with the observer's experience included as part of the interpretive understanding, principles of theory and practice are brought together, anchored in 'data' that can yield empirical hypotheses

These works are efforts in synthesis and integration; of old with new, body with mind. The results are partial and provisional. My hope is that by continuing to use the psychoanalytic method for research purposes, I will have paved the way for others to build upon. Finally; the fundamental premise of both works is that semiotic processes give rise to human meanings and mind, and therefore that meaning and mind are *one*, born of acts of signification.

References

Ackoff, R. L. (1975). *Redesigning the Future*. New York: John Wiley

Aragno, A. (1997/2016). *Symbolization: A Revised Psychoanalytic General Model of Mind*. New York: Psychoanalytic Books.

Aragno, A. (2008/2016). *Forms of Knowledge: A Psychoanalytic Study of Human Communication*. New York: Psychoanalytic Books.

Aragno, A. (2009). Meaning's Vessel; A Metapsychological Understanding of Metaphor. *Psychoanalytic Inquiry*, Vol. 29 (1); 30–47.

Aragno, A. (2011). Silent Cries, Dancing Tears...The Metapsychology of Art: Revisited, Revised. *Journal of the American Psychoanalytic* Association, 59 (2), pp 139–188.

Bateson, G. (1972). *Steps to an Ecology of Mind*. New York: Ballantine.

Bowlby, J. (1969). Attachment and Loss - Vol. 1. *Attachment*. New York: Basic Books.

Bowlby, J. (1973). Attachment and Loss - Vol. 2. *Separation*. New York: Basic Books.

Bowlby, J. (1980). Attachment and Loss - Vol. 3. *Loss*. New York: Basic Books.

Damasio, A. (1999). *The Feeling of What Happens* San Diego. New York, London: Harcourt, Inc.

Fauconnier, G. and Turner, M. (2002). *The way we Think: Conceptual Blending and the Mind's Hidden Complexities*. New York: Basic Books.

Freud, S. and Breuer, J. (1895–1895). *Studies on Hysteria*. Standard Edition, Vol. II, London: Hogarth Press.

Freud, S. (1900). *The Interpretation of Dreams*. Standard Edition. Vol. V, 1953, London: Hogarth Press.

Freud, S. (1915). *The Unconscious*, in *Papers on Metapsychology*. Standard Edition, Vol. XIV, London: Hogarth Press, 1957.

Freud, S. (1926). *Inhibitions, Symptoms and Anxiety*. Standard Edition, Vol. XX, London: Hogarth Press, 1959.

Freud, S. (1917). *Introductory Lectures Part III*. Standard Edition, Vol. XVI. London: Hogarth Press, 1963.

Goodman, N. (1984). *Of Mind and Other Matters*. Cambridge, Massachusetts. London, England: Harvard University Press.

Hegel, G. W. F. (1807). Introduction. *Lectures on the History of Philosophy*. Tr. T. M. Knox & A. V. Miller. Oxford: Oxford University Press, 1987.

Langer, S. K. (1942). *Philosophy in a New Key*. Cambridge MA: Harvard University Press.

Langer, S. K. (1967–1972). *Mind; An Essay on Human Feeling*. Vols I & II. Baltimore, MD: John Hopkins University Press.

Mahler, M., Pine, F., & Bergman, A. (1975). *Psychological Birth of the Human Infant: Symbiosis and Individuation*. New York: Basic Books.

Piaget, J. and Inhelder, B. (1969). *The Psychology of the Child*. New York: Basic Books.

Piaget, J. (1970). *Genetic Epistemology*. New York: Columbia University Press.

Russell, B. (1953). 'On Scientific Method in Philosophy'. In *Mysticism and Logic*, Penguin Books Ltd, Great Britain, pp 95–119.

von Bertalanffy, L. (1968). *General Systems Theory*. New York: Ballantine.

Vygotsky, L. (1978). *Mind in Society: The Development of Higher Psychological Processes*. M. Cole, V. John-Steiner, S. Scribner, and E. Souberman, eds. Cambridge, MA: Harvard University Press.

Weiner, N. (1948). *Cybernetics*. New York: John Wiley.

Werner, H. and Kaplan, B. (1963). *Symbol Formation*. New York: J. Wiley, 1967 Ed.

Whitehead, A. N. (1927). *Symbolism. Its meaning and Effect*. Fordham University Press.

Chapter 10

Unconscious Experience

Jon Mills

In previous work, I have introduced a systematic psychoanalytic metaphysics called "process psychology" or "dialectical psychoanalysis," which is largely derived from Hegel's dialectical logic (Mills, 2000, 2002b, 2005b). Having amended Hegel's dialectic to complement contemporary psychoanalytic paradigms,[1] I provide a process account of the coming into being of unconscious agency that conditions the subsequent emergence and organization of all other forms of psychic realty. As a result, I offer a novel treatise on the unconscious mind by explicating the origins of psychic experience. Although Anna Aragno (2008, 2019) has nicely argued for a biosemiotic multi-code model of forms of knowledge as unconscious communication patterns, I attempt to delineate in a systematic manner how unconscious semiotics are the preconditions for subjectivity and mental processes in general, including language, intersubjectivity and social relations, and ultimately human culture. Admittedly lofty in scope and design, dialectical psychoanalysis is therefore concerned with expatiating the ontological conditions that make knowledge and experience possible.

Dialectical psychoanalysis is an attempt to systematically explain how the unconscious generates mind and all facets of psychic reality. Reality is constituted by mind as agentic process that emerges, grows, and matures from its basal primitive form to more robust configurations of conscious life, self-reflection, and social order. Psychic reality begins as unconscious experience constituted through pre-subjective and pre-reflective events that collectively organize into an unconscious sense of agency. The coming into being of this agentic function signals the coming into being of subjectivity, which becomes

DOI: 10.4324/9781003090755-11

the fountainhead for future forms of psychic life to materialize and thrive. What this means is that before we can speak of the infant, before we can speak of the mother or the attachment system, before we can speak of culture or language, we have to account for the internally derived unconscious activity that makes consciousness, attachment, and social relations possible.

Process psychology shows how internally mediated relations become the ground and prototype for all external relations, as well as how the structures of unconscious subjectivity allow for intersubjective dynamics to unfold and transpire. The unconscious is real, although it is not an entity. It is more appropriately understood as a *series of spacings* or presencing of certain facets of psychic realty, having loci, shape, and force in the indefinite ways in which they manifest as both the interiorization and external expression of agentic events. Here we are mainly concerned with the reality of the unseen and the ontological invisibility of unconscious process. Process psychology displaces the primacy of language over the primacy and ubiquity of unconscious mentation, instead radicalizing an unconscious agency that modifies and differentiates itself, and disperses its essence throughout its dialectical activities.

For there to be psychic determination or causation, there must be a *determiner* or source of activity that executes this formal act of bringing about mental functioning to begin with, what we may equate with unconscious agency. Freud was never able to adequately answer to the question of a unifying agency because he divided the mind up into competing "agencies," "systems" (1900, p. 537), or "entities" (1923, pp. 23–26) culminating in his mature, tripartite structural theory of 1923. Although Freud did offer an adumbrated attempt to explain how the I (*Ich*) epigenetically developed out of the It (*Es*) as a differentiated and modified agency derived from its initial natural embodiment (see 1923, p. 25; 1926, p. 97), he was not able to explain this developmental process with any precision.

In *Origins: On the Genesis of Psychic Reality* (Mills, 2010), I further argue that the ontology of subjectivity is conditioned a priori by an unconscious agency that is responsible for the birth of consciousness. My reasoning relies upon the principle of sufficient reason, namely, that there must be an original ground for every mental event that stands in relation to every mental object. Psychic activity does not pop up ex nihilio; it must surface from an unconscious organizing principle I have metaphorically called the *abyss*. This unconscious abyss is itself a crude form of agency that performs executive functions and initiates determinate choices and actions through intentional maneuvers we are accustomed to refer to as drive derivatives, wishes, phantasies, defenses, compromise formations, self-states, dissociative enactments, or otherwise anything we may label as belonging to unconscious experience. The locus of this abyss rests within an agentic function that may be properly attributed to an unconscious ego that possesses formal capacities to execute intentional choice aimed toward purposeful ends, what I refer to as unconscious teleology. Here I would like to further elaborate upon these ideas in its applied bearing to the mind-body problem.

The *It* Remembers What the *I* Forgets

In *Studies on Hysteria*, Freud (1893–95) tells us that the origins of defense emanate from a psychical force that resists knowing certain pathogenic ideas through a process of censorship that is protective or insulating in its function (*SE* 2: 268–9),[2] a function we have commonly come to know as repression. Freud believes that this functional force in the mind is based on an "aversion on the part of the ego" that had originally driven threatening representations out of our awareness and that actively opposes their return to memory. Freud specifically states: "The idea in question was forced out of consciousness and out of memory. The psychical trace of it was apparently lost to view. Nevertheless that trace must be there" (269). This presumed *trace* becomes an unconscious artefact, not as a static unalterable truth about psychic reality awaiting to be unearthed in pristine form but, rather, as a *semiotic* that resists representation, that which resists being known. Following Hegel's (1812) logic of the dialectic, it becomes legitimate to assume that such a trace would persist in the abyss, given that all psychic phenomena, when negated or cancelled, must by extension be preserved to some degree within the repository of the unconscious, which Freud identifies as timeless and eternal. In fact, Freud (1925b) sees negation (*Verneinung*) as a "certificate of origin" (*SE* 14: 236), the signifier of repression.

Contra Freud, the trace is never preserved in its original perceptive form, as if it were merely a datum catalogued in a computer chip; rather, it is mutated the minute it is incorporated into the psychic register. According to process psychology, certain aspects of the trace must undergo transmogrification once subjected to the dominion of unconscious agency. And here I would argue that there is a selective retention performed by the microdynamic operations of agency inscribed on the psychic repository, an agentic process of memorialization that selectively preserves what it simultaneously alters due to unconscious emotional motivations, what Freud metaphorically equates with a malleable mnemonic tablet.

In his brief and playful essay, "A Note upon the 'Mystic Writing-Pad,'" Freud (1925a) draws an analogy between how unconscious representations are encoded and how a magnetic sketch pad records impressions on the surface that can be erased yet preserved underneath its structural interior.[3] Freud equates the perceptual system with the surface of sense impressions, which are ephemeral perceptual processes of the conscious mind that are passively received, filtered, unnoticed, and forgotten, yet that leave a "permanent trace" upon a subcortical level he equates with unconscious mnemonic representations. The former is a permeable and transient receptor of external stimuli that simultaneously acts as a "protective shield," while the latter is the hearty magnetic slab or, to invoke another computer analogy, the hard drive that records and preserves all software programs. Perceptual consciousness "has an unlimited receptive capacity for new perceptions," which "lays down permanent – even though not unalterable – memory-traces of them" (*se* 19: 228). Notice that a semiotic is "not unalterable." In fact, it is subject to all kinds of internal transformations, not to mention the way in which unconscious traces are construed, interpretively constructed, or understood within the patient-analyst dyad.

In describing the dynamics of unconscious teleonomy, Freud speculates that "cathectic innervations [*Besetzungsinnervationen*] are sent out and withdrawn in rapid periodic impulses from within" (*se* 19: 231) the unconscious into the perceptive apparatus of consciousness.[4] Note that Freud says that the origin of such activity, as a trajectory or occupation (*Besetzung*) of psychic energy, emanates "from within" and is directed into consciousness, where it receives perceptions and passes

them into the mnemonic reservoirs of the unconscious abyss. Here
mental process is directed and withdrawn as an active agentic function,
not merely as a biologic mechanism, or at least it is not reduced to
such. We may extend Freud here to show how both teleonomic and
teleologic aims (i.e., those belonging to economic and adaptational
aims and those belonging to more complex dynamic, purposeful [in-
tentional] activity governed by unconscious motivation) are mutually
operative. However, unlike Freud, a withdrawal of innervetic occupation or stimulation does not bring conscious life to a "standstill";
rather, the demarcation between the abyss and consciousness is sus-
pended through a process of inversion. In other words, the ego with-
draws into itself.

What is important to note is how unconscious telic activities, as
determinate aims executed by the unconscious ego, are channeled
into sensory perception, where they take the manifold sense impressions as their objects (hence making this the most permeable
aspect of a *Trieb*) and then withdraw back into its interior. Here
unconscious processes both breach and close up the porthole to
consciousness when outwardly directed stimuli are suddenly disrupted – stimuli that are subsequently aborted. Freud states that such
"interruptions" have an "external origin" (*SE* 19: 231). Like the
mystic pad, impressions penetrate the unconscious through the cel-
luloid register of the conscious apparatus and leave their mark. When
they are interrupted by external reality, the unconscious closes up and
inverts into its internal spacings. Here Freud (1920) returns to a
trauma motif, as he did when he introduced the death drive in *Beyond
the Pleasure Principle*. A protective or defensive retrograde reaction is
immediately instituted when an encroachment or intrusion is felt on
the telic trajectory of mental directionality. This closing of the
breach, this occlusive function of the psyche in the moment of intrusion, is introduced through a "discontinuity" – hence a gap – in
perceptual stimuli. Recall that, for Freud (1915a), the unconscious
reveals itself as phenomena through discontinuities. Here fore-
closures in perceptual stimuli signal the call for a retreat into the
unconscious. Sense impressions, perceptual impingements, images,
cognizing mediations, and so forth are internalized into the deep
structural configurations of unconscious memory and exposed to the
internal demands and economic pressures of the pulsions, where they

are further submitted to the ego's agentic autonomous manipulation by phantasy. Here lies the wishing well.

When speaking of the origins of dream-work, Freud (1900) states:

> There is often a passage in even the most thoroughly interpreted dream which has to be left obscure; this is because we become aware during the work of interpretation that at that point there is a tangle of dream-thoughts which cannot be unraveled and which moreover adds nothing to our knowledge of the content of the dream. This is the dream's navel, the spot where it reaches down into the unknown. The dream-thoughts to which we are led by interpretation cannot, from the nature of things, have any definite endings; they are bound to branch out in every direction into the intricate network of our world of thought. It is at some point where this meshwork is particularly close that the dream-wish grows up, like a mushroom out of its mycelium.
>
> (*SE* 5: 525)

Dream-work is an act of translation – translation with a limit, a point of blockage. This *nodus* is what Freud calls "the dream's navel" (*der Nabel des Traums*), where there is a "tangle" (*Knäuel*) that cannot be "unraveled" (*der sich nicht entwirren will*), as sometimes happens in a ball of yarn. Here there is a knot, a check, an obstacle – the occlusion of dream space – the meaning of which is "left obscure" (*Dunkel lassen*); hence, this is the limit of analysis itself. Freud points to the infinity of the abyss when he says that our dream-thoughts have no "definite endings" (*mussen bleiben ohne Abschluss*), only branches that spread out into an "intricate network" (*in die netzartige Verstrickung*) of unconscious semiotics. The wish – the content of desire – grows up out of a "meshwork" (*Geflecht*) of insoluble knots and tangled threads, what Derrida (1998) calls "the umbilicus" (16), "an unanalyzable synthesis" (15). The navel, the scar of birth, is an apt symbol for the trace – the semiotic – that signifies genesis, the seat of unconscious origin eclipsed from pure knowing. This semiotic is not only foreclosed, hence cast into the pit of the noumenal "unknown," but also the wellspring of desire, which blooms out of its convoluted mass. Spacings of the abyss awaiting to be born from its core "like a mushroom out of its mycelium."

Semeion

When I refer to semiotic, I am specifically inferring the Greek notion of *semeion* – a mark, trace, or distinctive inscription. As I have argued elsewhere (Mills, 2002a, b), the unconscious ego is awakened through a rupture brought about by its inner desire to externalize itself through the felt self-certainty it acquires via the negation of its confinement to its corporeal nature. It is in the formation of the unconscious ego prior to the birth of the infant that we have collapsed the sharp distinction between sensuous life and the realm of intelligibility, that is, between emotionality and thought. Desire is not only affective dialectical activity coming to presence, but it is also teleologically expressed through the inward awareness it has of itself as lacking; hence, presence and absence are cognized by the incipient mind in its initial dialectical moments. Desire is semiotic in that it differentiates and distinguishes through its sublating activity, always leaving behind the trace or inscription of its experiential movements as they are preserved within the abyss. Moreover, despite being qua absence, lack remains a *formal presence* in the mind. Recall that, while drive may be sated in its moment, desire may never be fulfilled or completed for mind would no longer long to move beyond itself, thus the dialectic would perish entirely, and the ego would cease to be. Lack is always an inscription within the psyche and, therefore, the seed of thought itself.

Unconscious self-consciousness is predicated on the level of awareness the soul attains for itself through its progressive dialectical achievements. Here we take Bion (1957) much further: the unconscious ego is dimly aware of its psychic reality prior to its birth into consciousness. In fact, the ego first and foremost becomes pre-reflectively aware of the lack that innately permeates its inner pulse of sentient-affective experience (Mills, 2002b). Desire is being-in-relation-to-lack as pure unrest, event, and internally derived activity, the very process that stimulates and fuels the dialectic (Mills, 2010). As a result, lack initially becomes the internal signifier for establishing a whole network of unconscious semiotic connections. This is arguably a radicalization of Klein's general notion of unconscious phantasy and Bion's theory of thinking, for the simple reason that it is preliminarily primed, arranged, and rehearsed prior to the ego's eruption into consciousness. Therefore, unconscious semiotics become the logical template for the acquisition of linguistic signification, concept formation, and language.

Lack – the presencing of absence – engenders its own forms of signification that are peculiar to the unconscious ego's unique subjective relationship to its own internality, such as the way it comes to experience its own sentience or affective reverberations as well as its prenatal environ. Being-in-relation-to-lack becomes the original form of representation – hence the representation of absence, of empty form – for it constantly imprints itself afresh in the psyche, thus it perpetually *re-presents* itself through the structural negativity informing the dialectic. With stipulations, we may loosely say that lack introduces a semiotic that both conveys something we sense or feel (the signifier) and think (the signified), thus conferring a relation between the sensuous and the receptive (apprehended), what we may more accurately refer to as preconceptual, pre-reflective apperception. Therefore, the signification of desire represents the object of lack or absence to the incipient mind. Here the relata of signification becomes triadic: at once desire signals and engenders a (1) *sign* or mark it institutes through its relation to the presencing of lack, thus producing (2) an *object* for itself that it (3) *re-presents* to itself through intro-reflection, hence pioneering its transition to thought. Yet thought at this level is not to be equated with the thinking of consciousness predicated on linguistic concept formation or the symbolic order; here it is merely formal, hence empty of concepts despite being registered by the agency of the ego as signifying absence. In fact, lack becomes the unconscious semiotic that signifies the very essence of the dialectic – namely, negativity, death, nothingness – the rotary drive behind appetition.

Because desire is a process relation between mutually implicative forms of opposition, thought is necessarily imbued with negativity. Here it becomes easy to see how unconscious phantasy is prepared by the dialectic to enter into internally divided, persecutory, and paranoiac relations characteristic of the paranoid-schizoid position, a process that formally transpires before birth. Klein and Bion require that the ego attain conscious experience before splitting, thinking, and symbol formation develop, while here I am pointing to the primordiality of unconscious signification that allows for conscious signification (e.g., metonymy and metaphor) to materialize through more rich and robust planes of experience, perception, and conceptual construction properly acquired through language and the structural laws of signification. What I wish to highlight is that not only does the dialectic generate and sustain unconscious semiotics, but it also establishes a whole fabric, network, or chain association of signification that is both prelinguistic and translinguistic, thus establishing the primacy of unconscious semiotic phantasy.

The reader should be aware that I concern myself with a narrow point of view with respect to the question, meaning, truth, and being of semiotic structure within a speculative ontological framework of unconscious process. I do not wish to engage the disparate and nuanced fields of linguistics and psycholinguistics, or the broader domains of structural and poststructural theories of language, which are derived from a wide body of research conducted in the social and human sciences (primarily in France), including anthropology, sociology, literary theory, cultural and political studies, and even mathematics. In fact, semiologists will likely object to my analysis based on the simple observation that language and signification are predicated on consciousness and culture. This is an assumption, however, I wish to challenge, or at least to qualify. Signification and meaning have archaic roots that emanate from the lived body, both evolutionarily and phylogenetically informed, at once a corporeal expression affectively animated by desire, drive, and sentience.[5]

Although not diminishing poststructuralism per se, I wish to distinguish myself from Lacan, who believes that the unconscious is "structured like a language" and, indeed, who equates the unconscious with language itself (see Lacan, 1955–56a, 11; 1955–56b, 119; 1955–56c, 166–7), which is predicated on consciousness and cultural determinism. For Lacan, because the symbolic temporally exists prior to the contingent birth of the subject, this, in turn, determines the essence of the subject. Therefore, the subject is constituted by the symbolic function. For Lacan, the subject is conditioned upon its "entrance into language" under the symbolic Law (*E*1957, 148),[6] which ultimately makes the unconscious a cultural category captured by his formula: "the unconscious is *'discours de l' Autre'* (discourse of the Other)"(*E*1960, 312). Because the symbolic order, namely, language and culture, is causally superimposed, this corresponds to the constitution of the human subject. Here Lacan precariously subverts the notion of freedom within psychic agency as if everything is conditioned on language. Furthermore, for Lacan, the ego is an "illusion of autonomy" based on its *méconnaissances* and imaginary relations to others (*E* 1936, 6); and, unlike Freud, even "man's desire is the *désir de l' Autre* (the desire of the Other)" (*E* 1960, 312). In Lacan, we may call into question whether human agency even exists, for he sees agency as belonging to the authority of the letter. For Lacan, human subjectivity is always constituted by something outside of itself.

Process psychology offers a rapprochement between the subject-object/otherness binary by supplanting the hegemony between the semiotic and the symbolic. But we do not wish to boil everything down to the sign, as postmodern theorists tend to do, because this reifies language, social causality, and linguistic determinism through the displacement of embodiment, biology, individuality and subjective qualia, personal agency, and freedom. Nor, for the same reason, do we wish to import Pierce's semiotics into process psychology as, like Lacan's, his system privileges a theory of language. Furthermore, while there are fruitful comparisons with regard to the role of signification and the tertiary functions that mediate higher modes of meaning relations, there are also divergences within our respective frameworks due to Lacan's emphasis on the symbolic as opposed to Peirce's emphasis on the sign. Although these theories of semiotics potentially possess pockets of compatibility with much of what I have to say, from my account, it is important not to subordinate the unconscious to linguistic processes alone, only to show how they are accommodated and subsumed within more sophisticated aspects of unconscious order with a clear respect for the notion of overdetermination.

On the potential compatibilities with Peirce, it is interesting to note that he delineates a triadic theory – or what Merrell (1997) refers to as a "tripodic" theory – of signification based on the interdependency of a *representamen* or representation (R), which is formally the sign, a semiotic object (O), and an interpretant (I). Here I would situate the function of agency within the interpretant as ego, which generates the meaning of relations between the signifier (sign) and signified (conceptual object). Here meaning is conferred and mediated between these interpenetrating events directed by a semiotic agent, which is necessarily contextual, variable, and nonlinear in its process relations and which, furthermore, supersedes the Saussurean *signifier-signified* dichotomy. What is of further fascination is that Peirce attributes the locus, origin, precipitant, or coming into being of this triadic relation – what he insists is a systemic unit – to a "cut" (*CP* 5 : 441).[7] This is the very language Lacan uses and which, as we have shown, is derived from Freud's (1915a) notion of the "gap," or discontinuity, in consciousness, itself the signification that unconscious processes are at work. For Peirce, the cut precedes his categories of immediate *Firstness*, dyadic *Secondness*, and mediate *Thirdness*, which form the basis of his theory of signs. Indeed, Peirce sees the cut as a marker or disfigurement of "nothingness" (*CP* 5 : 441) informing the ground or pure conditions for the emergence of semiotic possibility. Here I would extend this notion of nothingness, seeing it as a spacing that precedes all division and separation in the mind and in the relata of signification diachronically enacted and realized by unconscious agency. This *pre-beginning*, or primal nothingness, structurally imports the supremacy of negation. Following the logic of the dialectic, negation is enacted in every division or splitting of mental content. And the cut, like Freud's gap, guarantees that any act of signification, meaning relation, or symbolism would be marred by discontinuity emanating from the abyss.

Following Kristeva's (1974) emphasis on the semiotic, I am interested in exploring the realm of the presymbolic, what she has identified as the dimensions of subjectivity and meaning that exceed the structure of language and the laws of signification (Beardsworth, 2004). Bearing in mind the truest etymological sense of the ancients' emphasis on *semeion* as a distinctive trace (ἴχνος), we can easily appreciate how psychic reality would have to emerge from an underworld forging its marks along the way. Not only does consciousness (particularly the perceptual apparatus) leave a trace, or, more accurately, a combinatory of referential traces that serve as ongoing stimuli for one another in the associative matrix of signification, but unconscious processes themselves also institute distinctive inscriptions that are memorialized within unconscious structure and that serve as ongoing sources of internal stimulation. Here I would argue that the unconscious is ontologically prepared a priori by the dialectic both to generate and to acquire linguistic structures, not merely to have them causally and passively superimposed by virtue of our cultural thrownness. What is inferred from this position is that thought and ideas are not caused by a one-way relation, whereby external dictates (the Lacanian "demand") inscribe themselves on the blank slate of the mind through the superimposition of signifiers; rather, there is a two-way relation between the agentic processes that organize and institute signification and those experiences that are stimulated within the psychic register by what it encounters through sentient (desire/affect) and, later, conscious (perceptive/conceptual) impingements. Although the unconscious mind incorporates language and its formal operations introduced through the vehicle of consciousness, what it does with such information-carrying signs, symbolic communications, and meaning transmissions is conditioned by the unique intrapsychic microdynamic linkages performed by each individual ego, subject to the adroit manipulation of unconscious phantasy. Following the developmental unfolding of the ego, first there is an extended mediatory relation of interiority to externality – not the other way around. This means that the unconscious mind has the capacity to resist universal laws of signification that are properly attributed to the formal structures of language, instead forging its own modes of signification through desirous, defensive, libidinal, or aggressive processes sequestered from or dissociatively compartmentalized in opposition to more elaborate logical operations or rational restraints belonging to consciousness.

These sequestered, parallel processes typically fall under the influence of affective and somatic resonance states imbued with desire, conflicted motivations, wish-fulfilling properties, and so forth – under the direction of the pleasure principle and its derived variants. This principle of unconscious semiotics potentially explains how bodily and affective schemata are formally constituted by an agentic ego through phantasy operations that link content with form mediated by desire and emotionality, thus abstracting representations and interjecting them with coveted qualities and functions within the boundlessness of the abyss. But, as Bion (1959) points out, there are attacks on linking due to anxiety and threat, hence a defensive negation is employed by the dialectic based on a particular transitivism via projective identification.

The prelinguistic and translinguistic function of semiotics ensures that unconscious phantasy plays a definitive role in symbolic representations and concept formation, with affectivity or emotionality attached to thought and even adhering within the concepts the mind generates or conceives. What I have in mind here is a word, especially an antonym, that carries the possibility of being imbued with affect based solely on an archaic experiential meaning. For example, I had a patient whose father, upon greeting her each night at the end of his workday, told her, with great emotive delight, that she was his "little princess." The affirmative word "princess" acquired a very negating quality once she heard her jealous mother call her "little princess" in a scoffing tone accompanied by contorted facial expressions. To this day, for this patient, the word is inscribed with an affective semiotic that evokes disgust and negativity.

In traditional linguistics, affect has no place in semiotic structures, let alone in the irrational forces that beset mental activity. Here I am arguing that emotions are enlisted and potentially imbued in all objects of signification originally transpiring within the unconscious mind. In effect, unconscious qualia are structurally inscribed in the very meaning properties of a sign. These may be relatively benign, even pleasure-oriented, or aesthetically distasteful, dangerous, or malignant, depending upon how semiotic orders are linked to qualitative affect states associated with a particular event or piece of psychic datum. When the valences of competing psychic contents, forms, and their accompanying intensities overlap, interpenetrate, or are combined in an associational nexus orchestrated by the unconscious ego, a sign may take on very eccentric meaning properties specific to that individual subject's evoked internal experience filtered through their past developmental history. The potential radical subjectivity inherent to unconscious phenomenology ensures that semiotic structures are never completely severed or secured from the encroachment of competing psychic processes. Here a semiotic can never completely insulate itself from the underworld of striving pulsions, wishes, affects, conflicts, terrors, and so forth that can potentially attach to or bore into the sign itself, which it then disfigures, congregates, or makes its habitat. This would imply that the chain structure of signification would not be rigidly causal, unalterably laid down within memory, or harbour predetermined meanings in relation to signifiers.

It becomes easy to appreciate how certain signs have different meanings for different people, despite there being a collective consensual agreement around their range of potential meanings. Signification is initiated within the unconscious unfolding of the ego; therefore, thought in its rudimentary form is cognized within the initial internal splitting of the psyche as the desirous apperceptive soul takes itself as its object. Moreover, experience becomes semiotically etched or imprinted on the unconscious mind prior to the formal entrance into and acquisition of language, linguistic signification, and concept formation. What this means is that unconscious phantasy begets its own signs and deferral of signifiers attached to representations created by its own imaginary powers derived from the modification of desire and drive instituted through unconscious agency.

On Ideographs

I have been arguing that desire and lack, somatic and affective schemata, and the broader diachronic organization of unconscious semiotics are initially generated from within the nascent interior of the unconscious abyss only to become more vital and substantial during conscious ego development. On the level of unconscious experience, signification, symbol formation, and phantasy are radically subjective, thereby disfiguring language, in turn, reshaping it through self-imposed unconscious signifiers potentially defying universal laws or orders of sign classifications, or at least eclipsing them through determinate negation. When under the influence of anxiety or pathological currents, such as traumatic, schizoid, paranoid, and depressive phenomena, unconscious semiotics distort the laws of linguistic signification through the idiosyncratic medium of unconscious agency.

Let us turn to Bion's (1957) abbreviated theory of thinking as emanating from sight and pictorial symbol formation manifested in the form of "ideographs." What exactly does Bion mean by this term? He does not say. Let us extend his ambiguous speculation. I believe that rudimentary ideas, primarily based in visual sense data, are stimulated or evoked, symbolically interjected or encoded, and attached to objects of experience insofar as an object becomes an emergent representation signifying some form of meaning to the incipient mind. Recall that Bion (1957) specifically says that "some kind of thought, related to what we should call ideographs and sight rather than to words and hearing exists at the onset" (66). To my knowledge, this is his only statement on the concept of ideographs. Here Bion emphasizes "sight." But we have argued how this is preceded by the unconscious ego's felt self-relation in the desirous, somatic, and affective reverberations it ingressively encounters, shapes, and re-experiences while ensconced within its immediate fluid, corporeal monadic interiority. We must seriously question whether "sight" should be the prototype for ideographs.

Idea (ιδέα) in Greek refers to form, as "to form in," taken from *idein*, to see. Due to the evolution of the desirous apperceptive ego, the ideologic form of an unconscious idea must precede sight and the pictorial graphic symbols that represent such ideas or things. More pointedly, unconscious mentation originally takes the cognizing form of somatic and affective self-certainty: *feeling* becomes the proper form of such ideographs, itself the modification of desire. Unconscious cognition first cognizes itself as a desirous and sensuous felt-immediacy, only to differentiate and modify itself further as apperceptive sentience or unconscious self-consciousness. Given that the foetus in utero can hear and absorb many aspects of the prenatal environment within its self-enclosed cocoon, somatic sensations, affective urges, and audible sound precede a priori visual perception. Although still crude and inchoate, sight becomes the further elaboration of ideation inaugurated through the breach into consciousness. The manifold of sensation itself is subjected to the synthetic and unifying powers of the ego. When signification, concept formation, and symbolic meaning are introduced through linguistic structures, unconscious semiotics are further expanded and enriched. Bion is correct when he refers to ideographs as "some kind of thought." But notice that, in his definition, thought is only possible with the inception of perceptual consciousness. I wish to argue the opposite: perceptual consciousness bursts through the primitive meaning structures and networks of signification that first arise within the abyss prepared by the unconscious ego. Thought first lives underground – first emanating from the felt-sensuousness of its own self-interior – only to emerge as re-presentations of its original form. Archaic thought is formally interjected into all subsequent experiential encounters of perceptive cognition transpiring within the ego. It is the unconscious recapitulation of original form that allows new experience to be assimilated, organized, and transmuted within internal structure through the phenomenological robustness only consciousness affords. These a priori agentic orienting processes emitted from the abyss allow for structural variation and expanse, whereby the psychic register forges new pathways and networks of signification and synthetic meaning channels supplied by the multiple presentations, permutations, and multi-modal sources of information processing that ensue during the experiential flow of conscious perception. What this means is that representation is conditioned on the unconscious mobilization and assembly of original form that takes experience as a cognized object.

Representation

When we conceive of the process of representation, which is often associated with the reproduction of images in the mind, it is important to note that they are in fact re-presentations of original sensate (*sensus*) experience that are mnemonically encoded either as visual images, distinct sensations, or impressions aroused or imprinted in the embodied mind. Furthermore, they are specific sensory stimuli that have undergone inner transformations imbued with particular affective ideation and manipulated by the dexterous fingers of unconscious phantasy. The powers of imagination, both voluntarily willed or involuntary inscribed, re-present an original presentation (*Vorstellung*) that has been subjected to unconscious mediation and, hence, has potentially been altered in form and content when reproduced in the mind, whether consciously or unconsciously realized. Imagination re-presents these sensory experiences laid down in the microdynamics of memory arranged as differential schemata, which intermingle and gel with the infinite co-extensive matrices of semiotic connections, only on the condition that they reappear through translation and transmogrification of original form. What is reproduced as representation is in fact an alteration of form as well as the minutiae of content, despite the fact that certain subjective elements of memory and meaning are epistemologically clear or indubitably certain or extrinsically (i.e., objectively) verifiable. What this means is that representations are both translated and mediated psychic facts reconstructed through mnemonic retrieval mechanisms and potentially (albeit not necessarily) further constructed through phantasy relations and perceptual distortions that serve to fabricate sense data or real events due to primal anxieties or wish-fulfilment. These operations are metaphysical quandaries not open to direct empirical investigation, therefore they are inherently subject to duplicity and imprecision. On the other hand, the empirical observation, validation, falsification, or verity of their true facticity is not epistemically ascertainable, therefore such questions become mute and irrelevant. What is clinically germane, however, is how the lived phenomenology of the patient's psychic reality is experienced.

There is a doubling function inherent to the nature of re-presentation that must be acknowledged when we mnemonically re-trieve any previous experience or piece of psychic reality. Contemporary psychoanalytic theorists tend to focus on the con-structive aspect of representation, while classical theorists tend to emphasize the dichotomy of objective verses subjective elements. Here it becomes essential to note that there is always a dialectic be-tween these two parallel aspects of psychic functioning and that analysis itself should be equally concerned with attending to both of these issues simultaneously. The argument that everything is con-structed is untenable because it negates ipso facto the a priori ground that prepares constructive processes to begin with; and the argument that there are irrefutable lines that demarcate the object from the subject become untenable when mind and nature cannot be conceived or perceived without their dialectical symmetry. Representations are necessarily conditioned on how objects of experience – hence aspects of the world – are incorporated, transposed, and transformed by internally mediating processes. Therefore, pure constructivist and objectivist epistemologies only highlight one pole of dialectical to-tality and do not properly appreciate their systemic role in how op-positionality is conjoined in holistic order.

Imagination operates on both conscious and unconscious levels of organization. In conscious experience, we imagine an object, which is the recovery of a lost image (*imago*) brought back to immediational presence from the depths of the abyss. Therefore, representations, by definition, have already undergone some form of unconscious med-iation, the exact nature of which is left to critical speculation. If unconscious phantasy systems are particularly active and interested in attaching to a particular imago or presentation, thus investing it with particular or peculiar intentionality, what Freud would call a cathexis (*Besetzung*), then the representation would reappear as an alteration of the originally encoded experience due to the bimodal functions of the perceptual system that filters or distorts pure objects of internalization in the moment of cognizing them. Or they are subjected to other evoked intrapsychic operations that, by necessity, (perhaps defensively) transform initial sense impressions (e.g., the dissociation of traumatic events). Freud referred to how perceptual phenomena may undergo repression, disavowal, projection, and so forth during the initial act of presentation, while Morton Prince, Charcot, and Janet before him emphasized dissociation, a concept that is now currently in vogue. The main notion here is that re-presentation is a reconstructive retrieval based upon original sensory information processing units that had been transmuted during their perceptual reception, subjected to conceptual signification, and imbued with emotional properties that alter or reconfigure the presentation as it becomes an internal object. In this sense, the represented object acquires a different structure from its point of origination conceived in consciousness, and, hence, its initial impact on the psychic register becomes transposed.

Freud used the term *Vorstellung* – not idea – when he spoke of an object presented to the senses within the conscious mind. An idea is a later conceptual achievement based upon higher-order cognitively mediated events. For Freud, following from the entire history of German philosophy, presentations were distinct from thought. Presentations were associated with the processes and objects of perception while thought was connected to conceptual linguistic operations. Freud referred to the former as "thing-presentations" (*Dingvorstellung*), while he called the latter "word-presentations" (*Wortvorstellung*). In his essay "The Unconscious," Freud (1915b) conjectures that the perceptual system was advanced by conceptual thought through secondary process mentation linked to earlier object-presentations that belonged to the unconscious system. He specifically states: "The system *Ucs.* contains the thing-cathexes of the objects, the first and true object-cathexis; the system *Pcs.* comes about by this thing-presentation being hypercathected through being linked with the word-presentations corresponding to it" (*se* 14: 201–2). Despite the fact that conceptual thought, including reason, brings about a "higher psychical organization," Freud does not formally ascribe a semiotic function to the unconscious system, at least not in this earlier work, especially when he categorically commits to the notion that "the unconscious presentation is the presentation of the thing alone" (*se* 14: 201), hence devoid of language. He designates word-presentations as a function of consciousness. But this does not mean that the implications of his thought annul unconscious semiotics.

As I have previously argued, I do not uphold the same level of categoritization or bifurcation between thinking, emotion, and sensation, as if they are distinctly separated forms of cognition. On the contrary, I wish to dispose of any rigid antitheses between desire, sentience, affect, and thought. Although felt sentient life is the most primordial form of mentation, sentience thinks as it senses and, hence, represents its own corporeal experience to itself as rudimentary forms of unconscious cognitive mediation. This activity transpires within the elemental configurations of the agentic ego, where all mediatory cognitive relations are executed.

Freud is brilliant in arguing that the presentation resists a certain linguistic mediation belonging to consciousness, what he relegates to the operations of repression. As he puts it, what is denied "to the presentation is translation into words" (*se* 14: 202). Here Freud is speaking about unformulated experience, the unsymbolized, the unarticulated. But this does not mean that semiotic processes are not hard at work. On the contrary:

> Thought precedes in systems so far remote from the original perceptual residues that they have no longer retained anything of the qualities of those residues, and in order to become conscious, need to be reinforced by new qualities. Moreover, by linking with words, cathexes can be provided with quality even when they represent only *relations* between presentations of objects and are thus unable to derive any quality from perceptions. Such relations, which become comprehensible only through words, form a major part of our thought-processes.
>
> (ibid., emphasis in original)

Here Freud underscores the point that thought is based on a rudimentary form of relatedness between presentations and qualitative meaning, but because they are largely unmediated by language, they remain unformulated, hence unconscious. In his early monograph on aphasia, Freud put forth the notion that thing-presentations, or representations of sense objects, would remain an open system linked to "a large number of further impressions in the same chain of associations" (*SE* 14: 213), such as acoustic, tactile, and visual sense data. Word-presentations, however, were a relatively closed system with a limited number of semiotic associations, a claim the post-structuralists would overturn. But Freud does note that words acquire "*meaning* by being linked to an 'object-presentation'" or things (ibid., emphasis in original), and that the relation between words and things take on a "symbolic" function that objects in-themselves do not (214). Here the nature of representability is sublated through language. Moreover, representation becomes the re-presentation of *relationships* between internalized objects and words.

Recently, Keith Haartman (2006) argues that meaning is generated through relationality to our objects of attachment, where bonds of love and affection bind the symbol to the symbolized in the metaphorical mind. Clearly, our relatedness to other people, and particularly to our parents or primary attachment figures, provides a higher-order linkage to our emotional life – one that generates both integrative and debilitative semiotic meaning structures. Haartman emphasizes the sublated forms of the ego's ability to generate meaning through the incorporation of the primacy of the parents as significant functional objects – parents more so than any other people for the simple reason that they are emotionally powerful and imbued with value, hence meaning, that cannot be annulled or denied in psychic reality. Here we would be hard pressed to negate the priority of these internal objects. For Haartman, meaning is necessarily an object relation.

Notwithstanding Haartman's fine contributions, what I wish to highlight is that this object relation is predicated on a self-relation. Meaning is initially generated from within the subject's own self-relation to its inner unconscious experience and then transposed onto objects. The peculiar microdynamics of unconscious experience provide the prototype for future modes of object relatedness. This orienting principle is especially realized in relation to the M/other, the concrete attachment figure infused with the symbolic, who, in turn, acts as a mirror function to vitalize and extend value to the self-in-relation to others. Meaning becomes semiologically generated from the interiority of the abyss and given more functional currency and importance when linked through our relationality to love objects. What I have been attempting to argue is that, before such meaning structures become "comprehensible only though words" (*SE* 14: 202), they are prepared by the somatic and affective representations that predate our formal relations to others. Before we relate to other human beings, the first object the ego takes is itself.

Before the ego becomes aware of things or others presented to it in the stream of consciousness, it first finds itself in self-mediation with its own presented organic nature as soma, only to feel itself through bodily pulsions as self-certainty, which the unconscious apperceptive soul enjoys as cognized sentience. Freud (1915a) tells us that the unconscious discharges itself "into somatic innervation that leads to development of affect" (*SE* 14: 187–8). Here we have the rudiments of schematic representation, but the process is left unexplained. Elsewhere Freud (1923) returns to this theme when he declares that the ego projects itself onto the surface of its body, hence it takes its embodiment as its first form, which we may infer acquires emergent representational ideas associated with the pleasure and tension gradients of the ego's sensuous nature. Yet we have shown how this process originally transpires within the unconscious ego long before the ego is born into consciousness (i.e., conscious sense perception arising from within the ego itself). The forms of schematic representations as modes of differentiated embodiment have a prehistory. The original somatic and affective schemata experientially prepared within the unconscious soul become the archetype for latter conscious productions. Clinical evidence alerts us to how somatic and affective schemata are often dissociated from conscious insight and are resistant to linguistic mediation.[8] Recent developments in cognitive neuroscience have alerted us to the domain and role of somatic and emotional schemata (e.g., see Bucci, 1997, 2003), which introduce important insights to clinical theory. However, without exception, the fruits of such research have not offered us any coherent picture of how such prelinguistic processes are organized without appealing to general brain events. In fact, the whole field of neuropsychoanalysis runs the risk of always remaining under the specter of material reduction; however, well-intentioned it may be. From a philopsychoanalytic perspective, it becomes essential to explicate the logical, ontic, and developmental sequelea of how schemata are ontogenetically generated and dialectically emerge from unconscious process without devolving into reductive biologism or the mechanisms of the brain.

The Microdynamics of Unconscious Schemata

It proves instructive to note that the term *skhēma*, like *idea*, refers to the Greek notion of *form*. The unconscious ego is initially immersed in form, in a formal unity or universality confined to its own interiority from which it must break free. *Sēmeiōsis* is the organization of representational schemata originally instantiated within the corporeal and affective constituents of unconscious experience. Furthermore, bodily, pulsional, and emotional processes often resist being articulated or expressed through language, thus showing how embodied affective life has an ontological and developmental priority within psychic structure. This is why, in our clinical experience, the life of affect reigns supreme in the unconscious.[9] Affect fuels the substance of our greatest motivations and fears, from *primaevus* anxiety and destruction to the coveted attainment of love, ethical sensibility, and aesthetic sublimation. This ontological condition ensures that the realm of desire and the irrational will always hold sway over the masses.

By way of a brief clinical example, I had an analysand who had been prone to somatization her whole life. Particularly, she developed extreme conversion symptoms of colitis and irritable bowel syndrome when she became increasingly aware of her repressed and disavowed rage and hatred toward her mother. Her body bore the brunt of her emotional torment and conflicted unacceptable desire to kill her mother, which took the somatic form of defecating streams of blood. The repressed rage was submitted to a compromise that simultaneously expressed both the wish that her mother would die through her "shitting her out" of her entrails (symbolic of the purging of toxic introjects) and the need to harm and punish herself through obsessional worry, physical debilitation, guilt, and shame, thus leading to the acting out of further destructive repetitions. The bleeding stopped when she was able to conceptually form meaningful connections to her mother's past cruelties, which were traumatically absorbed within her psyche-soma yet never articulated in self-reflective conceptuality, hence never made actual. When her somatic and affective schemata were given a voice as narrative by being converted through proper conceptual thought, articulated in vivo, and validated by myself, there was an internal shift in her unconscious representations that allowed her to verbalize her unformulated, unsymbolized phantasies and oppressive conflicts rather than keeping them mired in more primitive representations.

The overall internal transmutation and psychic revamping that occur from microshifts in somatic and affective schemata allow for a sublation of conflict. Shifts from more primitive instantiations of representation to conceptually articulated thought and symbolic meaning allow unconscious schemata to transform and disperse their intensities through a redistribution of form.

Rudimentary ideas and their representations, what Bion refers to as "preconceptions" (hence, that which precedes linguistically mediated constructions belonging to advanced levels of thought), are better understood as affective and sensuously mediated experience that is semiotically assigned a functional meaning by the incipient ego when it encounters an object in consciousness. The ego's experience of objects is transient in nature and characterized by pre-reflexive immediate cognizing, particularly during the first few months of life, when mnemonic tracks are tenuous and only in the crude stages of being neurologically prepared. The emphasis here is on the ego's capacity to process immediate experience by its own novel engagement with objects presented to the senses, which are quickly lost as fleeting impressions. During the moment of engagement, objects are semiotically filtered through the psychic register and related to the original object of signification – *lack*. Here an object for consciousness becomes a presence rather than an absence, and, hence, the process of signification enters into other dialectical unfoldings based upon a multitude of sensible objects experientially presented to the ego. Ideation at this stage is not the mechanism of an a priori preconception mating with an object that produces a conception, as Bion would tell us; rather, it is a process of designated signification associated with the experiential *functions* objects serve.

I believe the preverbal ego constructs meaning not through concepts or words but through images, impressions, or sensory-tactile sensations that are internally processed in relation to a felt referent and related to objects encountered in unconscious phantasy, either real or imagined. Thought is originally the succession of sensory impressions imbued with emotional mediacy linked to functional meaning associated with objects of experience originally derived from the apperceptive sentient unconscious abyss of the ego.[10] What becomes encoded or imprinted on the psyche are the functional qualities, properties, and attributes of the experiential presencing of objects. Under the influence of internal drives and their derivatives – such as affect, wishes, and their vicissitudes – in relation to exogenous factors, the nascent ego constructs meaningful relations to objects through the functional attributions of phantasy that are subject to the anxieties or pleasure associated with its own internal impulses and eccentrically perceived object attachments. Images and sensory experience related to objects are imbued with functional meaning, linked to associative affect or corresponding feeling states, mnemonically recorded, and laid down as semiotic traces in the deep combinatory of signifiers in the unconscious, which are called forth when phantasy is mobilized. Such combinatorial operations highlight the overdetermined processes and multiple functions assigned by psychic agency.

We are justified, I believe, in further saying that the nascent ego performs such mediatory operations by attaching functional meaning to objects in the form of qualities and their related expectations, which take on the signification of the affects evoked corresponding to gratifying or anxiety-ridden associations. In effect, the ego assigns an object the experience of such a task or job, which is related to the quality and expectation it evokes, the represented meaning of which stands for the function the object serves. Hence, the function is the imbued purpose (*telos*) upon which the meaning is constructed. Sensory impressions become the original contents for the earliest modes of thought, which have their origins in the prenatal activity of the unconscious mind, where the embryonic ego senses its own internality along with its felt-sentience, urges, and affect arising within its constitutional embodiment. In the beginning stages of conscious life, the ego forms meaningful associations with objects based on the functional qualities and evoked affective states mediated through phantasy, a process that becomes more robust during language acquisition and formal concept formation. We may conclude that what Hegel (1830) refers to as the function of symbols and signs, and what Bion (1957) calls ideographs, occurs at the unconscious level of the feeling soul. Although the incipient ego does not think in concepts or words, the experiences of objects are dialectically mediated through projective identification in phantasy; they signify and are categorized by their various functional meanings in correlation to affect. It is only when language is introduced that such mediatory relations acquire conceptual signification in the form of phonemes, syllables, words, names, and proper linguistic signifiers.

Meaning is originally created privately, where imago and sign are gelled into a constellation of emotional properties and functional classifications. Here purposeful expectations are constructed, resulting in certain possible consequences that are perhaps even anticipated in response to desire and lack, thus resonating within the privatization of the nascent ego's interior language, which is assigned by its own affective organizing principles. This pre-reflective, affective-functional execution of signification, which mediates the infant's conscious experience of the object world, is dialectically prepared by unconscious semiotics. Such preparation allows for the receptivity and amalgamation of language that must converse with the ego's original forms of affect signification, thus producing a developmental revamping of the subject's intrapsychic semiotic linkages, which become more linguistically mediated over time. With the introduction of language, the question becomes: To what degree does the psyche partition off, via splitting, dissociation, and projective identification, somatic and affective schemata that are resistant to this new and more articulate form of signification, which is introduced through the medium of the spoken word and that gives rise to new capacities to symbolize and represent meaning?

In adopting Hegel's (1812) *Logic*, the dialectic is the ontological force behind the generation of multiplicity and complexity with regard to content and form, beginning as (1) embodied sentient life, progressing to (2) affective organization, then to (3) consciousness, and finally to (4) self-conscious self-reflection mediated by linguistic conceptualization and meaning. Because somatic and affective schemata are so intertwined despite having the capacity to appear as separate schematic representations (e.g., via compromise functions), the introduction of linguistic schemata in itself produces both a cleavage – hence a spacing – and a mode of unification between the inner world of embodiment and felt-sensation and the ability to represent such processes via conceptual thought and rational abstraction. At times signification may attain a triangulation of somatic-affective-linguistic linkages. But with concepts being applied to represent more embodied and emotional experiences, there is also a compartmentalization instituted between the ability of the subject to form linkages between bodily states, emotions, and conceptual thought, which may fall under the influence of dissociative strategies or militant forms of psychopathology. As Bion alerts us, perhaps there are inner intentional phenomena (as split-off or alienated desires) that attack other parts of the ego, what the Kleinians typically refer to as part-objects, or what more contemporary perspectives label as self-states, and therefore prevent the crystallization of junctions between soma, feeling, and thought. And if they are approximated, they are only partially forged. Regardless of the synthetic unification and compartmentalization processes at work, themselves the vacillation of the dialectic, the unconscious ego remains the executive agentic mediator of all psychical events and will be vigilant of the multitude of competing dangers, threats, and ancillary wishes vying for expression and victory over other competing processes pressing for fulfilment, defence, or censorship. Here we may say that the executive agentic activities of the unconscious ego merely perform a formal function of interceding, barring, and unifying opposition in the service of sublation. When this is not possible, the self falls under neurotic propensities subject to a variety of pathogenic potentials. In the case of trauma or overwhelming stress or fear, synthetic and integrating functions are compromised altogether; hence, behavioural action and adaptative responsiveness is rendered incapacitated. Here the dialect may become arrested or stymied in its sublating powers, or may regress to previous levels of functioning.

In more extreme forms of fear, danger, and trauma, the alienation, dissociation, and subsequent inability to form synthetic links will be more pronounced. Yet schemata belonging to these separate realms or orders of experience will fall back on the most original or regressed forms of signification that the mind feels it has previously mastered or that at least is most familiar to it when stress is present and threat reduction is summoned in the service of adaptive survival. This is one reason why so many traumatized patients, psychotics, schizoids, depressives, and alexithymics experience a fundamental gap between forming concepts about sequestered somatic and affective states. It is also why they are not able to enunciate and attach earlier dissociated body memories to emotional processes and their meaningful conceptual linkages. Here the dialectic resists synthesis and, instead, prefers to tarry in its previous modes of split-off division based on the negation of otherness. Or it regresses back to its previous, primitive mental divisions. It also becomes easy to imagine how the dialectic would inverse itself and withdraw to more emotive and somatic expressions that become represented, hence communicated, through affective dysregulation and bodily conversion symptoms guided by compromise formations. In effect, symptoms are accommodated by the unconscious ego. Here the cornucopia of mental illness can be seen as having its origin in disjointed, stifled, and segregated unconscious schemata barred from proper semiotic linkage, mediation, integration, and meaning construction.

But how are these split-off segregated schemata able to converse with one another or to intermingle, let alone to achieve some form of unification through conceptual mediation? A possible answer is to be found in understanding how schemata emerge out of basic units of unconscious organization that further differentiate themselves from their original unity and progressively modify in form through dialectical activity. This is why the mind should be conceived as emerging from a developmental monistic ontology, whereby sentient life gives birth to the realm of affect, which, in turn, gives rise to the phenomenology of consciousness. Here we must entertain the primordial ground of unconscious desire as it projects itself into higher tiers of articulated expression, culminating in the assimilation of earlier unconscious, embodied emotional activity within the conscious ego's conceptually self-reflexive mediation. Here it further becomes important to revisit the principle of archaic primacy: the past always saturates the present, which, in turn, conditions the ego's projection of a future as a desirous ideal state of affairs or wish-fulfilment. Each schematic system may also prove to successfully insulate itself from encroaching threats through defensive or dissociative strategies, which manage to keep the various schemata segregated. As a result, somatic, affective, and linguistic representations may appear at times as distinct organizations that are compartmentalized, although they are merely split-off relations that have not been formally integrated. Each differentiated schema or self-state is ontologically interconnected despite being modified from its original source, namely, desire as drive.

This brings to the fore the question of schematic structure. How is a schema constituted? What activity is at work within corporeal, affective, and conceptual order? As we have intimated in our treatment of the epigenesis of the unconscious ego, schemata emerge from the developmental architectonic thrust of the dialectic beginning with the most primordial form of (a) embodied sensuousness, then moving to (b) the life of feeling, then to (c) the robust explosion of consciousness that begets the higher fruition of lived experience. Schemata are originally constituted by splitting through the dividing function of negation carried out within the process of projective identification as sublating recapitulation. Hence lack – or the presencing of absence – becomes a semiotic function that brings the form of emptiness or nothingness into contact with the self-certainty the ego finds as itself, with the projection into otherness it comes to reincorporate back into its self. Recall that the unconscious ego comes into being through an implosion as externalized rupture, hence a negation of its constricted form of sleep, lethargy, or implicitness. The minute movements of the dialectic lend themselves to more cohesive forms: first the immediate self-sensuousness of the ego's embodiment (somatic schemata), then emotional reverberations within its interior (affective schemata), then a breaching into consciousness at birth and thereafter (perceptual, imagistic, iconic, symbolic, conceptual schemata, and so forth) – each schema emanating from its original ontic foundation yet differentiated over time into distinct interstices and groupings of mental spacings.

At this point, we need to look at how a differentiated mental form is organized from within its own interior constitution and how this is predicated on the prior shapes or movements of the dialectic. As we have seen, modification is achieved through the complex activity of projective identification as split-off, dissociated, or alienated feeling-properties, somatic-sensations, unconscious qualia, and self-states make a bid for integration or synthesis. Yet they are constantly fighting the tensions and elements that are resistant to amalgamation and fueled by opposition and defense that strive to maintain a compartmentalization between the schematic orders and their sub-components. Differentiated schemata stand in relation to one other, sometimes in rigid opposition and at other times in less resistant forms of engagement. Regardless of the malleability or mutability of schemata potentially interacting with one another, we have separate formations of inner experience that have their own spacings, press, valences, vectors, and qualities, such as biological impingements, urges, wishes, and conflicts that are opposed to other competing schemata, which inevitably produce discord with one another. We may assume a perspectival stance of understanding the internal dynamics of each schema and how it unfolds in relation to the rest. This requires us to think phenomenologically about the internal micro-dynamics of schematic activity within the broader ontological configurations that dialectically guide this process, through what I call an onto-phenomenological method.

Given the logical unfolding of the dialectic as progressing from (1) a general inner division to (2) external dispersal to (3) reincorporation, the internal activity of a schema would progress from (i) the immediacy of its somatic, sensual (or sensuous) pulsations;[11] to (ii) affective reverberations; to (iii) perceptual organization; then finally to (iv) conceptual (symbolic) order, each mode consisting of previously undifferentiated units of experience that have undergone modification in form and developed out of prior archaic shapes. A schema may be understood as first constituting a one-way internal relation to its own immediacy, only to dialectically transform through further division and modification that are sufficiently reorganized as separate pockets or units of experience having differences in content, form, valence, and intensity. Although there is a transactional, supraordinate system that is generated and maintained through the relata of schemata that are ultimately engineered by the unconscious ego, there still remains an internal relation that constitutes the intrinsic activity of each schema, what we may call the intrapsychic constituency of evolving mental form. Here a schema is viewed as participating within a subsystem or community of events that comprises the intrinsic constitution of each schematic structure or its representative; further, each differentiated schematic organization or category (i.e., somatic, affective, perceptual, conceptual) falls within the general organizational force of dialectical order. Here each schema has the potential to act with certain degrees of freedom. This potential may take both progressive and regressive forms, may marshal around certain aims for unification and communication with other schemata, or may coalesce around more compartmentalized organizations that delimit or annul the range of semiotic connections to (and awareness of) other schematic modalities that simultaneously exist and press for expression within unconscious mentation.

Given the level of semi-autonomous assertion inherent in schematic structure, we may readily appreciate that certain schemata may be dissociated or radically oppose coming into contact with other schemata due to the magnitude of conflict that may transpire. For example, a patient of mine who was sexually abused as a child had a somatic aversion to meat as an adult but was unable to understand why until she recovered repressed memories of having been raped by an uncle. Her having depersonalized throughout the trauma allowed certain body and affective schemata to remain compartmentalized and unintegrated within her perceptual and cognitive appraisals of the event. Remarkably, she recalled that, during her depersonalization, she had focused on a box of Kentucky Fried Chicken that had been left on the kitchen table. When these repressed memories came flooding back into consciousness, she was quick to conceptually link the horror of the abuse with what she psychically infused into the chicken box, which subsequently induced her generalized aversion to meat – the symbolic penis – as a means of keeping the memory buried. Before she had these insights, segregated schemata were presumably operative yet not integrated within conscious thought, despite taking the character of a compromise formation. This parallel unconscious activity supports the degree of autonomy various schemata may acquire and exert independently over other governing forces within the mind.

Given our logic of modification, each schematic subsystem or community acquires the capacity to mediate between other schemata once certain channels of communication are sufficiently compatible and less legislated by censorship or by the defensive maneuvers inherent to each schema. When this is favorable, schemata may undergo a transfigured relation, whereby they can absorb certain aspects of other schemata that are then incorporated within their own internal orders. When internal dynamics are unfavorable for cross-schematic interaction or fertilization, a schema may defend against other schemata and their imposed self-agendas through the inclination to cleave or abort linkages altogether. This points to the autonomy of agentic choice with regard to object and action at the hands of each differentiated or dissociated self-state that potentially inhabits schematic structure. This directionality of desire inherent within schematic structure also points to the selective retentive aspect of the dialectic, which is at odds with the mind's thrust towards unification and synthetic transcendence.

Figure 10.1 depicts the internal structure of a schema. Because schemata originally emerge from the primordial bedrock of the unconscious ego and encounters with psychic experience that the ego is condemned to organize, channel, and filter through the vast array of competing desires, endogenous impulses, teleologic pressures, counterdefenses, brushes with external impingements (e.g., social reality), and so forth, they may be viewed as differentiated and modified self-states that cluster into more functional units or subsystems that spawn their own organizational forms corresponding to specific modalities of embodiment and conceptual order. The pulsional mind generates thought

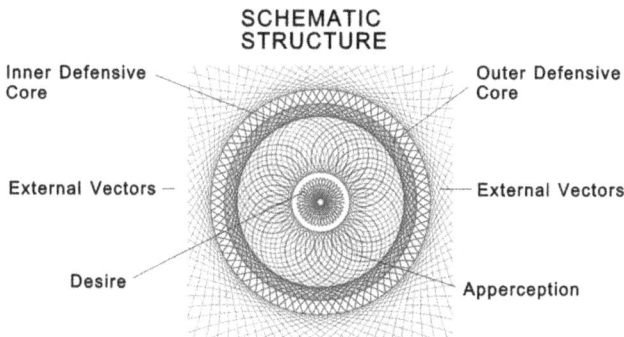

SCHEMATIC STRUCTURE

Inner Defensive Core

Outer Defensive Core

External Vectors

External Vectors

Desire

Apperception

Figure 10.1 Schematic Structure.

through desire, thought that first lives underground, confined to the circumscribed life of schematic structure. Because psychic modification is dialectically instantiated, all differentiated schematic forms must share and participate in the same essence. It is only in this way that multiplicity and diversity of psychic processes and their respective contents can interact, correspond, congeal, amalgamate, intertwine, or infuse with one another; yet they can equally oppose, negate, annul, and retreat from such linkages into fortified burrows forged through their own defensive constructions.

As desire gives rise to unconscious apperception, the ego generates both an inner defensive core and an outer defensive core, the former being an internal protective mechanism against intrapsychic and internally derived wishes, anxiety, and conflict, the latter being a shield against the encroachment of exterior impingements and environmental vectors. Here the rudimentary organization of the ego extends to schematic structure as schemata are modified self-states impregnated with ego-properties and their operations.

Because schemata share the same (modified) essence derived from unconscious process, they operate as self-contained ego-properties with their own locus of agency and internal organization assigned by the unconscious ego; however, they should not be conceived as entities that are separate or distinct from the ego. On the contrary, we have repeatedly maintained that the unconscious ego is the executor and directing force behind the unifying and telic operations of mind. In effect, the unconscious ego is a Grand Central Station that authorizes, dispatches, and attempts to unionize the multiple ego-states and their related contents that are alienated or dissociated from the ego itself into spacings of the abyss as they come back clamoring for rechanneling or resolve. Here the unconscious abyss becomes the cosmic storage bin, with labyrinthine tunnels forged through circuitous routes attempting to return to home base, only to be subverted and repetitiously sought and, perhaps, eventually retrieved or even called back to Grand Central. Although this banal metaphor does not do justice to the complexity and onus the unconscious ego ultimately shoulders, it may nevertheless serve as an analogue for the diverse activity of unconscious agency.

In psychoanalytic language, the unconscious ego disperses its internal content through projective identification. However, the content and ego-properties inherent in schemata have semi-autonomous modes of agency that take on a quasi-life of their own. They may revisit the executor (ego) or remain in the interstices of psychic space (like a planet in the solar system that maintains its own orbit regardless of whether it is ever discovered, stumbled upon, or bumped into by other objects in the cosmos). Here lies the universe of the abyss, populated with endless schemata and communities of schemata that may form substructures as process systems. The plurality of schematic forms and their combinations are virtually limitless. Some are more sophisticated, such as elaborate phantasy systems, while others are pithy and simple. The more schemata gather in communities, the more they gain in organization and strength. Communities can oppose one another, and, like our anthropological relations with other cultures and societies, they can have conflict and war. Dominant groups may attempt to capture and subdue other communities and assimilate them into their own social substructures. We may call this colonization. Colonies may oppose other colonies, or they may coexist in more harmonious fashions. Information may be transmitted or blocked by multiple overdetermined sources at once. The internal organization of each schema is ultimately determined by the dialectical mediations that transpire on micro and macro levels of order. This view of schematic structure is compatible with modern conflict theory in psychoanalysis today.

Because each schema is a modified and transmuted series of ego-states, whether sentient, affective, or conceptually mediated, it derives from the original process of unconscious desire and apperceptive self-certainty that is the ego's basal constitution. Here a schema is constructed by the unconscious ego and endowed with functional properties and qualia within representational structures and subjected to (as well as foreclosed from) semiotic meaning. Figure 10.1 attempts to show how each schema must necessarily participate in the unconscious ego's original form as desirous apperception, which must institute and execute internal defensive barriers that insulate it from the subjective contents both internally composed and derived from the network of external vectors impinging on the internal structure of each schema. External vectors are composed of the multitudinous forms of information processing within the psyche, along with its competing teleonomic pressures and teleologic trajectories laid down in the cosmic web of signification. The interactive and interactional dual cores form a three-way relation between the detection of inner experience, outer registrations, and the mediated object, which is a particular piece of datum (e.g., the material being appercepted or defended against). The dual defensive cores serve the double function of protecting against external peril and internal implosion and decay due to the self-destructive propensities of the death drive. The inner core safeguards the ego against self-annihilation, whereas the outer core protects against predation and external sources of discomfort and pain – both in the service of self-preservation through armament.

As the schemata divide and multiply, they acquire their own internal orders, which have varying degrees of complexity. This naturally means that more sophisticated forms of consciousness, such as perception and verbal concept formation, intervene in or are superimposed on earlier, more archaic and primitive forms of internal experience.

Figure 10.2 depicts how schemata can emerge out of one another as separated, differentiated modalities of inner experience, yet can also potentially interpenetrate one another when schematic receptors are reciprocally attuned and open to interaction, hence producing structural overlaps in content and form. When schemata defend against other schematic intrusions, they may operate as alienated or dissociated ego-states that work to guard against perceived invasions from other schemata that threaten their internal integrity or cohesion. As

Figure 10.2 Schematic Emergence.

mentioned, when schemata interpenetrate each other in content and form, they can give rise to higher-order complex structures that we may call colonies. As a general rule, these colonies are more sophisticated and dominate psychic valuation processes. In other words, they exert more force and influence over unconscious mentation. Of course, these colonies can be both positive and negative in content and form, hence susceptible to adaptive or pathological valences. Colonies are ingressive and can enter into other schemata; attempt to incorporate, subjugate, or oppose them; or strip them of their original properties. They may ban together with other colonies or maintain their unique autonomy. Colonies are tantamount to elaborate desirous phantasy systems that populate unconscious life. Here the dialectic is operative on multiple levels of annulment, supersession, and preservation within its sublating teleology.

Taken together as a system of differentiated agentic organization, each schema exerts a certain bid for freedom while falling under the governance of the dialectic executed by the telic functions of the unconscious ego. The diverse latitude of schematic autonomy may be said to account for resistance barriers and censorship as well as for open gates to communication via schematic redirection that allow for signification networks to engage one another, thus attempting to achieve some modicum of representational unification even if sifting filtration processes are operative.

I use the term "agency" rather than the term "entity" to denote the activity of a schema in order to avoid reifying the schema as a separate being or substance; however, I realize that the term "agency" can be just as problematic as the term "entity." I also realize that the reader may find the language I use to ascribe agency to psychic organizations existing as independent clusters in the mind to be highly anthropomorphic, interpreting them as hypostatized concrete entities. Of course, our human language imports psychological attributes when describing the observance of natural phenomena (e.g., when physicists ascribe the natural laws of repulsion and attraction to particles), but this is all the more reason to believe that subjectivity saturates every epistemological aspect of the natural world. Perhaps it is better to view a schema as a microagent or a distinctively organized self-state. What I wish to convey is that each schema, in principle, has a degree of freedom that compels it to act and that may fall under the sway of the drives, pulsional body, constitutional pressures, environmental forces, external vectors, or defensive functions that serve its optimal self-interests. Of course, each schema exists in relation to others that have potentially equal force, valence, and intensity, thereby ensuring systemic constellations of tension that the unconscious ego must mediate through redirective negotiated tactics or compromises. This potentially explains how certain elements of psychic phenomena appear alien to our own conscious intentions, desires, beliefs, and attitudes, thus accounting for conflictually ridden internal experiences, including dreams, slips, fantasies, and symptoms. We may refer to this alien process as Freud's *Es*, or, more broadly, the workings of the abyss. Despite the element of choice each schema possesses, it is important to keep in mind that these are differentiated aspects of the unconscious ego and are always subject to its executive powers. Hence, the ego is the *unifying unifier*; yet it is a unifier that, in principle, is not unified but, rather, is constituted as dynamic activity – fluid and in flux – yoked together by form.

The more autonomous, compartmentalized, or detached a schema becomes from the ego's synthetic hub, registry, or point of confluence, the more likely it may operate as an independent force in the mind. Here it is important to emphasize that the term "force" does not refer to homunculi operating in the mind but only to process. However, as any self-state, the schema is merely a differentiated element of the ego that retains its essence and thus seizes upon its internal capacity to act through dialectical mediation.

Let us attempt to summarize a few key points:

1   Schemata are the building blocks of the psyche and comprise the basic constituent movements of the dialectic. They operate as microagents with semi-autonomous powers of telic expression. Schemata build upon one other as epigenetic and architectonic achievements and can coalesce into higher organizations of complexity and order, just as consciousness proceeds from its unconscious foundation. In fact, schematic organizing principles allow for the emergence of higher-order forms of complexity.

2   The schematic underworld is composed of multitudinous complex subsystems or communities of associational and communicative networks harboring a combinatory of signifiers. Unconscious

semiotics are under the direction of implicit or unformulated phantasy systems within each schematic realm that partitions off objective content (i.e., perceptive data gathered from the senses about the object world) from subjective desire and wishes fraught by defense under the persecution of real or perceived threat and anxiety. Here interschematic communication constitutes ontic relations with potentially indefinite modes of intrarelations and interrelatedness.

3   Unconscious phantasy systems constitute the central activity of psychic life and become the locus of the abyss. In principle, there is a vast underworld of communities with smaller precincts or subcultures that are composed of various groupings or factions of schemata, each clustering around particular resonant states, affects, or symbolic ties that are potentially linked together by an extended chain of signification with a potentially infinite deferral of associations. It is here that imagination, and particularly phantasy, once again initiated and sustained by the ego, becomes a central nexus for appropriating and manipulating various schemata for unconscious semiotic expressions.

The term "community" is used to emphasize the communal nature of schematic communication and its mutual relata. For schemata to commune, they must maintain something in common (*communis*), hence they must have a shared essence, despite variance in content and form. There are some communities that are more self-governing and dominant over others, again, what we might call colonies. But these dominant settlements could be either positive or negative, depending upon a person's developmental history and life experiences. For example, it goes without saying that a child with relatively secure attachments would have different internal schemata than would a neglected, abused, or traumatized child. Furthermore, schematic processes enjoy a degree of liberty with regard to how they organize their internal structures, regardless of what extrinsic events transpire or are imposed. However, trauma can retard the growth, autonomy, and degrees of expressive freedom schemata can execute, not to mention the greater dynamic system we call mind.

Schematic communities may coalesce into certain dominant modes of organization, each assuming hierarchical levels of order, whereby some content is elevated and other content is subordinated in terms of importance or internal press. It is also conceivable that some communities will form more advanced, elaborate, compound, and reigning organizations, while others will struggle to thrive or peter out altogether. Once again, the potential for schematic subsystems to exist in harmony, tolerance, avoidance, or combat with one another mirrors cultural anthropology. Each may exist in engagement, proximity, or isolation from the others, but none is ever completely untouched or untouching. Plurality, independence, separateness, and interpenetration are conjoined under the rubric of dialectical unity.

Coda

Generally, we have identified the realm of: (1) *somatic schemata*, which are originally derived from the sentient pulsional body guided by desirous appetition; (2) *affective schemata*, which pertain to the feeling soul, which is the proper locus of emotions; (3) *perceptual schemata*, which are more consolidated, coherent imagistic clusters of cognitive-sensuous events; and (4) *conceptual schemata*, which belong to linguistic concept formation, symbolic signification, and rational understanding, the advanced domain of thought. Each classification of schemata has its own differentiated mode of mnemonic retention, synchrony, and semiotics that corresponds to its distinguishable form. However, when internal conditions are favorable, schemata may work together synergistically to form higher-order societies with more sophisticated modalities of generativity and creative meaning relations.

Overall, we may observe how the dialectic of desire has internally divided and modified itself through projective identification, which has prepared the developmental progression of each major schematic organization, whereby the lower relations remain subsumed within the higher yet are capable of retaining segregated relations that resist complete absorption into the sublated whole. Of course, phantasy systems may inhere in each type of schema under the direction of disunited ego-states. Here unconscious semiotic properties inherent in each schema may display various degrees of regulatory units of unconscious experience. The (a) *content* is highly contingent and variable, as are the levels of (b) *valence* (or the capacity to form conjoint relations with other schemata) and the structural (c) *intensity* of teleonomic pressures and telic trajectories of unconscious qualia. The more force or internal impulsion guided by quantitative (biologic) and qualitative (phenomenal) intensities, the more dynamic demand and economic constraint these schemata exert on the unconscious ego to mediate such tensions, which, in turn, exerts pressure on the whole dialectical system to intervene, arbitrate, or attempt sublation. It is within the threshold of these intensities that psychic life forms a nucleus of confluences that potentially answers to the mind-body problem as a complex totality of vital processes ontologically conjoined yet differentiated by form.

Here let us briefly consider the role of temporal mediacy on the spacings of the abyss. According to the principle of archaic primacy, the past has a primordial causal impetus within each psychic form or schema, exerting a powerful toll on its ontological status and motivational valences. Archaic primacy has an ontological privilege in the psyche for it encompasses the historicity of presubjectivity or, put another way, the prehistory of subjectivity, including the constitutional and phylogenetic dispositions that could be operative within psychic structure. Archaic primacy suffuses the immediational presence of being, which informs its projective teleology towards its future state of becoming. Here unconscious semiotics must necessarily take into account its various filterings of previously encoded content as concrete data within all three temporal contexts that pressurize one another in the infinite multitude of subsystems that exist within each classification of form. No small task indeed.

What this amounts to is that the unconscious ego has the onerous job of attempting to satiate the teleonomic pressures conforming to bodily pulsions or constitutional organic laws, which, in turn, are subject to higher-order teleological directives that forge the cosmic underworld of unconscious schemata and their semiotic correlates. This means that inscriptive markers or traces that are structurally inscribed in each specific schema, and of which there are potentially (at least in theory) an infinite number within the abyss, incubate, gestate, and possess some active life-force or energetic load clamoring for redirective expression or discharge. Here lies the inherent autonomy and freedom of psychic event clustered into precincts of permissible versus barred zones of delivery, each of which are brimming with various degrees of excitation, slumber or inactivation, and heightened modes of action potential. Just as the free association method of psychoanalysis can potentially lead to an endless stream of productions, so the conceivable associational branches of signification between the competing instantiations of schemata are as vast as a universe, and all of them are subject to the synthetic-mediating agentic activity directed by the dialectic. In fact, the structural complexity, functional operations, and teleological organizations governing the microdynamics of unconscious experience truly underscore the awesome capacities of mind.

Notes

1 What is important for process psychology is understanding the essential structure of the dialectic as sublation (*Aufhebung*) denoted by these three simultaneous movements: at once, they cancel or annul, transcend or surpass, retain or preserve – aspects of every transmutation. In offering amendments to Hegel's dialectic, I have argued that mind also has a dual tendency to fixate on earlier developmental experiences, dialectically regress or withdraw back to previous states of disposition and comportment, and become mired in neurosis, psychopathology, and trauma it cannot transcend in its natural progressive drive toward sublation.

2 All references to Freud's *Standard Edition* will be designated by *SE* followed by the volume and page numbers.

3 This is a child's toy, which, today, would be referred to as an "Etch-a-Sketch" or something similar.

4 What the reader may observe is how Freud's technical language in his "Mystic Pad" paper is wed to the biologics of his earlier homeostatic model of economics. But we can also see that, clearly, by this time, he has introduced his structural or process theory of psychic agencies and that the topography of psychic spacings have been expanded and subsumed within the economic, dynamic, and adaptive aspects of mental functioning.

5 It can be argued that waves of theoretical compatibility potentially exist between process psychology and the promising new discourse on biosemiotics; however, I wish to emphasize the primacy of the unconscious, which appropriates and executes biological and semiotic processes without reducing informational processing systems and communications networks to reductive frameworks. In my opinion, the language of unconscious mediation more broadly encompasses biosemiotics within a process paradigm of dialectical organizations that may find their expression in the most minute structural level of organic life (e.g., intercellular signaling) as well as in the higher forms of signification and communication that properly belong to animal behavior and human linguistic patterns.

6 All references to Lacan's *Écrits* is designed by *E*.

7 Peirce's *Collective Papers* is referred to as *CP*.
8 Refer to my extensive theoretical commentary on dissociation and my clinical treatment of a case of ritualistic trauma discussed in Chapter 10 of *Treating Attachment Pathology* (Mills, 2005a).
9 Although distinctions can be made between affect (as sentient, psychophysiological manifestations of mental events) and emotions (as more qualitatively organized threads of experiential feeling), for the sake of parsimony, here I refer to each synonymously. In psychoanalysis, affects are generally seen as complex psycho-physiological phenomena encompassing cognitive, physical, and qualitative sub-jective, experiential elements. Moore and Fine (1990) distinguish between affects, emotions, and feelings, although we are accustomed to view each as an inter-changeable construct. *Feelings* refer to subjective experiential states that may or may not be accessible to consciousness, while *emotions* are viewed as outwardly observable manifestations of feelings. *Affects*, on the other hand, are broad and enveloping, comprising all qualitative and quantitative instantiations, from the most primordial to the most cognitively differentiated complex psychic state under the direction of both conscious and unconscious forces. In contrast, *moods* may be viewed as prolonged and enduring affect states dominated by unconscious phan-tasy. It can be argued that emotionality is imbued with affect and that they are one and the same. Emotion is the implosional interiorization of affect. That is, affect is as implosive as it is expressive. Emotionality is merely a return – a slippage – to its rumbling beginnings, which are externally directed albeit internally experienced.
10 This is in contradistinction to what Freud privileged: namely, that judgment denotes the process of thinking based on concept formation, a claim Cavell (2003) recently upholds following from contemporary analytic philosophy.
11 There is a logical and developmental necessity to conceive of internal sensuous experience as derived from somatic sources that organically and constitutionally stimulate desire as being-in-relation-to lack and drive, as both libidinous (hence sensual) and destructive activity, hence as interiorized conflict and negation, which prefigures our sense experience belonging to conscious qualia.

References

Aragno, A. (2008). *Forms of Knowledge: A Psychoanalytic Study of Human Communication*. Baltimore: Publish America.
Aragno, A. (2019). "Semiotic Realms: Codes, Language, Mind. A Psychoanalytic Perspective." *Biosystems* 182: 21–29.
Beardsworth, S. (2004). *Julia Kristeva: Psychoanalysis and Modernity*. Albany, NY: SUNY Press.
Bion, W.R. (1957). "Differentiation of the Psychotic from the Non-Psychotic Personalities." In E.B. Spillius (Ed.), *Melanie Klein Today: Developments in Theory and Practice*. Vol. 1: *Mainly Theory*, 1988, 61–78. London: Routledge.

Bion, W.R. (1959). "Attacks on Linking." In E.B. Spillius (Ed.), *Melanie Klein Today: Developments in Theory and Practice*. Vol. 1: *Mainly Theory*, 1988, 87–101. London: Routledge.

Bucci, W. (2003). "Varieties of Dissociative Experiences: A Multiple Code Account and a Discussion of Bromberg's Case of 'William.'" *Psychoanalytic Psychology* 20, 3: 542–557.

Bucci, W. (1997). *Psychoanalysis and Cognitive Science: A Multiple Code Theory*. New York: Guildford Press.

Cavell, M. (2003). "The Social Character of Thinking." *Journal of the American Psychoanalytic Association* 51, 3: 803–824.

Derrida, J. (1998). *Resistances of Psychoanalysis*. Trans. P. Kamuf, P.A. Brault, and M. Naas. Stanford: Stanford University Press.

Freud, (1923). *The Ego and the Id. SE*, Vol. 19: 1–63.

Freud, S. (1968 [1940–52]). *Gesammelte Werke, Chronologisch Geordnet*, A. Freud, E. Bibring, W. Hoffer, E. Kris, and O. Isakower (Eds.), in collaboration with Marie Bonaparte. 18 vols. London/Frankfurt am Main: Imago Publishing Co. Ltd.

Freud, S. (1966–95 [1886–1940]). *The Standard Edition of the Complete Psychological Works of Sigmund Freud*, 24 vols. Trans. and gen. ed.J. Strachey, in collaboration with Anna Freud, assisted by Alix Strachey and Alan Tyson. London: Hogarth Press.

Freud, S. (1893–95). *Studies on Hysteria* (with Josef Breuer). *SE*, Vol. 2.

Freud, S. (1900). *The Interpretation of Dreams. SE*, Vols. 4-5.

Freud, S. (1915a). "Instincts and Their Vicissitudes." *SE*, Vol. 14, 109–140.

Freud, S. (1915b). "The Unconscious." *SE*, Vol. 14: 159–216.

Freud, S. (1920). *Beyond the Pleasure Principle. SE*, Vol. 18: 1–144.

Freud, S. (1925a). "A Note upon the 'Mystic Writing-Pad.'" *SE*, Vol. 19, 226–232.

Freud, S. (1925b.) "Negation." *SE*, Vol. 19, 234–239.

Freud, S. (1926). *Inhibitions, Symptoms and Anxiety. SE*, Vol. 20. London: Hogarth Press.

Haartman, K. (2006). "Attachment, Metaphor, and the Relationality of Meaning." In J. Mills (Ed.), *Other Banalities: Melanie Klein Revisited*, 188–216. London: Routledge.

Hegel, G.W.F. (1812/1831). *Science of Logic*. Trans. A.V. Miller. London: George Allen and Unwin Ltd., 1969.

Hegel, G.W.F. (1830). *Philosophy of Spirit*. In *Hegel's Philosophy of Subjective Spirit*. Vol. 3: *Phenomenology and Psychology*. Trans. and Ed. M.J. Petry. Dordrecht, Holland: D. Reidel Publishing Company, 1978.

Kristeva, J. (1974). *Revolution in Poetic Language*. Trans. M. Waller. New York: Columbia University Press.

Lacan, J. (1936 [1949]). "The Mirror Stage as Formative of the Function of the I." In *Écrits: A Selection*. Trans. Alan Sheridan, 1977, 1–7. New York: Norton.

Lacan, J. (1955–56a). "Introduction to the Question of Psychoses." In *The Seminar of Jacques Lacan. Book 3: The Psychoses, 1955-1956*. Trans. R. Grigg, ed. J.-A. Miller, 1–58. New York: Norton, 1993.

Lacan, J. (1955–56b). "The Other and Psychoses." In *The Seminar of Jacques Lacan. Book 3: The Psychoses, 1955–1956*. Trans. R. Grigg, ed. J.-A. Miller, 29–43. New York: Norton, 1993.

Lacan, J. (1955–56c). "The Hysteric's Question." In *The Seminar of Jacques Lacan. Book 3: The Psychoses,1955–1956*. Trans. R. Grigg, ed. J.-A. Miller, 161–172. New York: Norton, 1993.

Lacan, J. (1957). "The Agency of the Letter in the Unconscious or Reason since Freud." In *Écrits: A Selection*. Trans. A. Sheridan, 1977, 146–178. New York: Norton.

Lacan, J. (1960). "The Subversion of the Subject and the Dialectic of Desire in the Freudian Unconscious." In *Écrits: A Selection*. Trans. Alan Sheridan, 1977, 292–325. New York: Norton.

Merrell, F. (1997). *Peirce, Signs, and Meaning*. Toronto: University of Toronto Press.

Mills, J. (2000). Dialectical psychoanalysis: Toward process psychology. *Psychoanalysis and Contemporary Thought* 23(3), 20–54.

Mills, J. (2002a). "Deciphering the "Genesis Problem": On the Dialectical Origins of Psychic Reality." *The Psychoanalytic Review* 89 (6), 763–809.

Mills, J. (2002b). *The Unconscious Abyss: Hegel's Anticipation of Psychoanalysis*. Albany, NY: SUNY Press.

Mills, J. (2005a). *Treating Attachment Pathology*. Lantham, MD: Aronson/ Rowman and Littlefield.

Mills, J. (2005b). "Process psychology." In J. Mills (Ed.), *Relational and Intersubjective Perspectives in Psychoanalysis: A Critique*. Lanham, MD: Rowman & Littlefield.

Mills, J. (2010). *Origins: On the Genesis of Psychic Reality*. Montreal: McGill-Queens University Press.

Moore, B.E., & B.D. Fine (Eds.) (1990). *Psychoanalytic Terms and Concepts*. New Haven: American Psychoanalytic Association/ Yale University Press.

Peirce, C.S. (1931–35). *Collected Papers of Charles Sanders Peirce*, C. Hartshorne and P. Weiss. (Eds.), Vols. *1–6*. Cambridge, MA: Harvard University Press.

Chapter 11

The Plumbing of Political Economy: Marxism and Psychoanalysis Down the Toilet

Adrian Johnston

From Anus to Brain and Beyond: Psychoanalysis and a Materialism of Drives

Psychoanalysis indeed has much to say regarding the perennial mind-problem. I would argue that Sigmund Freud's most fruitful suggestions apropos the rapport between the mental and the bodily flow from his theory of drives (*Triebe*). I also would contend that the distinctive psychoanalytic concept of *Trieb*, given what it indicates as concerns the mind-body problem, places Freud unknowingly close to the theoretical tradition of dialectic materialism, a tradition inseparable from Marxism. In fact, I read Freud as (unconsciously) a spontaneous dialectical materialist, with Jacques Lacan, following in his footsteps, as an avowed one.[1]

I am far from alone in forwarding this contention to the effect that Freudian (as well as Lacanian) psychoanalysis cross-resonates with Marxist materialism, including via the analytic concept of drive. With permutations of what loosely could be labeled "Freudo-Marxism," such pioneering figures of the early-to-mid-twentieth century as the Soviets Alexander Luria[2] and Lev Vygotsky[3] as well as the Europeans Wilhelm Reich,[4] Otto Fenichel,[5] and Herbert Marcuse[6] all agree on the central role of psychoanalytic drive theory in a synthesis of psychoanalysis and dialectical/historical materialism. They interpret the interplay of somatic and psychical dimensions and components within each and every analytic *Trieb* as permitting the attribution to Freudian metapsychology of a materialist dialectics bringing Freud the psychoanalyst into proximity with Marx the

DOI: 10.4324/9781003090755-12

materialist. From this perspective, the Freudian drive is akin to the Cartesian pineal gland, with both serving to connect mental *res cogitans* and somatic *res extensa*.[7]

An oft-cited paragraph in Freud's 1915 metapsychological paper "Drives and Their Vicissitudes" directly applies the concept of *Trieb* to the distinction between mind and body. Freud famously states:

> If we now apply ourselves to considering mental life (*Seelenlebens*) from a *biological* point of view, an "instinct" (*der "Trieb"*) appears to us as a concept on the frontier between the mental and the somatic (*ein Grenzbegriff zwischenSeelischem und Somatischem*), as the psychical representative of the stimuli originating from within the organism (*Körperinnern*) and reaching the mind, as a measure of the demand made upon the mind for work in consequence of its connection with the body.[8]

As already indicated by the founding document of drive theory, Freud's 1905 *Three Essays on the Theory of Sexuality*, the anatomical sources (*Quellen*) of each and every drive—these sources include the oral and anal orifices as well as the genital organs—are the sites within soma from which emanate the pressures (*Dränge*), the "demands for work" (*Arbeitsanforderungen*), of the drives (whether oral, anal, genital, or whatever other additional type[s]).[9] The drives' sources and pressures of somatic origin motivate the human organism's turn to and navigation of the ideational representations (*Vorstellungen*) of drives' aims (*Ziele*) and objects (*Objekte*). These representations are constituted in and through psychical systems shaped by their ongoing interactions with natural and social external realities. With all drives, by Freud's metapsychological definition, composed of sources, pressures, aims, and objects,[10] drives bring together body/soma (as sources and pressures) with mind/psyche (as aims and objects). This clarifies Freud's characterization of *Trieb* as "a concept on the frontier between the mental and the somatic" (*ein Grenzbegriff zwischen Seelischem und Somatischem*).

My construal of Freud's corpus as containing a dialectical-materialist-style approach to the mind-body relationship best brought out through bringing a combination of Marxism and Lacanianism (i.e., a Lacano-Marxism) to bear on this corpus leads me to focus specifically on psychoanalysis's anal drive and its vicissitudes. In general,

Freud proposes an ontogenetic link according to which processes affecting the somatic side of drives (i.e., "organs" as orifices and genitals) in persons' early life histories give rise to the psychical side of "characters" and "character-traits" (as personalities, dispositions, attitudes, outlooks, tendencies, habits, etc.). This proposal can easily be made to resonate with a famous statement from Karl Marx and Friedrich Engels's 1845 *The German Ideology* according to which, "It is not consciousness that determines life, but life that determines consciousness"[11]—with Marxist life as Freudian organ and Marxist consciousness as Freudian character.

And, Freud emphasizes the organ-character bond most pointedly apropos anality in particular, especially in the papers "Character and Anal Erotism" (1908)[12] and "On Transformations of Instinct as Exemplified in Anal Erotism" (1917).[13] According to this Freud, rightly so-called anal personalities are ontogenetic outcomes of the vicissitudes of the anal drive. Furthermore, in both of these papers on anality as well as elsewhere, Freud repeatedly highlights associations conjoining gold/money and feces.[14] These associations are rich in implications for, among other fields, the Marxist critique of capitalist political economy. As an aside, it would be fair to say that anal character-types are pulled for by and tend to prosper under highly administered, bureaucratized industrial and post-industrial socio-economic orders.

For a Freudo-Marxist historical materialism, Freud's equation of wealth with shit (via anal erotism and its permutations) opens up possibilities for a non-reductive rapprochement between psychoanalysis and the critique of political economy (a rapprochement I will touch upon below and have explored at much greater length in other contexts[15]). For a Lacano-Marxist dialectical materialism, the general metapsychological theory of drive promises to allow for the construction of a rigorously materialist (even partly naturalist), and yet staunchly anti-reductive, rendition of minded psychical subjectivity able to take on board myriad crucial insights uniquely furnished by Marxism. Furthermore, just as historical and dialectical materialism are inextricably intertwined with each other in Marxism starting with Marx and Engels themselves,[16] so too are problems of political economy (as per historical materialism) and problems of the mind-body rapport (as per dialectical materialism) entangled. This entanglement is due to the social mediations of both mind and body acknowledged by Marxism and psychoanalysis alike.

Additionally, various of the Freudo-Marxists (particularly Reich, Fenichel, and Marcuse) seek to establish parallels between the psychoanalytic version of the soma-psyche configuration and a non-reductive (i.e., anti-economistic) historical materialist handling of infrastructure-superstructure interaction. Their shared hunch is that Marxism's analyses of the dynamics of complex social structures provide a macro-scale delineation of patterns operative within the microcosm zoomed in on by the traditional philosophical topic of the mind vis-à-vis the body. According to this Freudo-Marxist analogy, mind would be analogous to superstructure and body would be analogous to infrastructure.[17]

Probably due to repressions triggered and cemented in place by shame and disgust, philosophers preoccupied with the mind-body enigma, including dialectical materialist thinkers, have avoided examining biological loci such as the rectum and sphincter for clues to this stubbornly enduring mystery. Nobody wants to look in the toilet or up malodorous backsides when one's attention instead can be focused on the dazzling central nervous system and the technologically illuminated wonders of its celestial-like synaptic constellations. Most people, including most intellectuals, would like to believe that they genuinely prefer concerning themselves with the sublime heavenly cleanliness of heads rather than the ridiculous earthy filthiness of bottoms. Even radically materialist philosophies of mind, whether reductive or not, favor the neurological over the proctological. They do not acknowledge what psychoanalysis gestures at in terms of a body-body problem as an issue involving the (repressed) linkages between the organs of drives (including the anus and its anal drive) and the organ of the brain. Alongside the "gut brain" identified by contemporary biology, perhaps there also is an anus brain. And, as Bruno Bosteels perspicuously highlights, Louis Althusser enjoys the merit of being the at-least-one (Marxist) philosopher who underscores that philosophers do, in truth, have backsides.[18] They too poop, and, like everyone else, their shit stinks.

Likewise, as will be seen later, Lacan points out that the same sort of repression intellectually inhibits thinkers occupied with the terrain of political economy. On one occasion, he draws his audiences' attention to the solid waste disposal business. Simply put, toilets and everything servicing them count as "infrastructure" in both its technical Marxist sense (as socially essential economic industry) and its non-technical everyday sense (as plumbing, sewers, and septic systems, in addition to roads, canals, railways, subways, airports, power grids, communications networks, etc.). As Lacan notes, Marxist and non-Marxist political economists alike tend to be silent about sewage treatment as an absolutely indispensable rock-bottom dimension of social infrastructures (again, in both senses of "infrastructure").

Moreover, Slavoj Žižek's Lacan-inspired reflections on lavatories help further clarify both the convergences between Marxism and psychoanalysis as well as, within Marxism, the positioning of infrastructure and superstructure with respect to each other. Žižek accomplishes this precisely by bringing the body in its crudest aspects back into view, by putting the base back into the economic base of Marxist materialism. Anti-reductive historical and dialectical materialisms, even and especially in their struggles against idealisms, cannot, despite their sophistication, dispense with a certain vulgar materialism (one best developed by psychoanalysis). History may not march on its head, but it can get nowhere without its gluteus maximus.

Lacanian Economics: An Inquiry into the Poverty of Capitalism

In a recent piece, Fredric Jameson makes a straightforward case for prioritizing the specifically Lacanian version of psychoanalysis as a partner for Marxism in any rapprochement between the two fields (including one that would be concerned with the mind-body problem *à la* Marx *avec* Freud). Jameson's reading of Lacan situates him as a thinker of the *zoon politikon* in a lineage starting with Aristotle and continuing with both G.W.F. Hegel and Marx. Jameson explains:

> The primacy of desire in Freud remained essentially personal, and included the 'otherness' of the family in a merely causal fashion. Lacan was able to insert otherness into the heart of Freud's pathbreaking conception of desire, and to offer a picture of desire from which the presence of the Other—big or small— is never

absent, so that in a sense, or rather in all possible senses, individual desire is the desire of the Other, is the Other's desire. This socialization of desire itself now at one stroke renders the attempts to build a bridge between Freud and Marx, between the two great scientific discoveries which characterize modernity, unnecessary. For now the psyche is already essentially social, and the existence of the Other is at the very heart of the libidinal, just as all our social passions are already drenched in the psychic.[19]

He continues:

The fundamental superiority of Lacanian doctrine over the multitude of other psychoanalyses on offer, including Freud's original one, lies in the way it grasps the Other as being structurally internal to subjectivity itself...[20]

Finally, Jameson adds:

Here the stereotypical (and ideological) opposition between "the individual" and "society" cannot obtain, since the two are inseparable in an inextricable dialectic of identity and difference. To put it methodologically, where in other systems the operation of transcoding is unavoidable—we must pass from a language of subjective or psychological individuality to a very different terminology governing the social or the collective (a passage involving a mediation I tend to describe in terms of a translation process)— here transcoding is unnecessary and the same code can apply to either reality. Thus where for Freud, in *Group Dynamics and the Analysis of theEgo*, the superego is somehow outside the self, in the form of the dictator and object of fascination he constitutes, here the Lacanian big Other is within subjectivity, constituting it fully as much as it might be seen to influence it; nor is it some projection of my private desires, as when the Leader somehow symbolically resolves my own oedipal traumas (as for Erickson).[21]

There are three reservations I have about these passages. First, I worry about reading Lacan as radically liquidating any distinction between individual and social dimensions by dissolving the former into the latter. This renders him difficult to distinguish from, for instance, Jungians hypothesizing a collective mind/unconscious (a hypothesis Lacan rejects).

Second, apropos the Freudian super-ego specifically, what about Freud's repeated characterizations of the ego-ideal and the super-ego as each a "differentiated grade within the ego?"[22] Rather than the ego-ideal and/or super-ego being "somehow outside the self" as per 1921's *Group Psychology and the Analysis of the Ego*—even here, the external leader figure gets internalized via identification, with the 11th and final chapter of this book entitled by Freud "A Differentiating Grade in the Ego"[23]—are not the ego-ideal or super-ego *qua* differentiated grade(s) within the ego arguably "within subjectivity" just as much as are the Lacanian *petits autres* and *grand Autre*? Is Freud not sufficiently emphatic about this?

Third and relatedly, Jameson's extremely sharp contrast between Freud and Lacan on exogenous sociality/alterity is exaggerated. For instance, the ontogenetic zero-level prematurational helplessness (*Hilflosigkeit*) of the Freudian neonate, as per 1895's *Project for a Scientific Psychology*, renders the human psyche naturally inclined towards the dominance of nurture over nature, compelled to be socially related to others from the very get-go.[24] Moreover, Freud is not Thomas Hobbes, namely, he does not posit a purely and thoroughly pre/non-social individual at the core of his theoretical framework.[25] Instead, the Freudian psyche is fundamentally ambivalent about others, torn between Eros's relational inclinations towards others and the *Todestrieb*'s anti-social negativities. Freud's human being can be characterized by Immanuel Kant's internally conflicted "unsocial sociability" (*die ungesellige Geselligkeit der Menschen*)[26] rather than any unequivocal unsociability. Freud has at least one foot planted squarely within the *zoon politikon* intellectual tradition (along with Hegel and Marx).[27]

Despite my reservations about Jameson's contrasting of Freud with Lacan, there still is something to his insistence on Lacan as the best psychoanalytic partner for a Marxism motivated to ally itself with psychoanalysis. The Hegelian-Kojèvian sensibilities Lacan brings to his "return to Freud" indeed render Lacanian psychoanalysis much easier to blend with Marxism. This is thanks in no small part to the facts both that Marx is heavily influenced by Hegel and that Alexandre Kojève interprets Hegel's 1807 Jena *Phenomenology of Spirit* partly through the lenses of Marxism.[28] Yet, a general socialization of the unconscious does not make Lacan (or anyone else) a Marxist. Fortunately, Lacan himself helpfully specifies multiple precise points of convergence between his rendition of psychoanalysis and Marxist materialisms.

Some readers might be surprised to learn of the later Lacan's strong embrace of political economy in the context of the period of his most detailed and sustained dialogue with Marxism. Specifically, in his 16th (*From an Other to the other* [1968–1969]) and 17th (*The Other Side of Psychoanalysis* [1969–1970]) seminars, he advocates replacing Freud's reliance on the natural-scientific discipline of physics for metapsychological metaphors and models with the social/human-scientific discipline of economics instead.[29] This replacement would seem to entail a leap from the natural (of the *Naturwissenschaften*) to the non/more-than-natural (of the *Geisteswissenschaften*), even from the material to the spiritual (*als geistig*). Yet, in *Seminar XVI*, Lacan warns that this shift from a libidinal-psychical economy pictured on the basis of Freud's naturalist energetics to this same economy recast on the basis of socio-historical political economy involves no lessening or loss of materialist credentials, no backsliding into idealism.[30] This warning, along with lots of surrounding textual evidence, indicates that the political economy Lacan proposes as a disciplinary partner for analytic metapsychology is none other than that of the historical materialist critique of political economy established by Marx.

Seminar XVII offers additional elaborations apropos the combination of psychoanalysis with political economy. During the February 11, 1970 session of this academic year, right after talking about Marx and "surplus *jouissance*" (*plus-de-jouir*),[31] Lacan proclaims:

> From time to time I stick my nose into a stack of authors who are economists. And we can see the extent to which this is of interest for us analysts, because if there is something that remains to be done in analysis, it is to institute this other field of energetics (*cet autre champ énergétique*), which would demand other structures than those of physics, and which is the field of *jouissance*.[32]

In the following week's session of the 17th seminar, he invokes one of Freud's own references to capitalist economics in which Freud links this field to libidinal economics. Specifically, Lacan refers to Freud's analogy between the capitalist-entrepreneur relationship and, in terms of the analytic theory of dreams, the rapport between the unconscious infantile wish (analogous to the capitalist) and the day residues (analogous to the entrepreneur) triggering the production of a dream with its manifest content.[33] For Freud, just as the entrepreneur's productive powers are on loan from the capitalist funding the enterprise, so too are the day residues' powers to set in motion the production of a dream funded and fueled by archaic repressed impulses and ideas (i.e., unconscious infantile wishes).[34]

Lacan draws certain consequences from Freud's dream-theoretic analogy involving the capitalist and the entrepreneur. In particular, he links this analogy to his account of *jouissance*:

> Freud... tells us that one must not forget that a dream stands on two feet, and that it is not sufficient that it represent a decision, a lively desire (*un vif désir du sujet*), by the subject as to the present. There must be something that gives it support in a desire from childhood (*un désir de l'enfance*). And here, he takes as his reference—this is usually taken as a display of elegance—the entrepreneur, the entrepreneur of decisions, in his relationship to the capitalist whose accumulated resources, the capital of libido, will enable this decision to pass into action (*passer en acte*).[35]

Lacan continues:

> These are things that look like they are a metaphor. Isn't it amusing to see how this takes on a different value after what I have been telling you concerning the relationship between capitalism and the function of the master—concerning the altogether distinct nature of what can be done with the process of accumulation in the presence of surplus *jouissance* (*plus-de-jouir*)—in the very presence of this surplus *jouissance*, to the exclusion of the big fat *jouissance*, plain *jouissance*, *jouissance* that is realized in copulation in the raw (*bon gros jouir, le jouir simple, le jouir qui se réalise dans lacopulation toute nue*)? Isn't this precisely where infantile desire gets its force from, its force of accumulation with respect to this object that constitutes the cause of desire (*cet objet qui fait la cause du désir*),

namely that which is accumulated as libido capital by virtue, precisely, of infantile non-maturity, the exclusion of *jouissance* that others will call normal? There you have what suddenly gives Freud's metaphor its proper connotation when he refers to the capitalist.[36]

I suspect that Lacan is tacitly tapping into capitalist ideology's myths about the origins of capital. More precisely, this would be the moralizing fiction, flattering to capitalists themselves, according to which the (primitive) accumulation of capital originates in abstinence, namely, the virtuous self-renunciations and ethico-pragmatic frugality through which the righteous chosen few elevate themselves to their well-deserved class position as masters of the economy. What is more, given that, as Freud observes, anal personalities often are parsimonious, even capitalist ideology itself (inadvertently) confesses that capitalism is tied to anality, that it comes out of the anus. It really is shit, even by its own (unintended) admission. Althusser's claim that ideology is as much allusion as illusion is perfectly apt here.[37]

With Freud's analogy linking the figure of the capitalist to repressed infantile wishes (as the latent dream-thoughts involved in the dream work), Lacan proposes that such "desire from childhood" (*désir de l'enfance*) funding the production of dreams is itself a result of a process of accumulation. However, such saving or storing up is not the result of an inaugural decision or choice on the part of the (dreaming) subject (with "the entrepreneur of decisions" coming on the scene only with the day residues of adulthood, that is, long after the period of childhood to which the latent dream-thoughts are tied). Rather, "infantile non-maturity," as the prolonged prematurational helplessness into which birth hurls the human being, forces abstinence and, hence, the accumulation of "libido capital" upon the infant and pre-pubescent child. This abstinence is a necessity, not a virtue. And, with the capitalist, it becomes a vice bound up with yet other vices.

Lacan here draws attention to a facet of Freudian *Hilflosigkeit*, namely, the child's inability, its impotence, to engage in genital sexual relations with its adult significant others.[38] Such sexual helplessness brings with it, as Lacan puts it, "the exclusion of the big fat *jouissance*, plain *jouissance*, *jouissance* that is realized in copulation in the raw (*bon gros jouir, le jouir simple, le jouir qui se réalise dans la co-pulation toute nue*)" and "the exclusion of *jouissance* that others will call normal." By Lacan's lights, "the capital of libido" is the product of a period of primitive accumulation imposed upon the psychical subject(-to-be) by the brute biological facticity of its specifically sexual prematuration. This prematuration, lasting until puberty, is especially prolonged in human animals (as is the dependence on others for bare survival too, this being another crucial aspect of human *Hilflosigkeit*). For Lacan, a libidinal-economic primitive accumulation generates desire (*désir*) as surplus *jouissance* with its corresponding object, namely, *objet petit a qua* object-cause of desire (i.e., "this object that constitutes the cause of desire" [*cet objet qui fait la cause du désir*]).[39]

As Lacan points out the following year in *Seminar XVIII* (*D'un discours qui ne serait pas du semblant* [1971]), the accumulation of *jouissance* in the form of the surplus of *plus-de-jouir* renders enjoyment "impossible."[40] On this occasion, Lacan contends that all economies, including the psyche's libidinal economy, are "a fact of discourse" (*un fait de discours*).[41] As soon as the neonate's psyche begins primitively accumulating undischarged *jouissance*, it also, given the "throw" (*als werfen*) of birth, already is caught within the webs of intersubjective and trans-subjective relations, entangled in networks involving languages, institutions, interests, practices, fantasies, ideologies, and so on.

According to Lacan, the socio-symbolic mediation brought about in and through the signifiers and social links of *discours* renders "big fat *jouissance*, plain *jouissance*, *jouissance* that is realized in copulation in the raw" impossible (*à la* such Lacanian pronouncements as "*jouissance* is prohibited [*interdite*] to whoever speaks, as such"[42]). That is to say, even when the child in (post-)pubescent maturity comes to engage in what others then deem the "normal *jouissance*" of genital copulation, there inevitably will be an unbridgeable discrepancy between the "*jouissance* expected," crystallized in the childhood-in-origin fantasies ($ \Diamond$ *a*) funded by the "libido capital" of accumulated *plus-de-jouir*, and the "*jouissance* obtained" in frustratingly unfulfilling fulfillment of these fantasies via an adult copulation that never can measure up to the pregenital anticipatory fantasies orchestrating these later genital encounters. What is more, even if the child improbably were to go to the Sadean libertine extreme of transgressing the prohibition on incest, he/she still would confront the disappointing gap between fantasmatic expectation and actual obtainment.[43] Considering Lacan's emphasis on "infantile non-maturity" as the sexual side of *Hilflosigkeit*, the incest prohibition interestingly is superfluous (forbidding what is anyway impossible) for the child him/her-self.

But, what, if any, are the upshots of the later Lacan's linking of his libidinal economics (as centered on *jouissance*, desire, object *a*, etc.) to political economics generally and the historical materialist critique of political economy specifically? Likewise, how should one construe Lacan's glosses on Freud's capitalist-entrepreneur analogy as regards interfacing psychoanalysis with Marxism? Samo Tomšič, in his 2015 study *The Capitalist Unconscious: Marx and Lacan*, addresses this second question thusly:

> Freud does not say what the Freudo-Marxists will claim later, that the unconscious explains capitalism; he states precisely the opposite: it is capitalism that elucidates the unconscious. The unconscious discovered in the *Interpretation of Dreams* is nothing other than the capitalist unconscious, the intertwining of unconscious satisfaction with the structure and the logic of the capitalist mode of production.[44]

I have two hesitations about Tomšič's reading. First, from a Lacanian perspective at least, I am concerned that he runs the risk of excessively historicizing the psychoanalytic unconscious. Neither Lacan nor I would disagree that the structures and dynamics of the unconscious are significantly inflected by socio-historical forces and factors, including those of capitalism. But, I believe Lacan would maintain that capitalist modernity's contributions to the discovery and theorization of the Freudian unconscious are an instance of Marx's "Human anatomy contains a key to the anatomy of the ape."[45] Put differently, the explicit surfacing of the analytic unconscious within modern capitalism reveals a metapsychology already implicitly operative within the species *homo sapiens* long before the rise of the capitalist mode of production.

But, if Tomšič means by "the capitalist unconscious" the "inter-twining" of a transhistorical unconscious with capitalism as a med-iating historical social formation, then this first reservation of mine is mild or even moot. Lacan himself, again in *Seminar XVII*, provides an example of his openness to this intertwining approach when, once more appealing to Marx, he acknowledges that, under capitalism, "the interests of the subject" (i.e., the subject's drives, desires, etc.) are "entirely commercial" (*entièrement marchands*).[46] That is to say, there is an intertwining of libidinal and political economies such that, within a capitalist socioeconomic (and symbolic) order, the subject's libidinal interests are mediated and inflected by the demands and dictates of the mode of production characterizing this trans-subjective enveloping order. Similarly, Lacan, already in *Seminar XIV* (*The Logic of Fantasy* [1966–1967]), suggests that, under capit-alism, humans' love lives are themselves commodified through sexual and amorous encounters being arranged by the commerce of the so-called "meat market"[47] (a point Lacan would see being even more relevant nowadays considering the roles of the internet, social media, and dating apps in orchestrating libidinally-charged couplings).

My second hesitation regarding Tomšič is not so easily allayed. On the one hand, I concur with him that pre/non-Lacanian variants of Freudo-Marxism (including and especially those associated with the Frankfurt School) tend to err in one-sidedly having psychoanalysis explain capitalism but not *vice versa*. And, Tomšič is quite correct that a Lacanian approach, as per what one might label Lacano-Marxism, tends to offset this Freudo-Marxist one-sidedness by stressing how capitalism explains psychoanalysis. Lacan's afore-mentioned appeals to political economy *à la* Marxism as indis-pensable for conceptualizing libidinal economics confirms this aspect of Tomšič's interpretation.

Yet, on the other hand, Tomšič appears to favor one sort of one-sidedness (i.e., a Lacano-Marxist elucidation of psychoanalysis through capitalism) against another sort of one-sidedness (i.e., a Freudo-Marxist elucidation of capitalism through psychoanalysis). In my view, what this leaves unaccomplished in its playing off of Lacano-against Freudo-Marxisms is a revisiting of how psycho-analysis illuminates capitalism after passing through Lacan's reflec-tions on how capitalism illuminates psychoanalysis. Failing to do so amounts to foregoing certain insights undiscovered by more traditional Freudo-Marxism. In other words, a Lacano-Marxist illumination of capitalism by psychoanalysis brings certain facets to light left languishing in darkness by Freudo-Marxism's one-sided illumination of capitalism by psychoanalysis.

In terms of a Lacano-Marxist explaining of capitalism via psychoanalysis, Lacan's Freud-prompted parallels between the capitalist and the accumulator of "libido capital" *qua plus-de-jouir* suggest that, even for capitalists themselves, capitalism is not organized around anyone's contentment, fulfillment, gratification, satisfaction, or the like. Just as with the Lacanian dynamics of surplus *jouissance*, in which desire ceaselessly chases without end after the infinitely receding fantasmatic *objet petit a*, so too with capital's accumulation of surplus-value: The quantitative surplus of surplus-value is, as quantitative, an in-principle potential infinity which, as such, offers no prospect for the closure of completion and satiety to the pursuers of this ever-expanding numerical excess. There is no economic version of the finality of a well-rounded whole of "big fat *jouissance*" waiting for even the most successful of capitalists perfectly obeying the logic of capital.[48]

Yet, capitalists keep chasing the dragon as though there were some final point to be aimed at and reached. This indicates that the drive of/as capital, the circuit of M-C-M', is nothing if not a death-drive-like painful repetition compulsion (*Wiederholungszwang*) even for the most privileged bearers/personifications of capital. Both critics and defenders of capitalism frequently contend that this socioeconomic system is animated by the private narcissistic motivations of acquisitiveness, greed, self-seeking, and the like. But, seeing the closed loop of M-C-M' as akin to Lacanian *jouissance* strongly hints that the capitalist drive, the very motor of this mode of production, is something other than personal pleasures pursued through the enlightened cynicism of cold pragmatic calculations of measurable gains and losses.[49]

Although the bulk of the Lacanian ground I just covered is situated during the period of Lacan's teaching at the end of the 1960s and beginning of the 1970s, his fourteenth seminar of the mid-1960s lays the foundations for much of what he subsequently says about the topic of the economy as per (political) economics. First of all, in the April 12, 1967 session of *Seminar XIV*, Lacan portrays Marxism and psychoanalysis as sharing in common a focus on "economy" in the broad sense of latent structure.[50] Subsequent remarks to the same effect in the 16th seminar confirm that the classical (*circa* 1965) and then-contemporaneous quasi-structuralist recasting of Marx by Althusser is Lacan's source of inspiration here.[51]

Of course, this Althusser already draws on psychoanalysis (including of the Lacanian sort) in portraying socioeconomic structures according to historical materialism as involving various unconscious dimensions and dynamics. Moreover, this same Althusser deploys the interlinked concepts of "structural causality"[52] (blending Spinozism and structuralism) and "overdetermination"[53] (borrowed directly and avowedly from psychoanalysis) to capture how the whole of a given social formation (as infrastructure and superstructure combined) immanently-yet-invisibly converges upon and configures entities and events situated within such formations. Such historical materialist causation and determining *à la* Althusser is very much akin to Lacan's portrayals of the influences of the symbolic order *qua* big Other in shaping speaking subjects subjected to socio-linguistic signifiers.

A week after this Althusser-inspired identification of overdetermining structure as a common denominator between Marxism and psychoanalysis, in the April 19, 1967 session of *Seminar XIV*, Lacan speaks of the economy of the psychoanalytic unconscious. He states, "*Jouissance*-value... is at the source of the economy of the unconscious" (*La valeur de jouissance... est au principe de l'économie de l'Inconscient*).[54] Then, during the April 26, 1967 session of this seminar, he remarks that "the economy of the unconscious... is commonly called primary process" (*l'économie de l'inconscient... ce qu'on appelle communément le processus primaire*).[55] Lacan's use, once again, of the phrase "*jouissance*-value" signals that he has Marxist theory in mind when speaking of matters economic in this 1967 context. But, what does the thesis that the economy formed by the primary processes of the unconscious is organized around "*la valeur de jouissance*" contribute, especially as regards the implications of psychoanalysis for Marxism?

The April 26, 1967 session of the 14th seminar also contains some revealing specifications apropos Lacan's account of *jouissance*, specifications with clear implications for the related concept of *jouissance*-value. In particular, Lacan therein makes a reference to

Sophocles's *Oedipus Rex* as providing Freud with a founding myth for psychoanalysis. Through implying that Oedipus himself is an Oedipal subject who dares actually to succeed in transgressing the fundamental prohibitions against parricide and maternal incest,[56] Lacan proposes that the tragic conclusion of Sophocles's play reveals the guilt-ridden rottenness, the horrifying putrescence, of the ultimate forbidden fruit if and when it is seized. In being seized, this fruit unexpectedly goes from being tantalizing (when inaccessible) to becoming repulsive (when accessed).[57] The fulfillment of fantasies, as the transformation of *jouissance* expected into *jouissance* obtained, does not provide the ultimate in intensely, purely enjoyable Enjoyment-with-a-capital-E—quite the contrary.[58]

As an aside apropos *Oedipus Rex*, one should note that, at its conclusion, Oedipus turns himself into both excretory apparatus and excrement, traumatically expelling himself from Thebes. With the remainder of Sophocles's *Oedipus* trilogy, one has the self-expelled former King miserably floating around before being finally flushed out of the picture for good in *Oedipus at Colonus* (or Colon-anus). And, in *Antigone*, one of Oedipus's unfortunate sons, Polynices, is pushed out of Thebes by Creon to become excrement through animals eating (and then excreting) his unburied corpse. But, this admittedly is a shitty reading of Sophocles.

That said, the economy of the Lacanian unconscious, with its primary processes, is organized as a dynamic of interminably beating around a bush (i.e., *jouissance*) as if there were a desire to accomplish the terminal deed of really hitting the bush. Yet, despite the appearance of this "as if," the whole point is precisely not ever to hit the bush. If the bush gets hit, it disappears and, in so doing, reveals that it always marked an absence, namely, what the Lacan of *Seminar VII* (*The Ethics of Psychoanalysis* [1959–1960]) describes as the "vacuole of *das Ding*."[59]

If and when this disappearance and revelation transpire, the whole unconscious economy orbiting around the (absent) center of *jouissance* would grind to a halt and come crashing down. There would be a psychical market collapse causing the libidinal economy to sink into the depression of "subjective destitution." The primal repression concealing from the libidinal investor the truth that the economy he/she participates in is, in a sense, one giant Ponzi scheme erected on nothing more than empty promises of "big fat *jouissance*, plain *jouissance, jouissance* that is realized in copulation in the raw" (as per the already-quoted Lacan of *Seminar XVII*) would be lifted and the jig would be up. A libidinal investor who would go to King Oedipus's bitter end and try to cash out for good would end up empty handed or, perhaps worse still, with a handful of delivered shit in place of promised gold.

Taking the immediately preceding clarifications regarding *jouissance* into account as involved in Lacan's notion of *jouissance*-value, what does all this indicate regarding economics not only as per psychoanalysis's libidinal economics, but also apropos Marxism's historical materialist critique of political economy? In *Seminar XIV* and elsewhere, Lacan clearly intends to suggest that his reflections on *jouissance* and *jouissance*-value are of direct relevance to a Marxist-type analysis of capitalism. But, what exactly is this relevance?

Through the phrases "*jouissance*-value" and "surplus-*jouissance*" (*plus-de-jouir*), the Lacan of the 1960s and 1970s signals the relevance of his concept of *jouissance* especially for the *telos* around which the capitalist mode of production organizes itself, namely, surplus-value (as the "'" in M-C-M'). During a 1972 talk in Milan, Lacan, speaking of capitalism, observes, "There is only this that makes the system work. It's surplus-value."[60] So, if surplus-value is akin to *jouissance* (as *jouissance*-value and/or surplus-*jouissance*), then capitalist societies revolve around the unenjoyable incessant pursuit of an elusive, impossible-to-obtain enjoyment.[61] The carnivalesque merry-go-round marketplace is far from all fun and games.

If, as per Lacan, capitalism is ultimately about *jouissance* rather than pleasure, this runs conspicuously contrary to the image of capitalism as straightforwardly and unabashedly hedonistic, as sustained and strengthened by gratifications, happinesses, satisfactions, titillations, and so on of countless sorts. Not only do the exploited non-capitalists under capitalism not get to enjoy the surpluses extorted out of them; not only are capitalism's consumers kept in a constant state of agitated, dissatisfied want so as to keep them restlessly moving along the unending chain from purchase to purchase, with no bought commodity ever delivering the fulfillment advertised—even the capitalists themselves, including the biggest of the big bourgeoisie, prostrate and exhaust themselves in the endless quest after ever-more (infinitely more, in principle) surplus-value. In fact, the consumerist chasing of the dragon in the sphere of exchange, with its commodities, is itself an effect, a mere echo, of the capitalist chasing of the dragon in the sphere of production, with its surplus-values. For all capitalists and workers as well as producers and consumers alike, what could be called capitalism's Thing (as per Lacan's conception of *das Ding*) sustains everyone caught up in its socioeconomic system in a permanent state of discontented, restless seeking.[62] Capitalism doth make junkies of us all. Everyone ends up impoverished by it in one way or another.

The Political Economy of Shit: The Dirty Business of Business

I wish to begin moving towards a conclusion with one other hint Lacan offers about bringing together Marxism and psychoanalysis—a hint also pregnant with implications for a psychoanalytic approach to mind/psyche in relation to body/soma. In a 1968 talk given to psychiatrists-in-training, Lacan unexpectedly broaches the topic of the political economics of the solid waste disposal business:

> Unlike what happens at every level of the animal kingdom—which starts with elephants and hippos and ends with jellyfish—man is naturally characterized by the extraordinary embarrassment (*embarras*) he feels about—what should we call it? By the simplest name we can find, by God—the evacuation of shit.[63]

He continues:

> Man is the only animal for whom this is a problem, and it's a prodigious one. You don't realize, because you have little devices that evacuate it. You have no idea where it goes afterwards. It all goes through pipes and is collected in fantastic places you have no idea of, and then there are factories that take it in, transform it and make all sorts of things that go back into circulation (*lacirculation*) through the intermediary of human industry, and human industry is a completely circular industry (*une industrie très bouclée*). It is striking that there is not, to my knowledge, any

course on political economy that devotes a lesson or two to it. This
is a phenomenon of repression which, like all phenomena of
repression, is bound up with the need for decorum (*la bienséance*).[64]

In relation to the traditional philosophical project of identifying
those features distinguishing human beings as unique within the full
sweep of creation, Lacan, very much as a psychoanalyst, highlights
humanity's awkwardness and discomfort in the face of its own excrement. This is by contrast with nonhuman animals' comparatively
unperturbed attitude regarding their poops. Unlike all other living
beings, humans angst over their own shit. They are troubled by it, by
how to dispose of it and what to do with it.

Uniquely for humanity, there is, as per the title of a 1978 book by
Dominique Laporte, a "history of shit," namely, an evolution over
time of shifting strategies and tactics for how socio-symbolic subjects,
both individually and collectively, handle and cope with their ex-
crements. In the aforementioned quotations, Lacan indicates that
humans' rapport with their own shit is another instance of them
being naturally destined for (self-)denaturalization, for (self-)
alienation from animality ("man is naturally characterized," "Man
is the only animal for whom this is a problem"). As per a dialectical
naturalism also exemplified by the metapsychological significance of
biologically determined prolonged prematurational helplessness—
this *Hilflosigkeit* is tantamount to a natural determination not to be
naturally determined, a natural facilitation of the predominance of
social nurture over biological nature[65]—humanity's excremental self-
revulsion would be a natural inclination to rebel against nature.

From Lacan's analytic perspective, repression-inducing shame (i.e.,
"extraordinary embarrassment [*embarras*]," "the need for decorum
[*la bienséance*]") inhibits those interested in economics, whether they
be Marxists or not, from looking into such topics as the political
economy of shit. Moreover, in the second of the two preceding block
quotations, Lacan maintains that the treatment of excrement under
industrial capitalism reveals essential aspects of capitalism as a whole.
He portrays the fecal matter of capitalism's subjects as circulating
through looping circuits of pipes and factories. Then, this looping
(*boucler*) quality is attributed not only to industrial solid waste processing, but also to "human industry" *tout court* ("human industry is

a completely circular industry [*une industrie très bouclée*]"). Lacan could be said to move from the political economy of shit in particular to capitalism's shitty political economy in general.

So, following Lacan's insinuations, the loop of M-C-M', as the underlying structural dynamic of capitalism *überhaupt*, is a kind of socioeconomic anal-expulsive drive. The figure of the pre/non-capitalist miser, repeatedly compared and contrasted with the bourgeois capitalist by Marx, obeys an anal-retentive drive, since the miser hoards (i.e., retains) wealth. But, the capitalist, unlike the miser, spends (i.e., expels into circulation) money in order to make yet more money.

What is more, following the lead of the Freud who sets up the psychoanalytic association of gold/money with feces, capitalism is nothing if not the frenetic perpetual production, circulation, and accumulation of ever more shit. In addition to generating gold/money, it gives rise to mountains of commodities and/as garbage as well as the parasitic recycling industries resembling Lacan's description of the sewage-treatment business. With recycling, ecology, and the like in view, it justifiably could be said that the greening of capitalism is also its browning.

In fact, the full circuit of capitalism's shitty looping *ad nauseam* runs from the capitalist's anal-expulsive drive (more precisely, M-C-M' as a sublimation of this *Trieb*) setting in motion production to the consumer's oral-incorporative drive sustained and stimulated by the capitalist's drive. Somewhat relatedly, Laporte observes that both of capitalism's two main classes, capitalists and laborers/consumers, associate the other class with shit (with the poor person's scorn for the obscene "filthy lucre" of the wealthy and the rich person's scorn for the dirt and grime of the impoverished).[66] The logic of capital is nothing if not scatological.

Taking into account capitalism's extended circuit running through the spheres of production, distribution, exchange, and consumption, capitalism shows itself to be, in the psychoanalytic terms advanced by both Freud and Lacan, one giant loop formed by connecting capitalists' anality with consumers' orality. It composes a disgusting closed coprophagic circle in which shit keeps passing from the productive-expulsive anuses of capitalists into the consumptive-incorporative mouths of consumers, and back again, over and over. This is a manic binge-purge ceaseless oscillation in which, inverting the standard bulimic sequence where binging comes first, purging (as capitalist anal expulsion) precedes and conditions binging (as consumerist oral incorporation).

The capitalist socioeconomic system in its entirety thus resembles a person who shoves his own head up his own ass precisely in order to eat his own shit, or a snake that swallows its own tail specifically so as to consume its own feces. From a Lacanian vantage point especially, this whole vile *boucle* outlines the contours of a central negativity: the black hole of the vacuole of capitalism's Thing, the infinite abyss of the bottomless, self-voiding rectum of absent (unenjoyable) enjoyment. Paraphrasing Leo Bersani, perhaps surplus-value is a rectum, a rectum that also is a grave. With reference to a certain punchline ("Rectum? Damn near killed him!"), capitalism is ever nearer to driving all its subjects into early graves (especially its would-be exploited "grave diggers"[67]), wrecking them at a continually accelerating pace (as per Marx's image of "whole hecatombs of workers" as the sacrificial victims of capitalism's ritual-like repeated socioeconomic crises[68]). The ring of the traced rim of the loop M-C-M′ is simultaneously both the political- and the libidinal-economic sphincter at the heart of capitalism in its totality as a massively shitty political economy.

Hence, for psychoanalysis, particularly in its Lacanian version, literal and figurative sphincters function as Cartesian-style pineal glands stitching together the body and the body politic. As Richard Boothby, engaging with Freud and Lacan, insightfully articulates, "the anal sphincter, despite the socially rehearsed repugnance that attaches to everything excremental—or rather precisely because of that repugnance—must be considered the most profoundly social organ of the body."[69] And, in a now-famous set of meditations on national differences in European toilet design, Žižek permits seeing the literal bodily sphincter as a metaphorical pineal gland connecting historical materialism's distinct social levels of economic infrastructure and more-than-economic (including ideological) superstructure (just as, for Althusser, a mode of production's relations of production constitute the pineal-gland-like switch-point, within the economic base, where superstructure and infrastructure converge and interact[70]).

Žižek prefaces his reflections on toilets with a theoretical qualification about appeals to ostensibly no-nonsense, brass-tacks practical usefulness—"in everyday life, ideology is at work especially in the apparently innocent reference to pure utility."[71] With this important caveat about utility in place, Žižek soon proceeds to address the matter of European lavatories. He observes:

> In a traditional German lavatory, the hole in which shit disappears after we flush water is way in front, so that the shit is first laid out for us to sniff at and inspect for traces of some illness; in the typical French lavatory, on the contrary, the hole is in the back—that is, the shit is supposed to disappear as soon as possible; finally, the Anglo-Saxon (English or American) lavatory presents a kind of synthesis, a mediation between these two opposed poles—the basin is full of water, so that the shit floats in it—visible, but not to be inspected... It is clear that none of these versions can be accounted for in purely utilitarian terms: a certain ideological perception of how the subject should relate to the unpleasant excrement which comes from within our body is clearly discernible.[72]

Since all three types of toilets are equally effective in getting the job of disposing of poop done—they enjoy the same level of the essential use-value of being-a-toilet—their differences cannot be explained on the basis of any one design being more utilitarian than the others. This ruling out of a seemingly non-ideological utilitarian explanation includes the apparently utilitarian Anglo-Saxon lavatory design.

As Žižek has claimed ("the Anglo-Saxon (English or American) lavatory presents a kind of synthesis, a mediation between these two opposed poles") and will claim again in the quotation immediately below, the Anglo-Saxon style of "utilitarian" toilet is itself not a default original design but, instead, a secondary synthesis, a sort of compromise formation, between German and French lavatory designs. Žižek goes on:

> Hegel was among the first to interpret the geographical triad Germany-France-England as expressing three different existential attitudes: German reflective thoroughness, French revolutionary hastiness, English moderate utilitarian pragmatism; in terms of political stance, this triad can be read as German conservatism,

French revolutionary radicalism and English moderate liberalism; in terms of the predominance of one of the spheres of social life, it is German metaphysics and poetry versus French politics and English economy. The reference to lavatories enables us not only to discern the same triad in the most intimate domain of performing the excremental function, but also to generate the underlying mechanism of this triad in the three different attitudes towards excremental excess: ambiguous contemplative fascination; the hasty attempt to get rid of the unpleasant excess as fast as possible; the pragmatic approach to treat the excess as an ordinary object to be disposed of in an appropriate way. So it is easy for an academic to claim at a round table that we live in a post-ideological universe—the moment he visits the restroom after the heated discussion, he is again knee-deep in ideology. The ideological investment of such references to utility is attested by their *dialogical* character: the Anglo-Saxon lavatory acquires its meaning only through its differential relation to French and German lavatories. We have such a multitude of the lavatory types because there is a traumatic excess which each of them tries to accommodate—according to Lacan, one of the features which distinguishes man from the animals is precisely that with humans the disposal of shit becomes a problem.[73]

Žižek, with this closing reference to Lacan tying off the discussion of toilets, brings things full circle, as it were, to my earlier deployment of Lacan's 1968 remarks about the political economy of shit. As seen, these remarks push off from Lacan's observation about humanity's embarrassment regarding its own excrement. And, as my reflections unfolding in-between quoting that Lacan a while ago and quoting this Žižek just now reveal, Lacan's musings about the political economy of shit also turn out to imply the shitty (anal-expulsive, scatological, coprophagic) quality of capitalist political economy as such (i.e., Lacan's "completely circular industry" epitomized by the distinctively "human industry" of shit, with capitalism as the "circulation" of both shit and other [by-]products).

Furthermore, as Žižek very well knows, the Hegel he invokes here subsequently colors the Marxist tradition. The European spiritual trinity constituted by German, French, and Anglo-Saxon socio-cultural formations comes to be referred to by V.I. Lenin, among others, as furnishing "The Three Sources and Three Component Parts of Marxism" (as per the title of a 1913 essay by him).[74] On this view, Marx's thought takes shape at the crossroads of German philosophy (as Hegelian speculative dialectics), French politics (as the radical left-wing currents tied to the Revolution of 1789 and its protracted aftermath), and British economics (as the classical labor theory of value put forward first and foremost by Adam Smith and David Ricardo). Despite the humorous quality of Žižek's musings about European toilet designs, he is sincere in this context about using the differences between lavatory types to make some quite serious theoretical points at the intersection of Hegelian philosophy, Lacanian psychoanalysis, and Marxist critique. For psychoanalysis, starting with Freud's 1905 *Jokes and Their Relation to the Unconscious*, humor enables normally repressed unconscious truths to reveal themselves, with laughter both inside and outside the analytic consulting room as a not-uncommon sign that such truths have been registered.[75]

For my present purposes, what is most valuable in the Žižekian account of the significance of European toilets are its implications for rethinking both the Marxism-psychoanalysis rapport as well as the infrastructure-superstructure link as per historical materialism. Žižek's hybrid Lacanian-Althusserian conception(s) of the unconscious and/as ideology are pivotal in this context. From Lacan, Žižek takes the account of the unconscious as existing primarily in the forms of a manifest material-objective-real exteriority at the socio-symbolic level—albeit with those subjected to this manifest exteriority having eyes not to see it. Obviously, this Lacanian re-envisioning of the unconscious is diametrically opposed to the commonplace image of the unconscious as a hidden mental-subjective-ideal interiority, as per the picture of psychoanalysis as a hermeneutic depth psychology.

From Althusser, Žižek takes the account of the "materiality of ideology."[76] This account amounts to Althusser's de-psychologization of the ideological, parallel, and related to, Lacan's de-psychologization of the unconscious. According to the distinctively Althusserian theory of ideology, the ideological (despite the etymology of the very word "ideology") is not mainly ideas internal to individual persons' heads, in the guises of the misleading thoughts of false consciousness. Rather, ideology exists first and foremost in the extra-mental guises of external beings, of palpably tangible institutions, practices, rituals, and the like as the incarnate materials of fleshly bodies, concrete buildings, physical objects, and so on. Ideology for Althusser, like the unconscious and its truths for Lacan, is, so to speak, "out there," instantiated in the shared public spaces of socio-symbolic networks (including public restrooms).

Žižek sees in the diversity of European lavatory styles a condensed quotidian embodiment of unconscious ideology as per a combination of Lacan with Althusser, a condensation with consequences for Marxism, psychoanalysis, and their relationship. In light of Žižek's reflections, bathrooms now can be illuminated as sites of intersection for infrastructural and superstructural dimensions. To begin with, solid waste disposal involves infrastructure in both its technical Marxist sense and its non-technical everyday sense.

Moreover, as Žižek compellingly demonstrates, toilets also involve, in addition to their infrastructural use- and exchange-values, non-utilitarian influences and mediations irreducible to purely pragmatic economic considerations and calculations. These influences and mediations are attributed by Žižek to the superstructural *qua* ideological, the more-than-economic domain of what Marx and Engels, in *The German Ideology*, list as "politics, laws, morality, religion, metaphysics, and so on of a people" (*der Politik, der Gesetze, der Moral, der Religion, Metaphysik usw. eines Volkes*) as well as "all the rest of ideology" (*sonstige Ideologie*).[77] Obviously, the German, French, and Anglo-Saxon sociocultural constellations identified by Hegel, influencing Marx, and invoked by Žižek count, for Marxist historical materialism, as superstructures.

Insofar as toilet types reflect these sociocultural constellations in their shiny porcelain, they exhibit how pieces of infrastructure (in both senses, Marxist and non-Marxist) can be and are suffused with superstructure too. Dovetailing with Žižek observing that here, "a certain ideological perception of how the subject should relate to the unpleasant excrement which comes from within our body is clearly discernible," Laporte raises the question, "When considering the history of the senses alongside the history of modes of production and circulation, we must ask, which lights the way for the other?"[78]

Between German toilets and German speculative metaphysics, between French toilets and French revolutionary politics, between Anglo-Saxon toilets and Anglo-Saxon utilitarian economics—one is faced in each instance with the same apparent chicken-and-egg dilemma.

When Žižek claims, "We have such a multitude of the lavatory types because there is a traumatic excess which each of them tries to accommodate," he signals his endorsement of a Lacanian psychoanalytic resolution of the chicken-and-egg problem with which Laporte's *histoire de la merde* confronts Marxist historical materialism. Žižek's "traumatic excess" would be the Real of excrement which the realities of all different lavatory types are designed to deal with in their distinct, more-than-utilitarian ways. Yet, one still could ask of this Žižek whether, through his insightful discussion of toilets, he means to elevate Lacanianism over Marxism. More precisely, is his position that a somatic or psychical Real *à la* psychoanalysis enjoys explanatory priority vis-à-vis the infrastructural (i.e., the economic base *qua* mode of production) as per traditional historical materialism?

Although I am not entirely certain how Žižek would respond to this question, I am inclined to interpret Žižek's Lacanian Real of excrement as not neatly separate from (and, in its separateness, explanatorily competing with) Marx's Real of modes of production. That is to say, I do not believe, and do not believe that Žižek believes, that one has to choose between privileging this Lacanianism over historical materialism or *vice versa*. Why not?

The notion of need connects Lacan on defecation with Marx on the economy. In Lacan's metapsychological theory of the libidinal economy, the primarily somatic sources and pressures of the Freudian drives, the anal drive included, amount to biologically innate human needs that make "demands for work" (as Freud phrases it) on the psyche in terms of clamoring for satisfaction, for the gratifications of discharge, sating, and slaking. As such, need (*besoin*) *à la* Lacan clearly would be a driving force for the *praxes* of social laboring constituting the economic motor of history as per Marxism, with the "economic" intended by Marx in a broad but carefully defined sense. To be even more exact along Lacanian lines, Žižek's "traumatic excess" would be strictly "extimate" (i.e., intimately foreign and internally excluded) in relation to the infrastructural economic base.[79]

I wish to point out in passing that today's theoretical humanities are blessed or cursed, depending on one's perspective, by a continually proliferating series of "'x' theory" fields (e.g., affect theory, play theory, various identity category theories, and so on). Adding to this proliferation, maybe yet another new intellectual discipline, one sublating the convergences between Marxism and psychoanalysis, needs to be established. This would be "shit theory," a framework that could be said to foreground the bung(hole) in *Aufhebung*.

Shit theory easily could spread everywhere. For instance, a linguistic-semiological variant of it could be developed starting with an analysis of how and why the very word "shit" (like another profanity, "fuck") can signify anything and everything under the sun (as well as places where the sun does not shine). Shit as a signifier in symbolic systems is indeed like gold and money *qua* "universal equivalents" in economic systems. Both shit and gold/money can stand in for all other things, thus adding an additional buttress to Freud's equation of wealth with feces.

It seems fitting to conclude with a well-known proclamation by Lenin regarding the topic of toilets. In a November 6–7, 1921 article in *Pravda* marking the occasion of the fourth anniversary of the October 1917 Bolshevik Revolution, he proposes, "When we are victorious on a world scale I think we shall use gold for the purpose of building public lavatories in the streets of some of the largest cities in the world."[80] The proposal is that revolutionaries, after both seizing control of the levers of state power as well as grasping the reins of the means of production, must lay their hands on peoples' libidinal economies too. Although this revolutionary storming of bourgeois bathrooms (hopefully) will not be televised, videos of it likely will turn up in unseemly corners of the internet.

In all seriousness, Lenin's declaration indicates the importance of revolutionaries exercising an inverse Midas touch bringing about a liberatory desublimation (by contrast with Marcusian repressive desublimation[81]) turning gold back into the feces from whence, according to Freud, it ontogenetically came. Would not one of the best critiques of commodity fetishism be taking a literal shit on its condensed material epitomization? By the combined lights of Marxism and psychoanalysis, a transformative path here comes into view going from the plumbing of the capitalist financial system to the plumbing of the communist sewage system via a restructuring of the plumbing of the libidinal system (with hydraulic metaphors abounding in Freud's characterizations of the libidinal economy). Through this revolutionary restructuring, "new men," unlike the commodity fetishists of old, will come casually to defile gold without a second thought, nonchalantly producing their own, and not someone else's, dirty money on a daily basis. Lenin's toilets concretize a Pascalian-Althusserian anticipation having it that if you free your ass, your mind will follow.[82] To change the psyche with its ideas, one must change the body with its functions. A psychoanalytically minded Leninist might conclude that one knows communism truly has triumphed only if and when shit starts to happen differently.

Notes

1 (Adrian Johnston, "Freud and Continental Philosophy," *The History of Continental Philosophy*, eight volumes [ed. Alan D. Schrift], *Volume III: The New Century—Bergsonism, Phenomenology, and Responses to Modern Science* [ed. Keith Ansell-Pearson and Alan D. Schrift], Durham: Acumen, 2010, pg. 319–346)
(Adrian Johnston, "The Weakness of Nature: Hegel, Freud, Lacan, and Negativity Materialized," *Hegel and the Infinite: Religion, Politics, and Dialectic* [ed. Slavoj Žižek, Clayton Crockett, and Creston Davis], New York: Columbia University Press, 2011, pg. 159–179)
(Adrian Johnston, "Philosophy and psychoanalysis," *The Routledge Handbook of Psychoanalysis in the Social Sciences and Humanities* [ed. Anthony Elliott and Jeffrey Prager], New York: Routledge, 2016, pg. 278–299)
(Adrian Johnston, *Adventures in Transcendental Materialism: Dialogues with Contemporary Thinkers*, Edinburgh: Edinburgh University Press, 2014, pg. 65–107)
(Adrian Johnston, *Prolegomena to Any Future Materialism, Volume Two: A Weak Nature Alone*, Evanston: Northwestern University Press, 2019, pg. 187–255)
(Adrian Johnston, *Infinite Greed: Money, Marxism, Psychoanalysis*, New York: Columbia University Press [under review])
2 (A.R. Luria, "Psychoanalysis as a System of Monistic Psychology," *Soviet Psychology*, vol. 16, no. 2, 1977, pg. 22, 24–25)
3 (Lev Vygotsky and Alexander Luria, "Introduction to the Russian translation of Freud's *Beyond the pleasure principle*," *The Vygotsky Reader* [ed. René van der Veer and Jaan Valsiner], Oxford: Blackwell, 1994, pg. 14)
4 (Wilhelm Reich, *Dialectical Materialism and Psychoanalysis*, London: Socialist Reproduction, 1972, pg. 21–21)
5 (Otto Fenichel, "Psychoanalysis as the Nucleus of a Future Dialectical-Materialist Psychology" [ed. Suzette H. Annin and Hanna Fenichel; trans. Olga Barsis], *American Imago*, vol. 24, no. 4, Winter 1967, pg. 295–296, 302, 306)

6 (Herbert Marcuse, *Eros and Civilization: A Philosophical Inquiry into Freud*, Boston: Beacon Press, 1974, pg. 11–12, 21, 31)

7 (Johnston, *Infinite Greed*)

8 (*GW* 10: 214)
  (*SE* 14: 121–122)

9 (*SE* 7: 168)

10 (*SE* 14: 122–123)

11 (Karl Marx and Friedrich Engels, *The German Ideology*, Amherst: Prometheus, 1998, pg. 42)

12 (*SE* 9: 167–175)

13 (*SE* 17: 125–133)

14 (*SE* 1: 243, 273)
  (*SE* 4: 200)
  (*SE* 5: 403)
  (*SE* 9: 168, 173–174)
  (*SE* 11: 106)
  (*SE* 12: 187-190, 196–197)
  (*SE* 17: 72–74, 76, 82, 127–128, 130–132)

15 (Adrian Johnston, "Humanity, That Sickness: Louis Althusser and the Helplessness of Psychoanalysis," *Crisis and Critique*, special issue: "*Reading Capital* and *For Marx*: 50 Years Later" [ed. Frank Ruda and Agon Hamza], vol. 2, no. 2, 2015, pg. 217–261)
  (Adrian Johnston, "From Closed Need to Infinite Greed: Marx's Drive Theory," *Continental Thought and Theory: A Journal of Intellectual Freedom*, special issue: "Reading Marx's *Capital* 150 Years On" [ed. Mike Grimshaw and Cindy Zeiher], vol. 1, no. 4, October 2017, pg. 270–346)
  (Adrian Johnston, "The Triumph of Theological Economics: God Goes Underground," *Philosophy Today*, special issue: "Marxism and New Materialisms," vol. 64, no. 1, Winter 2020, pp. 3–50)
  (Adrian Johnston, "'I am nothing, but I make everything': Marx, Lacan, and the Labor Theory of Suture," *Parallax: The Dependence of Reality on Its Subjective Constitution* [ed. Dominik Finkelde, Christoph Menke, and Slavoj Žižek], London: Bloomsbury, 2021 [forthcoming])
  (Adrian Johnston, "The Self-Cleaning Fetish: Repression Under the Shadow of Fictitious Capital," *Objective Fictions: Between Philosophy and Psychoanalysis* [ed. Adrian Johnston, Boštjan Nedoh, and Alenka Zupančič], Edinburgh: Edinburgh University Press, 2022 [forthcoming])
  (Johnston, *Infinite Greed*)

16 (Johnston, *Prolegomena to Any Future Materialism, Volume Two*, pg. 71–183)

17 (Reich, *Dialectical Materialism and Psychoanalysis*, pg. 20–21, 56)
  (Fenichel, "Psychoanalysis as the Nucleus of a Future Dialectical-Materialist Psychology," pg. 294–296, 311)
  (Marcuse, *Eros and Civilization*, pg. 132–133)
  (Johnston, *Infinite Greed*)

18 (Louis Althusser, "Philosophy and Marxism: Interviews with Fernanda Navarro, 1984–87," *Philosophy of the Encounter: Later Writings, 1978-1987* [ed. François Matheron and Oliver Corpet; trans. G.M. Goshgarian], London: Verso, 2006, pg. 275–276)
    (Bruno Bosteels, *Badiou and Politics*, Durham: Duke University Press, 2011, pg. 48)

19 (Frederic Jameson, "An American Utopia," *An American Utopia: Dual Power and the Universal Army* [ed. Slavoj Žižek], New York: Verso, 2016, pg. 73–74)

20 (Jameson, "An American Utopia," pg. 74)

21 (Jameson, "An American Utopia," pg. 75)

22 (*SE* 14: 93-97, 100–102)
    (*SE* 16: 428–429)
    (*SE* 19: 28)
    (*SE* 22: 64–66)

23 (*SE* 18: 108–110, 112–114, 116, 129–133)

24 (*SE* 1: 318, 331)
    (Johnston, "Humanity, That Sickness," pg. 217–261)
    (Johnston, *Infinite Greed*)

25 (Philip Rieff, *Freud: The Mind of the Moralist*, Chicago: University of Chicago Press, 1979, pg. 221–222)
    (Louis Althusser, *Psychoanalysis and the Human Sciences* [trans. Steven Rendall], New York: Columbia University Press, 2016, pg. 60–63)
    (Martin Jay, *The Dialectical Imagination: A History of the Frankfurt School and the Institute of Social Research, 1923-1950*, Boston: Little, Brown and Company, 1973, pg. 105)
    (Jean Roy, *Hobbes and Freud* [trans. Thomas G. Osler], Toronto: Canadian Philosophical Monographs, 1984, pg. viii, 59–60)

26 (Immanuel Kant, *"Idee zu einer allgemeinen Geschichte in weltbürgerlicher Absicht,"* *Werkausgabe XI: Schriften zur Anthropologie, Geschichtsphilosophie, Politik und Pädagogik* [ed. Wilhelm Weischedel], Frankfurt am Main: Suhrkamp, 1977, pg. 37)
    (Immanuel Kant, "Idea for a Universal History with a Cosmopolitan Intent," *Perpetual Peace and Other Essays on Politics, History, and Morals* [trans. Ted Humphrey], Indianapolis: Hackett, 1983, pg. 31–32)

27 (Johnston, *Infinite Greed*)

28 (Alexandre Kojève, *Introduction to the Reading of Hegel: Lectures on the Phenomenology of Spirit* [ed. Raymond Queneau and Allan Bloom; trans. James H. Nichols, Jr.], Ithaca: Cornell University Press, 1980, pg. 65, 102, 159, 215, 259)

29 (Jacques Lacan, *Le Séminaire de Jacques Lacan, Livre XVI: D'un Autre à l'autre, 1968-1969* [ed. Jacques-Alain Miller], Paris: Éditions du Seuil, 2006, pg. 32)
    (Jacques Lacan, *The Seminar of Jacques Lacan, Book XVII: The Other Side of Psychoanalysis, 1969-1970* [ed. Jacques-Alain Miller; trans. Russell Grigg], New York: W.W. Norton and Company, 2007, pg. 81, 98)

30 (Lacan, *Le Séminaire de Jacques Lacan, Livre XVI*, pg. 32)

31 (Lacan, *Le Séminaire de Jacques Lacan, Livre XVI*, pg. 16–18, 29–30, 64–65, 172)
    (Lacan, *The Seminar of Jacques Lacan, Book XVII*, pg. 20, 79, 81, 107–108, 177)
32 (Jacques Lacan, *Le Séminaire de Jacques Lacan, Livre XVII: L'envers de la psychanalyse, 1969-1970* [ed. Jacques-Alain Miller], Paris: Éditions du Seuil, 1991, pg. 93)
    (Lacan, *The Seminar of Jacques Lacan, Book XVII*, pg. 81)
33 (Lacan, *The Seminar of Jacques Lacan, Book XVII*, pg. 98)
34 (*SE* 5: 561)
    (*SE* 15: 226)
35 (Lacan, *Le Séminaire de Jacques Lacan, Livre XVII*, pg. 111)
    (Lacan, *The Seminar of Jacques Lacan, Book XVII*, pg. 98)
36 (Lacan, *Le Séminaire de Jacques Lacan, Livre XVII*, pg. 111–112)
    (Lacan, *The Seminar of Jacques Lacan, Book XVII*, pg. 98)
37 (Louis Althusser, *On the Reproduction of Capitalism: Ideology and Ideological State Apparatuses* [trans. G.M. Goshgarian], London: Verso, 2014, pg. 181)
38 (Adrian Johnston, "The Late Innate: Jean Laplanche, Jaak Panksepp, and the Distinction Between Sexual Drives and Instincts," *Inheritance in Psychoanalysis* [ed. Joel Goldbach and James A. Godley], Albany: State University of New York Press, 2018, pg. 57–84)
39 (Johnston, *Infinite Greed*)
40 (Jacques Lacan, *Le Séminaire de Jacques Lacan, Livre XVIII: D'un discours qui ne serait pas du semblant, 1971* [ed. Jacques-Alain Miller], Paris: Éditions du Seuil, 2006, pg. 21)
41 (Lacan, *Le Séminaire de Jacques Lacan, Livre XVIII*, pg. 21)
42 (Jacques Lacan, "The Subversion of the Subject and the Dialectic of Desire in the Freudian Unconscious," *Écrits: The First Complete Edition in English* [trans. Bruce Fink], New York: W.W. Norton and Company, 2006, pg. 696)
43 (Adrian Johnston, *Time Driven: Metapsychology and the Splitting of the Drive*, Evanston: Northwestern University Press, 2005, pg. xix–xxiv, 184–341)
44 (Samo Tomšič, *The Capitalist Unconscious: Marx and Lacan*, London: Verso, 2015, pg. 108–109)
45 (Karl Marx, *Grundrisse: Foundations of the Critique of Political Economy (Rough Draft)* [trans. Martin Nicolaus], New York: Penguin, 1973, pg. 105)
46 (Lacan, *Le Séminaire de Jacques Lacan, Livre XVII*, pg. 105)
    (Lacan, *The Seminar of Jacques Lacan, Book XVII*, pg. 92)
47 (Jacques Lacan, *Le Séminaire de Jacques Lacan, Livre XIV: La logique du fantasme, 1966-1967* [unpublished typescript], session of June 21, 1967)
48 (Johnston, *Infinite Greed*)
49 (Johnston, *Infinite Greed*)
50 (Lacan, *Le Séminaire de Jacques Lacan, Livre XIV*, session of April 12, 1967)
51 (Lacan, *Le Séminaire de Jacques Lacan, Livre XVI*, pg. 29–30)
52 (Louis Althusser, "The Object of *Capital*," in Louis Althusser, Étienne Balibar, Roger Establet, Pierre Macherey, and Jacques Rancière, *Reading Capital: The*

Complete Edition [trans. Ben Brewster and David Fernbach], London: Verso, 2015, pg. 255, 334, 341–343)

53 (Althusser, "The Object of *Capital*," pg. 254, 343)
(Louis Althusser, "Contradiction and Overdetermination: Notes for an Investigation," *For Marx* [trans. Ben Brewster], London: Verso, 2005, pg. 87–128)
(Louis Althusser, "On the Materialist Dialectic: On the Unevenness of Origins," *For Marx*, pg. 204–206, 209–210, 213–214, 216–217)
(Louis Althusser, "Marxism and Humanism," *For Marx*, pg. 233–234)

54 (Lacan, *Le Séminaire de Jacques Lacan, Livre XIV*, session of April 19, 1967)

55 (Lacan, *Le Séminaire de Jacques Lacan, Livre XIV*, session of April 26, 1967)

56 (Johnston, *Time Driven*, pg. xix–xxiv)

57 (Lacan, *Le Séminaire de Jacques Lacan, Livre XIV*, session of April 26, 1967)

58 (Johnston, *Time Driven*, pg. xxiv, xxxiv–xxxv, 184–341)

59 (Jacques Lacan, *The Seminar of Jacques Lacan, Book VII: The Ethics of Psychoanalysis, 1959-1960* [ed. Jacques-Alain Miller; trans. Dennis Porter], New York: W.W. Norton and Company, 1992, pg. 150, 152)

60 (Jacques Lacan, "*Du discours psychanalytique*," *Lacan in Italia, 1953-1978*, Milan: La Salamandra, 1978, pg. 49)

61 (Lacan, *Le Séminaire de Jacques Lacan, Livre XVI*, pg. 333)
(Lacan, *The Seminar of Jacques Lacan, Book XVII*, pg. 79)
(Lacan, *Le Séminaire de Jacques Lacan, Livre XVIII*, pg. 49–50)
(Jacques Lacan, *Le Séminaire de Jacques Lacan, Livre XIX: ...ou pire, 1971-1972* [ed. Jacques-Alain Miller], Paris: Éditions du Seuil, 2011, pg. 52)
(Jacques Lacan, "*Discours à l'École freudienne de Paris*," *Autres écrits* [ed. Jacques-Alain Miller], Paris: Éditions du Seuil, 2001, pg. 278)
(Jacques Lacan, "*Radiophonie*," *Autres écrits*, pg. 424, 434–435)
(Jacques Lacan, "*Postface au Séminaire XI*," *Autres écrits*, pg. 505)
(Jacques Lacan, "*En guise de conclusion*," *Lettres de l'École freudienne*, no. 8, 1971, pg. 211–212)
(Jacques Lacan, "*Un homme et une femme*," *Bulletin de l'Association freudienne*, no. 54, September 1993, pg. 14)
(Lacan, "*Du discours psychanalytique*," *Lacan in Italia*, pg. 46, 49, 51)
(Jacques Lacan, "*La troisième*," *Lettres de l'École freudienne*, no. 16, 1975, pg. 189, 199–200)
(Jacques Lacan, "*Journées d'étude des cartels de l'École freudienne: Séance de cloture*," *Lettres de l'École freudienne*, no. 18, 1976, pg. 268)
(Johnston, *Infinite Greed*)

62 (Johnston, *Infinite Greed*)

63 (Jacques Lacan, "*Mon enseignement, sa nature et ses fins*," *Mon enseignement* [ed. Jacques-Alain Miller], Paris: Éditions du Seuil, 2005, pg. 82–83)
(Jacques Lacan, "My Teaching, Its Nature and Its Ends," *My Teaching* [ed. Jacques-Alain Miller; trans. David Macey], London: Verso, 2008, pg. 64)

64 (Lacan, "*Mon enseignement, sa nature et ses fins*," pg. 83)
(Lacan, "My Teaching, Its Nature and Its Ends," pg. 64)

65   (Johnston, *Prolegomena to Any Future Materialism, Volume Two*, pg. xix–xx,
     117–118, 132–134, 187, 200, 207–221)
     (Johnston, *Infinite Greed*)
66   (Dominique Laporte, *History of Shit* [trans. Nadia Benabid and Rodolphe el-
     Khoury], Cambridge: MIT Press, 2000, pg. 40)
67   (Karl Marx and Friedrich Engels, *The Communist Manifesto* [trans. Samuel
     Moore], *Karl Marx: Selected Writings* [ed. David McLellan], Oxford: Oxford
     University Press, 1977, pg. 231)
68   (Karl Marx, *Wage-Labour and Capital*, *Wage-Labour and Capital/Value, Price
     and Profit*, New York: International Publishers, 1976, pg. 48)
69   (Richard Boothby, *Freud as Philosopher: Metapsychology After Lacan*, New
     York: Routledge, 2001, pg. 249)
70   (Althusser, *On the Reproduction of Capitalism*, pg. 20-21, 52, 140, 148–149,
     246–247)
71   (Slavoj Žižek, *The Plague of Fantasies*, London: Verso, 1997, pg. 4)
72   (Zizek, *The Plague of Fantasies*, pg. 4–5)
73   (Žižek, *The Plague of Fantasies*, pg. 5)
74   (V.I. Lenin, "The Three Sources and Three Component Parts of Marxism," *The
     Lenin Anthology* [ed. Robert C. Tucker], New York: W.W. Norton and
     Company, 1975, pg. 640–644)
75   (*SE* 8: 170–171, 204)
     (*SE* 11: 233–234)
     (*SE* 21: 161–166)
76   (Althusser, *On the Reproduction of Capitalism*, pg. 76–77, 172–173, 175, 184–187)
     (Louis Althusser, *Que faire?*, Paris: Presses Universitaires de France, 2018, pg.
     33–34, 93–94, 110)
     (Louis Althusser, *How to Be a Marxist in Philosophy* [ed. and trans. G.M.
     Goshgarian], London: Bloomsbury, 2017, pg. 124–125)
77   (Karl Marx and Friedrich Engels, *Die deutsche Ideologie*, Berlin: Dietz Verlag,
     1953, pg. 22–23)
78   (Laporte, *History of Shit*, pg. 37)
79   (Lacan, *The Seminar of Jacques Lacan, Book VII*, pg. 139)
     (Jacques Lacan, *The Seminar of Jacques Lacan, Book XI: The Four Fundamental
     Concepts of Psychoanalysis, 1964* [ed. Jacques-Alain Miller; trans. Alan
     Sheridan], New York: W.W. Norton and Company, 1977, pg. 268)
     (Lacan, *Le Séminaire de Jacques Lacan, Livre XVI*, pg. 224–225, 249)
80   (V.I. Lenin, "The Importance of Gold Now and After the Complete Victory of
     Socialism," *The Lenin Anthology*, pg. 515)
81   (Marcuse, *Eros and Civilization*, pg. 99–101, 224–225)
     (Herbert Marcuse, *One-Dimensional Man: Studies in the Ideology of Advanced
     Industrial Society*, Boston: Beacon Press, 1964, pg. 72)
     (Herbert Marcuse, *An Essay on Liberation*, Boston: Beacon Press, 1969, pg. 9)
     (Herbert Marcuse, "Progress and Freud's Theory of Instincts," *Five Lectures:*

Psychoanalysis, Politics, and Utopia [trans. Jeremy J. Shapiro and Shierry M. Weber], Boston: Beacon Press, 1970, pg. 38–39)

(Herbert Marcuse, "The Obsolescence of the Freudian Concept of Man," *Five Lectures*, pg. 57–58)

(Herbert Marcuse, *Counterrevolution and Revolt*, Boston: Beacon Press, 1972, pg. 59–60, 76, 80, 113)

(Herbert Marcuse, "Repressive Tolerance," in Robert Paul Wolff, Barrington Moore, Jr., and Herbert Marcuse, *A Critique of Pure Tolerance*, Boston: Beacon Press, 1969, pg. 114–115)

82 (Althusser, *On the Reproduction of Capitalism*, pg. 186)

(Louis Althusser, "Ideology and Ideological State Apparatuses (Notes towards an Investigation)," *On the Reproduction of Capitalism*, pg. 260)

Chapter 12

The Dionysian Primate: Goethe, Nietzsche, Jung and Psychedelic Neuroscience

Gary Clark

Thoas: It is not a god that speaks: it is your heart.
Iphigenia: It is only through human hearts that gods can speak.
Goethe, *Iphigenia in Tauris*, Act 1 SCENE III. [1]

Growing Young Again: Goethe, the Unconscious and Dionysian Aesthetics

In September 1786, at the age of 37, Goethe travelled to Italy in part to expunge the spiritual malaise he was experiencing in his position as Privy Counsellor at the Weimar Court. Essentially, Goethe had suffered what today we would probably call a nervous breakdown, and Italy, with its rich history and culture, was to become the panacea for his fraught spiritual condition. As he writes of his experience in *Italian Journey*, an account based on the diaries he kept while travelling:

> Roman antiquity is beginning to give me about as much pleasure as Greek. History, inscriptions, coins, in which hitherto I took no interest, are forcing themselves on my attention. My experience with natural history is repeating itself here, for the entire history of the world is linked up with this city, and I rekon my second life, a very rebirth, from the day when I entered Rome.
>
> (von Goethe, 1970, p. 148)

Goethe goes on to describe how the old habits of thought that he developed in Germany had to be given up before he could find a new

DOI: 10.4324/9781003090755-13

centre of gravity within his personality; as he writes 'the more I give up my old habits of thought the happier I am.' The changes he experienced while in Italy were not merely intellectual, but involved the entirety of his being – as he continues 'I am convinced my moral sense is undergoing as great a transformation as my aesthetic' (von Goethe, 1970, p. 51). Such a process of transformation was not the result of a sudden change, but of an organic process, one that like the processes of growth in nature, unfolds over time – as Goethe reminds his reader: 'The rebirth which is transforming me from within continues' (von Goethe, 1970, p. 51).

Goethe is here describing the transformation of the aesthetic and moral aspects of his personality – that is the development and unfolding of his creative self. Interestingly, Goethe elsewhere offered a developmental perspective on the process of creative experience that provides a useful gloss on his comments in *Italian Journey*. For example, when discussing the creative and productive achievement of artists in their later years, he stated that 'they seem constantly to grow young again for a time, and this is what I call repeated puberty' (Goethe quoted in Bishop, 2008, p. 165).

Goethe also developed ideas about inborn and learned aspects of human psychology that are germane to his reflections on aesthetics and creativity. As he writes 'the organs of the human being, by means of practice, theory, reflection...link, unconsciously and in free activity, the acquired with the inborn, so that the result is a unity which astonishes the world' (Goethe quoted in Bishop, 2008, p. 157). By the acquired, we would today mean the human capacity for learning – what Goethe calls practice, theory and reflection – while inborn traits would consist of those that are genetically based or inherited. In this sense, Goethe seems to be arguing that the goal of human life is to integrate our genetically evolved or inborn emotions and instincts with our capacity for learning, cognition and acquired thought and behaviour patterns. Elaborating further on his theory of aesthetics, Goethe avers that the aim of life and art is to integrate 'sensuality and reason, imagination and common sense...into a coherent whole' (Goethe quoted in Bishop, 2008, p. 170). He also stated that 'man can not dwell for long in consciousness or in a conscious state. He must again take refuge in the unconscious, for that is where his life is rooted' (Goethe quoted in Bishop, 2007, p. 9).

Goethe's writing on the unconscious and creativity – what Faust describes as 'the deep and secret wonders of my heart' (Faust, Part1, lines 3233–3234) – had significant impact on psychoanalysis and analytical psychology (Bishop, 2007, 2008; Brown, 2014; Ellenberger, 1970). As Ellenberger writes in *The Discovery of the Unconscious*, Freud's aim was 'to incorporate into scientific psychology those hidden realms of the human psyche that had been grasped intuitively by the Greek tragedians, Shakespeare, Goethe, and other great writers.' (Ellenberger, 1970, p. 571). Echoing this notion Jane Brown argues Goethe had developed a complex response to the problem of representing the hidden and unconscious aspects of the personality. As she writes, the workings of the 'subconscious or unconscious part of the psyche...are largely inaccessible to the conscious or rational part of the mind.' Goethe, particularly in *Faust* had explored these unconscious domains of experience and had developed a theatrical technique that made the 'unconscious accessible to language,' enabling the artistic representation of 'what by definition cannot be known rationally' (Brown, 2014, pp. 7 and 9). Goethe's acknowledgment of the importance of the unconscious, and his ability to represent this domain of the psyche artistically, was also a major influence on Jung's thought (Bishop, 2007, 2008; Edinger, 1990).

Significantly, Nietzsche considered Goethe's conception of human psychology to have affinities with the transformations of consciousness he believed to have characterised ancient Greek ritual – as Bishop avers 'Nietzsche...uses Goethe's *Faust* as an intertext in describing the effect of the Dionysian' (Bishop, 1995, p. 111). As Nietzsche writes, linking Goethe's aesthetic to the Dionysian rituals of rebirth, Goethe 'strove against the separation of reason, sensuality, feeling [and] will...he disciplined himself into a whole.' Nietzsche continues, claiming that Goethe possessed the 'highest of all possible faiths: I have baptised it with the name Dionysus.' (Nietzsche, 1990, p. 114). Further, echoing the descent to 'The Mothers' section of *Faust*, Nietzsche writes: 'by the mystical triumphant cry of Dionysus...the way lies open to the Mothers of Being, to the innermost heart of things' (Nietzsche, 1993, p. 76).

Importantly, Paul Bishop has argued that in addition to Goethe, Nietzsche was one of the seminal influences on Jung's thinking.

Reflecting on Nietzsche's concept of the Dionysian, Bishop argues that Jung's uniquely Nietzschean approach 'lay in the construction of a Dionysian Self which, through the dialectic of consciousness and the Unconscious, permits the Ego to die and be reborn anew' (Bishop, 1995, p. 17). Further, this Dionysian framing of Jungian psychology conceives of the Self as 'an integrated wholeness in which the conscious and unconscious aspects of the individual psyche are united' (Bishop, 1995, p. 222). This integration of ego consciousness with the unconscious is essentially what Jung's concept of individuation entails (Jung, Adler, & Hull, 1980, p. 222).

Significantly, in *The Birth of Tragedy*, Nietzsche wrote about ritualised transformations of consciousness induced by mind altering substances: 'Under the influence of the narcotic potion hymned by all primitive men and peoples, or in the powerful approach of spring, joyfully penetrating the whole of nature, those Dionysiac urges are awakened, and as they grow more intense, subjectivity becomes a complete forgetting of the self' (Nietzsche, 1993, p. 17). Jung also argued that psychedelics offer a powerful means of accessing unconscious processes with numerous researchers suggesting his work provides a useful framework for analysis of the acute psychedelic state (Carhart-Harris & Friston, 2010; Carhart-Harris et al., 2014; Clark, 2020b; Hill, 2013). Significantly, psychedelics have been described as psychointegrators that facilitate the ritualised integration of phylogenetically ancient subcortical brain systems with more recently evolved cortical systems (Winkelman, 2001). In this chapter, I argue that such a process can be fruitfully analysed in terms of Jung's concept of individuation or the integration of the unconscious and consciousness.

Later in this chapter, I will explore Nietzsche's conception of the Dionysian as a 'forgetting of the self' in terms of what has been referred to in the psychedelic neuroscience literature as 'ego dissolution.' I will also use this model in an analysis of Goethe, Jung and examples of ritual transformations of consciousness taken from the ethnographic literature. Before doing so, however, I want to discuss research in developmental, evolutionary and psychedelic neuroscience in order to provide a context for that analysis.

The Evolution of Adolescence: From the Weird and Wonderful to the Tried and True

I now want to explore research on both the evolution of the human brain as well as its unfolding throughout development. This approach will also inform my analysis of the mind/body problem. One of the articulations of the mind/body problem sees it as arising from different perspectives – that is first person versus third person. The first-person perspective encompasses the subjective qualities of consciousness – that is the phenomenological nature of the *qualia* that we experience through introspection. The third person perspective on the other hand refers to understanding the putative neurobiological substrates of such experience that can be observed through empirical investigation. In this chapter, I will frame my discussion in terms of neurophenomenology – an approach that seeks to bridge the explanatory gap between these two perspectives (Khachouf, Poletti, & Pagnoni, 2013).

This approach will involve an exploration of the concept of dual aspect monism, which asserts brain states and the phenomenology of subjective states, are two aspects of the same phenomenon (Solms & Turnbull, 2010). More specifically, I explore evidence for this view from research in psychedelic neuroscience, where neurochemically induced alterations of brain connectivity correlate with archetypal religious experiences of 'ego dissolution' and 'oceanic boundlessness' (Carhart-Harris & Friston, 2019, pp. 317 and 336; Kettner, Gandy, Haijen, & Carhart-Harris, 2019, p. 4). I will suggest that the phenomenology of such experiences correlates with a phase transition from our more recently evolved secondary consciousness to a more primitive form of primary consciousness associated with emotionally laden subcortical brain systems. This research suggests that changes in the first person, subjective or qualitative nature of experience, are linked to changes in neural architecture that can be observed from a third person or empirical perspective. In fact, these two perspectives may be merely different ways of perceiving the same phenomena. That is the mind/body 'problem' may arise from two apparently (and I emphasise apparently) incommensurate perspectives – and not from two distinct kinds of phenomena in the objective world.

One of the unique features of humans when compared with other primates is the evolution of an adolescent period of growth – which is presumed to be the time when full maturation of our unique cognitive and linguistic capacities occurs (Locke & Bogin, 2006). For example, it is during this period that we see a transition from affect-based primary process control of behaviour to secondary process control associated with metacognition, theory of mind, mental time travel, and the development of the ego complex (Carhart-Harris & Friston, 2010; Fair et al., 2008; Jones, 2013).

There has been a long tradition in evolutionary thought that looks at the relationship between ontogeny (individual development) and phylogeny (evolution of species) – an idea first developed in the 19th century by the German naturalist Ernst Haeckel (Gould, 1977; Haeckel, 1887). It is worth noting that this conception of human evolution, and specifically as it applies to psychological development, had significant impact on the thinking of both Freud and Jung (Cambray, 2014). While this theory has been criticised by some researchers (Lovtrup, 1978), others have argued that there is an important relationship between ontogeny and phylogeny in human cognitive and linguistic evolution (Clark & Henneberg, 2017; Parker & McKinney, 2000). This is because the maturation of the human brain requires an extension of ontogeny with the evolution of such an extension being one of the key features of our phylogenetic emergence as a species. Additionally, it has been proposed that in both ontogeny and phylogeny, we see a gradual transition from subcortical affect-based control of behaviour, to higher-order control associated with self-consciousness and the ego complex (Carhart-Harris et al., 2014; Clark, 2020b).

This extension of ontogeny or life history relative to other primates means that humans have delayed schedules of dental eruption, cessation of brain development and delayed onset of sexual maturation (Hawkes, Paine, & Research, 2006; Minugh-Purvis & McNamara, 2002; Trevathan & Rosenberg, 2016). One of the consequences of this extension is that human childhood is longer than in other primates – in addition, we have an extra period of socio-cognitive and linguistic development that we refer to as adolescence which results in humans reaching sexual maturity some five to six years later than chimpanzees and bonobos (Bogin, 2003; Clark & Henneberg, 2015; Locke &

Bogin, 2006). Significantly, it is during this period that we see maturation of the default mode network and a transition from primary to secondary consciousness – that is from subcortical to more cortical control of behaviour (Fair et al., 2008; Jones, 2013).

When thinking about the transition from primary to secondary consciousness as we develop from children, into adolescents and adults, research into the maturation of the default mode network provides valuable insights. The default mode network is believed to be involved in a number of uniquely human cognitive capacities such as language and conceptual processing (Rilling et al., 2007), the construction of autobiographical narratives, the ability to project the self into the future, theory of mind as well as the uniquely human sense of self or ego (Carhart-Harris & Friston, 2010; Raichle & Snyder, 2007; Rilling et al., 2007; Spreng & Grady, 2010; Spreng, Mar, & Kim, 2008). Significantly, while infants show similarities with adults in the visual, sensorimotor, and auditory regions in the brain, the default mode network has yet to fully mature at this early stage of development (Fransson et al., 2007) and it is not until later stages of ontogeny that full integration of the default mode network occurs (Fair et al., 2008). It is also important to note that the default mode network has been implicated in various forms of psychopathology (Shim et al., 2010; Whitfield-Gabrieli and Ford, 2012), which seem to be associated with overly rigid or inflexible thinking (Carhart-Harris & Friston, 2019) and over active internal rumination (Zhou et al., 2020). The important point to consider here is that infants and children have a default mode network unlike the configuration evident in adolescents and adults – and they also lack the associated form of secondary consciousness. The implications are that human vulnerability to psychopathology may have involved the evolution of an adolescent period of growth during which the default mode network matures and during which we also see an ontogenetic transition from primary to secondary consciousness.

What is particularly relevant in this context are neuroscientific findings that as we age executive control related to development of the prefrontal cortex increases, while exploration, learning, divergent thinking and neural plasticity tend to decline – that is the brain becomes less entropic, with reduced plasticity and increased rigidity occurring throughout ontogeny (Carhart-Harris & Friston, 2010;

Carhart-Harris 2014; Gopnik, 2016; Gopnik, Griffiths, & Lucas, 2015; Gopnik et al., 2017). This seems to be associated with gradual accumulation of knowledge during childhood, and into adulthood, resulting in a decline in cognitive flexibility as we age and consolidate our knowledge of the world (Gopnik et al., 2017). This process seems to be associated with a proliferation of synaptic connections during the early period of development, with a process of pruning occurring as we age, transforming a more 'flexible, sensitive, and plastic brain into a more effective and controlled one' (Gopnik et al., 2017, p. 7893).

As Alison Gopnik and colleagues write, summarising this research, adults may sometimes be better at 'the tried and true, while children are more likely to discover the weird and wonderful. This may be because as we get older, we both know more and explore less' (Gopnik et al., 2015, p. 91). Significantly, the plasticity characteristic of the early stages of development can also be evident in adult cognitive life when 'disruptions to frontal control' may result 'in a more "child-like" brain' with improved performance in cognitive tasks that involve exploring a wide range of possibilities (Gopnik et al., 2015, p. 91). Developing this line of thought further, Gopnik notes that certain environments 'may lead to more flexible, exploratory and childlike learning, even in adulthood' (Gopnik et al., 2017, p. 7898).

Elaborating on this research, Gopnik notes that the less constrained brain of children is one that may be more creative than the adult brain – which, she suggests, may explain the literary trope of childhood as emblematic of the creative imagination. As she writes: 'the nineteenth century Romantics, [see] disorder as the wellspring of freedom, innovation, and creativity...for them, children were the quintessential example of the virtues of chaos' (Gopnik, 2016, pp 26–27). These observations may help explain the importance of childhood to poetic and literary traditions as well as possibly help illuminate, from an evolutionary and development point of view, the cross cultural child archetype analysed by Jung (Abrams, 1971, pp. 379–383; Jung, 2014, pp. 151–181). Reflecting on this aspect of his theory, Jung writes that 'in every adult there lurks a child...something that is always becoming, is never completed, and calls for unceasing care... That is the part of the human personality which wants to develop and become whole' (Jung & Adler, 2014, pp. 169–170). This model also provides a useful way approaching Goethe's concept of rebirth and 'growing young.' I will explore this perspective later in this chapter in my reading of Goethe's *Faust*.

Importantly, high-dose ingestion of serotonergic psychedelics seems to produce a collapse of top heavy neural hierarchies associated with the default mode network and secondary consciousness (Carhart-Harris & Friston, 2019; Carhart-Harris et al., 2014). This process is accompanied by reduced cognitive rigidity, increased plasticity and the emergence of sub-cortical, primary process brain systems into conscious awareness. Importantly, such experience of so-called ego-dissolution seems to result in increased global connectivity where different brain regions begin communicating with one another – that is the highly segregated and modular brain becomes desegrated under psychedelics (Carhart-Harris & Friston, 2010; Carhart-Harris & Friston, 2019; Carhart-Harris et al., 2012; Carhart-Harris et al., 2014; Muthukumaraswamy et al., 2013; Nour, Evans, & Carhart-Harris, 2017; Tagliazucchi et al., 2014).

Significantly, such alteration of neural architecture results in increases in neural and cognitive plasticity akin to the more plastic and flexible brain associated with the early stages of brain ontogeny. This alteration is believed to be associated with a phase transition from secondary consciousness to primary consciousness – that is a regression to a more primitive mode of consciousness that both Freud and Jung referred to as the unconscious (Carhart-Harris & Friston, 2019; Carhart-Harris et al., 2014). Such regression, and the accompanying experience of 'ego dissolution' (Nour et al., 2016; Tagliazucchi et al., 2016), provides an empirically grounded perspective on Nietzsche's Dionysian 'forgetting of the self' that he believed resulted from ingesting 'narcotic potions.' What is worth noting is that such perturbation of rigid and habituated thought patterns and neural architecture results in surprisingly effective recovery rates from treatment resistant depression when psychedelics are administered in caring and supportive clinical settings (Roseman, Nutt, & Carhart-Harris, 2018).

Alan Hobson has elaborated on the relationship between ontogeny and phylogeny and human brain evolution as it pertains to dream research and altered states of consciousness. Echoing the model outlined in this chapter, he argues that dream mentation represents the emergence into consciousness of phylogenetically ancient primary process brain systems. As he writes 'primary consciousness (or process) is more ontogenetically and phylogenetically primitive than secondary consciousness (or process).' Hobson continues, arguing that in both ontogeny and phylogeny, subcortical primary processes are superseded by upper brain cortical processes; as he writes while 'most animals, young and old, human and subhuman, have sub-cortical brains of comparable complexity, the complexity of the upper brain increases markedly in the early development of each lifetime and over eons of evolutionary time in the origin of the species' (Hobson, 2014, p. 109). Further, Hobson argues that psychoses, the phenomenology of altered states of consciousness such as the psychedelic state as well as dream mentation all seem to involve re-versions to primary process styles of thinking (Hobson, 1999, 2014; Hobson & Voss, 2011). Reflecting on these affinities, Hobson claims that in human dream life, we have our own naturally occurring parallel to the psychedelic experience – so much so that he claims dreams to be our own endogenous 'drug store' (Hobson, 2002).

Neuroscientist Jaak Panksepp has adopted a similar approach, arguing that dream mentation may be the expression of a phylo-genetically ancient primary process system that was superseded by our more recently evolved capacity for planning, free will and higher working memory. As he writes the REM mechanism, associated with periods of sleep during which vivid dreaming occurs, may have 'originally controlled a primitive form of waking arousal.' Over evolutionary time this primitive system, according to Panksepp, was overridden by higher cortical regions with the more ancient system being 'relegated to providing background function such as the in-tegration of emotional information that seems to occur during dreaming' (Panksepp, 2004, p. 135). Significantly, Nietzsche pro-posed a similar relation between dream life and the waking state of archaic humans: 'man still draws conclusions in his dreams as man-kind once did *in a waking state*' (Nietzsche, 1994, p. 21). In his commentary on this passage, Jung concurs with Nietzsche on this point, formulating his perspective in the context of evolutionary theory – as he writes: 'dream thinking [is]…a recapitulation of earlier evolutionary stages' (Jung et al., 2014b, p. 23).

In the following two sections of this chapter, I will discuss Goethe's *Faust* and the work of Jung using the aforementioned ideas to ground their work in evolutionary and developmental neuroscience. I will also explore affinities between Goethe's *Faust* and ritual transformations of consciousness evident in psychedelic rituals in both Africa and Latin America.

Faust and the Shamanic Quest: Purging Horror and Restoring Sacred Light

A common feature of human cultures is the belief in sprits, 'ghosts' or supernatural entities. Such phenomena seem to become manifest during rituals and other cultural practices that set out to alter consciousness. Some researchers have attributed this belief to the visualization of imagery either in dream or waking states. For example, Edward Tylor argued that belief in sprits, and the associated religious systems, originally grew out of dream life – a thesis that has found support from cognitive science and analysis of the significant role the emotionally potent imagery of dreams play in the religious and cultural life of our species (Bulkeley, 2016; Tylor, 2010).

In this context, it is worth considering the possible neurobiological substrates of experiential phenomena such as 'spirit entities' which are crucial aspects of shamanic healing and visionary states induced by psychedelic substances. For example, such entities are believed to arise from dissociated complexes in the unconscious that operate outside of ego consciousness – and that such a visually and emotionally rich modality represents a phylogenetically ancient form of primary consciousness based in 'somatic awareness and subjective feeling states' (Winkelman, 2010, pp. 12, 9, 205 and 207; 2017a, p. 7).

Significantly, Gloria Flaherty has argued that the dramatic trajectory of Goethe's *Faust* represents a modern incarnation of the shamanic quest. During the 18th century reports were returning to Europe from the New World on the cultural, religious and ritual practices of Indigenous people – reports that had an impact on Goethe's thinking. As Flaherty writes Goethe's *Faust*

is a consummate masterpiece that incorporates into the very scheme of European cultural evolution nearly everything the eighteenth century had heard or thought about shamanism. It elevates the phenomenon that had been considered diabolically aberrant, incredibly ludicrous, and then harmlessly exotic, and gives that phenomenon its significant place in the history as well as the prehistory of the West.

(Flaherty, 2014, p. 183)

Flaherty avers that Goethe 'suspected a connection between primeval forms of shamanism and the incipient mythology that in prehistoric times began to form the cultural basis of Europe' (Flaherty, 2014, p. 184). In this sense, Goethe's interest in these issues was focussed on both the thought and religious sensibility of European antiquity and prehistory as well as that of Indigenous peoples of the New World.

As Goethe writes, reflecting on reports of Indigenous cultures from the New World, tribal peoples sought to explain the world 'through fanciful, highly poetic symbolism' – what today we would refer to as mythological explanation. According to Goethe, such cultures – and here he refers to shamanism as sorcery – possess a more refined sense of affinity with the natural world than the modern rationalist culture of which he was a part; as he writes 'ancient magic and sorcery has style, the modern does not. Ancient magic is nature viewed humanly.' And emphasising the cultural contingency of our modern conception of human subjectivity he avers: 'Whereby then a particular difficulty arises for the moderns because as much as we wish, we find no easy substitute for the wondrous creatures, gods and soothsayers, and oracles of the ancients' (Goethe quoted in Flaherty, 2014, pp. 167–168).

As already intimated, my approach to *Faust* is that the play is structured around a phase transition from secondary to primary consciousness. That the dramatic trajectory of *Faust* represents a such phase transition is suggested when Faust and Mephistopheles sing at the start of the Walpurgis Night section: 'We have entered it seems/the realms of dreams and magic' (*Faust* Part 1, lines 3871–3872).

Additionally, as in shamanic practices spirits are associated in *Faust* with psychological healing. As I have noted such practices appear to engage visually and emotionally rich primary process cognitive modalities. Note in the following passage the reference to Ariel from Shakespeare's *The Tempest* – a figure that is believed to be a literary incarnation of early medieval folklore about spirits (Purkiss, 2000). In this section, Ariel sings to the spirits:

You who are floating in the air about his head,
offer him your elfin kindness,
assuage the bitter angst within his heart,
remove the red-hot arrows of remorse,
and purge his soul of horror!
Night has four phases;
be quick to make each friendly.
First place his head upon a cool pillow,
then bathe him in the cleansing waters of Lethe.
His body will soon recover from its lethargy
as sleep restores his strength to face the new day.
Perform your noble rite
and restore him to the sacred light!
              (*Faust* Part 2, lines 4621–4633)

In response the chorus of spirits sing:

Serenely sing of tranquillity,
cradle his soul in childhood's peace,
and upon his weary eyes
close the gates of daylight.
       (*Faust* Part 2, lines 4638–4641)

The evocation of emotionally rich primary processes is evident in the lines 'cradle his soul in childhood's peace' – a transition to earlier stages of ontogeny reminiscent of Goethe's reflections on creativity and 'growing young' discussed earlier. Similarly, emphasising that primary process emotion is the object of his quest Faust proclaims: 'I am not searching for salvation in rigidity/ Sublime dread is humankind's greatest gift/ and although our world suffocates feeling/if we are moved to the core we apprehend the Infinite' (*Faust* Part 2, lines 6271–6274).

As the play progresses, Mephistopheles instructs Faust about the realm of 'The Mothers': 'Reluctantly I will reveal a higher mystery./ Majestic goddesses enthroned in solitude/of no place and beyond time' (*Faust* Part 2, lines 6213–6215). As Faust continues his quest, he becomes more acquainted with the feminine dimension of life – and accompanying this process, the negativity that is burdening him is assuaged by spirts. In this sense, the function of his descent to 'The Mothers' is spiritual purification and illumination:

If there are spirits in the air
who exist between heaven and earth
descend from your golden haze
transport me to a renewed and brighter life!
(*Faust* Part 1, lines 1118–1121)

Further on Faust reflects on his condition: 'Darkness is becoming deeper and more profound,/ but from my inner being shines radiant light' (*Faust* Part 2, 11499–11500). In his *The Mothers in Faust: The Myth of Time and Creativity*, Harold Jantz argues that *Faust* extends a tradition that connects back to the myths and rites of ancient Greece and the various conceptions of the underworld associated with Orpheus and Persephone – traditions that are believed to symbolise descent into the unconscious (Hillman, 1979). As Jantz avers such rites make 'real to the initiate the meaning of death, total extinction, utter loneliness, and then lead him on, through deep ineffable terror, to the mystic glowing hearth of rebirth, of constantly renewed life, of the awareness of his oneness with the totality of life' (Jantz, 1994, p. 55). Significantly, a sense of oneness with the world, otherwise known as 'the unitive experience,' has been shown to accompany the experience of 'ego-dissolution' and the phase transition to primary process cognitive modes (Carhart-Harris et al., 2014). Interestingly, the feminine symbolism evident in 'The Mothers' and the Persephone myths and rites may be the expression of a much more ancient tradition that can be traced back through the archaeological record to the European Palaeolithic – a tradition where feminine symbolism may have been the expression an evolutionarily ancient matrilineal sociological complex (Clark, 2020a).

In his *Goethe, Nietzsche, and Wagner: Their Spinozan Epics of Love and Power*, T.K Seung argues that during his experience of rebirth and his descent to the realm of 'The Mothers,' Faust 'abandoned the cognitive mode of existence and embraced its affective mode' (Seung,

2006, p. 49). Significantly, while Seung writes that 'maternal instinct is the strongest blood tie that holds together a family' he also avers that 'paternal love is not any less caring than maternal love. Paternal care is the activation of the maternal principle in the father' (Seung, 2006, pp. 53, 117 and 136). It is such activation of the affective maternal principle in the male psyche that seems to facilitate Faust's rebirth. This perspective is consilient with research into the evolution of male care of offspring which seems to involve similar brain circuits and hormones evident in maternal nurturing, giving rise to a 'muted' version of the maternal experience in males (Wynne-Edwards, 2001; Wynne-Edwards & Reburn, 2000). Further, human fathers not only show reductions in testosterone but also a similar pattern of hormone concentration to human mothers when interacting with their new-born infants (Storey et al., 2000). It is worth noting that the affective basis of such social care seems to be based in primary process sub-cortical brain regions (Panksepp & Biven, 2012). Significantly, Seung argues that as Faust abandons the cognitive mode for the affective mode he 'recants his blinding egotism and gains the inner light of communal bonds.'(Seung, 2006, p. 117). Such a 'muted' version of the feminine in the male psyche seems to be what Jung had in mind with his concept of the anima – that is a less differentiated feminine aspect of male psychology that lay in the unconscious due to the predominance of male genes structuring the conscious mind (Jung & Kerényi, 2002, p. 112).

The phenomenology described in *Faust* is strikingly similar to that evident in the ethnographic literature on psychedelic states. For example, in his *Bwiti: an ethnography of the religious imagination in Africa*, anthropologist James Fernandez presents an extensive analysis of the ritualised use of the psychedelic iboga root by the Fang of Gabon. Echoing Goethe's poem, iboga visions involve encounters with the female principle of the universe – seen in various manifestations as a beautiful woman, as the moon, or transformed into a harp (Fernandez, 1982, pp. 484–485). Significantly, the rituals involve a process of purification and the attainment of a state of spiritual illumination – one that is phenomenologically comparable to that described in *Faust* as 'restoration' of 'sacred light.' To quote from one of the chants used in iboga rituals: 'Everything clean, clean. All is new, new. All is bright, bright' (Fernandez, 1982, pp. 488–499).

Significantly, the Fang believe that 'the younger a child is the closer he is to the ancestors' and that childhood represents a state of 'innocence propitious to passing over to the other side.' Additionally, the iboga rituals are believed to facilitate a 'return to infancy and to birth – to the life in the womb.' (Fernandez, 1982, pp. 491 and 556).

Similar phenomenology occurs during ritual ingestion of the psychedelic vine ayahuasca in the Amazon. For example, yaje (an Indigenous name for ayahuasca) is believed to be female with the vessel it is drunk from being decorated as a female body with the depiction of a vagina symbolising the 'door' through which the drinker will enter during trance. Significantly, informants call the visions 'a return to the maternal womb' (Reichel-Dolmatoff, 1975, pp. 148 and 180). Additionally, during trance shamans visit celestial 'subterranean and underwater dimensions' and experience an interior 'illumination that... makes things hidden in nature and in men's minds visible.' Yaje is also believed to be an 'emanation' that is thought to be directly 'derived from the sun' producing a 'strong inner light rendering visible all that is in darkness, all that is hidden from ordinary knowledge and reasoning' (Reichel-Dolmatoff, 1975, pp. 77 and 85). In the iboga and ayahuasca visions, we find the motifs of regressing to earlier stages of ontogeny, feminine symbolism and the experience of illumination. As I have shown, these are also the core elements of Faust's experience of rebirth.

In this context, it is worth noting Shanon's view that ayahuasca visions frequently involve the experience of rebirth – an experience involving inner illimination and feminine imagery such as the 'Ayahuasca *mama*, the mother of ayahuasca,' the 'Queen of the Forest' and the 'Holy Virgin' (Shanon, 2002, pp. 409, 434 and 115). Significantly, Shanon argues that the progression through Hell and Purgatory to Paradise and the 'Supreme Light' of Heaven that structures Dante's narrative of rebirth in *The Divine Comedy* provides a useful template for interpreting the trajectory of ayahuasca visions (Shanon, 2002, p. 106, p. 106). It seems the same could be said of *Faust*.

Jung and Uncharted Cognitive Domains: Exploring The Antipodes of the Mind

I now want to explore the work of Jung, and how his theory of archetypes and his evolutionary explanation for their emergence, is consonant with the theories outlined in this essay. Jung argued that the more phylogenetically ancient structures of the brain represent the neurobiological basis of archetypes giving rise to their unique affective qualities and associated imagery. These putatively more ancient brain structures, what Jung referred to as the collective unconscious, are believed to be 'environmentally closed, affective, innate and universal' (Goodwyn, 2012, p. 18). From this perspective, such structures preceded the emergence of consciousness in our species evolutionary history. Following the notion of a parallel between phylogeny and ontogeny, Jung also suggests that the emergence of individual consciousness during development is superimposed on more ancient collective or inherited brain structures.

In discussing the archetype of rebirth, Jung states that rituals produce a 'regressive identification with lower and more primitive states of consciousness…accompanied by a heightened sense of life' (Jung, 2014, p. 126). Significantly, Jung argues that the transformation of Faust into a boy at the end of the play and his admittance into the choir of blessed youths represents an example of the rebirth and transformation of the individual (Jung, 2014). This rebirth he avers is a variant of the child archetype or the notion of the 'child god' (Jung, 2014, pp. 158–159) – a formulation that is also reminiscent of Goethe's conception of creativity and 'growing young' discussed earlier. It should be noted, as argued by Abrams, the literary trope of childhood does not represent a nostalgic regression from adulthood to earlier stages of development but the incorporation and freshness of childhood perception into the higher maturity of adulthood (Abrams, 1971, p. 380). This is exactly how Jung suggests the child motif appears in therapy during the process of individuation – that is it represents a 'maturation process of personality' during which 'preconscious processes, gradually pass over into the conscious mind, or become conscious as dreams' (Jung, 2014, p. 159).

Jung also associates 'The Mothers' section of *Faust* with preconscious (or what I have called primary process) aspects of the psyche. For example, he argues that 'realm of the Mothers' represents a personification of the archetype of the feminine (or the anima) in the 'collective unconscious' – a dimension of the psyche that has a 'distinct tendency to influence the conscious conduct of life and, when this is not possible, to irrupt violently into consciousness in order to confront it with strange and seemingly incomprehensible contents' (Jung, 1959, p. 94). It will be remembered that I suggested earlier that the anima may represent a 'muted' or less differentiated form of the feminine in the male unconscious (Jung & Kerényi, 2002, p. 112) and that psychedelic rituals induce a regression to earlier stages of ontogeny – a regression that is, in a manner similar to Goethe's *Faust*, associated with feminine symbolism and imagery. This suggests that the commonalities evident when comparing *Faust* and psychedelic rituals arise from the activation of the anima archetype in the collective unconscious.

Jung argued that the collective unconscious was the inherited substrate that structures the human psyche – an idea not dissimilar to Goethe's notion of the 'inborn' aspects of human psychology noted earlier. And like Hobson, Jung believed that this phylogenetically ancient brain system is superseded in both ontogeny and phylogeny by our uniquely human form of consciousness – a distinction I have described in terms primary and secondary consciousness. It should be mentioned that while Jung adopted the notion that ontogeny recapitulates phylogeny in his analysis of dream life and myth, he did not accept the simplified notion that early human psychology was merely the equivalent of a child – or that the child recapitulates in any strict sense the phylogeny of the species. For example, he writes that in 'psychology a correspondence between ontogenesis and phylogenesis' suggests 'that infantile thinking and dream thinking are simply a recapitulation of earlier evolutionary stages' – a perspective on dream life, which I have already noted, was also proposed by Panksepp and Nietzsche. However, in qualifying this notion, Jung remarks that 'myth-inhabiting man was a grown reality and not a four-year-old child. Myth is certainly not an infantile phantasm, but one of the most important requisites of primitive life' (Jung et al., 2014b, pp. 23–25).

Significantly, Jung argues that children's dreams are frequently closer to the numinous and impersonal strata of the collective unconscious – that is 'big dreams' that are of a more spiritual nature and which represent powerful and meaning-rich content that often acts independent of the intentions or aims of ego consciousness (Adams, 2003; Bulkeley, 2016, p. 206, p. 206; Jung, 2012, p. 2). It will be remembered that the Fang believe that 'the younger a child is the closer he is to the ancestors' and that childhood represents a state of 'innocence propitious to passing over to the other side' – and that iboga rituals are believed to facilitate a 'return to infancy and to birth – to the life in the womb' (Fernandez, 1982, pp. 491 and 556). This sense of propinquity with the ancestors believed to characterise early childhood and infancy, if translated into scientific language, would amount to children being closer to the impersonal imagistic and emotionally potent layers of the collective unconscious – that is primary process brain systems that are 'environmentally closed, affective, innate and universal' (Goodwyn, 2012, p. 18).

Jung also believed that cross-cultural regularities in myth and religious symbolism resulted from the inheritance of such species-specific neural architecture. As he writes, the 'brain is inherited from its ancestors; it is the deposit of the psychic functioning of the whole human race' giving rise to the 'treasure-house of mythological motifs' and the 'revelatory' nature of religious symbols, which Jung argues are the 'spontaneous products of unconscious psychic activity' (Jung et al., 2014a, pp. 402 and 529). Elsewhere, Jung elaborates on which parts of the brain give rise to mythic motifs and religious archetypes. Note his attempt to bring together the 'first-person' experiential nature of the psyche with 'third-person' analysis of neurobiological correlates – that is putative neurophysiological substrates of subjective experience. If there is 'any analogy between psychic and physiological processes' Jung writes 'the organizing system of the brain must lie subcortically on the brain stem.' He goes on to argue that subcortical brain regions give rise to archetypes that are 'predominantly affective.' Consequently, he suggests that 'such a subcortical system might somehow reflect characteristics of the archetypal form of the unconscious' (Jung et al., 1960, pp. 270–271).

Using this evolutionary model, Jung approached one of the most difficult problems in the philosophy of consciousness: if we use our consciousness as the tool with which to grasp, and analyse the human mind, then how are we to grasp the unconscious domains of the psyche given they are by definition unconscious and inaccessible to consciousness? Jung also believed this to be a problem when analysing the history of religious, mystical and esoteric traditions which deal with domains of experience that are 'either unknown or barely accessible' (Jung et al., 1980, p. 3). It will be remembered that

Goethe's intuitive grasp of 'hidden realms of the human psyche' and his exploration of dimensions of experience 'largely inaccessible to the conscious or rational part of the mind' were a major influence on modern psychology and psychoanalysis (Brown, 2014, pp. 7 and 9; Ellenberger, 1970, p. 571).

As Jung writes, elaborating on the unconscious processes that seem to be inaccessible to normal conscious awareness:

> Consciousness grasps only a fraction of its own nature, because it is the product of a preconscious psychic life which made the development of consciousness possible in the first place. Consciousness always succumbs to the delusion that it developed out of itself, but scientific knowledge is well aware that all consciousness rests on unconscious premises.
>
> (Jung et al., 1980, pp. 432–433)

Significantly, Jung realised that psychedelics facilitate access to these unconscious processes. For example, in commenting on the psychedelic research of the 1950s and 1960s, he averred that such compounds 'lay bare a level of the unconscious that is otherwise accessible only under peculiar psychic conditions' giving rise to perceptions and experiences similar to those occurring 'either in mystical states or in the analysis of unconscious phenomena' (Jung, Adler, & Jaffé, 1976, p. 382).

In his essay 'The Psychological Foundation of Belief in Spirits', Jung develops the notion that belief in spirits and ghosts is derived from visual imagery and dream life – a notion proposed originally by Tylor and supported by more recent research in cognitive science (Bulkeley, 2016; Tylor, 2010). As Jung writes when commenting on so-called primitive cultures and the appearance of the dead in dreams: 'one of the most important sources of the primitive belief in spirits is dreams. People very often appear as the actors in dreams…The dream has for him an incomparably higher value than it has for civilized man.' The value attached to dreams in Indigenous cultures is something Jung lamented to be lacking in his contemporaries; as he avers 'if a European had to go through the same exercises and ceremonies which the medicine-man [shaman] performs in order to make the spirits visible, he would have the same experiences. He would interpret them differently, of course, and devalue them' (Jung et al., 2014a, p. 393).

This idea is echoed in the aforementioned notion of Goethe's that 'moderns' find it difficult to understand the 'wondrous creatures...and oracles of the ancients' (Goethe quoted in Flaherty, 2014, p. 167–168). As already intimated, the dramatic technique employed in *Faust* sought to address this cultural blind spot by personifying unconscious content and spirit entities on the stage thereby making the 'unconscious accessible to language' through the artistic representation of 'what by definition cannot be known rationally' (Brown, 2014, pp. 7 and 9). The ethnocentric devaluation of such states of consciousness referred to by Jung – and intimated in Goethe's comments – is beginning to ebb away as science investigates the neurophenomenology of these central aspects of the human experience.

Significantly, Shanon in *The Antipodes of the Mind: Charting the Phenomenology of the Ayahuasca Experience* argues that the phenomenology of the ayahuasca state undermines some of the central premises of Western thought and current conceptions of human psychology. As he writes of what he calls this 'uncharted cognitive domain':

> The visions and other non-ordinary experiential phenomena that Ayahuasca induces present a new, uncharted natural cognitive domain. Since the number of natural domains is very small, this makes the Ayahuasca experience of paramount interest for the student of mind... I am inclined to say that in various respects Ayahuasca brings us to the boundaries not only of science but also of the entire Western world view and its philosophies.
>
> (Shanon, 2002, pp. 34–35 and 39)

Jung, and Goethe before him, were pioneer explorers of this uncharted domain, which has for centuries remained alien to mainstream Western thought and experience. This intellectual insularity is beginning to fall away – but there is a paradox here. The Enlightenment project that laid the foundations of modern science and its inordinately rationalist epistemologies – what has been termed 'cortico-centric myopia' (Parvizi, 2009) – is now paradoxically revealing the limitations of its own assumptions and conceptions of the human mind. Science is now beginning to learn – or rediscover may be the better phrase – what Indigenous cultures of the Amazon take for granted as normative aspects of consciousness. But this rediscovery is not through an abandonment of the scientific project but a deepening and extension of it into aspects of neurophenomenology previously unexplored by science – that is a naturalistic conception of psychedelic spirituality grounded in neurocognitive mechanisms (Letheby, 2017). As Michael Winkelman writes, psychedelics help expose an 'ancient visual modality' that represents an 'area of human knowledge that has remained marginalized because of its notoriously subjective qualities.' Consequently, the scientific investigation of these modalities can help us

> better understand the nature of some of the ancient symbolic and conceptual capacities of the human brain and the kind of experiences that generate the human quest for transcendent knowledge and spirituality.
>
> (Winkelman, 2017b, p. 14)

Scientists and clinicians are now in a position to explore the ancient spiritual heritage of humankind and the unconscious strata of the psyche in an empirically rigorous manner – with all of the potential for healing, both personal and collective, that such exploration now makes possible. As opposed to science turning its back on the spiritual heritage and deeper religious sensitives of humanity in an attitude of rationalistic hubris, it can now seek to understand those sensitivities, and integrate them with our modern empirical consciousness and objectivist mindset. This implies that archaic or phylogenetic dispositions can be negated, forgotten or dissociated through individual, cultural or historical processes – however this does not mean that such dispositions are irretrievably lost as the quest for understating them can lead to holistic integration (Mills, 2010). Jung frequently criticised the Enlightenment project for its overemphasis on rationality. However, he never abandoned reason or empiricism, seeking to unite and integrate our modern consciousness with the archaic ground of being, that is the collective unconscious. In this sense, individuation is not only a personal but also a cultural and historical task – one that is central to the future civilisational development of our species. And this, I suggest, is the deeper significance of being the Dionysian Primate.

Note

1   All of the passages from Goethe's dramatic works quoted in this chapter are my own translations from the original German. However, I have consulted some of the most notable English translations – for example, the Faber edition of Louis McNeice's 1951 rhymed translation, as well as the more recent 2014 Princeton University edition, translated by Stuart Atkins. For the original German, I used volumes 2 and 3 of Bernt von Heisler's 1957 edition of Goethe's Gesammelter Werke.

References

Abrams, M. H. (1971). *Natural Supernaturalism: Tradition and Revolution in Romantic Literature*. Norton.

Adams, K. (2003). Children's Dreams: An exploration of Jung's concept of big dreams. *International Journal of Children's Spirituality*, 8(2), 105–114. 10.1080/13644360304632

Bishop, P. (1995). *The Dionysian Self: C.G. Jung's Reception of Friedrich Nietzsche*. W. de Gruyter.

Bishop, P. (2007). *Analytical Psychology and German Classical Aesthetics: Goethe, Schiller, and Jung, Volume 1: The Development of the Personality*. Taylor & Francis.

Bishop, P. (2008). *Analytical Psychology and German Classical Aesthetics: Goethe, Schiller, and Jung Volume 2: The Constellation of the Self*. Taylor & Francis.

Bogin, B. (2003). The human pattern of growth and development in paleontological perspective. In A. J. Nelson, G. E. Krovitz, & J. L. Thompson (Eds.), *Patterns of Growth and Development in the Genus Homo* (pp. 15–44). Cambridge: Cambridge University Press.

Brown, J. K. (2014). *Goethe's Allegories of Identity*. University of Pennsylvania Press, Incorporated.

Bulkeley, K. (2016). *Big Dreams: The Science of Dreaming and the Origins of Religion*. Oxford University Press.

Cambray, J. (2014). Romanticism and revolution in Jung's science. *Jung and the Question of Science*. Routledge.

Carhart-Harris, R. L., & Friston, K. J. (2010). The default-mode, ego-functions and free-energy: a neurobiological account of Freudian ideas. *Brain*, 133(4), 1265–1283. 10.1093/brain/awq010

Carhart-Harris, R. L., & Friston, K. J. (2019). REBUS and the anarchic brain: Toward a unified model of the brain action of psychedelics. *Pharmacological Reviews*, 71(3), 316. 10.1124/pr.118.017160

Carhart-Harris, R. L., Leech, R., Erritzoe, D., Williams, T. M., Stone, J. M., Evans, J., ... Nutt, D. J. (2012). Functional connectivity measures after psilocybin inform a novel hypothesis of early psychosis. *Schizophrenia Bulletin, 39*(6), 1343–1351. 10.1093/schbul/sbs117

Carhart-Harris, R. L., Leech, R., Hellyer, P. J., Shanahan, M., Feilding, A., Tagliazucchi, E., ... Nutt, D. (2014). The entropic brain: A theory of conscious states informed by neuroimaging research with psychedelic drugs. *Frontiers in Human Neuroscience, 8.* 10.3389/fnhum.2014.00020

Clark, G. (2020a). Carl Jung, John Layard and Jordan Peterson. *International Journal of Jungian Studies, 12*(2), 129. 10.1163/19409060-20201001

Clark, G. (2020b). Integrating the archaic and the modern: The red book, visual cognitive modalities and the neuroscience of altered states of consciousness. In M. Stein, Arzt T. (Ed.), *Jung's Red Book for Our Time: Searching for Soul under Postmodern Conditions* (Vol. 4). Asheville, N.C. USA: Chiron Publications.

Clark, G., & Henneberg, M. (2015). The life history of *Ardipithecus ramidus*: A heterochronic model of sexual and social maturation. *Anthropological Review, 78*(2), 109–132.

Clark, G., & Henneberg, M. (2017). *Ardipithecus ramidus* and the evolution of language and singing: An early origin for hominin vocal capability. *HOMO— Journal of Comparative Human Biology.* 10.1016/j.jchb.2017.03.001

Edinger, E. F. (1990). *Goethe's Faust: Notes for a Jungian Commentary.* Inner City Books.

Ellenberger, H. F. (1970). *The Discovery of the Unconscious: The History and Evolution of Dynamic Psychiatry.* New York: Basic Books.

Fair, D. A., Cohen, A. L., Dosenbach, N. U. F., Church, J. A., Miezin, F. M., Barch, D. M., ... Schlaggar, B. L. (2008). The maturing architecture of the brain's default network. *Proceedings of the National Academy of Sciences USA, 105*(10), 4028–4032. 10.1073/pnas.0800376105

Fernandez, J. W. (1982). *Bwiti: An Ethnography of the Religious Imagination in Africa.* Princeton University Press.

Flaherty, G. (2014). *Shamanism and the Eighteenth Century.* Princeton University Press.

Fransson, P. et al. (2007). Resting-state networks in the infant brain. *Proceedings of the National Academy of Sciences, 104*(39), 15531–15536.

Goodwyn, E. D. (2012). *The Neurobiology of the Gods: How Brain Physiology Shapes the Recurrent Imagery of Myth and Dreams.* Routledge.

Gopnik, A. (2016). *The Gardener and the Carpenter: What the New Science of Child Development Tells Us About the Relationship Between Parents and Children.* Farrar, Straus and Giroux.

Gopnik, A., Griffiths, T. L., & Lucas, C. G. (2015). When younger learners can be better (or at Least More Open-Minded) than older ones. *Current Directions in Psychological Science, 24*(2), 87–92. 10.1177/096372141455 6653

Gopnik, A., O'Grady, S., Lucas, C. G., Griffiths, T. L., Wente, A., Bridgers, S., ... Dahl, R. E. (2017). Changes in cognitive flexibility and hypothesis search across human life history from childhood to adolescence to adulthood. *Proceedings of the National Academy of Sciences USA, 114*(30), 7892–7899. 10.1073/pnas.1700811114

Gould, S. J. (1977). *Ontogeny and Phylogeny*. Belknap Press of Harvard University Press.

Haeckel, E. (1887). *The History of Creation, Or, the Development of the Earth and Its Inhabitants by the Action of Natural Causes: A Popular Exposition of the Doctrine of Evolution in General, and of that of Darwin, Goethe, and Lamarck in Particular* (E. R. Lankester, Trans.). D. Appleton.

Hawkes, K., Paine, R. R., & Research, S. O. A. (2006). *The Evolution of Human Life History*. School of American Research.

Hill, S. J. (2013). *Confrontation with the Unconscious: Jungian Depth Psychology and Psychedelic Experience*. Muswell Hill Press.

Hillman, J. (1979). *Dream and the Underworld*. HarperCollins.

Hobson, A. (1999). *Dreaming as Delirium: How the Brain Goes Out of Its Mind*. MIT Press.

Hobson, A. (2002). *The Dream Drugstore: Chemically Altered States of Consciousness*. MIT Press.

Hobson, A. (2014). *Psychodynamic Neurology: Dreams, Consciousness, and Virtual Reality*. Taylor & Francis.

Hobson, A., & Voss, U. (2011). A mind to go out of: Reflections on primary and secondary consciousness. *Conscious Cogn, 20*(4), 993–997. 10.1016/j.concog.2010.09.018

Jantz, H. S. (1994). *The Mothers in Faust: The Myth of Time and Creativity*. Johns Hopkins Press.

Jones, P. B. (2013). Adult mental health disorders and their age at onset. *The British Journal of Psychiatry, 202*(s54), s5–s10. 10.1192/bjp.bp.112.119164

Jung, C. G. (1959). *Flying Saucers: A Modern Myth of Things Seen in the Skies*. Harcourt, Brace.

Jung, C. G. (2012). *Children's Dreams: Notes from the Seminar Given in 1936-1940* (E. Falzeder, Trans.). Princeton University Press.

Jung, C. G. (2014). *Collected Works of C.G. Jung, Volume 9 (Part 1): Archetypes and the Collective Unconscious* (R. F. C. Hull, Trans.). Princeton University Press.

Jung, C. G., & Adler, G. (2014). *The Development of Personality*. Taylor & Francis.

Jung, C. G., Adler, G., Fordham, M., & Read, H. (2014a). *The Structure and Dynamics of the Psyche*. Taylor & Francis.

Jung, C. G., Adler, G., Fordham, M., & Read, H. (2014b). *Symbols of Transformation*. Taylor & Francis.

Jung, C. G., Adler, G., & Hull, R. F. C. (1980). *Collected Works of C.G. Jung, Volume 12*: *Psychology and Alchemy*: Princeton University Press.

Jung, C. G., Adler, G., & Jaffé, A. (1976). *Letters*. Routledge.

Jung, C. G., & Kerényi, C. (2002). *Science of Mythology: Essays on the Myth of the Divine Child and the Mysteries of Eleusis*. Routledge.

Jung, C. G., Read, H., Adler, G., & Fordham, M. S. M. (1960). *The Collected Works of C.G. Jung: The psychogenesis of mental disease*. Routledge & Kegan Paul.

Kettner, H., Gandy, S., Haijen, E. C. H. M., & Carhart-Harris, R. L. (2019). From egoism to ecoism: Psychedelics increase nature relatedness in a state-mediated and context-dependent manner. *International Journal of Environmental Research and Public Health*, *16*(24), 5147. 10.3390/ijerph1 6245147

Khachouf, O. T., Poletti, S., & Pagnoni, G. (2013). The embodied transcendental: A Kantian perspective on neurophenomenology. *Frontiers in Human Neuroscience*, *7*, 611-611. 10.3389/fnhum.2013.00611

Letheby, C. (2017). Naturalizing psychedelic spirituality. *Zygon®*, *52*(3), 623–642. 10.1111/zygo.12353

Locke, J. L., & Bogin, B. (2006). Language and life history: A new perspective on the development and evolution of human language. *Behavioral and Brain Sciences*, *29*(03). 10.1017/s0140525x0600906x

Lovtrup, S. (1978). On von Baerian and Haeckelian Recapitulation. *Systematic Zoology*, *27*(3), 348–352. 10.2307/2412887

Mills, J. (2010). *Origins: On the Genesis of Psychic Reality*. McGill-Queen's University Press.

Minugh-Purvis, N., & McNamara, K. J. (2002). *Human Evolution Through Developmental Change*. Johns Hopkins University Press.

Muthukumaraswamy, S. D., Carhart-Harris, R. L., Moran, R. J., Brookes, M. J., Williams, T. M., Errtizoe, D.,... Nutt, D. J. (2013). Broadband cortical desynchronization underlies the human psychedelic state. *Journal of Neuroscience*, *33*(38), 15171–15183. 10.1523/jneurosci.2063-13.2013

Nietzsche, F. (1990). *Twilight of Idols and Anti-Christ* (R. J. Hollingdale, Trans.). Penguin Books Limited.

Nietzsche, F. (1993). *The Birth of Tragedy: Out of the Spirit of Music* (S. Whiteside, Trans.). Penguin Books Limited.

Nietzsche, F. (1994). *Human, All Too Human*. Penguin Books Limited.

Nour, M. M., Evans, L., & Carhart-Harris, R. L. (2017). Psychedelics, personality and political perspectives. *J Psychoactive Drugs, 49*(3), 182–191. 10.1080/02791072.2017.1312643

Nour, M. M., Evans, L., Nutt, D., & Carhart-Harris, R. L. (2016). Ego-dissolution and psychedelics: Validation of the Ego-Dissolution Inventory (EDI). *Frontiers in Human Neuroscience, 10*(269). 10.3389/fnhum.2016.00269

Panksepp, J. (2004). *Affective Neuroscience: The Foundations of Human and Animal Emotions*. Oxford University Press.

Panksepp, J., & Biven, L. (2012). *The Archaeology of Mind: Neuroevolutionary Origins of Human Emotions*. W. W. Norton.

Parker, S. T., & McKinney, M. L. (2000). *Origins of Intelligence: The Evolution of Cognitive Development in Monkeys, Apes, and Humans*. Johns Hopkins University Press.

Parvizi, J. (2009). Corticocentric myopia: Old bias in new cognitive sciences. *Trends Cogn Sci, 13*(8), 354–359. 10.1016/j.tics.2009.04.008

Purkiss, D. (2000). *Troublesome Things: A History of Fairies and Fairy Stories*. Allen Lane.

Raichle, M. E., & Snyder, A. Z. (2007). A default mode of brain function: A brief history of an evolving idea. *NeuroImage, 37*(4), 1083–1090. 10.1016/j.neuroimage.2007.02.041

Reichel-Dolmatoff, G. (1975). *The Shaman and the Jaguar: A Study of Narcotic Drugs Among the Indians of Colombia*. Temple University Press.

Rilling, J. K., Barks, S. K., Parr, L. A., Preuss, T. M., Faber, T. L., Pagnoni, G., ... Votaw, J. R. (2007). A comparison of resting-state brain activity in humans and chimpanzees. *Proceedings of the National Academy of Sciences USA, 104*(43), 17146–17151. 10.1073/pnas.0705132104

Roseman, L., Nutt, D. J., & Carhart-Harris, R. L. (2018). Quality of acute psychedelic experience predicts therapeutic efficacy of psilocybin for treatment-resistant depression. *Frontiers in Pharmacology, 8*(974). 10.3389/fphar.2017.00974

Seung, T. K. (2006). *Goethe, Nietzsche, and Wagner: Their Spinozan Epics of Love and Power*. Lexington Books.

Shanon, B. (2002). *The Antipodes of the Mind: Charting the Phenomenology of the Ayahuasca Experience*. Oxford University Press.

Shim, G. et al. (2010). Altered resting-state connectivity in subjects at ultra-high risk for psychosis: an fMRI study. *Behavioral and Brain Functions, 6*(1), 58.

Solms, M., & Turnbull, O. (2010). *Brain and the Inner World: An Introduction to the Neuroscience of Subjective Experience*. Other Press.

Spreng, R. N., & Grady, C. L. (2010). Patterns of brain activity supporting autobiographical memory, prospection, and theory of mind, and their relationship to the default mode network. *Journal of Cognitive Neuroscience, 22*(6), 1112–1123. 10.1162/jocn.2009.21282

Spreng, R. N., Mar, R. A., & Kim, A. S. N. (2008). The common neural basis of autobiographical memory, prospection, navigation, theory of mind, and the default mode: A quantitative meta-analysis. *Journal of Cognitive Neuroscience, 21*(3), 489–510. 10.1162/jocn.2008.21029

Storey, A. E., Walsh, C. J., Quinton, R. L., & Wynne-Edwards, K. E. (2000). Hormonal correlates of paternal responsiveness in new and expectant fathers. *Evolution and Human Behavior, 21*(2), 79–95.

Tagliazucchi, E., Carhart-Harris, R., Leech, R., Nutt, D., & Chialvo, D. R. (2014). Enhanced repertoire of brain dynamical states during the psychedelic experience. *Human Brain Mapping, 35*(11), 5442–5456. 10.1002/hbm.22562

Tagliazucchi, E., Roseman, L., Kaelen, M., Orban, C., Muthukumaraswamy, Suresh D., Murphy, K., … Carhart-Harris, R. (2016). Increased global functional connectivity correlates with LSD-induced ego dissolution. *Current Biology, 26*(8), 1043–1050. 10.1016/j.cub.2016.02.010

Trevathan, W., & Rosenberg, K. R. (2016). *Costly and Cute: Helpless Infants and Human Evolution*. Albuquerque, New Mexico: University of New Mexico Press.

Tylor, E. B. (2010). *Primitive Culture: Researches Into the Development of Mythology, Philosophy, Religion, Art, and Custom*. Cambridge University Press.

von Goethe, J. W. (1970). *Italian Journey, 1786-1788* (W. H. Auden & E. Mayer, Trans.): Penguin Books.

von Goethe, J. W. (2014). *Faust I & II, Volume 2: Goethe's Collected Works—Updated Edition* (S. Atkins, Trans.). Princeton University Press.

Whitfield-Gabrieli, S. & Ford, J. M. (2012). Default mode network activity and connectivity in psychopathology. *Annual Review of Clinical Psychology, 8*(1), 49–76.

Winkelman, M. (2001). Psychointegrators: Multidisciplinary perspectives on the therapeutic effects of hallucinogens. *Complementary Health Practice Review, 6*(3), 219–237. 10.1177/153321010100600304

Winkelman, M. (2010). *Shamanism: A Biopsychosocial Paradigm of Consciousness and Healing*. Praeger.

Winkelman, M. (2017a). The mechanisms of psychedelic visionary experiences: Hypotheses from evolutionary psychology. *Frontiers in Neuroscience,* *11*(539). 10.3389/fnins.2017.00539

Winkelman, M. (2017b). The mechanisms of psychedelic visionary experiences: Hypotheses from evolutionary psychology. *Frontiers in Neuroscience,* *11*, 539-539. 10.3389/fnins.2017.00539

Wynne-Edwards, K. E. (2001). Hormonal changes in mammalian fathers. *Hormones and Behavior, 40*(2), 139–145. 10.1006/hbeh.2001.1699

Wynne-Edwards, K. E., & Reburn, C. J. (2000). Behavioral endocrinology of mammalian fatherhood. *Trends in Ecology & Evolution, 15*(11), 464–468.

Zhou, H.-X., Chen, X., Shen, Y.-Q., Li, L., Chen, N.-X., Zhu, Z.-C., … Yan, C.-G. (2020). Rumination and the default mode network: Meta-analysis of brain imaging studies and implications for depression. *NeuroImage, 206*, 116287. 10.1016/j.neuroimage.2019.116287

Chapter 13

Creativity in Cyborgs: Mind, Body and Technology

Plesnner's Spatial Phenomenology as a Basis for a Jungian Metaphysics

Joeri Pacolet[1]

Is it possible for cities to have dominant colours? Could London, for example, be mostly red and golden, while pale yellow and turquoise dominate Lisbon and Madrid is characterised by amber and terracotta? These particular hues are dominant in these capitals because they correspond with certain tones. But not only locations have music in them, but a careful consideration of variations in skin tone can also yield a musical experience. And if that were not enough, museum visits will never be the same again, as paintings can be both seen and heard. Vice versa, concerts produce colourful as well as tonal experiences.

Needless to say, the unconventional manifestations set out above are not yet available to the average person, but perhaps, they will be one day if people opt to become cyborgs. In this case, the experiences are those of artist and cyborg Neil Harbisson (2012, 2013). Via a technological extension (an antenna) implanted in his skull, Harbisson has turned his human defect achromatopsia (a severe form of colour blindness, which causes him to see only shades of grey) into a new faculty. The antenna enables him to convert colour frequencies into sound waves, so he hears the colour red as a sol, for example.

In this chapter, I will be using Harbisson's case to address an underexplored question in the mind-body problem, namely the role of technology in this debate. More specifically, I will use this case as a springboard to speculate on the relationship between Jungian psychology and the mind-body split. I will also consider what new insights might come out of the creation of a stable metaphysical foundation for analytical psychology, which would then facilitate a different analysis

DOI: 10.4324/9781003090755-14

of this case. I will argue that Jungian insights are unequal to the task of analysing the interaction between mind, body and technology in Harbisson's art, and put forward the spatial phenomenology of German philosopher Helmuth Plessner as a possible alternative.

Much has been written about Jung's (putative) phenomenological aspirations (Gray, 2013; Brooke, 2015), and there has been some work on the role of technology in Jung's writing (Jones, 2019), but never from a phenomenological perspective in which technology takes centre stage. In a debate about the role of technology in analytical psychology between Slater and Saban on the forum of the International Association for Jungian Studies (IAJS) (11 May, 2014), Saban asks: 'What more do we need to dream the Jungian myth onwards?' In this chapter, I argue that the answer is the development of a solid metaphysical basis that considers the influence of technological developments on our psyche. Plessner provides such a foundation.

Harbisson's Mozart

Over a decade ago, Harbisson started a project aimed at perceiving colour in a way other than through sight. He began by having a 10-pound computer on his back, linked to a webcam and earphones, which enabled him to hear colours. Later the transformation went one step further and Harbisson became a cyborg: the computer was replaced by a chip and an antenna implanted into Harbisson's skull (Harbisson, 2013). A whole new world opened up to him, one that is inaccessible to us. He even began to dream in colour tones (Harbisson, 2012).

Harbisson's artwork *Mozart* provides an entry into his world of tonal colours. We know the work of Wolfgang Amadeus Mozart as one of the pinnacles of classical music. But no music aficionado would ever associate Mozart's musical virtuosity with an abstract artwork with vivid colour patterns, as they do in Harbisson's work. To Harbisson, these specific combinations evoke the exalted experience of listening to Mozart's music. His creative translation of colours into sounds and vice versa are not limited to Mozart: he has also translated Vivaldi's *The Four Seasons* and rendered famous speeches by Martin Luther King and Adolf Hitler in colour.

As mentioned, Harbisson's cybernetics enables him to establish associations that we, non-cyborgs, cannot make. By doing so he updates the age-old philosophical-anthropological questions: what is man, and how does man relate to technology? Ever since Descartes ushered in the age of modern western philosophy, the relationship between *res extensa* and *res cogitans* has been one of the key problems in philosophical anthropology. Descartes is frequently seen, either rightly or wrongly, as the forerunner of substance dualism.[2] In the 19th and 20th centuries, case studies such as that of Phineas Gage have problematised substance dualism[3] (Damasio, 1994). Gage's case illustrates the problem of interaction: how can Gage's personality change when mind and body are to be viewed as two autonomous substances?

In technology, Harbisson's case introduces a third important partner into this debate and raises a question similar to Gage's case: if Harbisson dreams in colour tones, then what is the relationship between mind, body and technology? With this in mind, we can take a critical look at a possible underlying metaphysics in analytical psychology and its potential for understanding the complex triangular relationship between mind, body and technology. But before I introduce technology as a possible 'partner,' I want to first look at the mind-body dichotomy in the work of Jung.

Dualism in Jung

Although Jung never explicitly situated his theories of archetypes and the individuation process in a metaphysical framework (Cambray, 2014), he is often accused of being a substance dualist. Brooke (2015), for example, posits that Jung, saddled with a Cartesian legacy, describes our lived experience as first and foremost something that happens in our mind and reduces the external world to the cold, calculable and mechanical reality of the Cartesian *res extensa*. Looking at the dualistic influences in Jung's work, Gray (2013) identifies 'the fog argument.'

The Fog Argument

In his *CW* 8, Jung writes:

> It is my mind, with its store of images, that gives the world colour and sound ... 'experience' is, in its most simple form, an exceedingly complicated structure of mental images. Thus there

is, in a certain sense, nothing that is directly experienced except the mind itself ... So thick and deceptive is this fog about us that we had to invent the exact sciences in order to catch at least a glimmer of the so-called 'real' nature of things.

(Jung, 1969, p. 623)

In this argument, Jung sketches the relationship between our lived experience and our external world. According to Gray, we cannot infer from this that Jung is a substance dualist. Although Jung certainly makes a distinction between body and mind, Gray argues that he does so not from an ontological, but from an epistemological position, in an effort to explore the possibility of knowing the external world. All we have direct access to, according to Jung, are our conscious mental states. From this, it does not necessarily follow that Jung calls into question the existence of the external world. What's more, Jung assumes that the mind and body interact via the central nervous system (Jung, 1969, pp. 606–607) and views mind and body as 'the expression of a single entity whose essential nature is not knowable either from its outward material manifestation or from inner, direct perception' (Jung, 1969, p. 619).

Jung propagates a particular form of methodological dualism in which he wonders to what extent we should distinguish between mind and body in order to explain certain of our experiences. Significantly, Jung distinguishes between the content of an experience and having those experiences. Patients who confided in Jung certain transcendent experiences of spirits or the divine were of particular interest to him because of the personal relevance of those experiences to these patients. In other words, the ontological status of the content of these experiences differs from the ontological status of having them. Jung's distinction between mind and body is then no longer an ontological distinction in the form of a substance dualism, but more of a methodological tool for speaking two 'languages' as it were that allows him to do justice to the complexity of human experience.

If the metaphysical position that best suits Jung is not substance dualism, then the question is which ontology can provide fertile ground for his core concepts. Goodwyn (2019) concludes it is a Neoplatonic version of neutral monism. In neutral monism, mind and body sprout from a more fundamental neutral substance that is not directly visible. This neutral monism offers a haven for Jung's notion of archetypes as a priori structuring principles that give rise to consciousness and qualia. What is significant here is that archetypes are no longer empirical concepts that can be studied in an experimental setting. They occupy the status of ontological concepts that must be justified, not proven, in a metaphysical analysis.

Goodwyn also rightly points out that 'metaphysical concepts aren't "proven," they are foundational givens. Such concepts are then evaluated for how much they are able to explain without contradiction or quandary' (p. 78), but it is precisely because of the explanatory scope of a metaphysical theory that I worry about the future of analytical psychology. Even if a Neoplatonic version best fits classic Jungian theory, as Goodwyn argues, we must ask whether this metaphysical system is able to explain the effect of modern technological developments, such as Harbisson's cybernetics, on our human experiences. In Raphael's *School of Athens*, the image of Plato with his finger pointing heavenwards reminds us of the philosopher's hierarchical system in which the unchanging, transcendent world of Ideas takes precedence over the immanent and highly changeable physical world. Jung may be cleared of his perceived Cartesian heritage, at least to some extent, but what does his Platonic legacy mean for an analysis of the triangular relationship in Harbisson's case?

From Duality to Trinity: Technology as Inferior Partner in the Triangular Relationship

In his book *Two Souls Alas,* Saban (2019) alerts us to a hierarchical system in Jung's psychology in which the inner world always prevails over the external world. While Jung makes the correction of one-sidedness a core principle in the individuation process, his own personality is characterised by a one-sidedness that clearly finds expression in a marked preference for introversion, interiority, aloneness and secrets in his theory. The inconsistency prompts Saban to conclude the following: 'Jung hereby ring-fences individuation in such a way that it excludes the possibility that psychological growth might occur through an encounter with the outer other, whether in the form of the outer collective or in the form of the outer person' (p. 173). This one-sidedness has repercussions not just for individuation, but also for the value assigned to technology in the mind-body problem I want to address in this chapter.

So although Jung does not fall foul of substance dualism, I would argue, following Saban's critique, that he is guilty of a form of value dualism in which technology is the inferior partner in the triangular relationship between mind, body and technology. We speak of value dualism when, in the combination of two terms, one is seen as superior to the other (Gray, 2013). In Jung's case, this leads to the equation of our inner world with the unconscious, nature and psychological growth[4] and the association of our external world with technology, alienation and stagnation.

In his *CW7* (par. 428), Jung (1972) links the rhythm of work of the farmer tilling his land to a deeper, unconscious and symbolic dimension of fertility, and contrasts it with the monotonous, deadening labour of the factory worker. Jung concludes that from this close bond with the land 'we city-dwellers, we modern machine-minders, are far removed' (par. 428).

In a letter, Jung wrote to the editorial board of the *Zurcher Student*[5] entitled 'The Effect of Technology on the Human Psyche' (Sabini, 2016), he elaborates on the aforementioned comparison, writing that 'the technologist has something of the same problem as the factory worker. Since he has to do mainly with mechanical factors, there is a danger of his other mental capacities atrophying' (p. 153). The problem here is not so much Jung's nostalgic account of an obsolete agricultural society, but the way in which he positions technology. In the same letter, Jung argues that the threats posed by new technologies say less about that technology itself, but all the more so about our inability to rein in our unconscious instincts and to prevent us from harnessing certain technologies for destructive purposes. Jung here holds an instrumental view of technology.

Instrumentalism posits that technology is merely a tool, a means to certain ends. How this instrument is used is largely determined by those who use it. From this, it follows that technology cannot be accorded an autonomous status (Verbeek, 2000). That this view does not do justice to technology is illustrated by Verbeek (2000) with the following example: in the Romanian city of Cluj, the mayor proposed to considerably shorten the handles of rakes, as the longer ones were thought to encourage idling. More than a tool for raking, the rake therefore also played an active role in the mediation between the gardeners and the public parks and gardens where they worked. Is it not true that what is said here about a tool as simple as a rake must certainly apply to the far more complex cybernetics deployed by Harbisson? Are the uses of technology fixed, or does technology to some extent have a life of its own, irrespective of our intentions? Prior to the implantation of the chip, Harbisson preferred clothing that fit well; afterwards he favoured clothes that sounded good (Harbisson, 2013). Should we not also understand Harbisson's cybernetics as a mediator between himself and his clothing?

As I said before, Harbisson's case also raises the question what such a fusion between man and machine means for the human being himself. A passage from *CW18*, par. 603, 605 affords us a glimpse of Jung's view of mankind. In it, he argues that the essence of man is his symbol-producing unconscious (Jung, 1976). Jung's 'crusade' for depth psychology can be understood as an adjustment to a one-sided tendency seen in recent decades to focus solely on quantifiable, calculable and observable effects in the external world, but he slides into an equally one-sided focus on the interior and wholly neglects the potential impact of technological developments on our inner world. So we are justified in asking what tools Jung hands us to come to grips with Harbisson's creative 'juggling' with colour. When Jungian scholars rely too heavily on Jung, they continue to fall foul of a value dualism in which technology comes off second best and they are just as far removed from a well-founded understanding of Harbisson's cybernetics as modern urbanites are from the archaic peasant in the quote earlier.

Helmuth Plessner: A Nearly Forgotten Phenomenologist

Technology not only covers evocative developments such as Harbisson's cybernetics but also things such as pots, pans, hammers and nails. The German phenomenologist Helmuth Plessner (1892–1985) condemns the lack of philosophical interest in simple tools. He argues:

> The substantive character of tools, even the simplest – ladder, hammer, knife, and so forth – is usually overlooked, along with

the fact, essential to their existence, that they are detachable from the process of their invention.

(Plessner, 2019, p. 298)

This quote was taken from the 2019 English translation of Plessner's magnum opus, *Levels of Organic Life and the Human. An Introduction to Philosophical Anthropology*,[6] which is testament to a burgeoning awareness of the work of a philosopher who is not mentioned in leading resources such as *The Routledge Encyclopedia of Philosophy*. It is only in recent decades, and in part in response to a growing interest in the philosophy of technology, that Plessner has begun to come out of the shadows of his immensely popular contemporary Martin Heidegger (De Mul, 2014a).

Unlike Heidegger's concept of *Dasein*, which is linked to time and finiteness, Plessner develops a kind of phenomenology of spatiality in which finitude is related to his core concept: the positionality of various life forms. As it assigns a central place to technology, Plessner's concept offers us the tools to understand the relationship between Harbisson's cybernetics and his physicality. My argument, however, is that Plessner is not only more relevant than Jung in understanding Harbisson's colour-sound transformations, but above all that his philosophy can be used to demonstrate that the role of technology in analytical psychology is in need of major revision. Early in the 21st century, we find ourselves in a rapidly changing technological landscape. Ihde (1990) goes as far as to describe our lives as 'technologically textured' (p. 1). To subject the aforementioned triangular relationship to a rigorous analysis, we need a 'return to the things.' Plessner makes this return possible, whereas analytical psychology does not (yet).

A possible objection here is that Jung's primary concern was not technology, but his patients' mental problems. That said, Jung did not limit himself to these psychological issues, but also put forward an image of man in which the unconscious takes precedence and technology occupies an inferior role. When viewed from such a perspective, the major role of technology in Harbisson's creative colour-and-sound transformations will remain underexposed. Although Plessner does not say anything about Jung in his main work, he does touch upon Freud and psychoanalysis, and so his critique is also relevant to the development of analytical psychology. Responding to a psychologisation of man's nature, Plessner argues that a psychological reading of humankind does not go far enough to fully understand what it means to be human.

Plessner is not unsympathetic to psychoanalysis, but criticises it for its 'philosophical misuse of psychoanalytic ideas' (Plessner, 2019, p. 295). In place of a psychological reading, Plessner posits the following: 'Culture [does not] amount to an overcompensation for inferiority complexes but points to a prepsychological, ontic necessity' (p. 295). The fact that man cannot accept the fate nature has bestowed on him can ultimately not be attributed to his urges or repression mechanisms, but to his eccentric positionality. In other words, Plessner wants to return to a metaphysical basis from which we can understand different life forms.

Do Jungians not also need such a metaphysical foundation to lend Jung's insights greater explanatory power so they too can undertake a more informed analysis of the mind-body-technology problem? In his *Two Souls Alas,* Saban (2019) points out that human relationships are all too easily reduced to archetypes in analytical psychology, just as the various women in Jung's life were relegated to anima figures populating his interior. In the debate between Slater and Saban (11 May, 2014), which I referred to in the introduction, Saban also argues that the latest technological advances offer immense potential for arriving at new insights into the unconscious. Following this, I want to argue that not only should analytical psychology be more attentive to human relationships without psychologising them, but it should also look more closely at non-human entities. In the following section, I will illustrate how Plessner's spatial phenomenology does this by placing technology back at the forefront.

Inside and Outside: Plessner's Spatial Phenomenology

Plessner was not only a philosopher, but a biologist too. His work is effectively a fusion between a philosophical biology and hermeneutic spatial phenomenology (De Mul, 2014a). As early as the opening decades of the 20th century, Plessner suggested that from a biological standpoint, it was possible to mechanically create new lifeforms and that biologists can explain *how* this life manifests itself on earth and develops. But what biologists cannot do is explain *what* life is. Herein lay the core task of philosophy, according to Plessner (De Mul, 2014b). He viewed life from a psycho-physical perspective and was firmly opposed to a strict separation of body and mind (Plessner, 2019).

A starting point for a better understanding of Plessner's spatial phenomenology is his Neo-Kantian, transcendentalist influence. Like Kant, Plessner sought an a priori basis from which to understand all life forms. Unlike Kant, however, Plessner did not start from a cognitive a priori, but from an a priori that considered the entire living organism. The categories deployed by Plessner are therefore vital categories and they consist of boundaries, positionality and double aspectivity (De Mul, 2014b).

Plessner defines the concept of boundary as the minimal condition for life and in so doing makes a distinction between living and inanimate things (Plessner, 2019). Every living being is characterised by its positionality, or by the way this being relates to its boundaries. Inanimate objects, such as rocks, do not have such a relationship. Rocks are separated from the rest of the world by what Plessner refers to as contours. Significantly, this distinction enables him to describe the difference between inside and outside without resorting to a form of substance dualism. Compared to boundaries, contours are a relatively static property typical of the lifeless entity they belong to. Their only function is to delimit this entity from the rest of the external world. The boundaries of living beings, on the other hand, are determined by their movements inwards and outwards, such as eating, singing and listening to music, and are therefore much more dynamic; 'living bodies differ from nonliving bodies in that the former claim space while the latter merely occupy it' (Plessner, 2019, p. 123). A living body only has a boundary in the external sense of the word in that it ends at some point; a boundary is therefore an intersection of movements crossing in and out. On the one hand, boundaries offer the possibility of delimiting a body from the rest of the external world, while on the other hand, they also enable that body to open up to the world.

So there is no strict separation between inside and outside here. This same fluidity comes increasingly to the fore in cyborgs like Harbisson. In short, the new era, which Harbisson (2013) labels the era of cyborgism, has no room for substance dualism, because this approach offers no space for understanding how, in Harbisson's case, inside and outside and subject and object continuously constitute and blend into each other. For Harbisson, boundaries have clearly moved beyond his skin; his cybernetics are no longer merely an extension, but a crucial part of his body. Harbisson no longer has technology; he is technology.

At this point, we might ask how big the difference between Harbisson and non-cyborgs is. Surely technology plays a less constituent role in people without cybernetic implants than it does in Harbisson? Plessner's spatial phenomenology offers us a theory in which technology is understood as a critical component of our humanity. In order to understand the difference between Harbisson and non-cyborgs as a gradual one, we can draw on Plessner's three forms of positionality, the last of which forms the basis for his third vital category of double aspectivity.

Three Forms of Positionality

According to Plessner, the differences between a plant, animal and human being can be explained with reference to their various forms of positionality. A plant possesses an open positionality. An open positionality is characterised by the absence of a centre; in other words, there is a 'boundary which has no one or nothing on either side, neither subject nor object' (De Mul, 2010, p. 226). Unlike a plant, an animal has a closed, or centric positionality. Animals, therefore, do have a centre, namely a nervous system. This centre enables an animal to not only be its body but also be in its body. A human being, finally, differs from other life forms by not only having a centre but also an awareness of it and the ability to reflect on and about this centre. Plessner describes man as eccentric because what we see at work here is a second mediation; 'he not only lives and experiences his life, but he also experiences his experience... we are not where we think, and we do not think where we are' (De Mul, 2010, p. 226).[7] With respect to human physicality, we can conclude: 'Man is a body, in his body (as inner experience) and outside of his body, as the perspective from which he is both' (De Mul, 2010, p. 226).

Human beings therefore live in three worlds: an external world ('Aussenwelt'), an inner world ('Innenwelt') and the shared world of culture ('Mitwelt'). The final vital category Plessner introduces here is 'double aspectivity.' Double aspectivity refers to the fact that humans have relationships 'with both sides of their constitutive boundary, the interior and the exterior' (De Mul, 2010, p. 225). A body is at once a thing among things, a *res extensa* taking up space, as well as a living body that functions as the centre of our perception and actions. On the one hand, our inner world is the 'source of our psychic life' and, on the other, 'the plaything of the psychic processes' (De Mul, 2010, p. 226). Finally, with respect to our culture, we are both 'an I (*Ich*) that helps create this world, and a We (*Wir*) insofar as we are supported and formed by this world' (De Mul, 2010, p. 226). In other words, with his concept of double aspectivity, Plessner still does justice to people's everyday experience which boasts a distinction between someone who has an experience and something that is experienced. As Verbeek (2000) rightly suggests, 'A philosophy that seeks to understand the everyday reality of people...will have to start from this distinction, and ultimately show that this reality is not underpinned by an actual distinction' (p. 186). That this distinction does not occur at the ontological level finds unambiguous expression in Plessner's anthropological laws.

Plessner's Law of Natural Artificiality

That the distinction between *techne* (technique, craftsmanship) and *fysis* (nature) requires some nuance and that man is by nature a defective being (*Mängelwesen*) who interferes in his surroundings with the help of technology is pointed up in Stiegler's concept of 'originary technicity' (Stiegler, 1998) and in Haraway's phrase 'the cyborg is our ontology' (Haraway, 1991). These concepts suggest there has never been a clear divide between man and technology and what makes us human is precisely the fact that we are constantly bettering ourselves.

These insights originate in Plessner's law of natural artificiality[8] which posits that thanks to his eccentric positionality man is characterised by his 'constitutive homelessness' (Plessner, 2019, p. 288); he is always on his way home to himself and can, unlike an animal, never be one with his centre. For that reason, Verbeek (2014) describes eccentricity as 'the experience of a permanent imperfection' (p. 449). We do not simply exist, but our existence also involves a task. We are constantly seeking to compensate for the deficiency within ourselves with technology and culture. Looking at it through the prism of Plessner's law, technology should be understood not primarily as an instrument of survival, but as an 'ontic necessity.' According to De Mul (2016), this means that human beings 'have always been cyborgs, that is: hybrid beings composed of organic, technological and cultural components' (p. 74). If true, does that mean we can no longer differentiate between biological humans and cyborgs? Spreen (2014) reads this less literally and argues that we are not so much naturally cyborgs, but that Plessner certainly makes clear that concepts such as 'physicality, self-constitution and society cannot be imagined without conceptually taking technology into consideration' (p. 429). However, we understand this thesis of cyborgism, Plessner's theory enables us to argue that technology must always play a role in the mind-body problem, whether we have had cybernetics implanted in us or not.

Conclusion

In the introduction, I mentioned that Harbisson's cybernetic colour art has been used both to highlight the importance of technology to the mind-body problem and to address value dualism in analytical psychology, in which compared to nature technology always represents the dark side. I argued that Jung may be cleared of a Cartesian legacy, but if Jungian psychology deploys Neoplatonic metaphysics, it does not have the scope to analyse contemporary technological constructs, such as Harbisson's cybernetics. What do we need to dream the Jungian myth onwards?

In the second part of the chapter, I outlined Plessner's spatial phenomenology as a potential alternative with which to critique Jung's misplaced opposition between nature and technology; a critical analysis that does justice to the complex relationship between inner and outer world without lapsing into substance dualism. Elaborating Saban's argument, I demonstrated that both human and non-human relationships matter, and by doing so heeded the call to 'return to the things' from the philosophy of technology. There are various other reasons why Plessner's philosophy offers fertile ground for analytical psychology, the main ones being: Jungians may take inspiration from Plessner's philosophy because his concept of positionality underscores the fluidity of the boundaries between our inner and external worlds. If, following Plessner, we assume that human beings are characterised by their relationship to their boundaries then technology plays an important role in stretching those boundaries. Jung's view of man is that of the creative being and it is up to (post-) Jungians to research its compatibility with Plessner's first law of natural artificiality. Constant changes in a thoroughly technology external world are coupled with constant changes in our psychological inner world. On that basis, we can conclude that any form of archetypal reduction and essentialism fails to do justice to the complexity of the Plessnerian eccentrically positioned man who constantly reinvents himself.

Conversely, a conspicuous (and perhaps deliberate) absence from Plessner's key work is the concept of the unconscious. Would a case such as Harbisson's not benefit from the idea of a technological unconscious to explain, for example, the relationship between man and cybernetics? If there are any scholars who, inspired by Jung, want to take this on board, it is up to them to draw on the concept of the unconscious and engineer a return to the things without losing sight of the rich complexity of our creative, symbolic expressions.

Notes

1 Translated by Laura Vroomen.
2 Gray (2013) argues that Descartes' position was more nuanced than many of his critics initially surmised. She posits that 'Descartes' affirmation of the union of mind and body in *Meditation VI* ... is often overlooked by those anxious to point the finger at his unredeemable dualism.' (p. 24–25).
3 Phineas Gage underwent a radical change in personality after sustaining a serious brain injury (Damasio, 1994).
4 In the preface to her collection *C. G. Jung on Nature. Technology & Modern Life*, Sabini (2016) argues that one of the recurring motifs in Jung's oeuvre is the exploration of 'the loss of connection with nature' (p. xi). She also alerts us to the fact that Jung broadens his definition of the natural and does not limit it to the visual, physical domain. In other words, he also links the unconscious to the natural.
5 A newspaper published by the Federal Polytechnic Institute in Zurich.
6 Plessner's magnum opus was originally published in Germany in 1928 as *Die Stufen des Organischen und der Mensch: Einleitung in die Philosophische Anthropologie.*

7 Eccentric here refers to the ability to occupy a position outside the centre and must not be confused with an eccentric personality. According to Plessner, this positionality was the final stage in the development of man. De Mul (2014) and Verbeek (2014) have exposed the naivety of this standpoint by pointing to new forms of positionality: poly-eccentric and meta-eccentric.

8 Plessner describes two further laws: the second is the law of mediated immediacy and the third the law of utopian position. In summary, Plessner's second law refers to the various potential side effects of technology. As technology is partially beyond the human sphere of influence we can never have complete control over it. In his third law, Plessner stresses that we can never be one with our centre (not even with the help of technology). It draws on the literal meaning of utopian as signifying without a foundation. You are literally standing nowhere. This law precludes an overly optimistic view of cyborgs.

References

Brooke, R. (2015 [1991]). *Jung and Phenomenology*. London: Routledge.

Cambray, J. (2014). 'German Romantic Influences on Jung and Pauli.' In H. Atmanspacher & C. A. Fuchs (Eds.), *The Pauli-Jung Conjecture and its Impact Today*. (pp. 37–57). La Vergne: Ingram Books.

Damasio, A. R. (1994). *Descartes' Error – Emotion, Reason and the Human Brain*. New York: G. P. Putnam's Sons.

Goodwyn, E. (2019). 'Jung and the Mind-Body Problem.' In J. Mills (Ed.), *Jung and Philosophy*. (pp. 67–86). London: Routledge.

Gray, F. (2013). *Cartesian Philosophy and the Flesh. Reflections on Incarnation in Analytical Psychology*. London: Routledge.

Haraway, D. (1991). 'A Cyborg Manifesto: Science, Technology, and Socialist-Feminism in the Late Twentieth Century.' In D. Haraway (Ed.), *Simians, Cyborgs and Women: The Reinvention of Nature*. (pp. 149–181). London: Routledge.

Harbisson, N. (2012, July). *I Listen to Color* [Videofyle]. Retrieved from https://www.youtube.com/watch?v=ygRNoieAnzI

Harbisson, N. (2013, February). *The Human Eyeborg* [Videofyle]. Retrieved from https://www.youtube.com/watch?v=d_mmwrbDGac

Ihde, D. (1990). *Technology and the Lifeworld. From Garden to Earth*. Indianapolis, IN: Indiana University Press.

Jones, R. (2019). 'Jung, Science and Technology.' In J. Mills (Ed.), *Jung and Philosophy*. (pp. 289–304). London: Routledge.

Jung, C. G. (1969 [1947]). *The Structure and Dynamics of the Psyche*. In H. Read, et al. (Eds.), *The Collected Works of C. G. Jung*. (second edition). (vol. 8). New York: Princeton University press.

Jung, C. G. (1972 [1953]). Two Essays in Analytical Psychology. In H. Read, et al. (Eds.), *The Collected Works of C. G. Jung*. (vol. 7). New York: Princeton University press.

Jung, C. G. (1976 [1950]). The Symbolic Life. Miscellaneous Writings. In H. Read, et al. (Eds.), *The Collected Works of C. G. Jung*. (vol. 18). New York: Princeton University press.

Jung, C. G. (2016 [1949]). 'The Effect of Technology on the Human Psyche.' In M. Sabini (Ed.), *C. G. Jung on Nature, Technology & Modern Life*. (pp. 152–153). Berkeley, CA: North Atlantic Books.

de Mul, J. (2010 [2002]). *Cyberspace Odyssee*, Klement: Utrecht.

de Mul, J. (2014a). 'Artificial by Nature. An Introduction to Plessner's Philosophical Anthropology.' In J. de Mul (Ed.), *Plessner's Philosophical Anthropology. Perspectives and Prospects*. (pp. 11–37). Amsterdam: Amsterdam University Press.

de Mul, J. (2014b). 'Philosophical Anthropology 2.0. Reading Plessner in the Age of Converging Technologies.' In J. de Mul (Ed.), *Plessner's Philosophical Anthropology. Perspectives and Prospects*. (pp. 457–474). Amsterdam: Amsterdam University Press.

de Mul, J. (2016). *Kunstmatig van Nature. Onderweg naar Homo Sapiens 3.0*. Rotterdam: Lemniscaat.

Plessner, H. (2019 [1928]). *Levels of Organic Life and the Human. An Introduction to Philosophical Anthropology*. (M. Hyatt, Trans.). New York: Fordham University Press.

Saban, M. & Slater, G. (2014, 11 May). 'Debate about The Cyborg Psyche.' Proceedings at International Association for Jungian Studies (IAJS).

Sabini, M. (2016 [2002]). Foreword. In M. Sabini (Ed.), *C. G. Jung on Nature, Technology & Modern Life*. (pp. xi–xiii). Berkeley, CA: North Atlantic Books.

Spreen, D. (2014). 'Not Terminated. Cyborgized Men Still Remain Human Beings.' In J. de Mul (Ed.), *Plessner's Philosophical Anthropology. Perspectives and Prospects*. (pp. 425–442). Amsterdam: Amsterdam University Press.

Stiegler, B. (1998). *Technics and Time*, Volume 1: *The Fault of Epimetheus*. (R. Beardsworth & G. Collins, Trans.). Stanford, CA: Stanford University Press.

Verbeek, P. P. (2000). *De Daadkracht der Dingen*. Amsterdam: Boom.

Verbeek, P. P. (2014). 'Plessner and Technology. Philosophical Anthropology Meets the Posthuman.' In J. de Mul (Ed.), *Plessner's Philosophical Anthropology. Perspectives and Prospects*. (pp. 443–456). Amsterdam: Amsterdam University Press.

Chapter 14

The Embodied Analyst: The Mind-Body Impact of Sustained Clinical Practice

Alan Michael Karbelnig

The unusual, arguably absurd work of psychoanalysts offers scholars of the mind-body problem a unique example, a specimen, a sample for evaluation. It might serve, for them, the equivalent of a newly discovered bacteria for microbiologists. And, certainly, the mind of the practicing psychoanalyst is easier to understand than that of a bat (Nagel, 1974). Haunting philosophy since the dawn of civilization, the dualism inherent in the name of the problem itself, "mind-body," remains unsolved. Perhaps, as McGinn (1989) believes, it is unsolvable. Chalmers (2002) summarizes the divergent theories of understanding the mind-body problem, ranging from behaviorism to identity theory, from functionalism to mechanism, and from supervenience to epiphenomena. These offer intriguing, yet hardly complete, answers to the dualism conundrum.

Rather than introduce another model, or expand upon one, I explore the intricacies of practicing psychoanalysis, specifically its psychophysiological effects. The year 2019 marked my 40th year of clinical practice. My long-standing curiosity about the personal impact of such work, fueled by my personal experience with three significant medical crises in the past decade, motivated the investigation. I fear readers may view the ensuing discussion as the rant of a burned-out practitioner. However, my life's work has been, and continues to be, nothing less than thrilling. I feel honored at having walked alongside many patients navigating their way through life. Ideally, psychoanalysts facilitate natural transformational processes in patients. Burn out, exhaustion, or depletion most commonly occurs in psychoanalysts who impose an agenda on patients, or who,

DOI: 10.4324/9781003090755-15

like physicians, strive to return patients to an assumed "normal" state of mental functioning. Novelist Henry Miller (1941) describes how psychoanalysts who seek to cure, rather than cooperatively facilitating transformations, harm patients:

> Instead of exposing the secret of health and balance by example, they [psychoanalysts] elect to adopt the lazier course, usually a disastrous one, of transmitting the secret to their patients. Instead of remaining human, they seek to cure and convert, to become life-giving saviors, only to find in the end that they have crucified themselves. (p. 32)

I avoided crucifying myself by not imposing socially acceptable cures. However—and crucify is too dramatic a term—my deeply engaging in intimate if asymmetrical relationships with hundreds of patients over 40 years has taken a toll on me. I have worked with patients who find feces sexually stimulating, who became bored performing intricate surgeries, who lost their "only true love," and who repeatedly participated in ultra-marathons. Before describing the work in gritty detail, a few background assumptions require attention.

Foundational Assumptions

The primary assumption is non-dualism—a foundation which, ironically, proves impossible to explain using language. Describing non-dualism necessarily requires dualism, a subject and object, a reader and writer. Loy (1988), who explores non-dualistic philosophies, writes, "the problem with philosophy is that its attempt to grasp non-duality conceptually is inherently dualistic and thus self-defeating," adding that "philosophy originated in the need of the alienated subject to understand itself and its relation to the objective world it finds itself in" (p. 5). One of the words sprinkled throughout this discussion—psychophysiology—itself splits the mind from the body.

I render the impossible possible by utilizing perspectives or viewpoints. In regard to the mind-body split, for example, and writing two centuries ago, Spinoza (1677/2007) proposed aspect versus substance dualism. He considered human subjectivity but one viewpoint of psycho-biology, which, in turn, exists nested in geographical, historical, social, cultural, and other dynamically interacting stances. Nietzsche (1878/2002) similarly used the term perspectivism, a concept traceable to the ancient Greeks. I must, of necessity, present the experience of the practicing psychoanalyst in a dualistic manner; the primary assumption remains, nonetheless, that phenomena are non-dualistic. I "too" utilize perspectives, ranging from words like psychophysiology to psychoanalytic concepts like the unconscious, to describe phenomena.

One might analogize our world, especially given the epistemological limitations identified by Kant (1788/2018), to a ball of cotton. It can only be studied from various angles. Dissection opens up various viewpoints—the fiber, the seeds, and the underlying molecular structures. But cotton cannot be completely understood unless fully integrating the effects of water, sunlight, minerals in the soil, atmospheric gases, and endless other causal factors. Godel's incompleteness theorem (Nagel & Newman, 2001) demonstrated the impossibility of even creating a comprehensive mathematical model. Any such representation must encompass the act of the model-maker making the model, an infinite regress. Essentially, then, all models, systems, or theories, are necessarily incomplete. Maps always stray from terrains, and in my view the terrain is non-dual.

In investigating psychophysiology, I rely upon two perspectives— one from psychoanalysis and another from eastern philosophy. From psychoanalysis, Winnicott (1949/1975) coined the term, "psyche-soma" (p. 244), to describe the mind-body. He writes:

> The mind does not exist as an entity in the individual's scheme of things provided the individual psyche-soma or body scheme has come satisfactorily through the very early developmental stages; mind is then no more than a special case of the functioning of the psyche-soma.
>
> (Winnicott, 1949/1975, p. 244)

From Eastern philosophy, the term, *xin,* commonly translated from Chinese as "heart-mind," similarly reflects a blending of the mental and the physical. Thich Nhat Hanh's (2017) translation of the heart-mind sutra, part of Buddhist-Mahayana literature, reads in part:

all phenomena bear the mark of emptiness [...];

That is why in emptiness, body, feelings, perceptions, mental formations and consciousness are not separate self-entities.

(pp. 25–6)

Not separate self-entities, indeed, and thus non-dualism.

Psychoanalysis obviously rests on a number of assumptions. Psychoanalysts choose various perspectives, a psychoanalytic model of mind, for example, or an intervention, in working with their patients' subjectivities. These subjectivities—which emerge from a dizzying array of DNA, culture, socioeconomic forces, historicity, early social learning and more—exist in dynamic interaction with one another. They unfold over time. Their dynamism and temporality render them unimaginably complex (Karbelnig, 2014, 2018).

However, and regardless of theoretical model, clinical psychoanalysts concern themselves with four basic phenomena: the unconscious, and its manifestation in the repetition compulsion, transference, and dreams (or other signifiers of the unconscious). These trends are precisely that—*phenomena*. They exist regardless of how psychoanalytic scholars name, categorize, or signify them. The existence of the unconscious has been firmly established within and without psychoanalysis, including by contemporary cognitive scientists (Lakoff & Johnson, 1999). Psychoanalysts argue over how much drive, internal object relations, or early attachment relationships create the unconscious. But they agree on its existence. And they share a deep and abiding interest in it. It resides at the far side of a spectrum of subjectivity, which present most obviously as conscious states. For example, many patients harbor secrets they are barely able to tell themselves, let alone another person. Some disavow conscious phenomena, emotions like envy, for example, or habits like drinking too much. Moving along the continuum towards the dynamic unconscious, psychoanalysts use terms like dissociated or repressed states. To describe still deeper unconscious phenomena, terms like unconscious phantasy, dynamic structures, ego, id, and superego, or recurrent intersubjective transactions provide the nomenclature. The final assumption, then, concerns psychoanalysts' use of varied perspectives, particularly signifiers of the unconscious, the repetition compulsion, transference, and dreams (or other indicators of the unconscious mind).

The Nature of Practicing Psychoanalysis

In brief, it is the intensely personal nature of psychoanalysts' professional relationships that makes the work difficult. When psychoanalysts prepare to encounter their patients, they ready themselves for a type of theatrical performance. Patients enact their unconscious internal dramas within their psychoanalytic relationships (Karbelnig, 2016, 2018). Psychoanalysts typically experience a form of performance anxiety. From the moment they greet patients in the waiting room until they terminate their sessions, psychoanalysts are engaged in deeply intimate, if asymmetrical, relationships (Aron, 1996). Further, they use their bodies as instruments. Like actors, they use themselves, their *beings*. Paralleling Huston's (1993) description of actors' processes, psychoanalysts also play roles. They facilitate transformational processes—a dialectical process of ritual (facilitating the psychoanalytic process) and spontaneity (riding the unexpected twisting and turning waves of each psychoanalytic journey) (Hoffman, 1998). Psychoanalysts process projections ranging from fantastic idealizations to horrific devaluations; they absorb emotions ranging from the euphoric to the tragic, and they ingest, participate in, and engage with their patients' thoughts, attitudes, and feelings. Involvement in these always-intense transformational relationships affects psychoanalysts' psyche-somas and heart-minds.

Analogies to the social roles of lover, exorcist, and critic offer useful means of understanding psychoanalytic work. The first one, the lover, provokes intense controversy. Not to be taken literally, obviously, but psychoanalysts listen, respect, attend to, and otherwise receive what patients tell them—without judgment—much like lovers do. Their basic attunement to their patients—and even their actual care and love—form the absolute foundation for their transformative work. Conservative depth psychotherapists tend to relate to their patients in a formal fashion. They rely on abstinence (avoiding gratifying patients' needs in the process) and neutrality (striving to react evenly to what patients report, whether a hostile thought or a painful memory). They believe in *understanding* rather than *caring* for their patients.

Nonetheless, and despite allegedly withholding affection for patients, these conservative psychoanalysts still listen intensely to them—an attentiveness often perceived by patients as love or care. Liberal depth psychotherapists use less abstinence or neutrality, may self-disclose, and privilege the interpersonal relationship as a transformative tool.

How might psychoanalysts behave as exorcists? An interpreter of Freudian psychoanalysis, Jacques Lacan (2002) writes that psychoanalysts give their patients language, desire, and being. The part language plays is self-evident. It takes the form of the typical verbal interventions ranging from communicating empathy to interpreting unconscious themes. Lacan (2002) believed psychoanalysts lend their *own* desire to understand the unconscious mind to their patients. His final category, namely that psychoanalysts give with their *beings,* explains the analogy to exorcists. Psychoanalysts take in, and contain—literally psycho-physiologically—their patients' projections. They identify with these projected emotions, cognitions, and scripts; they introject them, meaning just that: they receive, and are moved by, these experiences. The logic is simple. Humans want to rid themselves of pain, and the interpersonal world provides a ready crucible. For example, people haunted by excessive self-criticism tend to perceive others as critical of them. By unconsciously projecting their internal critic into another person, they lessen their own internal conflict. Although they may wither at others' critiques, or become angry at them, they experience less *internal* discomfort through externalization. Psychoanalysts often have the visceral experience of *being* the rejecting father, the abandoning mother, or the unappreciative child. Consequently, they often feel a range of disturbing emotions from panic to angst, from sadness to unbounded despair, from mourning to melancholia. They require a high tolerance for pain. Gabbard (2016) reduces psychoanalytic interventions to *responding* rather than *reacting* to these introjects.

Fairbairn (1952) believes patients cling to what is, for them, the only family they have—their internal one. They often experience any change to the elements of the internal family, even toning down the voice of harsh internal critics, as deeply rejecting, disorienting. Poetically describing psychoanalysts' introjection of projections, Fairbairn (1941) identifies them as "the true successor to the exorcist [... because he or she ...] is concerned, not only with the 'forgiveness of sins,' but also with 'the casting out of devils'" (p. 250). Here, Fairbairn, like Lacan (2002), identifies psychoanalysts as using their *beings* in their work. Patients project parts of their mind into their psychoanalysts. The clinicians, in turn, identify them and return them, in a metabolized fashion, back to patients. Another key Fairbairn (1941, 1952) idea: psychoanalysts compete with their patients' devotion to their internal dramas. Relationships between psychoanalysts and their patients must be intense enough to dislodge patients' deeply grooved, unconsciously preferred, internal relationships.

Finally, psychoanalysts mimic the process literary critics use in analyzing texts. They facilitate hermeneutical discussions with their patients—analyzing myriad themes and meanings. They critically explore manifestations of the unconscious as evident in verbal material, dreams, slips of the tongue, transference, and elsewhere. Other aspects of the patients lives, such as patterns of relationships, of mood, of interest, of occupational and recreational endeavors, also become subject to critical analysis. In partnership with their patients, psychoanalysts uncover and evaluate a variety of narrative themes guiding persons' images of themselves, others, and their life situations.

Other Ways Psychoanalysts' Psychophysiologies Are Affected by Their Work

As implied earlier, analysis of the transference is arguably the *sine qua non* psychoanalytic intervention. It allows for a real-time exploration of projections. Some patients project a deeply loving, caring figure onto the analyst; others a persecutory, critical one. Countertransference refers, roughly, to feelings psychoanalysts develop for their patients. These usually parallel transferences. These interpersonal phenomena *enter* the psyche-somas and heart-minds of psychoanalysts. They are usually intensely emotional experiences. Several other phenomena, comprising an always-incomplete list, uniquely stimulate psychophysiological reactions in both parties to the psychoanalytic enterprise. For example, and surprising for non-practitioners, psychoanalytic work is lonely. Because psychoanalysts focus on their *patients'* rather than their own experiences, their needs go unmet day-in and day-out. Their facilitation of structured, asymmetrical but intimate relationships deprive practitioners of the normal type of interpersonal reciprocity.

Additionally, psychoanalysts regularly reject patients who are often deeply attached to them. Such well-worn phrases, as "that's our time for today" or "we're at the end of our meeting," are uttered hourly by psychoanalysts. For patients who are in acute emotional distress, feel vulnerable, or perhaps have developed a dependency on their clinicians, these session endings may be particularly painful. Finally, clinicians often encounter severely distressed patients, sometimes *in extremis,* that is, in acutely suicidal states. Despite whatever training they might have had dealing with such patient crises, the psychophysiological impacts on them are profound. When psychoanalytic relationships reach their endpoint, whether fruitfully or haphazardly, a loss is felt. Even difficult patients, who perhaps have hated their clinicians for periods of time, often elicit pain upon departure. Psychoanalysts cannot help but wonder what will become of them. Will they find the meaningful path they lack, the love they seek, the joy always eluding them? These questions usually go un-answered. Offering these descriptions of typical ways psychoanalysts react cognitively, emotionally, and physically to their work, I turn now to presenting a fictionalized set of patient encounters.

A Morning of Clinical Sessions

The following sets of meetings—unusually difficult ones—do some-times occur in quick succession. Psychoanalysts typically provide three-to-five consecutive clinical hours, lasting 45 minutes each. They usually take a 15-minute break after each patient. The following description—an amalgamation of patients from actual practice with identifying information altered to maintain confidentiality—demonstrates how psychoanalytic work affects clinicians' heart-minds or psyche-somas. They include samples of the clinical phenomena described earlier. On this hypothetical day, I arrived at my office at 7:30 am, allowing enough time to unlock the office, turn on the lights, fluff up the couch, and otherwise prepare for greeting my first patient.

Mr. A—The Shock of an Abrupt Marital Split

The first patient, Mr. A of age 72, was consulting a psychoanalyst for the first time. He called me the prior week, telling me he wanted help to deal with a sudden, unexpected marital separation. To model a holding environment (Winnicott, 1949/1975), and avoid any sense of rejection, I opened the waiting room door at exactly his appointment time of 8 am. My introduction to new patients follows a standard routine. I introduce myself with, "Hello, Mr. A. I'm Alan Karbelnig." Purposefully eschewing formality, I observe whether they call me by my first name or if, alternatively, they select Dr. Karbelnig. Next, I lead them down a hallway toward my consulting room. As I gesture them into the room itself, I often joke about the presence of the couch ("of course"). I invite them to sit where they please, and observe where they locate themselves. I begin the meeting by saying something like, "Please tell me a bit about what brings you, and then I will tell you about me and how I work."

Mr. A sat forward apprehensively. He appeared tremulous. Tearing up, he told me how his wife of 35 years had abruptly ended their marriage one month previous. Two months before that, the couple had enjoyed their customary annual anniversary celebration at a mountain cabin. When she subsequently and abruptly announced the marriage as over, Mr. A's wife refused to discuss the situation. She declined marital counseling. She proclaimed, "Our marriage was over many years ago." Mr. A reacted with "absolute devastation." He pled with her to discuss her feelings, to listen to her accusations, or to consult a marriage therapist. She steadfastly refused. She moved out of the home, leaving Mr. A to care for their one child, a 19-year-old, autistic son, alone. Because it was an initial session, Mr. A did most of the talking. Within a few minutes of sharing the tale, Mr. A began weeping uncontrollably. Mostly, I sat with him in silence. On occasion, I offered empathy for his situation and curiosity about it, particularly why he considered his future with his wife hopeless.

The most striking feature of that particular meeting, in terms of the psyche-soma or heart-mind, is the intense personal pain I absorbed listening to Mr. A. Not only was he facing the typical loss of individuals freshly separated from spouses, he was, quite literally, in shock. He was having obsessive ruminations, intrusive recollections of his wife's abrupt departure, generalized anxiety, hopelessness, insomnia, and fatigue—all symptoms of post-traumatic stress disorder (PTSD). I felt immense care and compassion for him. I also identified with him, imagining what it might feel like to have my own wife of nearly 40 years suddenly leave. Of course, my own reactions were but a tiny fraction of his. I explained the unusual nature of his experiencing PTSD in addition to the more typical feelings of loss and grief. He worried about the future of his son. His identification with the abandonment felt by his son compounded his own. Towards the end of the session, I made some inquiries regarding his other relationships. His friends had rallied around him, and he was not feeling despair that included suicidal thoughts.

In a more typical initial session, I would have closed with explaining the nature of depth psychotherapy, obtaining Mr. A's verbal and written informed consent. But his level of distress precluded my reviewing the consent forms with him. I told him we would "deal with the paperwork" at our next meeting, which we then scheduled, together, for later that same week. He left the office, his collar wet with tears. I felt a great need for the ensuing 15-minute break. I returned several e-mails and checked my voicemail to distract myself from the pain. I made myself a cup of tea, almost feeling the projections of his intense pain gradually slough off. I readied myself for my second patient, a physician who had been meeting with me twice-weekly for around two years.

Dr. B—An Encounter with Primitive Psychopathology

I typically greet Dr. B with some degree of trepidation. His long-term behavior meets the criteria for narcissistic personality disorder (NPD), a disturbance characterized by a fragile, yet grandiose, self-image, which compensates, albeit barely, for profound fears of abandonment, mental instability, and proneness to fragmentation. Dr. B felt "constantly driven" throughout his life, motivating him through two difficult, Ivy League degrees—the first an undergraduate major in zoology, and the second a graduate degree in medicine. Ultimately specializing in nephrology, Dr. B found comfort in the primary focus on one organ. He had an almost-algorithmic way of assessing and treating patients. Because they tended to be severely ill, Dr. B took refuge in his white-coated invulnerability. Quite the opposite of Mr. A, whose desperation led him to seek psychotherapy, Dr. B also had his first experience in psychoanalysis with me—but only because the medical board ordered him to do so. Dr. B had physically threatened an office manager he believed stole from him. The employee filed criminal charges of assault; she also retained an attorney to pursue litigation alleging personal injury.

Patients with personality disorders tend to vacillate between idealizing and devaluing their psychoanalysts. However, and particularly because Dr. B had been remanded to treatment, devaluation dominated. I endured weeks of Dr. B telling me "talk therapy is worthless," "we are wasting our time," and the like. Gradually, I invited him into having some curiosity about his life. Why had he assaulted the employee, we wondered together? What was causing the remarkable instability in his personal relationships and the chronic, deep feelings of loneliness and longing? As we surveyed these topics, Dr. B's hostility lessened. He would, at times, transition into a more idealized view of me. For example, on occasion, he seemed genuinely touched that I tried to understand him, had identified problematic areas, and was eager to explore them with him. Nonetheless, Dr. B had a quick temper. Even slight disappointment triggered irritability, even overt anger.

Shortly after the session began, Dr. B asked me if I would be willing to make an appearance, that same night, at a meeting before the local hospital's credentialing board. His legal situation had also imperiled his hospital privileges. I had written several letters for Dr. B, mostly acknowledging that he was attending sessions regularly and punctually. Once before, he had requested my presence at a legal hearing. I was unwilling to attend, advising him my personal involvement was counter-therapeutic. Dr. B seemed to understand. His attorneys discouraged my presence. I reminded Dr. B of these prior discussions. I also pointed out to him how his request showed little understanding of my personal needs. Even if I were to meet with the hospital committee, why would he expect me to be able to do so with only a few hours notice?

Nonetheless, and despite the greater evenness in our relationship evident during the prior year, Dr. B abruptly became enraged. He accused me of adhering to my personal boundaries too closely. "I respond to my patients in emergencies," he told me, adding, "Why can't you?" In terms of the unfolding psychodynamics, Dr. B manifested metaphorical demonic possession. Unconsciously, he became the rejected child (who he had truly been). I, in turn, became the rejecting parent (who he truly had). Already uncomfortable with being relegated to the vulnerable, patient-position himself, Dr. B regressed. Despite my confidence in managing his intermittent anger, I felt considerable anxiety, and some degree of rejection, at Dr. B's withering attack. I kept my reactions to myself, allowing him to fully vent his ire. As he calmed down, I reminded Dr. B of the well-worn transference theme. During prior sessions, we had discussed his childhood history of being the victim of frequent verbal assaults, as well as outright rejection, by his father. His mother, an extremely narcissistic person, paid him little attention. With care, I suggested he was reliving this childhood theme.

Gradually, the intensity of his anger subsided. And, yet, Dr. B remained irritated with, and critical of, me the rest of the session. He accused me of lacking empathy. He again suggested that my failure to drop everything exemplified a basic lack of competency. Early in the course of our work together, these episodes elicited intense anger in me which I suppressed—an example of responding rather than re-acting (Gabbard, 2016). I spent most of the session acknowledging his disappointment in, and anger at, me. As often occurred, he observed the dynamic with more dispassion towards the end of the session. On this day, Dr. B exclaimed, "I know I can be an asshole sometimes," as he was literally walking towards the exit door of the suite. I nodded blankly, neither joining him in his negative self-assessment nor disabusing him of it.

My experience of stress, albeit strikingly different than the heart-mind reaction after my time with Mr. A, was palpable when Dr. B exited. In contrast to the empathy I felt with Mr. A, the session with Dr. B elicited distress. I had been directly emotionally assaulted. I had little planned for the break. I sat for a few minutes, looking out my office window. Gradually, my own anger and hurt feelings subsided. I reflected, with compassion, on the many childhood years Dr. B himself had similarly struggled with anger, pain, and self-doubt. In many ways, his intense motivation was driven to please his father, to demonstrate his own competence (e.g., through admission to Ivy League schools). Slowly, my emotions transitioned into feelings of sadness, even pity. We had danced this tango multiple times. Focusing on my breathing and allowing some time to pass left me in a better position to receive my third patient of the morning. I also decided, for further distraction, to type out progress notes on Mr. A and Dr. B.

Ms. C—The Pain of Termination

Ms. C, of age 47, who had consulted me for the prior four years on a two-time-per-week basis, was in the process of terminating our meetings. Only two more sessions remained. Our discussions centered around her associations to the termination. Ms. C had sustained an unusual number of losses for her age. She had been adopted at age two, describing the experience as "moving from one world of pain into another." Seeking an early exit from her traumatic childhood home, Ms. C had become engaged at age 17. Her fiancé died in an automobile accident shortly before their marriage. Some years later, her first and only husband died of a myocardial infarction. Additionally—and exemplifying the cliché of life being stranger than fiction—Ms. C lived two blocks away from the World Trade Center at the time of the 9/11 attacks. Our discussions ranged from processing her deep disappointment of her childhood situation, the pseudo-maturity she developed to cope with it, the deaths of her romantic partners, and the emotional impact of the World Trade Center disaster. The primary reason for her seeking psychoanalysis was, to use her words, she "had it with corporate America." She wanted to find a more independent, consultant-type occupation without sacrificing the health, disability, and other benefits her executive vice president position afforded her.

Although we, of course, addressed her occupational concerns, many sessions were devoted to working through her many personal losses. The meetings in which she described the 9/11 attack, including details of watching people jump from the buildings and seeing the first building collapse, were extremely emotional for both of us. Ms. C wept profusely. She also relived the terror, saying, "I felt, as did all of us running away, that we were under attack." She wondered if the fighter jets screaming through the New York skies, minutes after the attacks, were hostile forces.

Termination processes are highly complicated matters. Ms. C felt appreciative of our work together. However, and despite her active involvement in the process, Ms. C had "guarded her heart" to prepare herself for the ending. She anticipated a two-year process, having consulted another psychoanalyst for two years almost two decades earlier. She wanted to focus primarily on the work transition. Although I readily agreed with her desire to terminate, I also made it clear that additional sessions could benefit her—specifically in the area of unresolved early childhood trauma. I explained this to Ms. C. She understood, and she even agreed with me. But she anticipated a lessening in her income as she transitioned into another occupation. She feared she would lack the financial resources for continuing.

Ms. C had made considerable gains. She spent much time between sessions exploring alternative occupations. She considered leaving the corporate world entirely but, as a form of compromise, Ms. C found an occupation that allowed her to apply her management skills autonomously. She completed an intensive, one-year training in executive coaching. Additionally, Ms. C worked through many of the adult losses—specifically the fiancé, the husband, 9/11, and even the loss of her 15-year career. Despite her clear accomplishments, and the steadfastness of her decision, this session proved particularly painful for both of us. I reminded Ms. C that reducing from two to one session per week could allow her to continue as long as an additional half-year. She appreciated the suggestion but, fearing greater dependency, insisted that the next meeting would be our final one. Ms. C explained she preferred to stop completely, for now, and then perhaps return at a later date to further process her childhood pain. In retrospect, I believe I had encouraged the once-per-week meetings out of my own sadness at seeing her leave. This realization exemplifies the meaning of a countertransference enactment. In truth, the steadfastness of her decision represented part of her growth as well as remnants of the hyper-maturity. As often occurs toward the end of a psychotherapy process, Ms. C and I spent the session reviewing themes we had discussed over the years.

The session was followed by my usual break. This time, I became immersed in an entirely distinct set of emotions. Obviously, I had none of the shock I had felt after Mr. A left, and none of the anger or frustration after Dr. B exited. Mostly, I felt a sense of sadness and loss. It triggered feelings of loss in my own life, specifically my children growing up and leaving the home as well as memories of feelings of rejection from my own childhood. I again spent a few minutes looking out the window, typed clinical notes on Ms. C, and prepared myself to take in my final patient of the morning.

Ms. D—Managing a Break in Continuity

Ms. D occupies a unique position in my practice. No other patient has consulted me as long as her. Although she took several breaks along the way—one of them totaling six months—Ms. D had essentially attended regular sessions for 30 years. She had undergone an actual, four-times-per-week psychoanalysis with me, starting as a low-fee control case when I pursued psychoanalytic training in the 1990s. Ms. D had developed severe PTSD after a home invasion robbery. One year of weekly psychotherapy with another therapist was of little benefit. She lacked resources to pay for more intensive treatment, so my need for a control case worked well for both of us. As it turned out, severe and unresolved childhood trauma had exacerbated the PTSD. Having been one of eleven children, Ms. D remembers feeling neglected during her childhood. She "never mattered."

She married her childhood sweetheart, a man who claimed he was sterile, shortly after her high school graduation. She was disinterested in having children. Her husband lied about his infertility, and Ms. D became pregnant just before the marriage ceremony. Surprisingly to her, she enjoyed motherhood. She and her husband ended up having three children. Her husband died suddenly of a brain aneurism shortly after their third child was born. She never remarried. Ms. D worked as an administrative assistant for an aerospace company for nearly 30 years. However, because of the loss of her husband's income and the expenses of single motherhood, she struggled financially. After I completed psychoanalytic training, Ms. D applied for a governmental victims of crime fund, which paid for two more years of twice-weekly therapy. After that point, I continued to see her at a significantly reduced rate on a once-a-week basis.

The combination of the severe childhood neglect and neurobiological vulnerability led to Ms. D displaying a borderline personality disorder with its characteristic instability in mood and interpersonal relationships. She had none of the narcissistic features plaguing

Dr. B. Also, despite profound emotional insecurity and flashes of anger associated with this condition, Ms. D managed to maintain stable employment. Because of financial concerns following her retirement, she reduced session frequency to every-other-week. Around a decade later, when she became concerned about disability and aging, Ms. D resumed weekly appointments. Arthritis elicited chronic pain and also limited her mobility; she suffered a mild heart attack just two months before this session. Ms. D, who had begun consulting me when she was 49 years old, was now age 79. Our discussion during this session surrounded a three-week vacation I would be taking in one month. Knowing the depth of attachment difficulties in Ms. D, and problems that had arisen in the past when the regularity of sessions was disrupted, I anticipated a reaction. Ms. D reported memories of her own losses and abandonments ranging from her childhood experiences to the death of her husband. Also, her only grandson had just been diagnosed with a malignant brain tumor.

I reminded Ms. D that, during many prior breaks in our work, she had developed intense feelings of anger at me. On occasion, she had become convinced the relationship with me was too frustrating. It was a "set-up for feeling deprived." We explored these feelings in detail. I reminded her of the trend of deprivation in her life. Anything more than a one-week break in our work tended to stir up these losses and the unmet need-states related to them. We reviewed how these separations could elicit an impulsive urge to quit, avoiding a mutual assessment of whether a termination or a pause was in her best interest. I reminded her I was always open to her terminating therapy or taking a break. In essence, I was preparing Ms. D, in advance, for her reaction. She asked if I would be available by e-mail. I told her I would. Once again, and together, we reviewed the date that would represent our last session and the date when we would initiate sessions again. Compared to the other three patients of the morning, the psyche-soma and heart-mind impact of the session with Ms. D was the least intense. Ms. D and I had, in a sense, grown up together. I felt a slight sense of guilt at abandoning her, even though I knew, on another level, it was good for both her and me to have respites in our work. The experience with Ms. D most echoed that of Ms. C in terms of lingering feelings of sadness and loss.

The Psychophysiological Impact of Practicing Psychoanalysis

How might these various stressors, central to psychoanalytic work, affect psychoanalytic practitioners? Bessel van Der Kolk (2015), a contemporary researcher in stress, reviews the biochemical, physiological, and anatomic effects of trauma on the body in his book, *The Body Keeps the Score*. Earlier, he and his colleagues (van Der Kolk et al., 2005) differentiated between instrumental stressors (like exposure to combat, sustaining physical injuries, or enduring earthquakes) and interpersonal stress (like abuse, neglect, harassment and other forms of interpersonal mistreatment). They found that interpersonal trauma, specifically, results in higher incidences of affect dysregulation, deficits in memory and attention, negative self-perception, disrupted interpersonal relationships, somatization, and destructive systems of meaning. Equally well-known, Panskepp and Biven (2012), in their book, *The Archeology of Mind,* explore the neurobiology of emotion, identifying ancestral roots of seeking, rage, fear, care, and panic/grief. The fear and panic/grief systems are most relevant to sustained work as a psychoanalyst. The fear system passes through a trans-hypothalamic circuit; the panic/grief system through the anterior cingulate, the dorsomedial thalamus, the periaqueductal gray, and ancient parts of the cerebellum. Many of the interpersonal stressors identified in the case examples—mourning, loss, anger, sympathy, empathy—stimulate these regions of the brain.

Slavich (2016) established that even subtle stressors like social rejection result in increased blood cortisol levels, compromised immune system functioning, and generalized inflammation. Other effects include altered neurological functioning, cellular oxidation, and accelerated biological aging. These, in turn, often lead to disease states—even premature death. Murphy et al. (2015), Dedovic et al. (2016), and Kross et al. (2011) found that interpersonal loss, social rejection, and social pain affect the same regions of the brain as physical pain. The just-completed description of a typical morning of psychoanalytic practice reveals it as often involving social loss, rejection, and pain. Slavich and Irwin (2014) and Slavich, O'Donovan et al. (2010) demonstrated that individuals more neurobiologically sensitive to social stressors—such as psychoanalysis—develop greater inflammatory responses to social stress. These studies, and others like them, validate how interpersonal stressors involved in practicing psychoanalysis, may lead to chronic disease development. The combination of acute life events, that is, episodic rage in patients, and chronic difficulties, that is, listening to mental pain day-in and day-out, cumulatively affects the body (Lupien et al., 2009).

My Personal Medical Background

Before considering the impact of decades of work as a psychoanalyst, other contributing factors warrant review. These include a propensity toward compulsive overwork, intermittent involvement in stressful forensic consultations, including court testimony, and pressures of being the primary financial supporter of a family of four. However, the four decades of psychoanalytic practice obviously took its own toll on my psyche-soma and heart-mind. I enjoyed excellent physical health until the age of 51, when I developed increasingly severe pain in the lower back. Unbeknownst to me, bacteria had entered my bloodstream and infected two inter-vertebral discs—causing the back pain. At the same time, the bacteria silently ate away the aortic valve of my heart. Flu-like symptoms ultimately emerged. My internist, initially puzzled, became alarmed. She referred me to an infectious disease specialist who ordered a blood culture. It revealed sepsis, specifically endocarditis—a bacterial infection of the inner lining of the heart. When I met with her two days later at 1 p.m.—and I had a patient in my nearby office scheduled for 1:45 p.m.—I anticipated, at worst, a referral to an orthopedic surgeon for injection of a local corticosteroid. Instead, having discovered endocarditis, she insisted on my immediate hospitalization. Over the course of the next 20 days, I was treated with antibiotics to eliminate the bacteria, narcotics to dull the pain, and finally, open-heart surgery to remove the infected valve and replace it with a prosthetic one. The episode resulted in my having to exit my practice with 20 minutes notice. I returned to work after a two-month medical leave of absence.

Four years later, my internist discovered a mass in my neck. Further evaluation revealed micro-papillary thyroid cancer. The same internist, a physician and friend for more than 30-years, referred me to a laryngeal surgeon. He performed a six-hour, modified radical neck dissection, opening up my neck from my right ear to my clavicle, dissecting out 14 lymph nodes, removing the thyroid gland, and then referring me for a weekend of radioactive iodine treatment. Just when I hoped the thyroid cancer was the final insult of late middle age, I contracted an upper respiratory infection, considerable fatigue, and a short bout of fever, chills, and night sweats during the fall of 2018. The same infectious disease specialist ordered another blood culture, which proved positive for sepsis. She hospitalized me for administration of intravenous antibiotics. A transesophageal echocardiogram revealed damage to the prosthetic valve. Consulting the same thoracic surgeon who implanted the original prosthetic valve, I told him I hoped for another three to five years on the current valve. I figured the IV antibiotics had resolved the infection. He curtly replied, "Oh, no, Alan, the valve is damaged; this needs to be done in the next three weeks." I burst into tears, unready to undergo such a serious operation almost immediately. I tolerated the procedure well. Fueled by the compulsivity previously noted, I missed only six weeks of work.

Suffice to say, my sixth decade of life, peppered by the three major medical conditions, and capped by passing four decades of providing full-time depth psychotherapy, got me thinking: was there something unique about this line of work that created disease states? And, what were the specific mind-body interactions involved in psychoanalytic practice? The invitation to contribute a chapter to this book on the mind-body problem came at exactly the right moment. As it turns out, the relevant literature, combined with my personal experiences, reveals that, yes, the extended exposure to the types of social stressors just described, not to mention accepting pain and projections into my being likely, had the physiological effects just described. Those trends, from the compromised immune system to the proneness to inflammation, almost certainly contributed to the endocarditis and, perhaps, the thyroid cancer. Endocarditis most commonly occurs in IV drug abusers, not middle-aged professionals.

Discussion

Every occupation or profession carries with it various degrees of stress exposure. Coal miners get respiratory diseases, bank tellers suffer repetitive movement injuries, and carpenters may sever fingers. Physicians may harm patients, attorneys can lose cases, and accountants might make financial errors. All workers face interpersonal stressors specifically related to their work, not to mention the risk of overwork, sexual harassment, or even workplace violence. Psychoanalytic practice carries its own unique stressors. These result from the extremely interpersonal, even intimate nature of their work, rendering their heart-minds and psyche-somas uniquely and intensely subject to the slings and arrows of projection, introjection, empathy, and identification. Their work often triggers their own childhood traumas, unmet need states, unresolved conflicts, and neurobiological vulnerabilities.

> Wilfred Bion, the brilliant psychoanalyst of the late 20th century, reported this exchange with a patient. The man proclaimed,
>
> "I'm taken aback by how much you're charging me for sessions."
>
> Bion replied,
>
> "Imagine what they're costing *me*!"

And, psychoanalytic work certainly costs clinicians, in their psyche-somas and in their heart-minds. Psychoanalysts encounter the entire array of human suffering, greeting patients who have become physically ill, whose family or friends similarly face serious diseases, who have heartbreak, or whose work is boring and ungratifying. Some patients never experience true interpersonal intimacy. Others live boring work lives lacking the relief offered by hobbies or other forms of recreation. Further, psychoanalysts are the only professionals who work closely with patients with severe mental disorders such as personality, major affective, bipolar, dissociative, or psychotic conditions. They meet with highly self-destructive patients. It is common for psychoanalysts to lose several patients to suicide in the course of their careers. In addition to the simple exposure to this range of human pain, psychoanalysts reject patients when they end sessions. They suffer the social loss characteristic of planned or unplanned terminations. Finally, despite the outward impression of day-in and day-out conversations, their work is an intensely lonely endeavor.

This exploration of the psychophysiological price paid by the practitioner of the psychoanalytic psychotherapist will hopefully intrigue, and offer yet another vibrant subject for, those fascinated by the unendingly complex mind-body problem.

References

Aron, L. (1996). *A Meeting of Minds: Mutuality in Psychoanalysis*. Hillsdale: The Analytic Press.

Chalmers, D. J. (2002). *Philosophy of Mind: Classical and Contemporary Readings*. New York: Oxford.

Dedovic, K., Slavich, G., Muscatell, K., Irwin, M., Eisenberger, N. (2016). Dorsal anterior cingulate cortex responses to repeated social evaluative feedback in young women with and without a history of depression. *Frontiers in Behavioral Neuroscience*, 10: 64.

Fairbairn, W.R.D. (1941). A revised psychopathology of the psychoses and the Psychoneuroses. *International Journal of Psycho-Analysis*, 22:250–279.

Fairbairn, W.R.D. (1952). *Psychoanalytic Studies of the Personality*. New York, NY: Routledge.

Gabbard, G.O. (2016). *Boundaries and Boundary Violations in Psychoanalysis*. Second Edition. Washington, DC: American Psychiatric Association.

Hoffman, I. (1998). *Ritual and Spontaneity in the Psychoanalytic Process: A Dialectical-Constructivist View*. New York, NY: Routledge.

Huston, H. (1993). *The Actor's Instrument: Body, Theory, Stage*. Ann Arbor: University of Michigan Press.

Kant, I. (2018). *The Critique of Practical Reason [Kritik der praktischen vernuft]*. Ed. and Trans. J. M. D. Meiklejohn. New York: Digireads Publishing. (Original work published in 1788).

Karbelnig, A. M. (2014). The sanctuary of empathy and the invitation of engagement: psychic retreat, Kafka's "A Hunger Artist," and the psychoanalytic process. *The Psychoanalytic Review*.

Karbelnig, A. M. (2016). Stirred by Kafka's a country doctor: an exploration of psychoanalysts' styles, vulnerabilities, and surrealistic journeys. *The Psychoanalytic Review*, 54(2):322–350.

Karbelnig, A. M. (2018). Addressing psychoanalysis's post-tower of babel linguistic challenge: a proposal for a cross-theoretical, clinical nomenclature. *Contemporary Psychoanalysis*, 103(1): 69–109.

Kross, E., Berman, M., Mischel, W., Smith, E., & Wager, T. (2011). Social rejection shares somatosensory representations with physical pain. *Proceedings of the National Academy of Sciences of the United States of America*, 108:6270–6275.

Lacan, J. (2002). *Ecrits*. (B. Fink, Tran.). New York, NY: W. W. Norton & Company.

Lakoff, G. & Johnson, M. (1999). *Philosophy in the Flesh: The Embodied Mind and its Challenge to Western Thought*. New York: Basic Books.

Loy, D. (1988). *Non-Duality: A Study of Comparative Philosophy*. New York: Prometheus.

Lupien, S., McEwen, B., Gunnar, M., and Heim, C. (2009). Effects of stress throughout the lifespan on the brain, behaviour and cognition. *Nature Reviews Neuroscience*. 10:434–445.

McGinn, C. (1989). Can we solve the mind-body problem? *Mind*, 98:349–366. 10.1093/mind/XCVIII.391.340.

Miller, H. (1941). *The Wisdom of the Heart*. New York: New Direction Books.

Murphy, M., Slavich, G., Chen, E. & Miller, G. (2015). Targeted rejection predicts decreased anti-inflammatory gene expression and increased symptom severity in youth with asthma. *Psychological Science*, 26:111–121.

Nagel, T. (1974). What is it like to be a bat? *The Philosophical Review*, 83(4):435–450. 10.2307/2183914.

Nagel, E. & Newman, N.R. (2001). *Godel's Proof*. New York: New York Universities Press.

Nietzsche, F. (2002). *Human, All Too Human*. Trans. R.J. Hollingdale. Cambridge: Cambridge University Press. (Original work published in 1878).

Panskepp, J. & Biven, L. (2012), *The Archeology of Mind*. New York: Norton.

Slavich, G., Irwin, M. (2014). From stress to inflammation and major depressive disorder: A social signal transduction theory of depression. *Psychological Bulletin*, 140:774–815.

Slavich, G. M. (2016). Life stress and health: a review of conceptual issues and recent findings. *Teaching of Psychology*, 43(4):346–355.

Slavich, G., O'Donovan, A., Epel, E., & Kemeny, M. (2010). Black sheep get the blues: a psychobiological model of social rejection and depression. *Neuroscience and Biobehavioral Reviews*, 35:39–45.

Spinoza, B. (2007). *Ethics: Theological-Political Treatise*. (Ed. J. Israel). Trans. By. M. Silverthorne and J. Israel. Cambridge: Cambridge University Press. (Original work published in 1677).

Thich, Nhat Hanh (2017). *The Other Shore*. Berkeley: Parallax Press.

van Der Kolk, B., Roth, S., Pelcovitz, D., Sunday, S., & Spinnazola, J. (2005). Disorders of extreme stress: the empirical foundation of a complex adaptation to trauma. *Journal of Traumatic Stress*, 18(5): 389–399.

van Der Kolk, B. (2015). *The Body Keeps the Score: Brain, Mind, and Body in the Healing of Trauma*. New York: Viking Press.

Winnicott, D.W. (1949/1975). Mind and its relation to the psyche-soma. (Chapter 19, pp. 243-254). *Through Pediatrics to Psycho-Analysis*. International Psychoanalytic Library, 100:1-325. London: The Hogarth Press and the Institute of Psycho-Analysis.

Index

For Product Safety Concerns and Information please contact our EU
representative GPSR@taylorandfrancis.com
Taylor & Francis Verlag GmbH, Kaufingerstraße 24, 80331 München, Germany

9 780367 548308